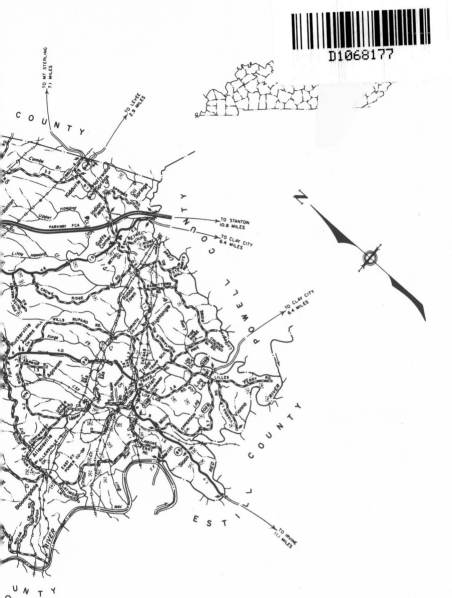

CLARK COUNTY
KENTUCKY

The Courthouse tower in Winchester. - *Photo courtesy of Jerry Schureman*

CLARK COUN

KENTUCKY

A History

CLARK COUNTY, KENTUCKY

A History

Thomas D. Clark

Clark County-Winchester Heritage Commission
The Clark County Historical Society
1995

First Edition

Library of Congress Catalog Card Number: 95-83436

Clark, Thomas Dionysius, 1903 -
    Clark County, Kentucky: A History

    Includes biographical references and index
    1. Clark County (Ky.) - History.   2. Kentucky - Civilization.   3. Westward Movement
    I. Title.
    ISBN 0-9648490-0-3

Published by Clark County-Winchester Heritage Commission and
Clark County Historical Society
34 S. Main St., Ofc. of the Judge-Executive
Winchester, KY 40391
Local Tel.: 606-745-0200

To the memory of Elizabeth Turner Clark
My beloved wife of sixty-two years

Without the diligent assistance of Betty Ellison this book could never have been written and published in so short an interval of time. She was masterful in the location of public records, manuscripts and other basic materials held in private hands. She must share full credit for the preparation of this history. I am certain that she shares with me the painful regret of having to leave so much detailed information and local anecdotal information behind.

Contents

Acknowledgements

The research and writing of a book of this nature places the author under deep obligations to many people. Interested persons in Clark County have been most generous with their time, making available their historic materials, and with their encouragement. Miss Kathryn Owens most graciously permitted me to use her invaluable scrap books from which I extracted much material and insights. Carolyn Sledd, a former student of mine, could not have been more generous in making her rich collection of materials available. Clara Houlihan Weidmann was tireless in her assistance and encouragement. She too made available valuable materials and information.

James Kirby was a staunch supporter and adviser from the beginning. Robert Coney has been most supportive. Richard Gamble of the Clark County Historical Commission gave tremendously important support. Judge James A. Allen, Jr., County Judge Executive and his assistants Linda M. Branhan and Elizabeth A. Miller not only made readily accessible the county's records, they patiently duplicated many of them. This was also true of Anita Jones, the Clark County Clerk. City manager Edallen Y. Burtner and City Clerk Marylyn Rowe were substantially helpful. Mrs. Rowe copied hundreds of pages of the Winchester City Records. I owe special thanks to Danby Williams and Jean Anne Kerr for their prompt responses to requests for information. No one could have been more supportive than William Blakeman and Betty Berryman. They not only gave of their personal support they generously opened the files of both the paper and the photograph collection of the Winchester Sun. Mrs. Louise Martin loaned considerable source materials. So did Robert Haggard, retired Clark County teacher.

Mr. and Mrs. William Sphar graciously showed me through the Hubbard Taylor House which gave me a feeling of the background of one of the most important men in Clark County history, Hubbard Taylor. Dr. and Mrs. James Glenn also gave me the privilege of seeing the John Martin-Samuel D. Martin House on Colbyville Road which once housed that renaissance man of Clark County, Dr. Samuel D. Martin. My former student, Ruth Gay Gaitskille, allowed me to use the impressive pictures of hemp growing and processing on the David S. Gay Farm. Jerry Schureman was most alert to the photographic possibilities of historic spots in Clark County. I still have to complete a visit with Dr. Peter Smith to the ruins of buildings and mills along that important artery of emigration and commerce, Lower Howard's Creek.

Jan Marshall and her staff in the Kentucky section of the Lexington Public Library permitted me free access to the original files of the Kentucky Gazette, the Lexington Reporter, and the Lexington Observer and Reporter. At the University of Kentucky I had free access to that enormously important Special Collections holdings, in the Margaret I. King Library. I especially want to thank William Marshall, Claire McCann, and Pam Brackett for their generous and indispensable assistance. I must thank Lynne Jackson who has typed all this book except the footnotes. Susan Short typed the footnotes, and to both of them I am indebted. I also wish to thank Teresa Robbins.

Finally I must again thank Betty Ellison especially for her intelligent and untiring assistance in every phase of the preparation of this book. As he has done for me several times in the past, David Berg did the copy editing of the manuscript with a deft hand. Paula Coney did a careful job of proofreading. Arthur "Whitey" Walson has given this product unselfish support from the outset. Will Hodgkin aided substantially in preparation of the book, and in the procurement of photographs.

No matter how much assistance an author receives in the preparation of a book, he, and he alone, must assume full responsibility for the writing and for the interpretations of facts and expressions of points of view. I assume this responsibility with full understanding of that, and I alone, must be held responsible for the writing, organization, and handling of facts and their interpretation. I saw enough materials along the way to support the writing of a half dozen monographs on Clark County history.

All of us, the author, the Clark County Historical Society, and the Clark County Heritage Commission are indebted to the Clark County Fiscal Court, and to the Winchester City Council for both their generous co-operation and tireless aid in the research. The Honorable Order of Kentucky Colonels, Inc. has been exceedingly generous in making the preparation and publication of this book possible.

Thomas D. Clark
December 12, 1995.

Introduction

In the writing of the history of a locality the historian comes into closer association with humanity than is true in dealing with the state or nation. This maxim has held true in the writing of this book. For more than two centuries one generation of human beings followed another, each leaving behind bodies of documents, artifacts, and monuments establishing the fact that they occupied the land. Historically, Clark County people lived close to, and off the largess of the land. Each succeeding generation bonded itself to place and region, and interwove the history of their being with events and institutions. Clark County's history might well be a prototype of all rural American development and progress. It has ever had those individuals in its midst who stood out from the crowd and assumed roles of leadership.

At this juncture it must be asserted emphatically that this study is not an excursion into the field of genealogy. I profess no competency whatsoever in this area of historical investigation. This aspect of Clark County's history must be left to the specialist. My interest and approach has been in the responses; social, cultural, political, and economic; that human beings have made to land and place. In Clark County's past these have been deeply personal and forceful. The writing of local history is akin to the editing and publishing of a country weekly newspaper; it of necessity must involve a multiplicity of personal names, some of notable and accomplished individuals, and some of more humble persons. In every county across the broad American continent there have existed coteries of individuals who have wielded heavy hands in the direction and conduct of public affairs. Repeated hundreds of times, groups of individuals, for one reason or another, have petitioned the state legislatures to permit the creation of counties and to name them for notable persons or distinctive natural features and landmarks. Courthouses across the land have been gathering places for elected officials, servitors of the courts, lawyers, and idling citizens. This has ever been true in Clark County's history. The courthouse in Winchester has been the scene of stirring court trials. Thus it towers high, not alone as a center of officialdom, but literally as a centralizing place of a "Little Kingdom" in all that this term implies. Within its walls social and political decisions were made which in some way touched the lives of every citizen.

A newly employed clerk or bill drafter in 1792 attached the suffix "e" to the name of the newly created county. The county was named for George Rogers Clark, commander of the Great Northwest Campaign in 1779-1780 and then against the Shawnee villages in 1781. Consistently in the collected and published papers of George Rogers Clark, in his signature on signed documents, and in the numerous biographies, including the biographical sketch in the *Dictionary of American Biography*, Clark's name appears without the suffix "e". The "e" was, however, added to the county's title down to 1865 or thereabouts with no discernible explanation being given as to the dropping of the "e". The name change appeared in the *Acts* of the Kentucky General Assembly for the legislative session of 1866-1867.

The history of Clark County and its governmental seat, Winchester, is a somewhat mixed one. No doubt the county and the town have been microcosmic prototypes of all the other Bluegrass counties. A degree of difference may be discernible however. There has ever prevailed in Clark County a provincial attachment to a variety of mores, social, cultural, and economic. These facts challenge the historian to sort out and be selective of the multiple historical strands which laced through the region's past.

The physical nature of the land, environmental impacts, and industrial influences, all have contributed heavily to molding the everyday way of life in Clark County. Throughout the last two centuries there have lingered vestigial reminders of closely knit family interrelationships and the sharing of common relationships by blood and by neighborhood attachments. The fact that several cohesive family and communal companies made the arduous trek from Virginia to the developing western frontier brought about a cohesiveness of families and communities from Clark County's historic beginnings. The family, immediate and extended, has ever been a force in shaping the course of history in Clark County, and so have been the profound human adaptations to the land itself. A cardinal fact in all provincial communities has been the cohesiveness of the family in the beginning and its disintegration with the passage of time and the outward flow of population. This has been true in Clark County.

There is a contradiction in Clark County's history, however, as is true in all of Kentucky. Why was the family so revered and the official leadership so laggard in providing adequate educational opportunities for the rising generations? Education considered in the broad context of a popular social and cultural movement is an intricate enough subject to merit in-depth research and the writing of a full scale book. Obviously a partial answer to the making of slow educational progress lay largely in the fact that settling in a virgin country; the construction of cabins, blockhouses, and outbuildings; and the extraction of a living from stump-and root-laden soil demanded the expenditures of backbreaking energy rather than intellectual applications. Too, there lingered on in Clark County the potential for local Indian raids, and the need for considerable militia forces to free the land from this danger. None of these tasks demanded learned skills. Added to these tasks were those of locating and opening roads, building warehouses and mill dams, constructing flatboats and propelling them south loaded with country produce. All these were labor-intensive undertakings.

The fact that Clark County was created by legislative fiat in 1792 is well documented but the political actions back of the creation are unrecorded. One has to infer from the list of petitioners something of the politics of the creation. The saga of the chartering and location of the county site, Winchester, and the location of the courthouse and its associated public structures is well documented. The courthouse with its public square has been the heart of county and town. Within the walls of the courthouse sat the courts, the county and circuit clerks, the sheriff, and other public functionaries. The clerks were essentially public diarists who recorded running accounts of public affairs. In the courthouse citizen disputes were reconciled or made more bitter, miscreants were led away to the nearby jail to sit out sentences, slaves were sold at public auction before the courthouse door, wills were probated and contested, and orphaned and indigent children were bonded out to guardians.

To the sitting court in the courthouse came masters requesting the manumission of faithful slaves, aliens came to take the oath of loyalty to the Republic and to become naturalized citizens, Mothers of bastard children came to court to point accusative fingers to errant fathers, widows sought equity in dower rights denied in the wills of departed husbands, and petty thieves were paraded before the bar of justice in the county court. Cattle breeders and log rafters came to register their private brands, and wolf scalp-ers brought their bloody specimens to claim bounties. The daily pageant of parading through the halls and offices of the courthouse was indeed akin to the comings and goings in a "Little Kingdom."

Clark County was a slaveholding domain, and, as in all slaveholding counties in Kentucky, the human side of the institution was historically a mixed one. There were masters who treated their charges with the same tenderness and care which they bestowed on their own families. There, however, were slave masters who were abusive and heartless toward their people. The public, including the commonwealth and the counties, were cruel in the administering of the traditional "thirty-nine lashes on bare backs" for even minor crimes. The public auction sale of slaves to interstate slave traders was in every case a heartless act, but especially so when such sales separated family members. In a far more human manner black slaves, in many instances, were allowed to attend religious services along with their masters, and, in some restricted instances, to hold church meetings of their own but under white surveillance. Much of the harsh treatment of slaves was mandatory by laws of the commonwealth, not by the county court. Perhaps one of the most disturbing conditions relating to slaveholding was the suspicion and underlying fears of outbreaks of slave violence. The presence of so-called patterollers was ever an irritation to master and slaves alike.

One of the most compelling moments in Clark County was the troubled decade 1860-1870. The issuance of the Emancipation Proclamation by President Abraham Lincoln in 1863 had a definite filtering effect on the county. The confusion in racial relations at the end of the Civil War caused by the generous issuance of exit passes by General J. M. Palmer to ex-slaves who wished to flee the state had some effect in Clark County. The final blow to slavery, however, was the adoption of the Twelfth, Thirteenth, and Fourteenth Amendments to the Constitution of the United States. This necessitated the making of major economic and social adjustments in the county. The struggle upward from enslavement to freedman status presented for both races challenges in the field of agriculture, town services, religious organizations, and, most important of all, the struggle to educate black youth.

Social, economic, and political changes in Clark County must at all times be viewed from the perspective of the rural-agrarian nature of the provincial society. From the penetration of the wilderness by Anglo-American settlers down to date, agriculture in the broadest sense has been the bedstone of Clark County's social and economic well-being. From the first tilling of the soil the more arable western portions of the county have yielded bountiful field corps and livestock. Even the more rugged ridgelands of the rising eastern Knobs and the swales and coves bordering the Red and Kentucky rivers nurtured a distinctive yeoman-agrarian population.

Until the latter half of the twentieth century basically the way of provincial life in Clark County was predominantly land based, with the family farm, like motherhood itself, being the foundation of every aspect of human life. By 1995 this ancient and revered institution was rapidly disappearing from the landscape. By the latter date only 950 family farms were said to be still in operation, as compared with 1,356 in 1954. Nevertheless, there were in 1984 farms occupying 95 percent of the landed area with 70 percent of the land in cultivation and pasturage. Clark County in that year ranked twenty-seventy in Kentucky in agricultural cash receipts, with 61 percent of this being derived from the sale of livestock and poultry.

Measured statistically, the landed area of Clark County has remained consistently as productive as ever in history. There has simply been a shifting away from the old methods of farming and land management. The modernization of the farming process has brought about revolutionary changes between agriculture and industry. In a final analysis the fundamental changes which have come in the rural-agrarian areas of life in Clark County have been in the nature and quality of human use of the land.

Throughout the entire scope of the nineteenth century the name of Clark County was synonymous with the breeding and raising of superior quality livestock. Local breeders engendered a brilliant chapter in the annals of American animal husbandry. The activities of the importers of purebred farm animals from abroad and the successes of local farmers and breeders border on being pure folk romance. The names of Patton, Gay, Taylor, Martin, Goff, Renick, Van Meter, Calmes, and others were deeply embedded in the annals of the county. These were the names which appeared in both the history and reports of the Kentucky Agricultural Society, the reports of the local societies and fairs, the herd books, the United States Patent Office reports on national agriculture, and the Kentucky and national farm journals.

The Clark County livestock breeders were countrymen well deserving of the title "Squire." They lived in their Georgian-style homes with numerous sons and daughters amidst their fields and pastures. In Winchester there were scores of personalities associated with both town and country. Winchester, county town, merited valid comparison with an English country market town. From the moment of its location all county roads led to Winchester. It had no competing town to stymie its growth or to sap its trade. By the latter quarter of the nineteenth century it was served, and misserved, by three railroads. Just as the order, will, deed, and road books attest, Winchester and

Clark County eloquently reflected the crosscurrents in Kentucky life itself. So did the minute books of town trustees and councilmen.

Both Clark County and its county seat Winchester have ever been subject to the changes which occurred in Kentucky and the nation after the end of World War I. The postwar years, the era of the Great Depression, and the advent of World War II literally hurled this rural-agrarian region into a new and highly complex age, the rising use of the automobile and motor truck, the building of modern roads, the coming of industries, and the introduction of both commercial and rural electrification along with rural water cooperatives wrought a social revolution in the county. The automobile, once a mechanical novelty on the streets of Winchester, lowered the barriers of provincialism and raised new management problems.

Despite James E. Garner's oft-quoted speech in 1888 entitled "Calf or Boy?" native sons and daughters have won state and national recognition in the fields of the arts and letters. The names of Hart, Tevis, Quisenberry, Tate, and Conkwright have added luster to pioneer family names.

Historians probably could produce a bookshelf of monographs dealing with special subjects during the two centuries of Clark County's existence. There lie dormant numerous stories of families and the anecdotes of their lives. Subjects of agriculture and animal husbandry, of religion and churches, of education and of pioneering, all await recording. In the writing of this history I have been constrained by space limitations, and often by a lack of dependable documentation. I have had to be selective of subjects and central issues, trying always to identify the forces and events which have given substance to the history of Clark County, keeping in mind the fact that Clark County must always be considered an integral part of the Bluegrass Region and of the Commonwealth of Kentucky. I have made an effort of draw information from original documentary sources and to document the text.

There is absolutely no connection between the name of Clark County and my surname. No relative of mine has ever been near Clark County as a resident. I have had no vested interest whatever in the county, and I hope no protagonists. My sole objective in this connection has been one of determining the main events of the history of the county as factually and objectively as possible. When I consented to members of the Clark County Historical Society to write this history I was fully cognizant of the fact I might have to deal objectively with some myths and legends, and always with personal histories.

At times in the preparation of this text the research and writing required the adeptness of Daniel Boone, the wisdom of Dr. Samuel D. Martin, the political insights of Hubbard Taylor and James Clark, and the astuteness and humor of James E. Garner. I undertook the writing of this history largely because years ago, as head of the Department of History in the University of Kentucky, I sought to bring together a group of scholars to produce a searching study of at least five representative counties in Kentucky to determine the grass roots dynamics of the state itself. The effort failed largely because of differing notions as to what might constitute an adequate local history. Since then I have had the intriguing experience of dealing with two representative sectional counties and their histories on my own. Nowhere in the nation has the county represented such intense and firm planting of human roots and a sense of place or the pervasiveness of a courthouse political ring of constantly changing shapes and personalities as in Clark County. Human kinships and relations have involved all the mores of the rural provincial American community in this county. The historic plights of the Kentucky counties have, since 1780, been the local breeding grounds of politics, of progress or lack of it, and of the shaping of what might be called the Kentucky "turn of mind.". The magic and deeply nostalgic word "home" and all the word implies has ever been cherished in Clark County. In its relative extension of the chronological scale of Kentucky history, this county has come to merit amply the relative modern political denomination "Little Kingdom."

The site of the southern Shawnee village of Eskippakithiki. The woods in the background no doubt are indicative of the site in the first half of the eighteenth century. It was here that John Finley came to trade and was robbed of his pack of goods and furs. - *Photo courtesy of Jerry Schureman*

CHAPTER 1

The Land, Its Resources,
Its People

The stream of human history in Clark county winds through three epochs of man's occupation of the land. Measured in the broad scope of time,
the presence of the Euro-American population has been of remarkable short
duration. There is uncertainty about the extent of the age of those first and
primitive tenants who wandered through the forest, across the ridges, and
pitched their encampments in secluded vales and flatlands. Modern archaeologists have made remarkable progress in piecing together information about
these early tenants. Their history has a fascination all its own, and is cast in its
own peculiar context.[1]

Despite the mist of elapsed time which has long enshrouded the travails
of prehistoric peoples who occupied the region north of the Kentucky River
and had familial connections with communities beyond the Ohio, there is
historical relevance and an essence of continuity which both relate and differentiate the eras of human presence in the region.[2] There has been at least one
cord of history which laces through the experience of all epochs of man in
Kentucky. That is the fact that in every period human beings have depended
heavily upon the resources of land, forest, and streams.

At the outset it must be emphasized, that despite the discovery of local
ancient sites, the patterns of cultures were spread over a broad geographical
area. Specifically in the case of Clark County, where modern scientific excavations have been made, evidence has been revealed of the presence of plant
and animal life, and of the mode of life of the primitive hunters and gatherers.[3] The historian is wholly dependent upon the findings of archaeologists,
paleontologists, and anthropologists for information about pre-recorded

peoples in this region. Though phenomenal progress has been made in the gathering of information about the primitive peoples who roamed through this area, there still remain unanswered questions about them.

There were no created explanatory documents in the first epoch of human history in Kentucky. Inferences and evidence have to be drawn from geography, the soil, and physical artifact remains. Happily for this generation, scientists in the fields of archaeology, paleontology, geology, and anthropology reached viable states of maturity in the commonwealth. Almost annually the body of knowledge in these fields has been greatly enlarged. Down to this date, modern scientists have developed many insights into the activities and mode of life of the prehistoric race.[4] By sophisticated excavation, classification, comparison, and perceptive interpretations they have moved the study of these prehistoric peoples well out of the morass of myth and legend. For instance, the excavation of a single site like the Goolman one on Bull Run Creek or the projected site of the J. K. Smith Electric Power Station has brought much more clearly into focus information about the seasonal occupancy of the land, foods, specimens of crude tools, and pottery, and the nature and form of shelter.[5]

There has now been established scientifically the fact that the general area in which Clark County is located was once a definite part of the domain of an ancient people, no doubt of the Fort Ancient group. Though there may still be lacking a precise knowledge of the narrow period of their occupation, some generalities relating to a broad era have been verified.[6] Questions prevail among archaeologists as to whether the ancient peoples were linked to a much broader culture group of the Fort Ancient people. Too, there was the question of whether the primitive people were seasonal or permanent occupants of Kentucky. William S. Webb and W.D. Funkhouser raised this question in 1920. Did the ancient race live in the area as a large group of people for short intervals of time, or were they here as a small group who lived in the country for a long time?[7] The fact has been established with a certainty that, no matter the length of time, an ancient people were present in some, if not all areas, of Clark County. Competent archaeologists have established irrefutable evidence of the existence of village or communal sites, and this evidence is backed up by the findings of a large amount of artifactual materials. Some of these silently document the physical and cultural way of life of the stone-age people. There has been established a fairly comprehensive understanding in bold outline of the close association of these people with the land, forest, wild plants and animals habits and existence.[8] Too, there is ample evidence that the early Kentuckians responded to geographical influences. Over the years a large number of artifacts have been garnered from the surface of the land, in the great majority of cases completely disassociated from evidentiary sites where scientific associations could be related with other materials and evidence.

From almost the dawning of recorded Kentucky history there has existed an interest in the fact that a prehistoric race had once wandered across the face of the commonwealth. In 1812, Humphrey Marshall published the first edition of his *History of Kentucky.* He reproduced as a prefatory essay Constantine Rafinesque's treatise on "Ancient Life in Kentucky", a study based upon the author's examination of some prehistoric sites, but even more upon consultation of secondary and widely diversified sources of varying degrees of relevancy to Kentucky. Perhaps the fact that Rafinesque made a table of existing monuments and sites in the region had far more importance than the text of his essay. In an explanatory note he said there were known to be 505 monuments (some kind of surviving evidence of the early presence of an ancient people). He said there were 148 sites in Kentucky, and that eighteen monuments and five sites were located in Clark County.[9]

In 1874, when Richard H. Collins prepared his eclectic *History of Kentucky* for publication, he appealed to his neighbor and friend, Dr. Thomas E. Pickett to prepare an article on prehistoric peoples in Kentucky. Dr. Pickett had been editor of the *Maysville Eagle,* but in 1871 he became editor of the Lexington *Intelligencer.* There is no evidence that he had more than a layman's interest in archaeology. He wrote in a flamboyant Kentucky oratorical style, describing what he conceived to be the presence in the region of prehistoric people. He said, "But antedating the utmost limits of human memory, and defying all ordinary methods of historic research, there still lies a mysterious past, embossoming a mighty civilization, which the modern eye sees, looming dimly through misty traditions and enigmatic remains."[10] It must be said in the author's defense that he viewed the misty past without the aid of carbon dating facilities or sophisticated comparative archaeological data. Instead Dr. Pickett relied heavily upon the writings of Constantine Rafinesque as sources of information in the preparation of his article.[11]

Unfortunately the science of archaeological research in Kentucky experienced appreciable periods of dormancy between the era of Rafinesque and the emergence of the new phase under the direction of Webb and Funkhouser. During the dormant periods much damage was done to archaeological sites all over Kentucky, and Clark County was no exception. Mounds were dug in to by careless and unscientific pot hunters or were plowed over by farmers; and in some cases nature itself eroded sites.[12] Conversely, amateur and casual

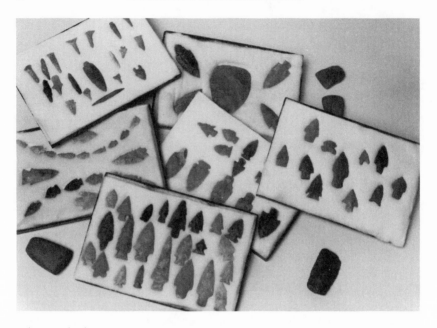

Indian arrowheads. - *Photo courtesy of Jerry Schureman*

collectors preserved a surprisingly good number of "surface" artifacts, gathering them without any associational importance they might have had to a specific site or area.

In 1923 Webb and Funkhouser published their *Ancient Life In Kentucky* with the Kentucky Geological surveys reporting series. The authors admitted their book was at best a preliminary study, but nevertheless it was seminal in its influence. It initiated a new era of scientific exploration and description of materials relating to the prehistoric inhabitants of Kentucky. Although the authors explained that they had made only a preliminary description of artifacts and excavation projects, they awakened Kentuckians to the richness of the artifactual treasures. Their work, though statewide in scope, had a pertinence to Clark County.[13]

Webb and Funkhouser wrote, "We know, for example, either that a large number of people inhabited Kentucky in prehistoric times for a short period, or that a small number were here for a very long time. This is evident by the enormous number of artifacts which have been found in the state." They explained further, "One is overwhelmed with the magnitude of the problem, [the establishing of chronology, classification, and identification of artifacts, and efforts to determine modes of prehistoric human life] especially as he comes to understand that many different people having different customs and degree of development and probably quite different origins, have lived over long and overlapping areas of our state, [perhaps widely separated periods]."[14] This observation most certainly applied to the politically and artificially created geographical entity, Clark County.

As indicated, over the years large numbers of artifacts have been gathered from the surface of the land. These inert objects, however, have a special appeal, partly because of the antiquity of their history, and partly because of the mist of elapsed time since another race lived and hunted on the land, lived by a different standard of subsistence and made particular responses to environmental conditions. The artifact is a tangible connector between times and cultures. Gradually scientifically trained archaeologists are making clearer facts about the prehistoric human forerunners of civilization in Kentucky.[15]

The excavations on the site proposed for construction of the J.K. Smith Power Plant, on the head of Bull Run Creek just north of the Kentucky River, revealed some fascinating evidence of both the presence and mode of life of a seasonal family or small communal group of individuals. The archaeologists, Christopher A. Turnbow, Cynthia Jobe, and Nancy O'Malley, estimate that this particular site was occupied sometime between 1400 and 1645 A.D. Their accounting of the fragmentary artifactual remains found along the waters of Bull Run Creek proved in good measure the occupation by the ancient race of the winter quarters site. The excavation took place on the 3, 120-acre property of the proposed power station and represented a modern approach to site analysis prior to its possible destruction on a construction area.[16] Not only did the prehistoric people leave behind fairly ample physical evidence of their having been present, they left enough evidence to indicate much of their way of life.

In subsequent years there came into existence the Indian trading post on the flat table land of Indian Old Fields. In this case there are written documentary records giving an insight into this moment of the dawning of the modern history of Clark County.[17] There was, however, a significant interval of time between the disappearance of the ancient race and the establishment of Eskippakithiki at the Old Fields. Surviving from the ancient epoch was the Great Warrior's Trace. Nobody knows precisely the time when this great arterial path was opened, but perhaps it was created in segments. Both animals and man padded out a clear and easily discernible passage way through the great wilderness, from Cumberland Gap by way of Flat Lick, Stinking Creek, the Goose and south forks of the Kentucky River, down Station Camp Creek to the Kentucky and the Red rivers, and across what is now Clark County, from Lulbegrud Creek to the Lower Blue Lick.[18] By the third decade of the eighteenth century Indians, from north and south traveled this way, as did white captives of the Indians. Then there were the French, Indian traders, and subsequently the Anglo-Pennsylvania traders who followed the great path. Not only was it a main artery of primitive travel across the broad waist of Kentucky, but it was also a central stem from which many subsidiary trails branched out to other licks and areas of the region.[19]

In what is now modern Clark County the Warriors Path skirted the 3500-acre tract of plane of land called Eskippakithiki or Indian Old Fields. This unusual corner of earth is located within the drainage apex of Upper Howards Creek and Lulebegrud Creek,[20] and subsequently near the tri-corner of Montgomery, Powell, and Clark counties. Documented history of the Indian Old Fields dates from the latter part of the third decade of the eighteenth century to 1755 and the conclusion of the French and Indian War. Basically the history of this peripheral Indian and French trading post may be divided into two phases. The site was occupied by a group of Shawnee Indians moving northward out of the South. Perhaps they were in the process of reuniting themselves with the main body of Shawnees beyond the Ohio.[21] The second phase was the brief use of the village as a trading post in what became the great rivalry between the English and the French for domination in the Ohio Valley. At one time there may have been several hundred people assembled at Eskippakithiki.[22]

There has ever hovered over the Indian Old Fields a veil of mystery and legend. The famous Shawnee chieftain Catahecassa, (Black Hoof), the father of Tecumseh, said he was born there. In one respect, a chapter of Kentucky history was associated with this remote trading post. In 1752 the aggressive Indian trader John Findley of Pennsylvania made his way down the Ohio and up the Kentucky River to Lulbegrud Creek, bringing with him a stock of trade goods. Findley was an unwelcomed competitor in the French trading domain. In an attack he lost both his trade goods and his accumulation of skins and furs. In making his escape he no doubt carried back to the Anglo-American settlements information which was far more valuable than skins and furs. He had gained considerable knowledge of the nature and lay of the land and the course of its streams.[23]

Two years later Findley served as a wagoner in General Edward Braddock's drive against the French and Indian stronghold of Fort Duquesne at the confluence of the Allegheny and Mononghahela rivers. A fellow wagoner, serving Major Edward Brice Dobb's North Carolina troops, was Daniel Boone. Findley told Boone of the great virgin lands which lay beyond the Appalachian Highlands. Perhaps this was the first time Boone had heard of the region.[24]

In March of 1932 Lucien Beckner read an extensive paper on the history of Eskippakithiki before members of the Filson Club in Louisville. He covered a fairly wide range of topics, including some description of his personally having done some excavation at Indian Old Fields. He cited a third-person story, Daniel Boone to Daniel Bryan to Lyman C. Draper, that John Findley had packed his trade goods in grass gathered from around Lancaster, Pennsylvania, and from it had sprouted the first bluegrass to grow in Kentucky. The grass, Beckner said, had been imported from England. Findley had dumped the grass down along the Upper Howard Creek.[25] This story must be considered of highly secondary origin with a considerable amount of time elapsing between Daniel Boone's account, and Lyman C. Draper's recording it. However, it way well have a foundation in fact. From other and more specific sources it is known that the colonial Indian traders, of both English and French origins, used grass padding to protect their goods. The history of bluegrass is complicated by the fact that there are said to be approximately fifty different varieties, and parental stock is known to grow in England, middle Europe, and Russia.[26]

Lucien Beckner implied in his essay that the name Kentucky evolved from the Iroquois word "Kenta", meaning "level". Those who have viewed the plain at Indian Old Fields can readily reconcile the implication of the Iroquois word.[27] This explanation of the origin of the name "Kentucky" is in direct contradiction to William E. Connelley's assertion that the name evolves from the Iroquois word, "Kentatha", meaning "Land of Tomorrow".[28]

By 1755 the village of Eskippakithiki had been abandoned, and its buildings were burned. This did not occur, however, until the powerful international and intersectional forces had been involved in fierce conflict, and control over the Indian trade and the Ohio Valley had been transferred to British hands, a fact which in a short time was to have a direct bearing on the history of Clark County.[29]

In a report of the soil survey made of Clark County in 1961 by the scientists Preston, Sims, Richardson, Blevins, and Taylor, no specific mention is made of the Indian Old Fields area. They describe the soil of this unusual tract of land as being within the Otway-Beasley Association of soil types. Earlier, 1916-1919, Arthur McQuiston Miller, a University of Kentucky geologist, described the unusual plat of ground as being a part of the Kentucky Knobs. He noted that the level of tract was an unusual formation within an otherwise high ridge area. Miller also observed that to date, 1919, no reasonable explanation had been forthcoming about this topographical-geographical anomaly.[30]

The desertion of Eskippakithiki by Indians and French traders, and the successes of the British and colonial Americans in the French and Indian War closed one chapter in the history of Clark County and opened a new one. Unleashed human energies eventually resulted in the great American westward movement and the population of the lands west of the Appalachian Mountains. The shaping of the mores of the new inrush of pioneers reflected the ever-powerful environmental influences of nature and geography. For more than two centuries the course of modern human history in Clark County has been charted largely through geographical influences.[31] Cast in a formative mold by natural forces over millions of years, the geography and topography of the region have been formed by the wearing impact of seasonal changes and erosion, forces which in subtle, but nevertheless powerful thrusts shaped the face of the land. The rolling hills, the deeply eroded defiles and valleys, the stone outcroppings, the sculpting of flat-faced and stratified palisades, and the complex coursing of streams all have physically reflected the passage of unrecorded time. All of these physical features have in some way exerted an influence on the shaping of the economic, social, and cultural patterns of Anglo-American occupation and exploitation of the region. For instance, the variations in soil types have over the years borne heavily upon the human progress and fortunes on the land. So has the topography of the region.[32]

All of the soil areas of Clark County are underlain with stone, which conditions both [the chemistry and the more physical] properties of the soils and influences the nature and variety of both forest and plant growth and species. Though inrushing and land-hungry pioneers no doubt came with the dream of planting a pastoral society in the expansive western country, it was geology, geography, and topography that conditioned the realization of the dream. The earliest land claimants applied only a few elementary criteria to the selections of claims.[33] They viewed the land as to its topography, the nature and size of trees and other vegetation, the nature of drainage; and they guessed as to soil fertility. Not one pioneer in Clark County had a dependable scientific notion of the diversity of soils or their chemical composition. They located farms and homesteads following general folk principles.[34] No competent scientist had in nearly two centuries made so detailed an analysis of soil compositions and types as did the soil specialists of the United States Department of Agriculture and the University of Kentucky Extension Service in 1961.[35]

Perhaps only a few, if any, inhabitants of Clark County were precisely aware that their home land was divided into eleven associational soil qualities and even more subgroups. Viewed on a varicolored map denoting the outcroppings of the various soil types, the area would reveal a veritable galaxy of variations. In more general geographical descriptions, Clark County is divided into four physiographic areas, if not in radical forms, then in subtle but definitely discernible differences.[36]

Since the moment the earliest Anglo-American settler arrived west of the mountains, the history, economy, and social organization of Clark County have been of an intense rural-agrarian cast with the area's own regional sense of place and folk mores.[37] This fact has been reflected in every aspect of social development and every period in the country's existence. In a little more than two centuries the approach to exploiting land resources has ever been consistent, ever conforming to a balance between the growing field of crops and hay and the production of livestock. The growing of corn, tobacco, and hay, along with some small grains, has all but remained fixed in a historical context. As an example, in 1850 there were 792 farms occupied by owners who lived on the land;[38] in 1950 there were 792; and in 1995, 947.[39] By the former date 150,000 of the county's 170,141 acres had been placed in some state of improvement. Only Fayette, Bourbon, and Woodford counties had improved greater proportions of their areas. In Clark County the scales were almost equally balanced between the production of field crops and the pasturing of livestock. Clark County was one of the four top livestock producers in the commonwealth in 1850 and was in the high upper echelon nationally.[40]

Again, in its aboriginal condition Clark County may have been one of

The Gay Mound, Pretty Run Road circa 1902. This mound is near the southeastern boundary of Indian Old Fields, and possibly belongs to the Adena culture. - *Photo courtesy of Jerry Schureman*

the most densely forested areas in the Inner Bluegrass region. Unfortunately there are no concentrated reports on the timber resources of the county. This information has to be gleaned from a variety of sources. There are frequent mentions of the wilderness in historical literature, and occasionally a contemporary observer noted the presence of the wilderness. Perhaps one of the best sources of information is the collection of estate inventories in the county order books. Listed in these are axes, saws, augurs, adzs, chains, and wedges. The remaining early homes contain a large amount of native wood, paneling, partitions, and flooring.[41] Also, the listing of vast amounts of maple sugar indicates the presence of large areas of these trees. So do the mention of mill dams, warehouses, and the rising flatboat trade. All of these indicated the availability of abundant timber. Most farm implements were of wood construction.[42]

As discussed earlier, some of the best evidence of the forest cover centers on the Indian Old Fields, or Eskippakithiki. John D. Shane's interview with a man named Rist contains a description of that site. Rist told Shane there were remaining stumps of hickory, black cherry, and locust. Sprouts of these trees had sprung up in the area.[43] Too, the numerous published descriptions of this place are evidentiary documents which indicate there were numerous log structures in the village trading post. A convincing aura which has hung consistently over the history of Eskippakithiki indicates that Clark County was heavily wooded at one stage. There does exist ample concrete evidence that fully 90 percent of the early dwellings, barns and out-utility buildings, plus hundreds of rods of worm fencing were products of the timbered lands. Even more convincing is the fact that the county courthouse, jail, stock and markethouse required a large supply of timbers.[44]

Every report of the United States Decennial Census down to 1850, in listing statistics of manufacturing industries and saw mills, documented generous consumption of wood in Clark County. Running throughout the economic statistics reported by the Bureau of the Census until a decade or so after the Civil War is the revelation that Clark County produced appreciable quantities of maple sugar. For instance, in 1840 the local maple woods yielded 71,155 pounds of syrup and sugar. In the same report there were listed twenty-one saw mills, two cabinet shops, and a wagon and carriage factory. In addition there was harvested 1,743 cords of firewood.[45]

Though no foreign visitor, following the "Grand Tour," came to Clark County, John Filson gave some vague description of it in his so-called *History of Kentucky,* especially on the accompanying map. The map indicates that the northeastern portion of the county was a cane-covered savanna. By this description Filson must surely have referred to the Indian Old Fields.[46]

Almost to the point of neglect Kentucky's historians have failed to indicate the basic social and economic importance of the rich forest resource in the planting of settlements in the region. They have consistently focused attention upon political, military, and personal accounts, and ignored too many of the natural resources. This is true of the accounts relating to Clark County. Though the forest stand may have been a deterrent to the opening of the lands for cultivation or served as cover for Indian marauders, it was one of the region's richest natural assets.

Again, the most tangible documentation of the existence of ample timber resources in early Clark County is found in the order books of the county, and also in the minutes of the town trustees of Winchester. Both of these sources make frequent mention of the [stands] of heavy oak, ash, walnut, and locust timbers.[47] The county court ordered that the original courthouse, jail, and stray pen be constructed of solid timbers of broad dimensions. Trustees of the newly chartered county seat town of Winchester engaged in the formulation of a limited building code when they prescribed the use of substantial log and other building materials in the construction of residences and stores. Obviously these heavy materials had to be readily available and near at hand. Presently, there is a degree of historical documentation in the fact that there is considerable growth of preclimatic timber growing in the deep ravines, coves, and ridges of the county. This growth contains a widely mixed variety of trees, including the ubiquitous red cedar.

By 1850 an overwhelming portion of the landed area of Clark County had been cleared of the forest growth and fell into the category designated by the United States Census Bureau as "improved."[49] This condition at mid-nineteenth century was indicative of the rapidity of the spread of being a virginal forest and an opened agricultural area was of almost remarkable brevity. A late-twentieth century survey of the county indicated there were only scattered remains of forest which might, by strained imagination, resemble the original forest cover.

Like the larger area of Kentucky itself, that of Clark County is literally a land of contrasts defined in terms of topography, drainage system, nature of farming, and social and political organization. In a sense the county historically has three points of orientation: the Kentucky River Valley, the area northward up the Licking River, and the overland channel in to the bluegrass plateau.[50] These facts have been revealed countless time in the location of land claims, the opening of trails and roads, the location of homesteads, and the outflow of trade and communication.

The surface of Clark County is lined literally with a spidery gossamer of stream courses. These branch off and flow in almost every point on the compass, often feeding into one or two secondary channels before they drain into the two main basins. In essence the stream pattern was a primeval blueprint of settlement before the first Euro-Americans ever saw the land. The names of the streams and places on the terrain constitute a veritable litany of geography and pioneer personification. There are Twomile, Fourmile, Stoner, Log Lick, and Pretty Run.[51] It seems that every pioneer family who crossed the Kentucky River plastered its name on a creek or place. There are Bush, Vivian, Johnson, Boone, Harris, Bybee, Hoods, Woodruff, Combes, Lulbegrud,[52] and on up every spring branch where a settler could build a cabin. All the names are reminiscent in some way of the past, but more significantly, they stand as virtually inerasable definitions of places.

In both microcosmic and historical perspectives, the human element and economy of Clark County have been cast firmly into the mold of geographical determinism, a condition which from the beginning of Anglo-American settlement, has shaped and conditioned man's relationship to the land. Politically there was thrust upon the region tremendous problems of administering land grants, adjudicating claims, and establishing a system of registry.[53] The increase in the population of Kentucky, 1775-1790,[54] was within itself a political phenomenon that no American authority had ever been called on to manage. In a single instance, the archaic metes and bounds plan of land surveys dated back to medieval times in Europe,[55] if not beyond to the ancient world. This ancient mode of land location and boundary establishment applied to the face of virgin Clark County magnified the topographical indentations and regional diversities. It might be argued the old world Virginia survey of metes and bounds was highly compatible with the ridge and stream contours of the county.[56]

Deed books of Clark County are filled with highly esoteric land boundary descriptions that border on being the fantasies of local surveyors. In most cases it appears that surveyors believed the boundary markings they described would exist throughout the time of man. Many landmarks are described as being stakes, axe hacks on trees, following the course of streams, the dividing of ridges, and meandering roadways. As indicated , the metes and bounds method was set long before Clark County was organized, but this in no way lessened the confusion of boundaries and litigation which resulted.[57]

The original land grants in the Clark County area were made in conformity with the Virginia land resolutions, and the law of 1779.[58] Reflected in the early claims in the county are evidence of the law of 1779, which permit-

As attractive to the first settlers as the land was a free flowing spring. This one is located in the knob section of Clark County near the confluence of the Red and Kentucky rivers. It once was used by the Merritt family in the making of whiskey. - *Photo courtesy of Cecil E. Walson*

ted claimants to establish almost instant ownership of four hundreds of acres and to pre-empt upon the payment of a modest fee, a thousand additional acres.[59] There was a veritable rash of claims in the years 1779 to 1785, with overlapping boundaries and what Henry Clay in later years called "fireside surveys." This meant the marking of boundaries was done carelessly, if done at all. So serious was this problem that as early as 1779 Virginia created a land court to attempt to bring order to land titles in Kentucky. This court was given the mandate to try and sort out the types, priorities, and validity of claims; to regulate application of the various land laws; and to institute an orderly system of warranty certification. All of these actions had a pertinency in Clark County prior to its creation in 1792.[60]

One has only to read the descriptions in Clark County land deeds to understand both the origins and nature of the irregularities in boundaries and the difficulty of reestablishing the boundaries after a short interval of time. The property of John Holder was described in 1803 as two hundred acres of land "Beginning at two locust [saplins] and running south fifty degrees west forty-five poles to a stone, thence south seventy degrees, East thirty-

The broad sweep of Indian Old Fields. It was to this spot that John Finley came in 1754 on a trading mission, and where he was robbed of his trade goods. The southern Shawnees had lingered in this village generally from sometime in the 1730's to 1754. - *Photo courtesy of Jerry Schureman*

six poles to a stone, thence South forty-one East sixty poles to two young hickories and a Walnut, thence North fifty-one degrees thirty E, one hundred and eight poles to a dead white oak, walnut, and ash in the line of Samuel R. Combs and with his line North twenty West one hundred and forty poles to two Hickories and a White Oak, thence South twenty degrees West One hundred and forty five poles to a hickory and red oak, thence south two East twenty-six poles to three Iron woods on the west side of [Jouetis] creek to a Hickory and Horn Beam, thence twenty three degrees East ninety-six poles to a stone, thence South thirty-nine degrees West twenty-six thirty poles to the beginning.[61] It is doubtful that many of the land-markers mentioned in this deed could be identified twenty years later. Few deeds could be more representative of the defects of the metes and bounds plan of land survey and markings.

These examples of descriptions written into land deeds are illustrative of the nature of the land survey of Clark County. If it were possible to exhibit on a comprehensive map in variegated colors the pattern of landholds in Clark County, the map would present a collage of patterns more bizarre than any created by a kaleidoscope.[62] This would be especially true for more rugged terrain marked by stream courses, deep but narrow valleys and vales, and steep ridges.

With most of the area of Clark County cleared of timber, its physical features are highly visible. Perhaps no markings on the land reveal more clearly the spread of population and the establishment of homesteads than do the meandering roadways. This manmade physical feature virtually outlines ridgetops, stream crossings, and the subdivision of the land and the spread of homesteads. Politically, the route of the Clark County roads reflect the more or less higgledy-piggledy process of road extensions by the order of the county court. The order books of this court are filled with the documentation of the opening of roads. There is scarcely a square mile of the county's surface which is not penetrated by a road of some sort, however secondary it may be.

Few or no more tangible bits of evidence of the spread of population and the occupancy of the land exist than the presence of roadways. Sociologically, the system of roads reflects the efforts to break the barriers of isolation, gaining access to public institutions and to a farm market. Clark County has a generous number of crossroads which in many instances became locations for churches, stores, schools, and fourth-class post offices. On the face of the map of Clark County appears a veritable litany of village names. There are Ruckersville, Schollsville, Pinchem, Wades Mill, Becknerville, Pine Grove, Trapp, Indian Fields, Rabbit Town, Goff's Corner, Flanigan, Pilot's View, and others. These places represented a rural-agrarian provincialism embodied within the broader one, the county. In a human context, these crossroad social concentrations represented sentimental attachments by individuals to a place and to an identifiable spot on maps.

In many ways the lay and quality of the land had a distinct bearing on the kind of society and economic welfare which sprang up on it. In the more fertile quadrant of the Inner Bluegrass part of the county the landholds were larger, and homes were built on a larger and more affluent scale in the midst of multi-hundred-acres tracts. In this area, as nearly as in any other part of Kentucky, the speculative dream of planting a thriving pastoral society became a reality. Interestingly, William M. Beckner published in 1890 a booklet entitled, *A Handbook of Clark County and the City of Winchester, Kentucky.* Obviously this publication was created with the intent to attract visitors to Clark County, and perhaps as a boost to the Newport News and Mississippi Valley Railroad (the subsequent Chesapeake and Ohio). In this profusely illustrated publication there is no single reference to the type of homes, stores, crossroads post offices, or country churches which existed in more than half the county. A traveler coming to Winchester in 1890 might have been startled by this fact.

Lower Howard's Creek - *Photo courtesy of Jerry Schureman*

CHAPTER 2

Travails In The "New Eden"

The history of Clark County, prior to its separation from Fayette and Bourbon Counties as an independent governing entity of the Commonwealth of Kentucky, falls into three fairly well-defined time epochs. As explained in the preceding chapter, there was the prehistoric era with indeterminant beginnings and endings. During the second quarter of the eighteenth century there was that brief habitation of a portion of Clark County by Shawnee Indians and French and American colonial traders. Of far greater importance was the opening of the great western settlement frontier by Anglo-American settlers who pushed into the western country on the waters of the Ohio to established fort stations at Boonesborough, St. Asaph's (Logan's), Harrod's and Bryan's Station.

Scattered over the landscape were blockhouses and minor safety stations. The establishment of these places was an initiatory indication that a new and aggressive civilization would come to possess the land.[1]

Immediately after 1775 there began to be plastered on the face of Kentucky a veritable crazy quilt pattern of land claims, and the raising of remote cabins and more substantial raid-resistant log houses. Basically the claiming of the land, the making of surveys, the registry of deeds, the adjudicating "shingled" plats of tracts, and the establishment of Clark County contemporaneously with the founding of the commonwealth are all matters of primary concern in presenting the history of the county.

A central fact, poorly defined by Kentucky historians, is that the arrival of the Anglo-American pioneers on the frontier west of the Appalachian Highlands in time completely disrupted the Indian presence and activities in the region.[2] This was a pastoral hunting ground claimed and fought over by rival tribes, north and south. With the arrival of long hunters and land speculators armed with axes, compasses, and poling chains the history of the Kentucky country assumed a new dimension. Once established, forts and stronghold stations became islands of safety from which land hunters spread out across the "waste" lands.[3]

The Anglo-American colonial settler made a radically different approach to the land from that made by the French and American skins and Indian trades goods invaders. For instance, the central focus of interest at Eskippakithiki was the Indian trade, not the land.[4] The new wave of settlers who arrived after 1775 came to stay, to clear away the forest, drive out the wild game, and turn grazing and browsing grounds into cultivated fields. Where once buffalo, deer, and elk browsed there now wandered through the woods herds of settlers' cattle and droves of their hogs. As impressive as these were to apprehensive Indian observers, the fact that the newcomers established a form of government, a land court, and organized militia companies was even more significant. This was no invasion of Indian traders and long hunters who gathered packs of skins and furs and went home.

There have always been moments in history when forces and circumstances have had so profound a bearing on future events. The era of the formation of Clark County was one of interesting timing. A combination of events and forces bore upon the decisions of the moment.[5] These were geographical location, environmental conditions, and early interstate rivalries, all of which helped shape the fortunes and character of the yeoman immigrant-settlers. First, the area of the new county was not only skirted by the Great Warriors Path, a lateral of which led to the Blue Licks and onto the Ohio, but was also not far removed from the well-padded buffalo trace which circled about the salt licks and then to an Ohio River crossing.[6] These historic passways became immigrant arteries for settlers and war trails for Indian resisters. These were the land routes of western penetration. The river systems were of monumental importance, and Clark County was bounded by the Kentucky and Red rivers on the south and east, and by lateral creeks which emptied into the Licking River to the north.[7]

After 1775 the Wilderness, or Boone Trail, which led up from Cumberland Gap to the south bank of the Kentucky River and to Boonesborough and Lexington, fed one party after another of land hungry immigrants onto the land. It was also a virtual trail of fire beset by angry Cherokee warriors who resented the overgenerous territorial cessions made in the Treaty of Sycamore Shoals in the winter of 1774-1775.[8]

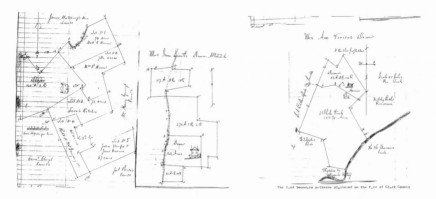

The land boundary patterns plastered on the face of Clark County challenges the imagination of the brightest student of plane geometry. These three plats reflect both the pattern of original surveys, and of the process of subdivision which has gone on in the county for two centuries. Two plats are dower right divisions of the lands of Sam Hume, Thomas Vivian, and John Smith, Sr. These subdivisions were made in 1860 and '61.

In many respects the area which became Clark County was a Kentucky frontier anomaly. There were not located in the area a major fort or many blockhouse or log resistant stations.[9] Perhaps for this reason there were no major incidents of Indian attacks. Nevertheless, the region was caught tangentially in the attacks on Boonesborough, Bryan's Station, and the Blue Licks.[10] British-Indian attacks on these places during the American Revolution had a profound influence upon the rate of settlement in the area.

Though of remarkably short duration, 1775-1776, the activities of Richard Henderson and his Transylvania Company partners at Boonesborough influenced the early approaches to land on both banks of the Kentucky River.[11] There remained after 1776 traces of the Virginia-North Carolina rivalry, especially in the relationships between Boonesborough and the settlements about Logan's, Harrodsburg, and Lexington. In the meantime there filtered through this sieve of southern and northern Indian raids and the settlement rivalries a surprisingly flush stream of settlers fleeing the potential ravages of war, land exhaustion, and the burdens of indebtedness back east. Most important, however, was the hope of establishing a more prosperous way of agrarian life on the new lands of the Kentucky frontier. Despite the theorizing of historians that these westward moving settlers came imbued with a desire to establish a true democratic society, it is exceedingly doubtful that the average immigrant head of household who came to Clark County knew little of the Jeffersonian views of this matter or was aware of the debates which had taken place in Richmond over the conflicting views of the settlers and the new lands.[12] They

were, however, acutely aware of the dangers threatened by British-Indian attacks on the settlements.

The timing of the opening of the Kentucky frontier was of the greatest
seminal importance. The year following the Declaration of Independence
was one of rather heavy immigration. The ensuing Revolutionary War placed
all but defeatist pressure against the opening settlements. Every fort, blockhouse, cabin, and camping place on the Wilderness Trail or landing place on
the Ohio River was subjected to assault by Indian raiders. So prevalent was
this fact that the earlier historians of Kentucky placed a major emphasis on
the conflicts.[13]

Precursor to the Indian raids to follow was the famous kidnapping incident at Boonesborough. On July 14, 1776, a small band of wandering
Shawnees, in what is now Clark County, seized the Boone and Calloway girls
and made off across the wilderness toward the Blue Licks and the Shawnee
Villages north of the Ohio.[14] This incident touched off one of the most dramatic rescue pursuits in Kentucky frontier history. No doubt because of its
romantic implications, plus the shrewd woodsman craft of Daniel Boone and
his fellow pursuers, this incident has been described many times over. Too, it
was given even wider notice in Karl Bodmer's famous painting of the seizure.
Not only was the rescue a triumphant outwitting of the Indians by both the
girls and their rescuers, but it in some measure marked the beginnings of
raids against the emerging settlements.[15]

Along with the fact that the Boone and Calloway girls were rescued was
the corralling of a stray horse wandering in the woods, but even more notable
was the fact that Boone and his party came on the cabin of William Bush.
This incident also emphasized the importance of the Warrior's Trace and the
Lower Blue Licks as major landmarks in the western country.[16]

In time the Clark County area was to stand on the perimeter of at least
four or five major Indian attacks against the Kentucky settlements. First of
these was the major drive and siege against Boonesborough on September 7-
18, 1778 by Indian forces under the command of Antoine DeQuindre and
Chief Blackfish. Earlier on April 15, 1777, Boonesborough was being attacked, Down the Kentucky River Logan's and Harrod's forts were under
siege in May and July, 1777. The great blow of the capture of Daniel Boone
and the salt makers at the Blue Lick on February 7, 1778, was to open an
extended drama of attacks against the settlements. No attack by the British
and Indians stirred frontier anger more than that of Colonel Henry Bird
against Ruddle's and Martin's stations on the Licking River. The atrocities
committed by the Indians against the settlers, though of limited military sig-

nificance, had a powerful impact on Kentucky settlements.[17] This was true of the defeat of the pioneers led by Captain James Estill at Little Mountain, now Mount Sterling, on March 22, 1782. Then came the defeat of Captain John Holder and a party of seventeen men at the Upper Blue Licks. Three days later Major William Caldwell, Alexander McKee, and Simon Girty led a warrior force against Bryan Station on August 15th, and in their retreat toward the Ohio they were followed by a hurriedly organized party of settlers. At the Blue Licks the Kentuckians suffered a defeat which has long imprinted in blood the lesson of using extreme caution in combatting war parties.[18]

During the years 1775-1782 the western backcountry settlements served as a line for checking British-Indian drives against the Virginia and Pennsylvania Revolutionary War rear. Following the Battle of the Blue Licks, August 19, 1782, Indian raids were more of a nuisance than life-threatening. Many of them were no more than horse stealing forays. Largely because there were no forts or major points of concentration of settlers the Clark County area never became the scene of a major British-Indian assault during the American Revolution, though it was a key territory between Bryan's Station and Boonesborough.[19]

There is some historically dramatic coincidence that both the Commonwealth of Kentucky and Clark County came into existence in one of the truly seminal moments in American frontier history. Neither the progress of the American Revolution nor the constant threats of Indian raiding seems to have deterred immigrants from coming west in search of new land and a new way of life. The Indian threat was in good part the yeast which fermented into a move for independent statehood for Kentucky. It was the pressure of attacks on the settlements which caused Benjamin Logan to call for a special convention of delegates from the counties to discuss the problems of the western country.[20]

Represented in the ten conventions which met, 1785-1792, in Danville was a full delegation from Fayette County. It is impossible to identify who among the delegates who went to Danville during the years of the conventions might be considered as either being from the Clark County area or contributing to the framing of the first constitution. Certainly many people in the area read the reports of the conventions which were published in the *Kentucky Gazette*. On a national stage the Constitutional Convention in Philadelphia had drafted the United States Constitution, and subsequently Kentuckians became involved in the ratification debates in Virginia.[21]

Contemporaneously with the national events, the Kentucky country was in a highly fermentive stage. Almost monthly the pressure of incoming popu-

The ravine opposite Boonesborough. It was near the mouth of this ravine that the Boone and
Calloway girls were captured. This spot appears as background in the famous Bodmer painting of the
capture. - *Photo courtesy of Jerry Schureman*

lation was felt in almost every aspect of the frontier territorial way of life. The
Clark County area was represented in all of the ten conventions by delegates
from Fayette County at large.[22] When a constitution for the Commonwealth
of Kentucky was finally drafted and adopted the state was admitted to the
Union on the arbitrary date of June 1, 1792. During the years 1775-1792
there had occurred almost revolutionary changes in every aspect of life on the
Kentucky frontier.[23] By the latter date the central area of the commonwealth
has largely passed through the raw stages of pioneering and had now become
a settled region generating its own problems of political organization, economy,
and concern with the still daunting problem of Spanish control of the Lower
Mississippi. The actual impetus for separating from Virginia and establishing
an independent state was that of bringing an administrative authority closer
to the people.

When Isaac Shelby and his official aides rode horseback from Danville to
Lexington on June 4, 1793, to formerly institute the government of the Commonwealth of Kentucky, they may even have proclaimed an ending of the old
frontier itself.[24] At that moment the conflicts with the Indians of the Northwest Territory had moved northward to the Great Lakes region. Colonel John

Hardin and a Major Trueman were on their way to discuss opening commu-
nications with the tribes along the River Auglaize. These peace emissaries
were murdered, an act which fueled both Kentucky and national official anger.[25] A major military campaign was organized under the command of General Anthony Wayne to advance northward over the route where previous
militia and military forces had met stinging defeats.[26]

General Wayne's well-planned and successful drive through the Northwest Indian territory, the culminating victory in the Battle of Fallen Timbers,
and the subsequent negotiation of the Treaty of Greenville ostensibly ended
Indian raids on the Kentucky settlements.[27] Almost as a grand finale to a
quarter of a century of warring, a small band of warriors struck a fatal blow in
the Clark County area. On March 23, 1795, the horse stealing band broke
into the house of a backwoods family near the Bourbon Furnace and killed
three black slaves and a white man, woman, and child. Later, in May that
year, two settlers in Madison County were hunting for stray horses when they
were fired on by Indians and one of the settlers was killed. He may have been
one of the last victims of northern Indian raiders. At last the Kentucky settlements were free of menace which had hovered over the settlements ever since
James Harrod had led his party to the headwaters of the Salt River in 1774.
Certainly the settlers in the Clark County area could now breathe more easily; their homesteads were no longer threatened with deadly attacks.[28]

Historians of Kentucky in the earlier years paid too little attention to the
technical and social aspects of pioneering. They concerned themselves with
military conflicts, politics, and personalities.[29] Aside from politics if there was
any single constant in Kentucky's history, it has been the human sensitivities
generated by two centuries of issues arising from the possession of the land.
As indicated, land was the drawing magnet which brought streams of settlers
up the Wilderness Road or down the Ohio in search of fortune and economic
and social security. Long before the first settlers arrived the Kentucky Territory was a pawn between Britain and France.[30] After the Revolutionary War
it became for Virginia a means of granting bonuses to its military veterans.

The land pattern which was fixed on the face of Clark County was designed far from the boundaries of the Kentucky frontier. There has been no
more significant fact relating to the county than the acquisition, occupation,
and bringing under cultivation of the virgin wilderness. This central theme of
Clark County history is eloquently documented in its ever-expanding volumes of deed recordings and in the county and circuit court case files and
order books. After the formation of Clark County scarcely a meeting of the
county court took place when some issue pertaining to land ownership was

not on the docket. The case files of the circuit court contain a considerable accumulation of documentary evidence of land disputes and the vagaries of human nature. Some of the depositions are eloquent testimonials of the trials and tribulations of planting a civilization in the western country.[31]

Whatever complaints the American colonists had against the British crown, none charged it with having failed to develop an orderly system of land surveys and orderly recording of deeds and other records of private ownership. Instead the land problem in the western country was complicated by competitive rivalries of the speculative land companies, such as the Ohio, Loyal, and Transylvania seekers broad expanses of territory. All of these had a direct bearing on the land system and settlement of Kentucky. In addition there was the rivalry between Britain and France for possession of the Ohio and Mississippi valleys. The French and Indian War left Britain in control of the West by the Treaty of Paris of 1763. On October 2, that year the crown undertook to halt settler movement into the Indian lands of the West by issuing the famous Proclamation of 1763.[32] This royal decree undertook to establish an official dividing line along the watershed of the Appalachian Highlands all the way from Quebec to the Spanish territorial boundary on the 31st degree parallel. This vague line of demarcation was ignored by traders, land scouts, and land speculators. In the brief interval of time, 1763 to 1776, settler pressure was building up in Pennsylvania, Maryland, Virginia, and the Carolinas. The Declaration of Independence and the occurrence of the American Revolutionary War changed completely the approach to the trans-Appalachian frontier.[33] Long hunters had explored extensively the Kentucky region; so had Daniel Boone, Simon Kenton, and others. No longer was the land on the western waters one of mystery. In 1763 it was only a matter of a brief time before the region would begin to be settled.

Before the advent of the Declaration of Independence no colonial state government had the official power either to make land grants in the West or to establish a policy of management for the outlying lands in the Ohio Valley. By 1776 the matter of making land grants and registering them in the Kentucky country had become a highly involved and complex one. Directly bearing upon the history of future Clark County was the coming of the Transylvania Company speculators and settlers to the south bank of the Kentucky River at Boonesborough. Under the leadership of Richard Henderson and a company of partners a treaty cession, more nearly a lease, was concluded with the Cherokee Indians at Sycamore Shoals in present eastern Tennessee. The partners of the Transylvania Company and Richard Henderson had the grandiose idea of establishing a fourteenth American colony.[34]

An intriguing chapter in Kentucky history is that of the role of Daniel Boone in the affairs of the Transylvania Company. Certainly his wide knowledge of the Kentucky country was of vital importance. His immediate service to the company, however, was the blazing of a wilderness trail from the point where the Warriors Trail veered off at Flat Lick to the southern bank of the Kentucky River.[35] The adventures of Boone and his trailblazing party were not without grave danger. Indians attacked the party with fatal results at what became known as Twetty's Defeat, or Little Fort, a site near present-day Richmond. This trailblazing expedition generated two interesting firsthand descriptions of the task and the countryside. William Calk kept a journal which in a cryptic vernacular style graphically described the ordeal of traveling on a narrow path across a sprawling wilderness. Felix Walker, a member of the Daniel Boone party, also kept a journal which reflected the almost utopian dreams of the first wave of settlers to the Kentucky country.[36] That dream, however, was severely darkened when the author suffered a wound at the hand of an Indian.[37] The arrival of Daniel Boone and his trailblazers underneath the southern bluff of the Kentucky River on March 28, 1775, was in fact a cardinal event in the history of Clark County. The location of the headquarters of the Transylvania Company on the Kentucky River was to figure prominently in the future of the region on the north side of the river.[38]

This was also true of the beginnings of settlements at Harrod's and Logan's and McClellan's forts. Almost immediately there developed a sharp intercolony rivalry between the North Carolinians at Boonesborough and the Virginians at the other settlements. In 1775 there appeared at Harrod's Fort one of the most impressive personal figures in American frontier history. George Rogers Clark, himself a land hunter, quickly sensed the developing rivalry between the colonial groups and the increasing danger of the Indian raids. At a called meeting at Harrod's Fort, Clark and John Gabriel Jones were chosen representatives to go back to Richmond, Virginia to solicit aid for the western settlements. They sought to convince the Virginia officials to assert the colony's authority over the western country.[39] A political result of Clark and Jones' representation was the creation of trans-Appalachian County to come into existence on December 31, 1776, six months after the Declaration of Independence was proclaimed.[40] The creation of this blanket county out of Fincastle County marked the beginning of a long history of Kentucky county creations. Clark and Jones were also given a limited supply of arms and ammunition with which to protect the western settlements. These acts of the Virginia Assembly also introduced into western country an archaic political system which was more adaptable to pastoral England and the Virginia Tidewater than to the frontier. In 1812 Humphrey Marshall succinctly described the political situation of the western settlements. "As part of Fincastle County," he wrote, "they [Kentucky settlers] had in fact, no part, or lot, in its policy; nor could they vote at elections for representatives--receive military protection, or be distinctly heard in the legislature, in consequence of their detached situation; but composing a county themselves, they, by the constitution of the state, were to be thence forth entitled to two representatives of their own choosing. They were also entitled to have a county court of civil jurisdiction of matters in both law; and equity--justice of the peace--militia sheriff--coroner, and surveyor; in fine, to be a civil, and military, municipality; or corporation; with powers competent to their own government, agreeably to the general laws of the commonwealth."[41] Essentially this statement contained the seeds of a declaration of western country independence.

Though the formation of Clark County was to be almost a decade and a half away, the issues which arose in the opening years of the Kentucky frontier had fundamental bearings on its future. There were few if any political figures east of the Appalachians who truly had any basic concept of the rugged environmental conditions of the western country, the challenges of cutting holes in the great wilderness, and the planting of a civilization amidst constant threats of militant resistance.[42]

In no aspect of the opening of the Kentucky frontier was the lack of policy and planning more evident than in administration of the distribution of public lands, management of natural resources such as streams, control of the building of mill dams and the operation of ferries, and the art of making

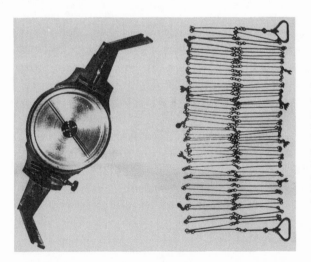

The chain and compass were two of the most important instruments in establishing land boundaries, in the settlement of disputed boundaries, and in the subdivisions of the larger landholds in Clark County. - *Photo courtesy of Clark, Historic Maps of Kentucky*

competent land surveys. No doubt Virginia officials in 1776 were too intently involved in the issues of independence and the impending Revolutionary War to give the western problem much more than a cursory notice. For
the long span of the history of Kentucky this was the cardinal moment setting precedents; political, social, and institutional; in the first great moment
of interregional migration in American history.[43]

There was in Richmond, Virginia, despite preoccupation with the emer-
gencies of independence and war, an awareness that some attention had to be
given the West. Under the circumstances they could not have done otherwise. Again, Humphrey Marshall summed up the reasons for action. He wrote,
"in mentioning the incidents of 1776, the visit of George Rogers Clark, who
will hereafter occupy a distinguished place in this history, also demands attention. His appearance, [in Richmond] well calculated to attract attention,
was rendered particularly agreeable, by the manliness of his deportment, the
intelligence of his conversation; but above all, by the vivacity, and boldness of
his spirit for enterprise, and determination he expressed of becoming an inhabitant of the country."[44] Thus it was for vivacity, boldness, and enterprise
that in 1792 the founding fathers of the new county named it Clark.

The history of the opening of the western country cast against the background of the revolutionary era is a highly complex one. There was a veritable
entangled legal web of trying to arrive at a workable public land management
policy on the part of the Virginia leaders and the general assembly members.
There were sharp differences of approach to the enactment of legislation governing the lands of the West. There was a hint that Jefferson, Henry, Mason,
and others wanted to populate the projected Kentucky County with yeoman
settlers on the theory that they were a solid democratic element who would
escape many of the evils of the old landed colonial society of Tidewater Virginia.[45] On December 7, 1776 the Virginia General Assembly created Kentucky County. It also removed Richard Henderson and the Transylvania
Company as a rival by granting Henderson's company 200,000 acres of land
on the Green River, thus placing the settlement about Boonesborough in an
entirely new political and administrative context.[46]

Opponents of the creation of Kentucky County and the further opening
of the western country to settlement brought forth some interesting oppos-
ing arguments. It was feared that the new lands would draw off an important
body of the older area's population, having significant economic effects on
the state. Too, it was contended that immigration to the West would result in
the loss of military manpower in the Virginia continental forces.[47]

The constitution of the State of Virginia went into force on July 5, 1776.

Not only did it outline that structure of government, but it defined the boundaries of the state and forbade the purchase of lands from the Indians except as the state might do so. There was written into the document a clear presumption that a new state or states would be formed from the western lands included in the treaty between Britain and France in 1763. The precise statement was, "By act of this legislature, one or more governments be established west of the Allegheny Mountains." Thus the fortune of the western frontier was set: in time Kentucky County would evolve into a state.[48]

Six months prior to the creation of Kentucky County, the Virginians understood to deal with the tangled western land question. On June 24, 1776, the assembly adopted a resolution that the claims of private purchasers of lands from the Indians would be forbidden. This action in fact was intended to nullify specifically the Transylvania transactions with the Cherokees at the Sycamore Shoals in March 1775 and the claims of the Ohio and Loyal land companies. There was more to this matter than the revocation of land transactions. Clearly there were numerous conflicting special interests involved and issues which revealed the personal connections of many of the current Virginia leadership.[49]

The resolution of 1776, adopted in the midmoment when the colonies were advancing toward independence, perhaps lacked the force of law and in actuality settled nothing. Already in Kentucky there had occurred many rather extensive surveys. There were those made by Hancock Taylor, James Douglas, John Floyd, Thomas Walker. In 1773 Captain Thomas Bullitt had made an agreement with the Shawnee Indians to make a survey and a settlement on lands about the Falls of the Ohio.[50] Then there were other landseekers before 1776 who had been in the Kentucky country. It may be true that Thomas Jefferson, Patrick Henry, and their inner circle of prowestern associates may have entertained the idea that the tracts of western lands should be restricted to a size which would probably maintain a family with the hope that the region would be populated by a yeoman class. But in coldly realistic and objective historical terms the administration of Virginia's western lands was careless at best and negligent in fact.

Between the adoption of the June 1776 resolution and 1779 it became urgently clear that more positive action was necessary to establish some kind of order in the granting of land claims, the warranteeing of their prior ownership, and the registering of deeds. The intervening law of October 1777 made provision for the registration of claims made prior to June 24, 1776. It also assured that prior claimants were to be enabled to register title to 400 acres of land in the region of the "western waters." Each claimant was required to make a serious gesture of occupation and settlement by having cleared a plot and planted corn and, later, to have built some kind of crude cabin structure on it. This law was modified to permit a claimant to preempt 1,000 acres upon the payment of a modest fee. By 1778 landholds in Kentucky County were either poorly surveyed or in many cases were located almost by a wave of the hand and by blazing trees and driving down stakes.[51] As a result across the whole Kentucky frontier, occurred the overlapping of boundaries, or "shingling," as it was often called. It may have happened that the arrival of every immigrant party signaled more complications in the locating and claiming of homesteads. Boonesborough, Bryan's Station, and Logan's and Harrod's forts served largely as islands of safety while land claimants moved out into the countryside to locate tracts of land. By 1785 a good part of the area which is now Clark County was plastered over with a patchwork of claims, many of which overlapped prior claims. In some cases there might have been three or four shinglings overlapping a tract, a fact that took a wise and patient court to disentangle.[52]

The Virginia General Assembly asserted in the new law "that a great number of people have settled in the country upon the western waters, upon waste and unappropriated lands, for which they have been hitherto prevented from suing out patents or obtaining legal titles as the King of Great Britain's proclamation or instructions to his governors, or by the late change of governments, and the present war having delayed until now the opening of land office, and the establishment of any certain terms for granting lands, and it is just that those settling under such circumstances should have some reasonable allowance for the charge and risk they have incurred, and that the property so acquired should be secured to them."[53]

When one moves across the modern Clark County landscape he or she has in view boundary outlines in the form of fences, rows of trees, and the outlines of fields and meadows; all of these monumental registries of the impact to the complex lands laws passed in the latter quarter of the eighteenth century by the Virginia General Assembly are physical documentation of the transforming of a wilderness into fields and meadows. In 1792 the Kentucky General Assembly took up the governing of land matters where the Virginia General Assembly had left off, and the volume of land legislation has grown with each succeeding century.

It was clear to Virginia governors and legislators by 1779 that some definite steps should be taken to provide for the certification of land claims and for settling prior claimant contests. By 1778 the massive confusion in land surveys and the establishment of valid deeds called for an enormous amount of judicial wisdom and courage to establish even a semblance of order. The Land Court created by the law of 1779 was to consist of four judges or commissioners and a clerk. Prefatory to this legislation was a considerable amount of philosophical discussion and the reconciliation of various self-interest. The four appointed judges were William Fleming, a Scotch-born immigrant of bright and practical mind; James Barbour, scion of an old and established family, a former member of the General Assembly, and an officer in the Virginia armed forces; Colonel Edmund Lyne, also the son of a planter family; and James Steptoe, a county clerk for forty years, a graduate of William and Mary College, and a lifelong friend of Thomas Jefferson. The fifth member of the court was Stephen Trigg, who bore the title of "colonel" and was a native of Augusta County. He was a nephew by marriage of the influential surveyor general William Christian. Trigg had actively participated in the organization of Bottetourt County, and, two years later, lost his life in the Battle of Blue Licks. John Williams, Jr. served as clerk.[54]

By October 1777 a majority of the commissioners had arrived at Logan's Fort and begun the laborious task of taking depositions, scanning crudely drawn land survey plats, and undertaking to determine who was in fact the prior claimant. The judges of the Land Court were empowered to recommend the issuance of warrants. The law of 1779 was explicit and all-inclusive. It provided that, "The said commissioners shall have the power to hear and determine all titles claimed in consideration of settlements, to lands, to which person hath any other legal title, and the right of all persons claiming pre-emption to any lands within their respective districts, as also the rights of all persons claiming any unpatented lands, surveyed by order of council for sundry companies, by having settled themselves under the faith of the terms of sale publicly offered by such companies, or their agents, and shall, immediately upon receipt of their commissions, give at least twenty days previous notice by advertisements at the forts, churches, meeting-houses, and other publick places in their district, of the time and place at which they plan to meet, for the purpose of collecting, hearing, and determining the claims and titles, requiring persons interested therein to attend and put their claims, and may adjourn from place, to place, and time to time, as their business may require."[55]

"They shall appoint and administer an oath of office of their clerk; be attended by a sheriff, or one of the under sheriffs of the county; be empowered to administer oaths to witnesses or others, necessary for the discharge of their office...they shall have free access to the county surveyor's books, and may order the same to be laid before them at any place or time of their sit-

The ferry site at Boonesborough over which both emigrants and travelers were crossed for several decades. More important it was a strategic connector between Clark County and the Wilderness Road. - *Photo courtesy of Jerry Schureman*

ting." This law had fundamental meaning for the settlers of the Clark County area in 1779-80.[56]

The first session of the Kentucky Land Court was held at St. Asaph (Logan's) Fort. By the onset of the extremely cold and devastating winter of 1789-80, the judges had held eight sessions. The two most directly applying to Clark County land claimants sat at Boonesborough and Bryan's Station. In the very heart of a paralyzing ice and snow storm that court sat at Boonesborough on December 19 to 26, 1779, and then moved on to Bryan's Station to sit there, January 3 to 19, 1780.[57] Except for many of the warranty deeds appearing in the Clark-Fayette county deed books, there are no precise data available about individuals who were favored with warranty approvals. Frequently present-day individuals will produce land warrants signed by Thomas Jefferson, Patrick Henry, and other Virginia governors.

It is pertinent to mention in connection with the early land history of Clark County that the "great freeze" of 1779-1780 was a landmark incident in Kentucky history. Daniel Trabue, a contemporary observer, recorded a graphic first-hand account of the hardships suffered by settlers and animals. He wrote, "This hard winter began about the first of November 1779 and broak up the last of February 1780. The turkeys was almost all dead. The buffeloes had got poore. Peoples cattle mostly Dead. No corn or but very little in the cuntry. The people was in great Distress. Many in the wilderness frostbit. Some Dead. Some eat of the dead cattle and horses. When broak the men would go and kill the buffeloes and bring them home to eat but they was so poore. A number of people would be Taken sick and did acutly Die for the want of solid food. The most of the people had to go to the falls of the Ohio for corn to plant which was brought down the Ohio."[58]

William Fleming confirmed Daniel Trabue's account of the devastating winter. He wrote, "Dec. 3rd and 4th. Did a little business and adjourned to Elkhorn (i.e., Bryan's Station). It continued excessive cold. Col. Barbour proposed to leave us. The 5th A storm of snow fell and the Kentucky rose, which made us alter our appointments from Elkhorn to Boonesborough. 6th continued cold with snow. The inhabitants averred they never knew so severe weather at that season, the winter generally setting in about Christmas and continuing about six weeks."[59]

One of the basic problems which the Kentucky Land Court could not solve was the inefficiency of the hoard of deputy surveyors. Kentucky pioneer surveyors used the three instruments in current usage: the jacobs staff and compass, the four pole linked chain, and the axe. Doubtless most of the patronage deputy surveyors were too inexperienced to make the necessary time declinations to establish the true north or to set precisely the bearings showing on the face of the compass. An even greater chance of error was the use of chains which had been dragged over gritty grounds until their links had become worn or enlarged. Even if chainmen had been most careful in making their measurements, which they were not, the chains were so inaccurate that measurements could not be repeated with the same results. In wooded country it was difficult, if not impossible, for the early surveyors to set bearings and chain boundaries. Indisputably chainmen were either too lazy or indifferent to make deep notches in trees or other durable marks which could be identified in later years. The Virginia law of 1779 specified that substantial marks be made on trees, but chainmen in the old Fayette countryside frequently cited bushes and stakes. Finally, surveyors specified trees of a general class without identifying the particular variety, a fact which created disputes in the future.[60]

Because of the haphazard mode of establishing land boundaries in frontier Kentucky, plots of land got left out of deeds and off of assessor rolls. These "wild lands" also created future problems. Thus one reads the land pattern in Clark County pretty much as an historian reads a documentary source. The local land pattern is in fact a physical and legal testimonial to the early pioneer Kentucky settler's approach to the land before any official prior survey of it had been made. The early Virginia laws which were enacted with the hope that order could be established in land granting in the Kentucky counties were little more than legal gestures.[61]

One may well ask what actually the Kentucky Land Court accomplished in its brief moment of existence? What direct impact did its decisions have on the establishment of land claims in Clark County, of combatting the threatening virus of overlapping claims? The deed books of Clark County bear eloquent testimony to the vagueness of written boundary descriptions, the lack of investigations by deputy surveyors regarding established land ownerships, and, most important of all, designating of calls which did not meet or close. No doubt the best-known Kentucky deputy land surveyor was Daniel Boone. He was highly trusted as a judge of quality land, the location of free-flowing springs, and other attractive features. He is said to have made surveys which were little more than a wave of the hand or an educated guess as to the types of trees in a boundary, the meanderings of streams, and the "quartering" of ridges. Later Henry Clay described these off the ground surveys as a "fireside" creation. Court records and even deeds in Clark County contain testimony in land disputes given by Daniel Boone. He seems to have been an infallible authority on boundaries and land grants.

The petitioners seeking the creation of Clark County made no mention of the total population of the area nor did the legislators in drafting the law authorizing its organization. Had there been such a statement it would have been inaccurate within a month's time. There were said to be an estimated 73,000 souls in Kentucky in 1793. The United States' second census, 1800, indicated there were in Clark County 5,998 whites and 1,358 black slaves, or a total population of the astonishing number 7,526 in all. More revealing than mere numbers is the fact that males and females were almost equally balanced. This is contrary to the general assumption by historians about the frontier that males far outnumbered females. Three-fourths of the population was under twenty-six years of age, with young children being the most populous. The newly formed county seat, Winchester, had a population of 127 individuals, of whom 28 were slaves. This was a rural, land-dwelling population.[62]

What motivated immigrants to move into the Clark County area? Clearly, the availability of fertile lands was a chief attraction. A central question is why did so many people brave the environmental hardships, the threats of Indian attacks, and the arduous challenge of performing the physical labor to

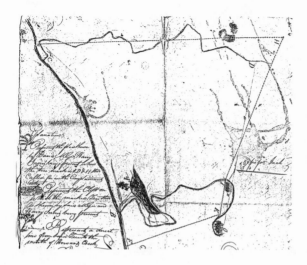

This plat of the land at the mouth of Lower Howard's Creek and the Kentucky River. It was involved in 1816 in the dispute over overlapping claims between Matthew Jouett and the heirs of John Holder.

exploit the land? There was in the closing quarter of the eighteenth century a virtual land-hungry frenzy created by word-of-mouth reports on the availability of rich western lands at modest cost. Without reasonable doubt the spread of the promotional propaganda of the "the great edenesque-great meadow promise" heightened the impulse to move west.[63]

Always it must be remembered that the exigencies of the Revolutionary War and the hardships it created for families in the east were a major factor. Large numbers of immigrants coming to the Kentucky frontier between 1775 and 1792 had faced economic crisis conditions back in Virginia or the Carolinas. It is questionable whether the mass of immigrants who came west were imbued with a burning desire to create a democratic society in their new country. Historians have dealt with the matter of a grassroots population moving onto the virgin frontier with a fixed dream of establishing a democratic, rural-agrarian yeoman type of social and cultural simplicity. Historically, one of the strong motivations for moving onto the Kentucky frontier was the granting of land bonuses to Revolutionary War veterans. For simple propertyless immigrant plodding his laborious way up the Wilderness Road in search of a new home there could have been no more eloquent testimony than the conversation reported by Moses Austin. "Ask these pilgrims," he wrote, "what they expect when they get to Kentucky the Answer is Land. have you any. No, but I expect I can git it. have you any thing to pay for land. No. did you Ever see the Country. No but Every Body says its good land. can any thing be more Absurd than the conduct of man, here is hundreds Travelling hundreds of miles of Miles, they Know not for what Nor Whither, except its to Kentucky, passing land almost as good and easy obtained, the Proprietors of which would gladly give on any terms, but it will not do its not Kentucky its not the Promised land its not the goodly inheritance the Land of Milk and Honey, and when arriv'd at this Heaven in Idea what do they find? A goodly land I will allow but to the forbidden Land, exhausted and worn down with distress and disappointment they are at least Obliged to become hewers of wood and Drawers of Water."[64]

Thus there moved onto the Clark County frontier, 1775-1792, a mixed economic and social class of population. They came for reasons almost as varied and vague as were their immigrant group organizations. They lugged along with them as cultural and social baggage folkways, religious beliefs, dreams of finding and establishing themselves on productive land, enjoying the blessings of a pastoral existence, and, no doubt, a vague notion of embracing some kind of political system which could be manipulated at the local institutional level.

A fact known very well to local genealogists was that there came west a veritable tapestry of interfamily relationships with background ties of blood kinship to piedmont Virginia and the Carolinas. Often it almost seemed that the intricacies of blood relationships, even many times removed, were a major human factor in attempts to explain the motivations for the great movement onto the lands of the "western waters" and into the area of future Clark County.

The Courthouse tower in Winchester might well be considered the magnetic center of the county. Here the tower stands out a dignified landmark of two centuries of politic history in the "Little Kingdom." - *Photo courtesy of Jerry Schureman*

CHAPTER 3

Forming The "Little Kingdom"

Kentucky in 1792 was rural, agrarian, and still a frontier. It had not really developed a local system of roads, and every group which settled down on isolated land claims soon found there was urgent need for access to both county and state governments. Perhaps few of the immigrants who arrived in Clark County in the formative years had little notion of how vital government would be to their safety and welfare. During the decade 1785-1795, the population in the areas of the three original counties grew phenomenally fast.[1] The expansive areas of Fayette, Lincoln, and Jefferson counties presented almost insoluble problems of hazardous travel, possible Indian skirmishes, and exposure of families to other possible dangers.[2]

The sprawling original county of Fayette was reduced appreciably in size by the creation of Bourbon County in 1785, but even so none of the problems of reaching the county seat, Lexington, were alleviated.[3] Petitioners in both Fayette and Bourbon counties, prior to 1792, revealed their dissatisfaction to the Virginia General Assembly by sending to Richmond a veritable stream of petitions, many of them outlining the boundaries for new counties in the area. Some claimed that citizens had to travel sixty-five miles to a county seat.[4]

The same threats of endangerment from Indian raids which provoked the calling of the first Danville Convention in 1785 agitated the early settlers of the Clark County area.[5] In a more Jeffersonian philosophical vein, early petitioners pleaded the fact that, "obtaining of justice should be made safe and easy as possible to all its [Virginia's] citizens."[6] Here it should be noted that while the movement was under way to effect separation of the Kentucky

District from Virginia, there was a definite drive locally to divide the large three counties into smaller units for much the same reasons delegates to the Danville Convention (1785-1792) gave for their efforts to create a separate state.[7]

Unfortunately there seems not to be in existence any formal record of just how the idea of creating Clark County originated or who placed the idea before the Kentucky General Assembly. It seems reasonable to assume that some, if not all, the supplicants were William Sudduth, John Strode, John Baker, James McMillan, John Holder, Robert Clarke, Jillson Payne, John McGuire, and Abijah Brooks.[8] The Clark County Petitioners had plenty of company in Frankfort in December 1792. There were groups seeking the creation of Green, Logan, Hardin, Scott, and Shelby counties who presented the same reasons for the creation of a new county as did those from Clark.[9] Historically, this was the beginning of transforming the landscape of Kentucky into a multiplicity of counties.

The legislative act creating Clark County, December 6, 1792, out of portions of Fayette and Bourbon counties is an unusually terse one. The law prescribed in more or less general terms the boundaries of the new county, which was to begin independent operation on February 1, 1793.[10] The boundaries began at the mouth of the Boon's Creek on the Kentucky River, thence up the same (Boon's) to the mouth of Welch's Fork, thence a direct line in the Bourbon line, such a course as will leave the house of John M'Creary, senior, one quarter of a mile to the westward, thence a straight line to Stoner's fork of Licking such a course as will leave Bourbon Courthouse eleven miles from the nearest part of the said line; thence a straight line to the line of Mason County, so as to leave the Blue Licks two miles to the northwest thereof, up the branch of the Licking along the line of Mason of Mason County to the head thereof; and the said line a direct course from the head of Licking to strike the nearest part of Cumberland Mountains; thence at the head of the Kentucky; thence down the same to the beginning."[11] Most of these boundaries would have challenged the imagination of the most skilled surveyor then in Kentucky. They were as vague in parts as were many of the internal deed descriptions of private landholds. Not a single bearing in the boundary was sufficiently well identified as to avoid future disputes. Two things seem clear: no one had the notion that Clark County would retain its original boundaries, and the boundaries were classic examples of what was popularly called a "fireside survey."[12] There was in neither the act of the General Assembly, nor in subsequent efforts to define the county boundaries evidence that anyone had access to a map; if so the map was a highly generalized one. In its act of creation, the General Assembly ordained that the broad territory described within the authorized boundaries would "be called and known by the name of Clarke," in honor of General George Rogers Clark's name when he never used the appending letter. Also it is possible that Clark had never visited the area of the county.[13]

Once the county was chartered and made a part of an expanding commonwealth, the Clark County Court held its first session on March 26, 1793, at the home of John Strode.[14] Justices or magistrates present on that date were Robert Clarke, Hubbard Taylor, John McGuire, James McMillan, John Holder, Enoch Smith, John Baker, Jillson Payne, William Sudduth, and Abijah Brooks. These may be considered the founding fathers of Clark County. One of the first matters of business for the new court was authorizing Robert Clark, Hubbard Taylor, and John McGuire to organize a court of quarter sessions![15] The other commissioners, or magistrates, were entrusted with the responsibility to organize the county court, to prepare themselves to review issues which came before it, to make decisions about appeals made to it, and to begin the business of creating a county government located within a county seat town and functioning in the necessary public buildings.[16] James Martin was appointed county clerk and administered the oath of office to his official colleagues. Technically March 26, 1793, may be considered the actual date on which government in Clark County began to function.[17] At that meeting John Martin presented a commission from Governor Isaac Shelby appointing him sheriff. His bondsmen were Hubbard Taylor and Benjamin Combs, who obligated themselves in the sum of $3,000, assuring that Martin would perform his duties in a proper manner. David Bullock was appointed county clerk pro tem, John Higgins was made "under sheriff" and John Strode was made coroner.[18]

Aside from creating the official organization of the county, one of the first acts by the newly formed court was to grant the Reverend Robert Elkins the authority "to celebrate the rites of matrimony according to solemnities required by law." The Reverend Elkins offered as evidence of his qualification to do so a certificate of convenience issued by the Baptist Society.

Once the court was seated there came before it a rising barrage of petitioners asking permission to construct mill dams across streams, an act which necessitated an impartial inspection of each site by a committee to assure that property owners up and down stream would not be injured by the dam. Surprisingly, the court was petitioned from the outset to make arrangements for the care of indigents. It had the responsibility of making estate appraisals and of insuring widows their dower rights. The court asked Enos Hardin to

Hubbard Taylor, a native of Virginia, in 1781 a deputy land surveyor for the sprawling county of Lincoln, a land speculator, a frequent correspondent with James Madison, in land and constitutional matters. A member of the House of Representatives from Fayette County in 1792. One, if not the founding father, of Clark County. Served in the Kentucky Senate 1792 a presidential elector 1805-1825. A key figure in the organization of the government of Clark County, and was the progenitor of a large and extended family. - *Photo courtesy of Clara Houlihan-Wiedemann*

establish a more accurate survey of the county's boundaries than those listed in the act of creation. John Martin declared that the public gaol or jail must be one of the first buildings constructed, which surely indicated that the county was still a rowdy frontier area.[19]

No issue which came before the court was more vital to the safety and economic welfare of the people than that of opening roads. It is now difficult to reconcile the fact that in the fall of 1792 the topography of Clark County was practically devoid of trails and roads. On this date three central or arterial connector roads were of primary interest. An open road to Lexington which could be used in wagon travel was an all but urgent necessity. This road promised to become the main thoroughfare of economic, social, and political intercourse with the rest of the commonwealth.[20] A second main road which needed surveying and opening was one from Winchester to Mount Sterling, the outlying village of the county.[21] A third main connector road was needed from Boonesborough to Strode's Station.[22]

Over the years the opening and maintenance of roads became a major function of the county court. The court's practice from the beginning was to appoint a committee to travel along a proposed route, select the least difficult way along ridge tops, locate suitable stream crossings, and placate objecting property owners who did not want roads to cross their properties. The committee blazed trees as they went, following identically the process of marking internal land boundaries. The committee then reported its findings with rec-ommendation to the court. This is how a network of local roads was finally woven across the face of the county.[23]

The opening of a road across Clark County in the closing decade of the eighteenth century involved little more than chopping down trees, leaving the stumps below wagon axle height, and perhaps bridging some of the larger streams with primitive narrow log construction. No mention appeared in the court order books about any attempt to grade or otherwise improve road beds. The court specified that the new roads should be opened wide enough to permit the passage of wagons. As primitive as were the county court's directions for the opening of new roads, they documented the ending of the old packhorse era of travel and transportation. After its chartering and loca-tion on the John Baker lands in 1793, Winchester quickly became the hub of the roads, east and west north and south.[24]

Just as Clark County was unscored by roadways in 1793, so it was open grazing range country over which domestic animals wandered at will. The only method by which owners could identify their cattle, hogs, sheep, horses, and mules was by devising and registering distinctive brand marks. A duty of the county clerk was the recording of the marks and brands much in the same way they recorded land deeds. John Strode's herds and flocks bore an underheel crop in the ears, and I S on the "rear shoulder." John Baker's wandering herd bore a crop of the left ear, and J B on the rear buttock. William Sudduth cut a swallowtail fork slit and punched a hole in the right ear. Thomas Burras registered a crop in the right ear and an underheel in the left, and Daniel Dean's mark was a crop in the left ear and a half crop in the right.[25] As the human population and that of the herds and droves of animals grew it re-quired considerable imagination to devise a distinctive brand mark and ani-mal disfigurement to assert ownership. David Hughes met the challenge by punching a hole in the left ear, and burning a distinctive brand on the "near shoulder."[26] Primitive Clark County was a rangers free and open territory, roamed over by animals bearing private brands of picturesque devisement well before cattlemen in the Southwest began branding their herds.

Early sessions of the Clark County Court were of brief duration. The magistrates attended to the short agendas of business and went home for three months. As an example, the court directed Sheriff John Martin to meet with the sheriffs of Fayette and Bourbon counties to collect and prorate the tithes due each county for the period before Clark County was created. This applied to taxes collected after December 20, 1792.[27]

It was not until July 1793 that the magistrates began making plans for the construction of the four official structures which comprised the courthouse domain. These were to be built on the plot of ground purchased from John Baker and within the bounds of the future county seat town of Winchester. The Baker site had been approved by a majority of the magistrates. They were cautious, however; a committee consisting of James McMillan, John Holder, Enoch Smith, Jillson Payne, and William Sudduth was charged with overseeing the survey of the Baker land. The tract was near John Baker's house and enclosed the fresh flowing spring. The committeemen were requested to have their report ready for the late July sitting of the court.[28]

At the same session of court a second committee made up of James McMillan, William Robinson, John Judy, and John Vivian was requested to locate the nearest and best route for the road connecting the Clark County seat with the older town of Lexington.[29] It should be noted in this case that James McMillan was a deputy land surveyor. Another committee composed of John Baker and an unnamed party was to locate a road to the outlying county village of Mount Sterling.[30] A third committee of viewers was instructed to locate a road from John Holder's boatyard on the Kentucky River to John Baker's house. Thus were outlined by mid-1793 arterial roads which crisscrossed the county.[31]

No doubt the petitioners who sought the formation of Clark County also sought the chartering of the town of Winchester. The members of the court on October 22, 1793, anticipated this event when they began seriously planning for the construction of public buildings. It had been understood from the start that John Strode's Station would not be made the county seat. At the October session James McMillan, Jillson Payne, and William Sudduth went forth once more to view the land where John Baker lived and to begin the process of locating the site for the courthouse and associated structures. The court was adamant that the four acres deeded the county would include the spring; otherwise the site would be unacceptable.[32] James McMillan, a deputy surveyor, was asked to lay out, describe, and record the title to the Baker land. As indicated, all these actions preceded the actual chartering by the Kentucky General Assembly of the county seat town. There appeared to be no doubt that a charter would be forthcoming before the year's end and that the Baker land would be the site for the new town.

During the two decades of Clark County history 1792-1812, all tithes, costs of construction, legal fees, payment for services, and supplies were stated in pounds, shillings, and pence. Expenses for operating the county government cost approximately 1,200 pounds, and income from tithes (taxes) was approximately 1,400 pounds, or approximately $5,000.00. An interesting note for the expenses of the first year of operation: there did not appear among the meticulously itemized accounts any entries for office equipment and supplies.[33] Apparently the offices of the various officials were located wherever they hung their hats.

From the outset, however, the county clerk had in his possession deed, will, mortgage, and court order books. The formal recording of minutes, deeds, and committee reports was done in longhand, with the scribe using quill pens and iron-based ink. The clerks wrote good clear hands, and in some cases, provided elegantly written recordings. Aside from the surveyor descriptions of land surveys, most of the other recording officials gave evidence of some educational proficiency.

Again, in anticipation, of the organization of a county town, a commission comprised of Hubbard Taylor, Robert Clarke, Senior, Robert Clarke, Junior, and Clarence Hockaday was assigned the responsibilities of having a "log cabbin" courthouse, a jail, detention stocks, a stray pen, and a spring house constructed. They were told to advertise these projects for two weeks in the *Kentucky Gazette* and to accept the lowest and best bidders.[34]

Both John Baker and the founding fathers anticipated financial returns from the sale of town lots along Winchester's two projected main streets. From the beginning there were business entrepreneurs who anticipated economic returns from the establishment of the courthouse and the county seat town. These were merchants, tavern keepers, lawyers, doctors, and even surveyors. John Holder, a famous old frontiersman and Indian fighter, and then a justice of the peace, sought a license to keep an ordinary tavern or inn in the house occupied by William Harris. He named Sheriff John Martin and Daniel Bullock as his security bondsman. To create a county courthouse in earlier days without an ordinary or a doggery nearby was unthinkable.[35]

True to official anticipation, the Kentucky General Assembly on December 17, 1793, granted a charter to the county seat town of Winchester.[36] The name of this town, like so much of local Kentucky's nomenclature was of Virginia origin. Winchester, Kentucky, was named for the famous old frontier Virginia town located on the Cumberland Road at the head of the Ohio River. This road had figured prominently in the French and Indian War and the American Revolution. For Kentucky and Clark County it was a town through which thousands of emigrants to the West passed on their way to descend the Ohio aboard flatboats.

The trustees of the new town, as named in the act of creation, were David Bullock, William Bush, Josiah Hart, John Strode, John Elliott, and Benjamin Combs. Their first duty was to have the sixty-six-acre Baker land surveyed and laid off in town lots. These were to be sold, and John Baker was to be compensated from the proceeds. The chartering of Winchester was in fact the last official state act in the establishment of the new county.[39]

By January 1794 the Clark County Court was ready to begin the process of constructing the public buildings on the reserved courthouse square of four acres. A bidder was sought through an advertisement in the *Kentucky Gazette* to build a two-story log "cabbin" courthouse of four rooms. Two of these were to be twenty by twenty feet and two, ten by twenty feet.[39] The specifications for the buildings called for a prodigious use of heavy timbers. Log walls were to be made of oak or blue ash logs, and the floors were to be laid with thick, flat hardwood puncheons. The new courthouse, modeled largely after John Baker's house, was to be completed and ready for occupancy by the quarterly meeting of the court in its April session.[40]

Highly reflective of the raw frontier conditions of the Clark County area, the law creating the county was specific on the subject of free-ranging livestock and the nuisance of animals who wandered far away from their owners. The *Kentucky Gazette* regularly ran notices of strays which had been corralled. One of the first laws enacted by the newly formed General Assembly, June 28, 1792, dealt rather extensively with the matter of straying animals and their disposition.[41] The law mandated the construction of a stray pen in each county, and in the case of Clark County, the court asked William Bush to locate the site for a pen or corral nearby the "cabbin" courthouse. The pen was to be sixty by sixty feet square and constructed of stout hardwood post sunk two feet in the ground, ten foot rails of either oak or locust planking were to form the fencing slats, a gate was to be mounted on strong iron hinges; and a strong lock was to be provided. In short, the Clark County stray pen was to be hog tight, bull high, and sneak-owner proof.[42]

Just as the law provided for the corralling of stray livestock, so it ordered a stronghold for offenders of the law. The founding fathers of Clark County seemed at an early stage to be alert to the fact that there was at large in the county a fair number of criminals. A wooden jail was planned to be a mighty fortress of detention for offenders of the law and the commonwealth. Using the abundant heavy materials at hand, officials planned what they believed would be a pry-proof structure from which no prisoner could cut his way to freedom from the inside and no accomplice could pry him free from the outside. The extraordinary four-room structure was designed to be constructed of large oak logs, well notched at the corners and closely saddle fitted. Flat stones were to be driven into the interstices. The four two-foot square windows were to be barred with half-inch iron rods. Cell doors in the upper rooms were to be fifteen inches wide, just wide enough to squeeze a fat man through them. Every precaution was taken to prevent prying loose doors and windows. This heavy log structure, or public dungeon, with its tiny barred windows, narrow doors, and all but impenetrable oak sidewalls would have done creditable honor to a Haymarket Square Jail in ancient London, England. Certainly members of the Clark County meant to keep prisoners well in hand and in sight in darkened and austere quarters. Now even their visiting kinsfolk could stand outside and get a clear view of the prisoners.[43]

From some source, no doubt buried deep in the annals of medieval Anglo-Saxon law, Virginians dug up the idea of erecting public stocks on courthouse grounds. The Kentucky law creating Clark County perpetuated this tradition. The county as mandated to erect public stocks located on the courthouse grounds. There is some question as to the purpose of this humiliating public punishment device. In what capacity was it supplementary to the public jail? It is possibly true that the stocks were basically intended to punish recalcitrant slaves. Whatever the purpose, the justices of the peace or magistrates of the county court took the chartering law seriously, and on May 27, 1794, ordered the construction of double-yoke stocks on the public square.[44]

William Sudduth, John Baker, and David Bullock were given the task of planning and building the stocks. The heavy stanchions of the structure were to be ten feet long and braced by equally stout crossbars of wood. There were to be two sets of yokes, each containing three slots. The smaller slots were to bind the wrists of the prisoner while the larger middle holes collared his neck. Platforms were provided for the prisoners to stand on, and the neck and wrist yokes were to be mounted four feet high. No doubt the stocks must have been used at some time in Clark County, but the official record is silent on the subject.[45]

With the completion of the "cabbin" courthouse, jail, stray pen, and stocks the assemblage of public buildings was complete. The log courthouse, which was said to be a duplicate of John Baker's house, was occupied on May 24, 1794.[46] Up to this date the court had set in the residence of John Baker, a favor for which he was paid approximately five pounds for each session.[47]

Even though there are no illustrations of the appearance of Winchester and the courthouse array of buildings in 1800, the crude drawings of the planned buildings which appeared in the County Court Order Books give a rather good perception of the community's frontier setting. Both the official county buildings and the surrounding stores and dwelling houses were in fact a replication of the popular log-house community. Unfortunately no contemporary observer went to the pains to record a description in narrative form or to make a primitive drawing of this classic frontier village.[48]

Although there are no visual portrayals of early Clark County, there is evidence that it became a "Little Kingdom" from its beginnings. The annual fiscal accounting of public expenditures reflects payment of what amounted to patronage sums. William Sudduth, John Baker, James McMillan, and others were paid for their services in holding viva voce elections, attending court sessions, summonsing witnesses in court cases, accompanying and guarding prisoners, and providing care of indigents. Whether there actually was a "courthouse ring" aborning in 1793 may be questioned, but certainly the same names appeared repeatedly in the early official history of the county. For instance, the names of William Sudduth, John Strode, James McMillan, and John Baker seemed to be a part of every public auction. John Baker was paid for four shillings for guarding John Petty, a prisoner. James Kidd was paid nine shillings for guarding John Woods for ten days in 1794. John Baker also received payment for clearing the grounds for the construction of the public buildings. He also had a hand in the guarding John Wood, who appears to have been Clark County's first chronic offender. The arrest and incarceration of John Wood alone proved to be a source of income for several persons.[49] The names of John Holder, James McMillan, surveyor, and others of the founding fathers appear to have constituted an inner circle who received pay for their various services of locating roads, judging elections, serving as magistrates, and providing other services to both the county and court of quarter sessions.

One of the less taxing duties of the members of the county court was that of setting prices which tavern and ordinary keepers could charge their customers. In November 1793 the court prescribed the price for supper and breakfast as five shilling, six pence each. Stable and hay for a horse was one shilling, three pence, and if the guest chose to pamper his horse he could purchase two quarts of oats for six pence. He could drink a pint of country whiskey for eight pence; a half pint of madeira wine, for two shillings, three pence. He could bed down in a room with an indeterminate number of persons for six pence. In all, a guest could accommodate himself and his horse with food, feed, stabling, liquor, and lodging for approximately $1.50 a day.[50]

It must be noted that John Baker's disposition of the land surrounding the virile freshwater spring was by no means a matter of *pro bono publico*. John Baker seems to have been a shrewd acquirer of land, if not in fact a speculator. Once the land on the site of the new village of "Winchester was surveyed and staked into lots the court ordered that they be auctioned off to highest bidders on a future court day. In the meantime John Baker agreed to

Once this would not have been more than a commonplace sight in Winchester. There were Clark County farmers who contended they preferred oxen to mules at the plow, or drawing ground sleds and wagons.

accept a mortgage bond instead of cash payment for his land.[51] Following the procedures used in the organization of the pioneer town of Lexington, the Winchester trustees assumed authority to designate the nature of structures which would be built in the town.[52]

Duplicating the experience of the magistrates in organizing the Clark County government, the Winchester trustees held their first organizational meeting in the residence of John Baker on February 6, 1794. Daniel Bullock was appointed town clerk. Without stating a reason for his action, John Strode resigned from the board; perhaps he did so because he lived well outside any possible village limits. Hubbard Taylor was appointed in Strode's place.[53]

One of the first major concerns of the Winchester trustees was making certain that the big spring near John Baker's house would be included well within the town survey. This source of fresh water was of the utmost importance to the prospective population of the rising town. Characteristic of Kentucky's metes and bounds survey system, the boundaries of Winchester began at a landmark ask tree near the spot chosen for the courthouse, and followed the meandering of the spring branch.[54]

A week later the trustees held their second meeting. This time they adopted a more clearly defined plan for the new town which now had definitely been sited on the sixty-six acres of the Baker tract. A main street was to be laid off one hundred and twelve poles, four feet, and six inches long and eighty-two feet wide. An east to west street was to be ninety-four poles, eight feet and three inches long and eighty-two feet wide. The surveyor was instructed to have his work completed and a plat in hand by March 25, 1798. An advertisement would then be run in the *Kentucky Gazette* offering the lots for sale at the next meeting of the county court.[55]

Purchasers of the lots were required to give bond that they would construct buildings on them within eighteen months of the date of purchase. The Winchester trustees engaged in an elementary form of town planning and establishing a minimal building code on a virginal site. Houses were to be at least sixteen feet square, their sidewalls to be constructed of "good hewed logs." All other structural materials were to be of a solid and acceptable nature. Roofs were to be shingled over with hand-riven hardwood boards, and each housing unit was to have at least one chimney constructed of stone or brick. Failure to comply with the building restrictions within eighteen months of lot purchase would result in forfeiture of property.[56]

On the first advertised lot sales day, March 25, 1794, twenty town lots were sold. A month later, April 22, eight more were disposed of, and on July 22 six more were sold. By March 24, 1795, the sale of town lots was deemed completed when eight were disposed of to the highest bidders. Prices for lots ranged from twenty-one pounds for Lot 80 to four pounds for lot 20.[57]

Purchasers of the original lots of the town of Winchester included numerous heads of early Clark County families. It is noteworthy that John Strode bid in lot number one for nine pounds, William McMillan acquired lot 91, John Baker purchased several lots, and John Martin bid on and purchased lot eighteen. Interestingly, the names of William Sudduth, Hubbard Taylor, Robert Clarke, Junior, David Bullock, Jillson Payne, and William Bush do not appear in the official records as town lot purchasers, even though David Bullock was appointed town clerk in April 1795.[58]

The decade 1794 to 1805 was a period of constructing public buildings, devising basic ordinances, holding early sessions of courts, locating roads and streets, and establishing a commercial community. By 1801 both county court magistrates and town trustees could make an assessment of their accomplishments. The Winchester trustees sought to determine how many of the original bidders for town lots had defaulted in their payments. Thomas Scott and James Simpson were appointed to make an inventory of the delinquent bidders.[59] On March 25, 1794, John Baker had been employed to resurvey the town, but apparently he failed to do so; and in May 1801, James Simpson, James Ward, and John Spillman were asked to employ a surveyor to have the town resurveyed and have new lots laid out. They were commissioned to locate new streets and alleys and to clear away the courthouse square. In asking this committee to resurvey, and, in fact, virtually relocate the town, the trustees for about the fifth time emphasized the necessity for the protection of the public spring.[60] Without this natural source of fresh water Winchester would have been left in a precarious situation. The town seems to have had no alternative water supply. Specifically, the committee was admonished to have the surveyor split stakes out of seasoned and lasting hardwood eighteen inches long and three inches square. The stakes were to be driven into the ground at a depth of fourteen inches at lot corners and along street and alley rights-of way.[61]

The public spring was located on lot 79, and John Bruner was appointed a one-man commission to have a quarter of an acre of ground surrounding the spring to be set aside and enclosed in a stout post and rail fence.[62] Aside from this provision the trustees frequently concerned themselves with protecting that precious source of water. They may not have known much if anything about B-coli or hepatitis, but they did know muddy water when they saw it. They forbade, "The washing and renching of clothes within thirty feet of the public spring." Offenders were to be subjected to the modest fine of three pence. Since the ubiquitous mounted Kentuckians rode their horses into town on court day and watered and hitched anywhere there was water and a hitching post or tree limb,[63] the Winchester trustees ordained that they should keep their mounts at least thirty feet away from the spring. The ordinance read, "... those who watered their horse or gelding within thirty feet of the spring," should be fined three shillings. These thoughtless or slovenly who dipped dirty tubs and buckets into the fount were to pay three pence for their indiscretions. "Any wagoner," said the ordinance, "or any other person who shall tie or keep any horse, mare, or gelding, Cow or Ox, within thirty feet of the spring for the space of fifteen minutes shall for every offence be liable to a fine of three pence."[64] The town's trustees seemed to have been of the bizarre opinion that the microbes of pollution were incapable of drifting more than thirty feet. Even in their ignorance of the bacteria of infection they knew that the water supply of Winchester would be jeopardized by filth. If children or slaves were guilty of polluting, then their parents or masters were to be fined. In this case the term "child" was defined as anyone under twenty-one years of age. The ordinance authorized anyone witnessing the defiling of the public water source to make a citizen's arrest.

By the time Clark County and Winchester had advanced into the nineteenth century there arose a constant succession of public issues. It perhaps was little short of a miracle that most of the population was not invalidated by hepatitis. The village appeared to be dotted with what the trustees euphemistically called "necessaries." They mandated that none of these would be permitted to remain within twenty feet of a street, and those already in violation would have to be moved back. This ordinance seemed to have been provoked more for olfactory than sanitary reasons.[65]

At the same time that the town trustees were agitated over the matter of properly locating "necessaries," they considered for something like the tenth time the protection of the public spring. Supplementing former ordinances, they again forbade the keeping of livestock nearby. When the trustees were not hot on the trail of the spring polluter they were seeking ways to keep in bounds itinerate peddlers, liquor sellers, gingerbread purveyors, and dramatic performers. Kentucky county seat towns on court days drew money grubbers in droves. Too, these vendors flocked about the polls in the three-day *viva voce* elections. The county magistrates and the town trustees attempted to fend off purveyors by keeping them well outside the pale of the courthouse. They also undertook to keep persons from carrying liquor into the courtroom and offices. Interestingly, in this instance the town trustees cited the penalty in dollars. An offender caught violating the liquor ordinance would be fined $3.00. This seems to have been the first time American monetary species of dollars was entered into a Clark County public record.[66]

Except for plows, grain cradles, scythes, and broad axes these were the tools most often listed in the inventories of early Clark County estates. - *Photo courtesy of Kenneth Colebank*

As in numerous other Kentucky towns at the opening of the nineteenth century, Winchester's trustees were faced with establishing some degree of urban decorum. They outlawed racing horses up and down the streets, standing stud horses in full public streetside view, and the rowdy frontier sport of throwing long bullets. This latter activity or sport, if it could truly be called a sport, consisted of throwing knives, dirks, or tomahawks at a rolling wooden ball or log. The trustees ordained that violators of this ordinance were to be fined $3.00 a throw.[67]

Though Winchester was beginning to shed its primitive beginnings, much of Clark County was still virgin forest land. With the coming of settlers and the opening of farmsteads, human activities and nature were often thrown into conflict. Gone were the herds of buffalo that roamed the region, but left behind were their trails and pawed-out hardpan about the salt licks. Herds of deer and elk were rapidly surrendering to bovine interlopers that laid claim to the open range. The arrival of flocks of sheep and droves of hogs introduced into the area a new source of food supply for predators, especially for wolves. At its quarterly session in November 1805, the Clark County Court validated the wolf scalp claims of numerous individuals, paying twelve shillings for old wolf scalps and six each for those of pups.[68] Claimants brought in trophies to be inspected, destroyed, and paid for.[69]

Among the wolf bounty seekers were Moses and James Sharpe, Bartlett Woodward, William Parish, Samuel West, James Spillman, James Blackwell, and Richard Oldham.[70] These men brought in an astonishing number of wolf scalps. The fact that bounties appeared in the records of the county court for 1804-1805 was impressive documentary proof that there still prevailed in this part of the Kentucky and Licking river valleys appreciable areas of virgin forrest.[71]

In contrast to the documentary record of paying wolf scalp bounties, there exists a preponderance of documentary evidence that both Clark County and the town of Winchester were gradually emerging from the conditions of raw frontier log house and cabin days. The ordinance against open street horse racing and the throwing of long bullets is proof positive of this fact.[72]

No doubt the quarterly meetings of the county court were days of excitement and extraordinary interest. The meetings of both the county and circuit courts were magnetic occasions which drew to the courthouse demesne countrymen, lawyers, judges, horse jockeys, pitchmen, and itinerate showmen. Supplicants came to the county court bearing petitions for the opening of new roads and for permission to build mill dams, to have appraisers for estates appointed, and to seek care for the indigent. People flocked into Winchester on court days having no other objective than being a part of the crowd. They could always engage in a little whiskey drinking, perhaps having opportunities to settle old piques fist-and claw fashion; trade pocket knives, horses and saddles; or just mingle for the sake of gathering news and gossip. They could even be enthralled and deluded by eloquent candidates for public office. Rivaling the courtroom itself in excitement was the scene of "jockey row," a standard adjunct in every Kentucky courthouse town. This institution had a dual function. On certain seasonal meetings of the court the jockey row became in fact a livestock market place. Always present was the ubiquitous horse trader, one of the trickiest of all north American characters.[73]

Rivaling county court days were the more extended sessions of the circuit court, with its flocking of judges and lawyers along with prisoners at the bar and reluctant witnesses. Listening to the flights of oratory by backwoods Kentucky lawyers was in some respects the common man's brush with high drama.

Court days were peddler havens. There came tinware and clock peddlers, the compounders and purveyors of life-extending elixirs and golden medical discoveries of ancient and unidentified Indians, bearded "doctor men of science," and generous contributions from Kentucky distillers. As much a part of court and election days as judges, lawyers, and election judges were the purveyors of gingerbread. For some reason this homey culinary product enjoyed a rich patronage. County magistrates and town trustees undertook to control the pitchmen by requiring them to secure peddler licenses. Aside from the tradesmen, a prime target of the Winchester town fathers, however, were the tumblers, jugglers, rope and wire dancers, and show actors who presented drama, both "real and fictitious." These itinerants seemed to have impressed the town fathers with being a greater moral threat to local social decorum than the peddlers and horse jockeys. Performers who failed to procure a license were to be fined $10.00.[74]

While their colleagues, the Winchester town trustees, wrestled with the challenges of maintaining law and order in their domain, the county court magistrates held extensive hearings in cases of lawbreaking. One such was that pertaining to Jacob Smith, who was charged with having stolen a silver watch from Jonathan Baker's saddlery shop. The court made a capital issue of this felonious act. It commissioned Charles Lander, Ezekiel Pool, John Liggett, Lewis Sudduth, Samuel Darnaby, Jonathan Baker, Jonathan Morton, and Levi Lender to appear in court as witnesses. These were new names, perhaps those of the younger generation, an indication that new faces were appearing on the public scene. As for Jacob Smith, he was thrown upon the mercy of the up-coming session of the circuit court as a thieving felon who should receive stern punishment.[78]

Just as the town trustees concerned themselves frequently with issues relating to the public spring and Winchester's lifeline, the court magistrates had to deal with equally taxing matters. They were admonished by the law of the commonwealth to guard against the wanton location and building of mill dams. In a specific case, an overview committee was appointed in July 1805 to view the proposed site of an impoundment which Samuel McCreary proposed to build. Twelve men, "good and true," were chosen. These included Abraham Scholl, John Rankin, William Edwards, Senior, William Frame, Benjamin Combs, John Crisby, John Sidebottom, John Gibbs, William Frazer, William Thomas, William Henderson, and Isaac Scholl. They were instructed to view the site of the dam to make sure it would not create hazards of flooding upstream or drought downstream or a stagnate pool of water. The viewers recommended that McCreary be allowed to build the impoundment with the understanding that he would be liable for all damages it might cause. The commissioners staked out the limits of the projected ten-foot high dam and the land to be flooded. With this great show of official concern, the commissioners valued the site of the dam at no more than three shillings and ten pence.[76] Thus it was that the opening chapters of the founding of Clark County and the town of Winchester often turned on slender spindles. An expansion of the population, the opening of farms, the creation of outlying villages, and the need for outlets for an annually expanding production of agricultural crops and livestock speeded up the need for new roads and for the expansion of local ordinances and laws. Dealing with an ever-increasing number of law enforcement and estate settlement matters and the care of indigents created the complications of a maturing society.

The early history of Clark County and the town of Winchester was purely a masculine one. The historian combs through the somewhat voluminous documentary sources of the county and town and remains completely oblivious to the fact that there were women present. Except for the possible notation of an indigent woman or girl the order and minute books are silent on the subject. No woman's name appears among the numerous committees and commissions. Only the petitioners for the organization of a new county make somewhat oblique reference to women in their complaints that they have to leave their families exposed to possible Indian attacks and harm while they ride long distances to reach the county seat in Lexington or Paris. Women were present in both the county and town. The United States census count of 1800 reveals an almost numerical balance between the sexes.

A representative log cabin of solid construction. This cabin was located on Hingston Creek. - *Photo courtesy of Carolyn Sledd*

CHAPTER 4

The Way Of Life
On An Evolving Frontier

❦

A miracle of pioneering in Clark County is the fact that is took so few tools, farm implements, and household goods to clear the land and establish a livable log house homestead. Unfortunately there are no full inventories of what the earliest settlers to reach the Kentucky River Valley had in the way of tools. It is safe to guess they brought an axe, an augur, a broad axe, a drawing knife, and, perhaps, a foot adz.[1] Household furniture was too heavy and cumbersome to be brought up the Boone Trace or down the Ohio and then overland. Much of this had to be imported in the form of patterns and memories. Certainly one of the precious intangibilities some settlers brought to Kentucky were personal craft skills.[2]

Measured by mid-nineteenth century standards, it took only a minimal amount of farm and household furnishings to maintain a fairly stable way of life in early Clark County. Basically, log cabins and houses were havens of shelter and safety.[3] In their primitive fashion they provided a basic kind of efficiency. The building of a house in early Kentucky involved varying degrees of skill, expenditure of energy, and use of materials. This was also true of opening the land to cultivation.

By the year 1792 a Clark County pioneer could purchase from a Lexington merchant everything he needed to settle a family into a home. By that time the *Kentucky Gazette* published long lists of merchandise offered by both itinerant and resident merchants.[4]

A modern visitor to Clark County's homes in 1792 might have been astonished at the sparsity and drabness of the surroundings. Nevertheless there would be a fascination with how the occupants managed to perform the daily chores of living, preserving some sense of modesty, and of individuals fitting themselves into relatively large families in such limited spaces. Even enjoying some degree of comfort would be intriguing. All of this, however, would have to be viewed within the historical context and conditions of the times, and with some considerable admiration for the adaptability of the pioneering people.

Basically, the foundations of social, cultural, and economic life in Clark County during the first century were intensely rural and agrarian.[5] During much of this time the population had to depend on merchants in Lexington for their commercial goods. Even so almost everything needed to maintain a family was dredged from the land or garnered from forest and stream and from the growing herds, flocks, and droves of domestic animals. The preparation and cooking of foods was done by use of most elementary utensils and vessels. It is safe to assume that no main chimney was built without the installation of cranes, pothooks, trammels, and spits. Pothooks in many an early home bore constantly their burdens of cooking meats and vegetables. The spit was used to roast and baste meats, while the trammel was a raising and lowering device for pots.[6]

The log house fireplace might well be portrayed as the centralizing area of family life. It was here that the universal household utensil, the Dutch oven, was a permanent fixture. In fact it was the queen of the hearth. With its tight-fitting cast-iron lid it could be used for boiling, roasting, or baking.

There seems to have been no designated kitchen space in many earlier Clark County homes. Cooking and eating may have been done in the main room of the house. This was especially so during the cold weather. Traditionally the fireplace was topped by a mantel fastened parallel with the keystone lintel. The mantel was in fact a domestic depository for the family Bible, keys, medicines, small tools, bullet and spoon molds, combs, trinkets, and even guns. Once the Yankee clock peddler found his way to Kentucky, a clock became the traditional centerpiece of family fireplace mantels.[7]

By the very force of physical circumstance, of environmental and limited economic conditions, the early rural home-farmstead was largely self-contained. With the exception of tea, coffee, and salt, the family food came from the land. Pioneers lugged across the mountains as part of their folk cultural baggage the knowledge of curing meats, drying and preserving fruits and vegetables, and, most important of all, a basic knowledge of gardening and dirt farming. There was in early Clark County a super abundance of raw subsistence materials.[8]

Just as the local pioneers brought to Clark County knowledge of subsis-

tence farming, there were among them more or less experienced craftsmen
who could convert the rich wood materials into bedsteads, tables, chairs,
chest of drawers, cupboards, kegs and barrels, and spinning wheels and looms.
No Americans were ever more richly blessed at having such an abundance of
prime quality furniture made from timber resources which existed almost
just outside of every dwelling house door.[9]

Prior to 1840 the Clark County inventories of the properties of personal
estates reflected eloquently the necessary articles which were required to convert a log house into a comfortable and livable home.[10]

The utensils and tools to meet the needs of a frontier Clark County
household were of simple design and highly practical use. Among the basic
ones were, as mentioned above, the Dutch oven, wooden noggins or pails,
cranes, trammels, spinning wheels and looms, an augur, axe, broad axe, cards,
for processing wool and cotton, and home-made beds and cabinets.[11]

Gradually in early Clark County homes there were accumulated the essential materials to sustain a functional way of life. Household furnishings
were simple and limited. There were bedsteads, crude chests, a table or two,
some chairs of varying quality and design, a looking glass, and wall shelves.[12]
Everything but the mirror glass could be made with only a few basic tools,
and little or no actual furniture-making experience on the part of the amateur craftsman. Remarkably, the court-appointed estate appraisers seldom took
the pains to describe the style or wood contained in bedsteads; to them these
were commonplace fixtures. They also failed often to mention that beds consisted of three major components, the bedstead, the mattress, and the covering. No single inventory mentioned bed springs. Evidently shuck-and-straw
filled mattresses rested on either bed ropes or slats. There were two types of
mattresses, those stuffed with straw or corn shucks, and those containing
feathers. Occasionally there was mention of a trundle bed, which would be
pushed underneath a standard bed to save space during the day. All of these
things were homemade. The bedstead itself consisted of four posts and whip-
sawed lumber converted into headboards and footboards.[13] Some of the posts
may have been turned on crude foot lathes. Mattresses were made at home
and out of readily available stuffing materials. No doubt many an early Clark
countian slept on a corn-shuck mattress because there was a scarcity of feathers. However, there appeared repeatedly in estate inventories notations of
accumulations of feathers. Then there was the matter of what the appraisers
called "bed furnishings." These consisted of coverlets, quilts, and counterpanes.[14]

Quilts and coverlets of the earlier period in Clark County history may well be called expressions of folk art. Many a pioneer woman brought with her from the eastern states quilt patterns of traditional forms and drafts for the weaving of coverlets. The latter consisted of slips of paper with design forms inscribed by a series of long and short lines which indicated the mode of threading looms and the casting of shuttles.[15] No doubt it seemed a barren family room in an early Clark County home which did not have suspended from its ceiling a quilting frame. As with the drafts for weaving coverlet patterns, quilters followed traditional lines which possessed the prestige of special names. Quilting often became as much a social as a utilitarian act even in many a home. Women gathered to quilt, to gossip, and to boast of their talent at reproducing faithfully a pattern which had been passed down through several generations, and especially to demonstrate their ability at making fine regular stitches.[16]

Almost universally estate appraisals listed coverlets. This historic piece of bed covering was indigenous to American pioneering itself. It not only represented a distinct form of folk art, but by its sturdily woven fabric combining woolen, flax, and cotton threads it was as sturdy as the primeval forest itself. The coverlets' colorings were as distinctive as the patterns and weavings. There were varieties of dyes brewed from natural sources, such as the hulls of black walnut, the bark and cambrium lining of sassafras, various types of wild berries, and mineral earths.[17]

The absence from the early Clark County home of any of three types of spinning wheels, cards, slays, and looms might have well indicated a lack of skills on the part of the housewife. Basic to the fabrication of any type of cloth or woven or knitted garments were spinning wheels. In a majority of the estate inventories these were listed as to type of fiber they spun. There were the smaller flax and woolen wheels and the larger ones for spinning cotton. Winding blades and cards were indispensable parts of the spinning process. All of these found almost universal entry into the estate inventories along with quantities of wool, flax, and cotton.[18]

By no means were all garments or household goods woven on looms. Knitting perhaps was one of the most utilitarian of all the domestic arts. Family knitters produced socks and stockings, sweaters, scarves, headwear, and even underwear. Knitting was the prime fireside industry of the early years. This was one activity in which the artisan could be creative and carry on a conversation at the same time. There seems to be no local primary documentation of knitting, but the presence of spinning wheels, cards, winding blades, and wool and flax bundles in the estate inventories is *prima facie* evidence of this highly productive art.[19]

The home of John Martin, the first jailor of Clark County, and the father of the famous Dr. Samuel D. Martin.

Basic always to the production process of fabricated materials, as mentioned, were the three or four types of spinning wheels. With the exception of two pieces of metal, all types of wheels could be created by a craftsman of limited experience. The most important part was the wheel itself, with its grooved rim for spinning wool and flax, and the larger one for spinning wool and cotton.[20] All the fibrous materials had to undergo a process of straightening the fibers and rolling them into loose bats. Cards were constructed from two flat boards approximately six to fourteen inches in dimension. A face of each board was lined with fine metal or wooden teeth with enough flexibility to permit their being filled with fiber and the cards being drawn in opposite directions. Skilled carders could create a fantastic number of rolls in a brief period of time.

Numerous inventories listed cowhides and sheepskins. Cowhides were tanned for the making of shoe leather, pieces of harness, and leather strings. Tanned sheepskins had a multiplicity of purposes from the making of soft leather items to use as rugs. Along with these materials there appeared frequent inclusions of shoemaking tools, an indication that during the early years of Clark County families made and repaired their own shoes.[21] No doubt many of them were served by itinerant shoemakers who measured feet and made shoes on the spot. These artisans in this period, made straight last shoes which fitted either foot without the distinction of right and left conformations.[22]

Without exception inventories listed both cooking utensils and table-ware. As mentioned earlier, cranes, pothooks, pots, Dutch ovens, and roast-ing spits were standard cooking equipment fitted into family fireplaces. The mode of dining in early Clark County has to be drawn largely by inference. There does not appear to be a first-hand description of this activity now available, even though it is a most vital and commonplace event in daily life. Standard in the listings of household furnishings were the tables, sometimes described as "falling" tables, pewter "putter" basins, plates, and spoons and ladles. In many of the inventories there appeared listings of pewter spoon molds, indicative of the fact that some families, at least, cast their own table-ware.[23] There were frequent listings of assortments of knives and forks, but seldom if ever were these listed in the inventories in sufficient numbers to accommodate many members of even a most moderate-sized family. Thus one is left to speculate on how those without knife, fork, or spoon trans-ported food from plate to mouth.[24]

Despite the fact that tableware became available in the Lexington stores, there were Clark County families which were still without adequate supplies. Knives, forks, and spoons were prized. In May 1804, the county court was called into special session to hold a trial. With all the solemnity of a hearing of a fundamental constitutional case, the court was in session to hear evi-dence in the trial of William Dever, listed as a laborer. This worthy stood charged with having stolen from Saul Smith's house three pewtered-over iron spoons, appraised to be worth three shillings by Achilles Eubank, George W. Taylor, and Robert Clarke, Jr.

Prisoner Dever was escorted to the bar of justice with strict legal protocol by the jailer and the commonwealth's attorney. Dever, however, stood not alone. He was defended by James Clarke, a future governor of the common-wealth, and then a twenty-five-year-old attorney with a growing reputation as a defense lawyer. In this case, however, the court became obfuscated be-cause of a flaw in the records and ruled that laborer Dever, spoons or no spoons, had become the victim of clerical dilly-dallying and ordered that he be "then and there discharged out of custidy."[24] Thus the case of William Dever, charged with stealing three pewtered-over iron spoons, not only indi-cated how scarce these utensils were in Clark County at the time, but re-flected the fact that the processes of rendering justice in a new county dangled at the end of a slender thread.

In later nineteenth century inventories there were listed coffee mills. At the time green coffee beans were available in the Lexington stores. Earlier this commodity no doubt had been brought west by way of Baltimore and Philadelphia, thence to Pittsburgh and down the Ohio River by flatboat. After the steamboat appeared on the Ohio, generous supplies of coffee reached Kentucky from New Orleans. However this commodity reached the state, Clark County households possessed the simple little hand-turned mills for pulverizing parched coffee beans. The same thing was true of the importation of tea. Though no specific mention is made of the fact, earlier Clark County families, as was true of Kentuckians generally, drank herbal teas and tea made from sassafras roots.[26]

Just as the record is sometimes vague on the possession of tableware and cooking utensils, so it is in relation to other household furnishings. Almost every inventory contained a listing of candlesticks, sometimes no more than a pair. Along with them were candle molds to be used in converting beeswax and tallow into candles. Frequently bee gums were listed. Bees supplied both sweetening and wax for scores of uses. Nightfall in Clark County homes, prior to the kerosene age, meant a limiting of human activities to only those which could be performed in a narrow radius by candle or fireside light.[27]

Though hundreds of entries appear for cooking utensils and tableware, there is sparse mention of possible foodstuffs. There were frequent listings of grain and occasionally one of dried fruit, otherwise much of the early Clark County diet has to be inferred from the type of cooking vessels listed. Almost every inventory gave varying numbers of hogs, some of them in considerable numbers. Clearly indicated is the fact that the early county population was a generous consumer of pork, green and cured, and prodigious amounts of lard. From the outset cured meats and lard became commodities of the downriver trade which necessitated the maintenance of inspection stations on the Kentucky River.[28]

The inclusion of cowhides in many estate listings indicated that there was also an appreciable consumption of beef. There was also some consumption of mutton as indicated by the inventories of sheepskins. The universal listings of skillets, frying pans, spits, and Dutch ovens give a clear insight into the methods of food preparation and preservation. Much of the meat, pork, beef, mutton or chicken was fried. Strangely, in none of the inventories are there listings of chickens, ducks, or geese; yet, as indicated, there frequently appeared in the inventories listings of accumulations of feathers.[29]

Fortunately the historian has access to a full file of estate inventories which give insightful listings of the kinds of implements, tools, and household furnishings which early Clark County families accumulated. The public records suggest the ebb and flow of daily life on the emerging farms, the dress of the people, some indication of their dietary and drinking habits, and, maybe, a revealing look into their living-dining-bedrooms. [30] There is every indication that a main fireplace, in a living-kitchen-dining room, or in a side kitchen room was almost a centralizing family shrine about which members gathered.

The extensive and detailed appraisals of the worldly goods of deceased persons are primary historical sources of the first order. It must, however, be ever remembered that the appraisals submitted to the Clark County Court are only quasi-official documents. They give no information as to procedures in evaluating the holdings of an estate, of the role and reactions of surviving family members, or of articles which may have been removed from public viewing. The appraisers themselves qualified their reports by the notation, "Such goods as were presented for our viewing."[31]

With these evidentiary precautions, presented here as illustrative inventories are those of two individuals of normal economic conditions. When James Chilton departed this life in December 1797, he left behind an impressive accumulation of worldly goods for the times. He died possessed of eight horses, fifteen cows and calves, and twenty-five hogs. There were two cartwheels, the hind parts of a wagon, a whiskey still, mash tubs, five sickles, a pair of flatirons, a frow, a teakettle, a set of shoe making tools, flax hackles, three spinning wheels, a man's saddle, four hoes, three axes, two shovel plows, whiskey vessels, four hogsheads, a churn, a grindstone, twenty bushels of barley, three bushels of hemp seed, a teapot, a fireplace oven, a pothook, a pair of hames, a log chain, three bedsteads, a feather mattress, a bed cover, a table, seven chairs, a chest, and a razor.[32]

As hardy as the human pioneers were the flocks of sheep driven overland to the Kentucky frontier to supply wool for clothing and fleeces for rugs and padding. - *Photo courtesy of J. T. Evans*

In addition to the household goods, farm implements, and livestock, James Chilton died possessed of fourteen African slaves, which the appraisers listed by name, sex, and age. Too he must have been one of the most erudite men in early Clark County history. In 1797, Chilton's modest library collection contained copies of Morse's *Geography,* Ferguson's *Astronomy,* an English grammar, Sheldon's *Dictionary,* and Thomas Paine's *Rights of Man.*[33] All of these books were offered for sale in an advertisement of William Leavey's store which appeared in the *Kentucky Gazette,* June 6, 1793, and no doubt James Chilton bought them in Lexington.[33]

The tempo of the social and cultural way of life in Clark County seemed to level out into a plane of fixed routine and habits down to the opening of the ante bellum years in 1840. The variety of properties accumulated in homes during these years showed little change in either style or usage. The most impressive changes were in the increased number of possessions rather than any remarkable modernization. Illustration of this fact occurs the in the appraisal of the estate of William B. Smith, who died in the fall of 1821. As in the case of James Chilton, the court appraisers seemed to be highly conscientious in making a minutely detailed report of his worldly possessions. He owned three horses, five working steers, seven cows, and sixteen hogs. His farming implements consisted of a shovel plow, a bar share plow, four clevises, a scythe, a spade, a pitchfork, four stands of bees, a mattock, three hoes, a sidesaddle, a man's saddle and bridle, a set of blacksmith tools, a grindstone, a pair of steelyards, and two mandrels (no doubt to be used in constructing a turning lathe).[35]

Among William B. Smith's household furnishings were a loom, five tin pans, three basins, two crocks, a lot of tubs and kegs, a cupboard, a set of knives and forks, a looking glass, a table, two beds with coverlets and other furnishings, a flax wheel, a cotton wheel, a set of firedog irons and a shovel, two flatirons, ten undesignated pieces of bed clothing, a rifle gun and implements, a jug, a crock, and a drop-leaf table. In addition to the material objects of the estate Smith owned three African slaves, a mature woman and an adolescent boy and a girl.[36]

The Clark County Will Books are a veritable catalogue of the material things which people accumulated and which were necessary in the pursuit of daily living. Listings in the large number of estate appraisals are invaluable for their comparative information. If only one estate appraisal is read it would leave the impression that families were highly selective in what they produced for the viewing of appraisers. This, however, was surely not the case because of the nature and variety of implements and household furnishings which appear almost standard in scores of estate inventories. Obviously these sources are indispensable for the kinds of information they contain relating to the social, economic, and cultural facts of life in the earlier days in Clark County. They also have a highly reflective value for information they do not contain. For instance, there are no mentions in any of the inventories down to 1840 of buggies and carriages, and remarkably few of wagons. There was, however, almost universal mention of men's and women's saddles along with saddle-bags. A few listings mentioned packsaddles. These entries indicate that much of the traveling done in the first quarter of the nineteenth century was by horseback. Even more important the entries no doubt reflect the fact that despite frequent openings of new roads, the roads were not conducive to vehicular use. No doubt both stumps and mud were deterrents to the use of wheeled vehicles. Nevertheless an unusually large number of villages and named places appeared on the map, places which became the locales of stores, schools, and country churches.[37]

Although the inventory, without exception, listed the number of horses owned by the deceased, most also contained entries of work steers. These were, for many farms, the true draft animals. Along with these animals were entered log chains and oxcarts. The bar share plow, which appeared as standard farm equipment, was a heavy draft implement necessitating the use of oxen. This was the plow which broke the virgin soil of Clark County. Along with its cutting colter, it could withstand the rugged challenge of plowing through heavy ground cover, roots, and stumps.[38]

Remarkably, the early Clark County farms were cleared and cultivated with a limited number of hand tools and plows. Perhaps the most important central fact in the history of the new county was the rapidity with which its landed surface was cleared of a heavy forested growth and the land was fallowed for cultivation with lighter types of plows.[39]

Inferences can be drawn from articles listed in estate inventories about the tenor of life in the first half century of Clark County. Some of the more common articles listed in almost all the inventories were barrels, kettles, ferkins, and piggins.[40] There, however, appears not a hint of bathing and sanitary facilities. Perhaps some of the large pots answered this purpose. There is no mention of that sanitary vessel, so common in later homes, the china chamber pot, or bed pot. There is ample evidence that most of the male population were clean-shaven. Regularly razors, razor boxes, and strops were listed. Possibly every household could boast of having a least one looking glass, perhaps of modest size as there were no listings of full-sized dressing mirrors. There were no listings of towels and few of scissors. No doubt the soap in popular

Martin's Mill on Lower Howard's Creek. This mill was representative of those which lined this historic stream, and which ground the grain shipped aboard flatboats to the Lower South.

use was that made with a combination of alkali filtered from hardwood ashes and combined with scraps of fat meat.

One is left to speculate, because of the absence from inventory lists of the materials used in a more mature and refined way of life, about the habits and routines of the people. Doubtless some items in every estate were kept from the viewing of the court-appointed appraisers. As indicated above, the appraisers were cognizant of this fact. Only in a very few instances are there notations of personal clothing, and these are listed in the generalized form of a "bunch" or "lot."[40] There were frequent entries of bed sheets, coverlets, blankets, and mattresses but none of nightgowns or other garments. The fact that flax, cotton, and wool spinning wheels appear often in the inventories and so do bundles of flax, sacks of wool, and occasional bits of cotton, indicates the type and texture of the cloth from which both male and female garments were cut.

Except for the inclusion of cowhides and cobblers' tools in the estate properties, one is left to speculate on the kinds and appearances of the clothing the people of Clark County wore in the decades of 1792-1840. Stockings were of the knitted variety; men's clothing was coarse, heavy, and durable, like contemporary jeans. Female garments were made from the traditional frontier cloth, lindsey-woolsey. Skirts were long and heavy, coats and blouses were of the same handwoven materials. The inclusion of spinning wheels of three types, cards, slays, loom harnesses, and quantities of hemp and flax, along with a generous supply of wool, document the domestic industry of the women of early Clark County. There appeared in the record no hint of style of clothing or shoes.[41]

Since the earliest history of mankind both sexes adorned themselves with jewelry. In the early Clark County inventories, however, there is no mention of rings, bracelets, broaches, or any other type of jewelry. It is possible, of course, that family members withheld such things from public viewing. In all the inventories there was no mention of a single musical instrument. Surely several persons owned fiddles, guitars, and even Jew's harps, but none was listed. If the early population of Clark County did not engage in dancing, play party games, and singings, then it was unique among the Kentucky counties. In wills, court order books, estate inventories, and other sources there is, however, no hint of opposition to dancing or any other form of entertainment.

Upon an examination of the court orders, wills, land titles, and estate appraisals it becomes at once obvious that during the years down to 1840 Clark County was a male-dominated region. In every case of an examined estate it was the death of the male head of the family which necessitated an estate inventory. The only time feminine names appeared in the reports of the appraisers was when women were the purchasers of articles.

There is every indication that the people of Clark County, like Kentuckians in general, drank whiskey and wine. The fact that stills, mash tubs, stone jugs, kegs, and barrels appeared frequently in the inventories is indicative of this fact. Occasionally a still and other whiskey-making equipment appeared in the estate records.[43] In many of its quarterly sessions the county court was called upon to approve the operation of taverns or ordinaries and to set the rates which they could charge for lodging, meals, and liquor. Operation of an ordinary must have been a profitable business because there was an inordinate number of requests for a license to operate one. The Kentucky statutes outlining the county court's responsibilities contains the rather coy phrases, "Shall not suffer any person to tipple or drink more than is necessary."[44]

The county order and will books of Clark County and the United States decennial census give a rich insight into the presence and role of the slaves.[46] There appear almost universally in the appraisals of estates a pro forma listing of slaves as chattel property. A law enacted by the Kentucky General Assembly had a marked degree of pertinency for Clark County. This statute provided, "That slaves, so far as respects last wills and testaments, shall hereafter, within this commonwealth, be deemed as real estate, and shall pass by the last will and testament of persons possessed thereof in the same manner, and under the same regulations as land property; and nothing contained in the `An act to reduce in one the several acts concerning wills, and administrators,' or in the fourth session thereof, which enable persons above the age of eighteen years, to dispense of their chattels by will."[47] This dehumanizing law constituted the legal basis by which Clark County slaves, as with all other Kentucky slaves, were appraised in the same material category as land, livestock, and domestic furnishings.

In 1800 there were 1,535 slaves and 5,686 white persons in Clark County. In 1820 there were 3,463 slaves, and 8,142 whites; in 1830 4,514 slaves, and 7,960 whites; and in 1850, 4,840 slaves and 7,705 whites.[48] Almost consistently a third of the Clark County population down to the ante bellum years was comprised of slaves. The African slave population, like the white, were either pioneers who moved into Kentucky or were born soon thereafter. Like their white masters they had both family and sentimental roots firmly planted back in Virginia, Maryland, and the Carolinas. On the opening of the great western frontier they played active roles in defense against Indian attacks, clearing the land, raising cabins and double log houses, and cultivating the fields and caring for livestock.[49]

The undertones of many of the probated wills in Clark County appear to express both affection and concern by their masters for certain slaves. Unfortunately there seems to be no existing testamentary evidence of such sentiments expressed humanely in letters and diaries, but the wills do contain testaments of regard in legalistic language. Fundamentally slavery in Clark County was of the domestic small family type. No slaveholder in the county approached ownership of the number of slaves found on a Lower South cotton plantation. Because of this fact apparently there were far more interfamily relationships between master and servant families.[50]

The absence of surnames in the records of the county makes it difficult, if not impossible, to determine interpersonal relationships. Slaves were designated as "A woman, forty years of age, named Matilda," or "A man thirty years old, named Jeremiah, " and "A boy, twelve years old," and a "girl four years old." There was an almost inscrutable statutory provision that any "infant" above the age of eighteen years of age might make a will manumitting any slave he or she inherited.[51]

Numbers of Clark County slaves were manumitted by the simple process of their master appearing before the county clerk and requesting that a certificate of manumission be granted. In the May 1802 session of the county court George Boone came forward and asked that his forty-year-old man

In mid-twentieth century sheep bred and exhibited in the local and national livestock shows brought fame and considerable income to Clark County.

named Ben be manumitted. Boone assured the court that Ben would be well able to support himself and would not become a ward of the county. The court issued Ben a certificate of freedom.[52]

At the October 1808 sitting of the county court William Sudduth sought a certificate of manumission for his slave man named Soloman, and his petition was granted. In 1811 Roger Beckworth included a proviso in his will that his slaves, Joe, Nancy, Polly, Rachael, Nelly, and Becky be manumitted upon his death. When this will was probated the court expressed the opinion that certificates of emancipation should be issued and that no bond of security was required.[53]

Documentation of how well the manumitted slaves fared as free men and women is limited. There is every inferential indication that they became productive free laborers. In one case at least, a manumitted African slave woman named Fanny Cole was highly successful. When she made her last will and testament in 1849 she listed an appreciable amount of real estate, including two houses in Winchester, and substantial amounts of cash money and household goods. The will seemed to indicate that Fanny Cole had operated a store. The inventory of her possessions was full and informative. Listed were all the household furnishings commonly found in other inventories of the times, plus what no doubt was stock from Fanny's store.[54]

When the famous pioneer cattleman Matthew Patton reached what he described as a stage of infirm body, but soundness of mind, he dictated his last will and testament on May 2, 1803. Throughout a long and eventful life Matthew Patton had accumulated a considerable estate. It consisted of land, slaves, livestock, and household goods. He instructed that his slaves should be freed at different intervals following his death.[55] On that day in 1803 there may have been on Matthew Patton's mind and conscience a deeper personal concern for the future welfare of his slaves than was indicated in the usual will. He listed Cuff, Ruth, and David as mulattoes. He willed that the latter two slaves should be freed when they reached the age of twenty-four years and had "learned to read the bible distinctly." His man Henry was to be freed in ten years. Patton bequeathed to his wife a mulatto woman and her youngest child to be disposed of "As she may think proper." The court-appointed appraisers subsequently listed these slaves but gave no indication of their disposition. [56]

John Washington Buckner died in 1799 and left seven slaves as part of his estate. When the court appraisers came to view his worldly goods, they listed the slaves by name and assigned an estimated value to each of them stated in British pounds. Simon was said to be worth 100, Sam, 100, Daisy 75, Hannah 70, Celia 25, Patience 70, Milly 70, Judy and child, 80, a lame boy Bill, 15, Rueben, 25, Phebe, 20 and Adam, 25.[57]

Late in 1802 the well-known John Baker, the man who had owned the land on which Winchester and the Clark County seat were located, died possessed of ten slaves. These were valued also in pounds. Tom was appraised as being worth 90, Jarrard, 90, Daniel, 110, Henry, 40, Poll 50, Betty 33, Maud, 33, Tilly 95, Dark, 90, and Nate, 70.[58] The inventories described here were characteristic of other slave listings in the Clark County Order Books, 1792-1840. The appraisers' report of the inventory of the D. Collins estate in 1822 was stated in dollar values. Collins died possessed of eight slaves. These seem to have been members of a single family unit, and the individuals were valued as follows: Charles, an old man was said to be worth $100; Betty, an elderly woman, $100; William, twenty-four years of age, $550; Milford, eighteen years of age, $650. The remaining three slaves were children valued at $375 to $550. At the same time there was entered in the Court Order Book the fact that Williamson's five slaves brought comparable prices and appeared to be a single family group.[59]

The date appearing in the Clark County wills, the order books, and the estate appraisals give a clear picture of the existence of slavery in the county, the numbers of slaves around, the process of emancipation, and the stated worth of individual slaves; but lacking are descriptions of the daily lives and labors of the slaves, an account of master-slave relationships, and the life histories of those slaves who received manumission certificates form the county court. No doubt behind every will and estate inventory there was a story of human relationships, both pleasant and fractious.

A central theme of Clark County history is a highly personal one centered in the family and the broad human fabric of kinship and common origins. There appear in all the official records scores of personal names of officials and private citizens. Implied in these are the fact that perhaps most of the first wave of settlers to reach the county originated in a common Virginia neighborhood, and no doubt they were acquainted long before they set out for the West. Many of them were kin either by blood or by marriage.

Whatever the personal backgrounds and social relationships of the early Clark County settlers were, they all shared a common set of folk mores, taste for foods, mode of home building and domesticity, speech dialect and intonations. The numerous estate inventories reflected a common and almost uniform pattern of the physical surroundings and needs of the family. Families accumulated the same things, used the same tools and farm implements, had comparable herds and droves of livestock, planted common crops, and shared in a common market.

There came frequently before the court prospective guardians of orphaned children, or children who were being "bound out" for one reason or another.[60] The Clark County order books reflected over the years concern for the indigent, meagerly as they chose to spend on the social responsibility.[61] As time passed the court located and sustained a county poor house to care for the indigent persons within its jurisdiction.

Frequently there appeared in the Clark County Court persons requesting that either they or some other person be appointed guardian for orphaned or otherwise dependent children. Children were bound to guardians on an apprenticeship basis in which the guardian assumed certain obligations to train the child to engage in some useful occupation or calling. There are no records available to assess the success of this kind of social care, but no doubt in most of the cases the guardian was a relative of the dependent children.[62] In the case of manumitted slaves the Clark County officials were cautious. In most cases they required the master to post a bond that his ex-slaves would not become dependent upon the county for support.[63] Then there were those cases of bastardy in which a mother of an illegitimate child came into court and asked for support from the child's father. Sometimes a bastardy case no doubt raised the collective eyebrows of the community. Such a case was the one in which Nancy McDaniel charged James Brassfield with being the father of her bastard child. Brassfield was fined $180.00 by the court, the money to be used in the care of the child.[64]

The complex ramifications of the migration of a sizable population to a

A pioneer whiskey store
operated in Clark County
in mid nineteenth century
by Ellen Payne Blakemore.

fresh and virgin land from an older settled area necessitated a certain amount
of social and economic cohesiveness. In the case of Clark County these were
still the tag end threat of the Indian menace, the conquest of the forested
land, the arduous labors of fallowing the soil, the building of homes, and the
opening of roads. Every one of these challenges required a considerable amount
of neighborly cooperation. Added to these physical aspects of settling in the
western country were the intricacies of kinship through blood and social origins. At no time in American history was the family as a tightly knit unit
more pronounced than in the years when Clark County was emerging as a
mature political entity in the Commonwealth of Kentucky. Intertwining social and economic forces centered in the rise of the numerous community
"knottings" in the county, all of which eventually were linked to Winchester
umbilically by a network of rural roads.[65]

As a social, cultural, and political organization Clark County, during its
formative years, 1792-1840, might well be presented as a microcosm of local
social, cultural, economic, and political development all across the spreading
American frontier. Concentrated within the duration of this historic interval
were all the elements of planting and nurturing a viable provincial society
which underwent a constant bonding of human beings to one another, but
most importantly the collective bonding of human beings to a geographical
area and an environment. The population of Clark County over the years has
responded generously to these forces and since 1792 has developed an intense sense of loyalty to place.

The Boonesborough Ferry in operation in the 1920's was reminiscent of the long history at this crossing of the Kentucky River. Once this spot was crossed by Indian canoes, later by settler john boats. - *Photo courtesy of the Winchester Sun*

CHAPTER 5

Breaking The Ancient Bonds of Primeval Isolation

When the first Clark County Commissioners gathered in session on December 20, 1792, at the house of John Strode they were confronted by many challenges but none greater than that of opening roads into the most distant recesses of the then sprawling county domain. At that date no one was doubtful that the Kentucky General Assembly would charter a county seat town which would be centered about the big spring of John Baker's land.[1] This spot would immediately become the legal and commercial center of the county. Thus it was that the commissioners were positive that at least four main public roads should radiate out to all points of the compass. There existed no map or even fragmented platting of existing trails or of dips and elevations of the land.[2]

There were two fairly well worn and trampled pack horse trails in use, and less defined Indian and game trails. There was a connection between the Kentucky River opposite Boonesborough and Strode's Station, and an extension to Lexington.[3] By 1793 this rapidly developing town was becoming a central Kentucky mart where an ever expanding variety of merchandise became available.[4] To the north was Paris and Bourbon County, and to the east the outlying village of Mount Sterling,[5] all to be connected by roads with Winchester. Internally the spread of settlements and farmsteads, and the increase of agricultural products mandated the opening of a veritable web-work of rural fair weather roads.[6]

The tiny county seat village of Winchester, except for the presence of John Baker's cabin, was nestled down in virgin country. As yet the land surrounding it had not been streaked by muddy country roads leading inward to the courthouse square. As yet not even the Kentucky General Assembly had taken up the matter of creating a system of arterial public roads. In the enactment of the road law of 1797,[7] there were two clear implications. Kentucky's capital town was to be located in the center of the Commonwealth's public road network if possible, and locally all county roads should lead toward the courthouses.[8]

The Commonwealth of Kentucky in 1792 was faced with precisely the same problems of opening and maintaining roads as were its counties. Framers of the Kentucky Constitution were too much concerned with the technical forms of the government to look forward to the creation of public highways. In the opening years of state government legislators also neglected this subject. There does not appear in the Acts of the General Assembly, prior to 1797, a statutory guide to the opening, financing, and maintaining of roads, bridges, and ferries. The first legislation referring to roads was the act of 1795, which authorized the widening and improving of a stretch of the old Wilderness Trace between the Kentucky and Rockcastle rivers. This section was known as "Shelby's Wagon Road," because the Governor had personally promoted the project. He had raised some private funds to pay for improvements.[9]

As indicated, numerous buffalo and Indian trails wound around internally throughout Kentucky from one salt lick to another, or to popular hunting grounds. One of these was the trail from the Ohio River to the Blue Licks and on into the central bluegrass area. This trail, which was literally padded into a clearly discernible highway by in-coming emigrants, was known as the Limestone Road, a road which later was to become famous in American political history.[10] Unfortunately, in light of its early beginnings, the Clark County area was off both the Wilderness and the Limestone feeder roads. In the formative years of 1792, Kentucky had no plan for opening and maintenance of either a central or local road system. Certainly Virginia, before that date, had done absolutely nothing to build a road to its outlying western domain. In this era roads of the future had literally to be chopped out of the forest, and this meant they were not opened until there was settler population pressures for road outlets.

Again, the historians, local and regional, treating the spread of the great westward movement in American history, have devoted too little attention to the locating and opening of roads which became such a vital part of the folk movement into the virgin western territory. Road building was a slow and hap-hazard undertaking in early Kentucky largely because it was a backbreaking laborious process requiring the labors of many human beings.[11]

Historians, sociologists, and folklorists have written much about mutual aids and common workings on the frontier in connection with the clearing of the land, and about house and barn raisings, but virtually nothing about the legally mandated common workings connected with the opening and maintenance of roads. This effort was vital to the spread of settlement to the breaking of the gripping bondage of social and cultural stagnation, and to fully exploiting the resources of the land.[12] In its chrysalis stage of settlement Clark County had to open a network of roads almost mile-by-mile as new homesteads were established.[13] Without the opening of access roads, both local and inter county, it would have been impossible for pioneering farmers in Clark County to have delivered the produce of their newly opened fields, or to drive their flocks and herds of livestock to market points. This was also true in the gaining of access to iron works, saw mills, grist mills, and to river boat landings.[14] One of the numerous complaints to the Virginia General Assembly by western settlers was a lack of communication between outlying settlements and the seats of government.[15] The courthouse and the county seat town of Winchester, in subsequent years, became the centrifugal magnet of all the activities, political and commercial, after 1793. For this reason the main stems of the complex of local roads emanated largely from the courthouse square. Again, a dominant fact in the opening and maintenance of the ever-expanding ganglia of rural roads was of vital importance to the spreading of the local population, the opening of new farmsteads, the location of mills, of warehouses, and fording places and ferries across the streams. An important element of Clark County social and cultural history was the puddlings of population in a relatively large number of roadside villages. The chore of serving as a "viewer" of the location and opening of new roads during the first half century of Clark County's history became an almost professional one, but a low paying one. The county paid a dollar-a-day for this service.[16] In many respects the blazing on trees and the preparation by rough description of the routes of new roads bore a close similarity to that of locating and blazing the boundaries of landholds.

A multitude of problems was involved in laying out a road. There was the elementary task of laying out a thirty foot wide right of way across a densely forested landscape, and over the "easiest and best" topographical route, following always the county court's mandate to find such a route.[17] Then there was the delicate matter of locating a road across private property in such a way as to placate the owner. It was asking too much of human nature to expect that all landholders would be public spirited citizens and generous in granting rights-of-way without controversy. There were farmers who welcomed the opening of a road across their land, and if possible, over the most direct route possible. There were others who wanted roads to pass by their cabin doors regardless of the lay of the land. All the property owners had to be placated one way or another. It was unfortunate that the pattern of land boundaries were established ahead of the location of roads. The magistrates of the county court were quick to admonish viewers to locate roads along the most direct routes possible, but neither they nor the viewers had access to general surface or rough topographical maps. The viewers had little to go on in the way of making scientific instrumental surveys, and were dependent upon information from local settlers, or the following of ridgetops to wherever they led. The viewers had only a generalized knowledge of precise distances or mileages. Too, they had always to keep in mind that the making of cuts and of grading rights of way, and of bridging streams was well beyond the financial capability of the county to finance.[18]

There persisted the matter of the unevenness of the texture of the soils of Clark County with the results that soft and sloppy spots turned into bottomless mud holes. Routes of many country roads were thrown askew because of the difficulty in finding a firm enough fording place across streams, or the satisfactory location of a ferry. During the initial stages of road building, and despite the immediate availability of necessary timbers, only a limited number of narrow bridging was undertaken. By 1800 almost every mile of roads in Clark County passed through either cultivated farm land or across open range lands. The question of erecting gates across the public roads to keep free ranging domestic animals away from growing crops was a serious enough issue to necessitate legislative attention. The Clark County Court had the authority to approve or disapprove the location and erection of gates across roads, except no road was to be placed across a road over which star route mail was delivered to bar connector roads between the various county seat towns.

The matter of construction of gates across the roads had behind it a strong folk practice. Since the first emigrant drove hogs, cattle, sheep, and horses through Cumberland Gap, the open countryside of Kentucky was regarded largely as free range dominion, and so it had been for the herds of buffalo and their Indian hunters.[19] Once, however, when fields were cleared and a system of domestic agriculture was introduced there arose the conflict, sometimes bitter, between farmers and livestock raisers and drovers. This situation was documented in Clark County by the act of the creation; in the requirements was that one of the public structures near the central courthouse would be a stray pen.[20]

By 1797 it would have been miraculous if a public road of any mileage

PRINCIPAL STAGE ROUTES.								
1. *From Maysville*			Middletown, ...	7	126	*NASHVILLE,..*	6	173
to Louisville.	Miles	M.les.	*Louisville,*	12	138			
To *Washington,* .	4					3. *From Catletts-*		
May's Lick,.....	8	12	2. *From Louisville*			*burg to Frankfort.*		
Ellisburg,..... ..	13	25	*to Nashville.*			To Little Sandy, .	24	
Millersburg,.....	11	36	To West Point,..	21		Tripletts, ...	38	62
Paris,..........	7	43	*Elizabethtown,*...	22	43	*Owingsville,*.....	16	78
Lexington,......	18	61	*Munfordsville,* ...	27	70	*Mount Sterling,* ..	13	91
Versailles, ...	12	73	Three Forks, ...	15	85	*Winchester,*	15	106
FRANKFORT,.	13	86	Dripping Spring,.	10	95	*Lexington,*......	20	126
Hardinsville, ...	8	94	Smith's Grove, ..	3	98	*FRANKFORT,*.	25	151
Clay Village,....	8	102	*Bowling Green,*..	13	111			
Shelbyville,.....	5	107	Franklin, ...	20	131	4. *From Frankfort*		
Simpsonville, ...	8	115	Tyree Springs, ..	21	152	*to Nashville, Ten.*		
Boston,.........	4	119	Haysboro',......	15	167	To *Lawrenceburg,*	12	

Main Stage Routes in Kentucky 1835 showing Winchester on the route from Cattlettsburg to Frankfort.

could have been opened without crossing through cultivated fields. The gates which barred the roads were intended more to keep free ranging animals out of crops and on the open grazing lands. A careless user of the roads who left gates open could be responsible for the destruction of field crops. This legislators understood full well when they placed the responsibility for regulating the gates upon the local county courts.[21] Advertisements which appeared in the *Kentucky Gazette* during the early years give clear indications of the nuisance of wandering domestic livestock.[22]

On February 27, 1797, the Kentucky General Assembly enacted its first and somewhat extensive road law.[23] This legislation outlined the procedures for laying out and opening systems of public roads in the counties. It provided that when a person or persons wished to open a local road he or they should appear before the county court and request that a commission of viewers be appointed to locate and mark the route. The viewing commissioners, in turn were admonished by the court to locate the "nearest and best route" between a specified beginning and an ending of the proposed road.

In submitting their reports to the court, viewing commissioners often demonstrated that they had little knowledge of the physiographic and human difficulties which might effect the most efficient location of routes. The county court magistrates requested commissioners that in making their reports they would describe both the nature of the convenience and the inconveniences of the routes they were recommending.[24] This meant, obviously, a general notation of the nature of the terrain over which a proposed road would be opened, the nature of the soil, and the elevation of hills and ridges. Of particular interest to the magistrates were identifications of the owners of the lands over which new roads might cross. Veiled in the term "inconvenience," was a desire to avoid resistance and political controversy. Viewers were admonished by law to see that all main roads led to both the county seat, and through the county intersections to the state capital in Frankfort.[25]

When the three chosen Clark County commissioners had tramped over the route of a projected road and had reported their observations to the court, it was then the court's responsibility to call a meeting at some convenient place along the route to hear questions and to adjudicate disputes which might occur. In the case of controversies which could not be settled by compromise and persuasion, the court could assemble a twelve-man jury and hold a trial to settle the issue by judicial fiat.

At different intervals of years the Commonwealth ordered that the counties be organized into road precincts.[27] In the case of Clark County and twenty-eight others, this was not done until January 30, 1830.[28] By legislative act the county was, at the yearly election of members of the House of Representatives, to choose three road commissioners. After being duly sworn into office these three officials were instructed to lay off the county into road precincts. The legislation prescribed neither the number nor the size of the precincts. Each one, however, was to be under the supervision of an overseer who was empowered to make improvements and repairs on the roads. The elected commissioners were authorized to levy a special road tax of six and a fourth cents per hundred dollars assessed property, plus a dollar poll tax on each white male of legal age. For their services the commissioners were paid a dollar a day, but not more than fifty dollars in a single year.[29]

The new law permitted the commissioners to call out all males between the ages of fifteen and fifty years to donate a prescribed number of days of work on the roads. This meant the opening of new roadways, plowing and smoothing the road bed, cutting back obstructing trees and underbrush, bridging small streams, and erecting sign posts. The county clerk was required to make a list of every eligible "tyther" and supply it to the commissioners. The overseer was instructed to make tax collections, to call out citizens to work the roads and to see that they were kept in passable condition within the district or precinct, which meant that the early Clark County roads were segmented into districts, and often reflected the diligence, or lack of diligence on the part of the overseers and workers in the different jurisdictions.[30]

In addition to their other duties road overseers were instructed to have erected at every crossroads a directional sign post of stone or durable wood,

or placed on nearby trees bearing directional markers inscribed in bold letters, "directing to the most noted place to which the road leads."[31] One won-
ders if the Clark County surveyors in fact actually followed the letter of the
law and saw to it that all the roads in their districts were kept clearly marked.

The office of road surveyor in Clark County was an important one, if
that official conscientiously performed his duties. He could wield a certain
amount of political influence because it was within his power to initiate requests for individuals for roads and for changes of rights-of-way, he could
enforce the calling out of citizen-laborers to contribute their "tithe" obligations for road work. The surveyor could even grant releases for work to individuals. The most important of the engineer's duties, however, was the
exercising of his broad powers of locating and opening roads, of keeping
them in passable repair, and the straightening out of curves, and in making
major relocations of roads. Not only could he draft manpower, he could also
commandeer the use of horses, and ox teams, the use of plows and all other
farm implements necessary to keeping the roads "well plowed,"[32] In many
cases slaveowners sent their subjects to work in their place, and the surveyors
and overseers had to exercise special oversight over the involuntary workers.
Fortunately owners of teams, wagons, and plows were given work time credit
for their use. Later a state law permitted the county to purchase plows and
other equipment to be used on the roads.[33] The law, however, undertook to
restrict the use of public equipment for the benefit of private individuals.
This law ante-dated the latter practice of some magistrates offering it as patronage to faithful supporters.[34]

Reflective of the forest cover of a considerable portion of Clark County
and the casual frontier practices of felling trees across the road, restrictive
action was necessary. Under the law if a person was caught committing this
act of indiscretion and vandalism he was given forty eight hours to remove
the blockage or be fined ten dollars for every tree lying across the road.[35]

Unfortunately there seems to be no accounts by contemporary travelers
which describes the travail of moving over primitive "tithe" maintenance and
public roads in back country Clark County in most of the nineteenth century.[36] There is, however, a description of the toils and frustrations of the
famous old pioneer Indian fighter, Benjamin Logan. By 1796 Benjamin Logan
had moved away from Lincoln County and was living in Shelby county where
he was establishing himself as a farmer and miller. That year he entered the
race for the Kentucky governorship in opposition to James Garrard. In the
midst of the campaign he went to Winchester to solicit support. On the way
to the town he came on one of his wagons mired hub deep in mud. The

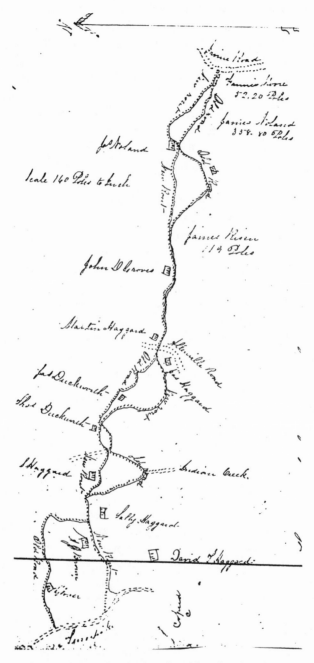

Redirecting the Road from Ruckersville to Allanville, July 1869.

wagon had been sent to the knobs near Mount Sterling to secure rock from which to chisel millstones. Logan, according to the story, dismounted and tried to help pry up the wheels of the vehicle, but in doing so muddied his shirt and had to remove it from his back. The other story has it that Logan removed his shirt, and while he was working with the wagon a cow chewed his shirt so badly that it was unwearable. Either way, the roads were miserable. When he arrived in Winchester shirtless he may have attracted attention, but the incident was hardly enough to cause him to lose the election to James Garrard.[36]

Indicative of the kinds of pressures which legislators and public officials were under in the administering of public roads, the General Assembly in December 1804, enacted a law exempting ministers of the gospel from enforced labor on the roads, and after the preachers came the halt, the lame and the self-proclaimed infirm to petition that they should not be required to perform such common peasant labors. These were requests which could be heard distinctly in the county court room, and in the legislative halls in Frankfort. No aspiring politician was going to deny such requests.[37]

Opening roads across the face of Clark County was of such vital necessity to its social and economic growth that the issue often was the prime one before the county court. By a propitious historical circumstance the Commonwealth of Kentucky and Clark County were confronted simultaneously with the vexing matters of developing roads in a virginal wilderness country. Emerging farmsteads and country cross roads villages made urgent demands for road outlets. Both state and county were impelled to act by the force of kindred pressures, the phenomenal increases in population, the raising annual yields of agricultural produce, the rapid expansion of the livestock herds, and the political ones of forming direct connections with the county seat and the courthouse, and then with the statehouse.[38] In Clark County a main commercial traffic road to Kentucky River boat landings and warehouses was a prime necessity. Too, livestock producers needed a connection with the great drover road to Cumberland Gap. By 1804 there had come to exist in the county a number of grain and saw mills along with the inspection stations established along the Kentucky River by acts of the General Assembly. All of these enterprises were dependent upon road outlets.[39] Even today one has to travel down Lower Howard's Creek to understand how vital a main road to the river landings and warehouses was to the economic well being of the region.

By the date of the second meeting of the Clark County Court, July 25, 1793, it had become a foregone conclusion that the county seat not be located at Strode's Station, but on the land of John Baker, and including the big spring. That site doubtless had by that time some connection with Boonesborough and the Kentucky River. This passage way may have been no more than primitive pack horse trail; the record is silent on this matter. Clearly, Boonesborough had been the stopping place for many emigrants entering central Kentucky after 1775, and the river presented no barrier to their crossing over in to the adjoining and available lands in the area of present-day Clark County. There were several settler communities which grew out of the appearance of communal emigrant parties. No clearer example of this type of settlement can be found in Clark County history than that of the "Bush Colony" on and near Lower Howard's Creek.[40] By 1798 the Kentucky River had become the economic lifeline for the county's farmers. For more than three decades the flatboat trade floating down stream from Boonesborough was an era of some romance in western river traffic annals.[41]

In the 1793 session of the Clark County Court a committee of viewers was appointed to tramp over the proposed route on the "nearest and best way" for the opening of a road from Holder's Boatyard to the place where the courthouse would be erected. This viewing committee was composed of "true" yeomen who swore they would do their duty. Members were James Frame and James Dunlap (Duncan). Not only were these men instructed to locate the nearest and best way to Holder's Warehouse and Boatyard; they were required to discover the conveniences and inconveniences of their choice of route.[42] The latter phrase, as indicated several times elsewhere had more profound meaning than a superficial description of physical contours. Always the court sought to have located roads which would serve the greatest number of settlers, cross the landholds of the most amenable owners, and not to irritate the cantankerous landholders any more than was necessary.

At the outset of the creation of the Clark County seat in Winchester succeeding magisterial members of the court realized it was important to form connection with the neighboring county towns. An interesting development in this instance was the chartering of Winchester,[43] a fact which made the opening of a road connecting the two towns mandatory. Historically, the chartering of Mount Sterling was promoted by a group of land speculators led by Enoch Smith. The petitioners whose names appear in the chartering act were Enoch Smith, Hugh Forbes, John Judy, and Sam Spurgin, all of whom owned parcels of the 540 acres of land on which the village was to be located. This site on "Small Mountain Creek" was described as if it were the transfer of an ordinary tract of land, which perhaps it was.[44] For four years, 1792 to 1796 settlers pushed deeper into the outlying areas of Clark County, and especially along the eastern periphery. One of the earliest settlers in the area was the famous Boone Trail diarist Journalist William Calk. This venturesome trailbreaker went out from Boonesborough in 1776 to scout the lands along the South Mount Creek. His party raised a crude log structure which became a famous area landmark, "Calk's Cabin." The Calk party no doubt followed an ancient Indian trail to the Little Mount area. In fact the trail may have been a bold and well traveled one.[45]

In March 1782 a band of Wyandotte warriors threatened Boonesborough with a surprise, but as it turned out, an abortive raid. They withdrew and menaced the weaker outlying cabin settlement along the trail to Little Mount. At this place, little more than a mile from the future village of Mount Sterling there occurred a brief but furious encounter between the Wyandotte party and the defenders of Estill's Station. Both sides suffered severe injuries in the so-called Estill's Defeat. James Estill was killed and so was the leader of the Indian raiders.[46] The bloody encounter at Little Mount was associated with the history of Clark County, and so was the subsequent devastating attack on Morgan's Station on Slate Creek on April 1, 1793. Settlers at the latter station were just beginning the planting of their crops when their station was overwhelmed by a raiding party.[47] There was some ironic significance to the Morgan Station attack. It was one of the last Indian raids to occur in Kentucky. It took place just prior to the crushing defeat of the northwestern tribes by Anthony Wayne's forces in the battle of Fallen Timbers which resulted in the signing of the Treaty of Greenville,[48] August 20, 1794. From this moment on the Clark County area was at peace, and the opening of roads into the developing back country became an important part of the county's highway history.

So common place was the poor condition of most of the rural roads of Clark County, or of Kentucky as a whole, no one seems to have found the subject worthy of extensive comment. Nevertheless, as times and conditions of human life changed there arose urgent demands for more efficient highways. A new era in Kentucky road building and management dawned in the decade of the 1830's, an era which demanded the relocation of winding roadways and all weather surfacing.[49] Clark County in 1830 had no tax base substantial enough to build even a mile of all weather road. An examination of expenditures on roads now seem utterly unbelievable. The old system of enforced or tithe labor on the roads was both impractical and fundamentally unworkable.[50] There was introduced a solution to highway construction and maintenance in the organization of quasi-private public turnpike companies. These were chartered by the Kentucky General Assembly, but managed by local boards of stockholders. This was a means of avoiding the institution of direct tax levies.[51]

Kentucky in the decades 1830-1850, pursued a will-o-the-wisp notion that its main arterial transportation problems could be solved by improving its navigable streams and use of the steamboat, this in an age when the building of railroads in the country was gaining momentum.[52] Clark County was vulnerable on this point because of its direct access to the Licking and Kentucky rivers.[53]

Nevertheless, Clark County, in 1834 was an inland region. There is no doubt that the Kentucky River with both its flatboat and later steamboats traffic was vital, but the future special and economic welfare of the county depended upon its roads as outlets. During the years 1830-1900, legislation pertaining to the chartering, operation, and defaulting of toll roads grew voluminous. So did the entries in the Clark County Order Books.[54] The toll gate companies were technically bound by detailed legislative regulation. They were controlled as to the width and structure of the McAdam roadbeds, the location every five miles of toll gates or pike poles, the objects which gave the roads the name turnpikes. Generally the standard specification of a turnpike was an eighteen foot wide roadway based on an eight or nine inch layer of crushed stone. The stone had to be crushed down to a size with a knapping hammer where it would pass through an iron ring with a three inch diameter. The stone bed was held in place by the MaCadam process of forcing the finely crushed limestone "metal" into the stone interstices.[55]

Apparently the earliest turnpike chartered in Kentucky was that which ran south from Louisville by way of the mouth of Salt River to Elizabethtown, Munfordsville, Bowling Green south to the Kentucky-Tennessee border at the famous "Black Jack" Corner in Simpson County.[56] The first Clark County Turnpike company to receive a charter seems to have been for the road connecting Winchester, Chilesburg, Colbyville, and Lexington.[57] This company was chartered February 4, 1834. The legislative mandate was that the toll road would be built to the same specifications as the Louisville one to the southern state border.[58] This meant use of the McAdam process. There were four groups of investors and directors who represented each Winchester, Chilesburg, Colbyville, and Lexington. The Winchester directors were Samuel D. Taylor, Richard Hawes, James B. Duncan, Jr., Joseph Decret, John Williams, and James Simpson. Those for Chilesburg were Thomas R. Dudley, Clifton R. Ferguson, Hubbard Taylor, Jr., Matthew Kennedy, and Edward Darmaby, for Colbyville C. H. Taylor, Dr. Samuel D. Martin, Dickinson Parrish, Edward D. Hockaday, William R. Smith, and William Price. From

Lexington, Elisha Warfield, Aaron K. Woolley, John Brand, Richard Higgins, and Charlton Hunt. This rather large board of directors contained many representatives of early Kentucky families, and certainly an impressive segment of power structures of Clark and Fayette counties.[59]

The legislative act, which in fact was a charter, of the Winchester, Chilesburg, Colbyville, and Lexington Turnpike Company appropriated $1500 per mile provided the stockholders raised a comparable amount. It also required that the company would locate the turnpike down a fifty foot wide right-of-way, and that the roadbed itself be from twelve to eighteen feet wide. Later this latter requirement was modified and the roadbed was reduced to eight feet. It was to be constructed by using the "artificial McAdam process."[60]

Toll gates or turnpikes, were to be established at five mile intervals, each to be attended by a toll keeper who was provided with a roadside residence or toll house. Toll rates were set by law, and no amount bickering and abusing of the toll keeper could change them.[61] No person traveling on weekdays and who pretended he was on his way to church or to a religious meeting was permitted to use this excuse for not paying toll.[62] On Sundays church goers were passed free of charge. From time to time the question of religious travelers was to be reviewed both by the Kentucky General Assembly and the Clark County Court.[63]

Travelers in general were required to pay a specified or classified rate of toll. Individuals riding, driving, or leading a horse or mule, or driving a herd of cattle, a drove of hogs, a flock of sheep, or riding in a sulky, a chair, a chase, a phaeton, a wagon or any other kind of pleasure or burden vehicle was to be halted at the pike poll until charges were paid. The rates were listed on a somewhat complicated scale. For twenty head of sheep or hogs, or other small stock (turkeys) the rate was six and a quarter cents for every ten head, the same for cattle. For large animals, horses and mules, the rate was four cents each, two-wheel pleasure carriages were charged eight cents, four wheel carriages sixteen cents. and wagons were charged by the width of their tires; narrow tired ones were charged sixteen cents, while those four inches or broader were assessed twenty five cents, and prices when up with the increasing width of tires. The draft animals were assessed separately. Thus it cost a patron traveling in a four wheel carriage from Winchester to Lexington a dollar and sixty cents the round trip.[64]

No mention was made of the rate charged for stage coaches. Yet there was at least one stage line operating from Lexington to Winchester, Mount Sterling, and the mouth of the Big Sandy River. The waybill of the scheduled stages which operated from Staunton, Virginia, to Harrodsburg in 1800 listed the Kentucky points of Mouth of Big Sandy, Olympia Springs, Mount Sterling, Winchester, Chilesburg, and Lexington.[65]

The chartering of the Winchester-Lexington Turnpike Company was to usher in a new era of road location, building, and administration in Clark County. Winchester was to become an even more important hub for the turnpike as it had been for the earlier rural roads. In 1845 the Paris and Winchester Company was chartered, the next year the Winchester and Mount Sterling Turnpike Company, and the Colbyville-Combs Ferry Company came into being. Between 1834 and 1900 there was a veritable rash of turnpike company charterings.[66]

Entries made in the Clark County Road Book by the road surveyor or commissioner are terse. Notations entered in the Order Books are somewhat fuller of details, but none of these official records give even a revealing hint of the actual use of the roads.[67] With the organization of the turnpike companies a significant change was made in the labor situation. Private companies could not have access to the old citizen tithe source of labor. The building of a MaCaddam road with the limited mechanical equipment available in the 1840's was a taxing challenge. Dirt was removed by use of carts, grading was done with horse drawn plows, and the stone seating was hand prepared. So was the fine adhesive limestone dusting. Without the official records even giving a hint of the source of labor, after the great Irish immigration following 1845 most stone work was performed by itinerate Irishmen.[68] Stone was hand crushed by use of heavy knapping hammers. Rock was crushed into approximately six ounce chunks. The road overseers used iron rings of three inch diameters to test the fineness of the crushed rock. The congealing or binding limestone "metal" had to be crushed into virtual dust to permit compaction.[69]

By 1860 there may have been as many as a half dozen privately owned turnpike roads in Clark County. There were also some toll bridges which were enclosed within gates. Too, ferries were operated across the Kentucky, Red, and Licking rivers. During the latter half of the nineteenth century nearly all the main road travel in the county was over turnpike roads. There seems, however, not to have prevailed the bitter anti-turnpike virus which spread so violently in some of the neighbor counties in the mid-1800's. Under cover of darkness toll gate raiders destroyed pike poles, intimidated toll collectors, and, in some instances, burned toll houses. The bitterest of the raids occurred in Washington, Anderson, Mason, Marion, Mercer, Franklin, Woodford, and Jessamine counties.[70]

The resistance to the private management of the roads actually started in Mason County when Dr. John A. Reed was denied passage through a toll gate when he was on his way to visit a patient. Dr. Reed was turned back either because he did not have money to pay the fare, or simply refused to pay it. This treatment of a popular physician was the act which touched off the era of vigilante activities. Beyond this it forced the Commonwealth to reassess its policy of public roads management.[71] The time was ripe for abandoning reliance on turnpike companies to assume such a heavy and vital public responsibility, and to return the obligation to the state and counties. The fact that the public record is littered with accounts of turnpike company failures or readjustments is indicative that the scheme was a defective solution to a vital public need in Clark County and the rest of Kentucky.[72]

For more than a century it was a rare meeting of the County Court when no petitioners appeared either for the opening of a new road, or the relocation of an older one in the Order Books diagrams of changes recommended by viewing commissions. Most of these concerned the straightening of unusually crooked stretches of road, or the relocation of roads around gullied and worn out sections. The brief descriptions accompanying the diagrams of

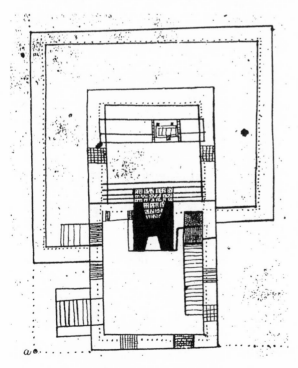

Floor plan of the Clark County Jail. This strong wood bastion was deemed stout enough to hold even the most rowdy miscreant. The big "H" was the nerve center of the jail.

route changes are vague, giving little more than the most elementary details of right of way changes. There were exceptions in some of the diagrams. The road viewers or surveyors not only drafted the route of the old road with one of the change, but the draftsman or court clerk drew houses bordering the road. There are indications that these rough drawings may have been indicative of the appearances of some of the earlier rural homes.[73]

Graphically reflective in both the statute of law of Kentucky and in the Clark County financial reports in the court order books is the fact of strong resistance to taxation. Neither county nor state embraced this idea. By the middle of the fourth decade of the nineteenth century, however, it became clearly evident that the old tithe labor system may have worked only moderately well in a pioneering situation, it must be branded a gross failure so far as the maintenance of an all-year passable network of rural roads was concerned. The tasks were too great to be accomplished with the use of reluctant enforced labor, and primitive equipment and supervision. This fact became clearly evident by the 1830's when the Commonwealth sought to partially solve its public road commitment by chartering semi-private companies to assume the responsibility for maintaining the state's complex maze of potentially navigable streams would solve the problems of transporting the rising tonnages of agricultural products to market.[74] The Commonwealth unwisely supported a chimerical plan of internal improvements which on one hand stymied the building of roads, and on the other failed to comprehend that the new age of transportation had already dawned in the great burst of American railroad building.[75]

As indicated above the resort to shifting public responsibilities onto the shoulders of private enterprise in the toll turnpike era was only moderately successful. Possibly the most positive observation that can be made of this experiment is the fact it introduced the process of hard surface roads to Kentucky, a state which had an abundance of the materials with which to construct Mcadamized roadbeds. The turnpike company scheme of highway building and management was destined from the beginning to meet with a troubled end. Operation of these turnpiked highways was concentrated in the hands of a limited number of stockholders, and the companies were only loosely administered by the state. If the prediction of growing public dissatisfaction with the management of the main roads had been written in the company charters it could not have been made clearer than was the case by the 1890's. Nevertheless the era of the toll or turnpike road drew to a lingering end in both Clark County and Kentucky.[76]

On July 6, 1892, and almost contemporary with the ratification of the fourth Kentucky Constitution, the General Assembly enacted a fourth and extensive revisionary highway law which had a genuine pertinency for the users of public roads in Clark County. It gave the turnpike companies legal protection for obtaining construction materials, including the acquisition of acre square plots on which to erect toll houses, to acquire rights of way, and access routes to rock quarries. In turn the companies were subjected to fines if they failed to maintain the toll roads in sound passable condition.[77]

For the first time in precisely a century of enactments of road laws, the General Assembly adopted rules for the use and travel on public roads. The law provided that drivers of vehicles could claim only half of the road. Passes were to be on the right hand side, faster moving vehicles going in the same direction could pass on the left hand. Loaded wagons or carts had the first choice of the road. The unsentimental legislators blithely trampled a cherished Kentucky tradition of the road. They ordered that, "no bells of any kind shall be carried on the animals drawing any vehicle." Drivers were to be fined five dollars for every day they ignored this law.[78] The august statesmen of Frankfort surely must have been unaware that Kentucky stock drovers felt downright ashamed if one lead head of their livestock entered an eastern city without being belled. No respectable wagoner could imagine a team on the road without tinkling bells. When that Kentuckian, William Becknell led his famous trading party down the Sante Christo Mountain into Santa Fe Mexico, he did so with bells tinkling on his mules. The New Kentucky road law forbade drivers to leave vehicles standing on the roads, and no teams were to be fed on roads. Drivers who violated this law were to be fined five dollars for each offense. Woe betide the sloven wretch who scattered stone, fifth, or other trash on the highway.[79]

An earlier law, April 10, 1890, dealt with a nagging problem along the Winchester-Mount Sterling Turnpike. Range roving livestock had a habit of bedding down on this public road, and no doubt threatened the safety of travelers. For every offense committed by a loitering head of livestock the owner was to be fined ten dollars, and if he did not pay it then the offending animal was subject to be sold and the money turned over to the county.[80]

Whatever progress Clark County made in developing an intricate system of both local and inter-county roads prior to 1913, many were still mud choked in winter and dust stifling in summer, and rough in all seasons. Clark County, like all of America, was to feel the rising pressures caused by the introduction of the automobile. By the latter date Kentucky became aware of the incipient good roads movement in the nation. The General Assembly responded by enacting still another comprehensive road law, this one far more sweeping in scope than any of the previous ones.[81] The plan was sound, and the promise bright, but as always in the past, no adequate provisions were made for financing it either at the state or local level.[82]

For both Kentucky and Clark County times at the opening of the twentieth century were changing rapidly. Demands for more efficiently managed public roads became too heavy to be satisfied by the old penny pinching practices of the past. By 1912 the Commonwealth of Kentucky began to feel the forces for constructing a more stable system of roads. By that date the automobile was coming into expanding common use, and the existing roads were ill-prepared for its arrival.[83] Since 1792 the Kentucky General Assembly had enacted at least four basic highway laws, but none looked beyond use by horse drawn vehicles.[84] Essentially the extensive law enacted in 1912 may be considered as the watershed of highway legislation of the past, and revolution of the immediate future. Essentially the law of 1912 created the offices of highway commissioner and engineer. It set specifications which looked to the building of more efficient roads, the mode of awarding construction contracts was prescribed, and for the first time in Kentucky history ordered the drafting of an official state road map.[85]

The new highway engineer was to be either a man of scientific training in the field, or one of extensive experience in highway planning and building. The engineer was given considerable power to oversee the county road system, even though the politically sensitive law made frequent gestures to the county courts and their road administering authority. Too, there was a consciousness that there were still turnpike companies and toll bridges and ferries.[86]

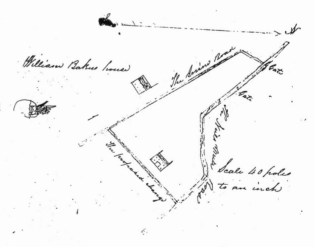

Straightening out a section of the Irvine and the Bush Road showing the relationship to the William Baker House and a second unnamed dwelling.

The law of 1912 reflected the fact that parts of Kentucky were still on a fringe of the frontier age. It prescribed a set of rules for keeping public roads free of all forms of obstruction, meaning gates, the cutting of trees across roads, and dumping trash. Legislators reflected a surprisingly mature aesthetics and environmental sensitivity by encouraging private individual landholders to plant at sixty foot intervals fruit and nut bearing, and shade trees. These were to be set back fifteen feet from the road center lines. Clinging to the past and serving the present, the law required certain bordering landholders to construct watering troughs, to be mounted at a height to accommodate horses and mules drawing loaded wagons. For this service the landowner could levy on the county for two dollars.[87]

Finally the law of 1912 abolished the ancient county offices of surveyor and overseer as provided in the law of 1797.[88] Though the law of 1912 impelled Clark County into the on-coming age of the automobile so far as state roads were concerned, there still remained an intricate matrix of local roads which fell outside the prescriptions of state control, and remained a responsibility of the Clark County. As mentioned above, there still lingered the necessity for coming to terms with the turnpike stock companies, and of moving into an age when the road users paid toll to one where there was a universal system of taxation, principally in the form of automobile license and gasoline taxes.[89] The age of the turnpike highway in Clark County ended almost as it began by having performed a vital service, but the system was no answer to the general public need for passable roads.

Road building nationally assumed a new and much broader dimension. The Congress, on July 11, 1916,[90] enacted the Federal Highway Law which initiated a joint state-federal governmental system in roads. These were to be built and maintained by federal specifications. In the case of Clark County this meant the designation of the historic highway connecting Lexington, Winchester, Mount Sterling, and Owingsville with the Big Sandy River. The designated Highway 60 followed generally over the original location of this route.[91]

Adding another important chapter to national highway modernization representatives of twenty-four states gathered in Washington in February 1925, to discuss problems arising from the creation of the national system of roadways. An age old problem was the creation of a uniform directional system which could keep travelers informed as to where they were and how to get to where they were going. Both states and counties had attempted to erect signage but there was a lack of uniformity.[92] The Washington assembly settled this issue by adoption of a uniform highway marketing system. Federal highways were to be indicated by even numbers embossed on the face of a metal shield. Even numbers to run east to west, and uneven numbers north to south. State roads were to be numbered inside circles.[93] Thus for Clark County the main east west road became Highway 60. In subsequent years all Clark County roads were numbered and standard signage placed at proper intervals.

Within two centuries the face of Clark County became etched with roadways, all of which was hard surfaced by 1994. The automobile and motor truck had taken over the roads. They brooked no toll gates, bridges or ferries. A classic example of the ever evolving history of highways in Clark County was the replacing of the Boonesborough ferry with a bridge which in less than half a century became archaic, and in May 1994 was replaced by a modern wide bed multi-million dollar one.[94] This bridge cost more than Clark County spent on highways in its first century and a half. The modern road from Winchester to Boonesborough is a far cry from the one which viewers blazed from Holder's Boatyard to Strode's Station in 1793.

Over the years Winchester not only became a highway hub for local roads, but for inter-county ones as well. No "settler" is now located more than three or four miles off an improved road. Gone are the freight wagons and carts drawn by oxen, mules, and horses, long ago the watering troughs were drained and crushed into road metal, the echoes of tinkling team bells silenced by unromantic legislators, and toll houses gave way to gasoline stations. Embalmed within the covers of the Clark County Order Books are the chronicles of weaving an intricate gossamer of roads over the landscape, stretch by stretch.[95] No modern Clark Countian can now recall the days when men and boys between the ages of sixteen and fifty were officially listed as "tithers" and were "warned out" to work the roads or when the farmers supplied teams and "barshare" plows to plow them.[96]

Throughout two centuries of highway history in Clark County there were many forces at work which brought about the constant changes in the management of the public roads. One such force, though shadowy at times, was a vigorous goad to effect road improvements. There was a close and intimate parallel relationship between the history of Kentucky roads and that of the United States Postal Service. At every chronological stage of opening and improving of main roads there also had to be a consideration of the delivery of mail.[97] During the primary settlement era of Kentucky communication with the eastern parts of the Nation was largely on a catch-as-catch-can basis. Post riders and travelers over uncertain intervals of time brought letters, newspapers, and word of mouth news. For a brief period of time after the organization of the United States Government in 1789 the Congress continued the archaic postal system of the Confederation. In 1792 and 1798 it enacted laws establishing a postal system which in time would serve an expanding republic.

The congressional laws had a direct bearing on Kentucky. Mails reached the western country either by post riders from Philadelphia, Baltimore, and Washington traveling through Virginia and North Carolina, and up the Wilderness Road to Danville, and subsequently to Lexington,[98] or they were floated down the Ohio on flatboats and carried to Lexington over the Limestone Road. After it began publication in 1787 the *Kentucky Gazette* ran periodic listings of letters and addresses. Bradford himself instituted a skeleton post rider service to facilitate the distribution of his newspaper.[99] Thus persons in early Clark County were served in a more or less casual manner. They perhaps sent few letters, and receive few. The Lexington postoffice was established in 1794, and two days later post riders went out from that office delivering mail to outlying communities. No doubt they left the mail with local tavern keepers. Certainly this was true of newspaper delivery.[100]

It was not until 1803 that a postoffice was established in Winchester with Edmund Calloway as postmaster. Early postal rates were based on the distances letters traveled, and most often the recipient paid the cost. At some undisclosed date in early nineteenth century Winchester became a central distribution point for mail delivered over the Winchester-Red River crossing road to Irvine. Post riders made these journeys twice a week. By the late 1820's contracts were awarded stage coach lines to carry all the mail from Lexington to surrounding towns, including Winchester. Holding the mail contract added prestige to the line, and even allowed a tolerance of a certain amount of arrogance on the part of the drivers.[101] The mail coaches did hold to a semblance of a regular schedule, but they served only towns on main roads.

Delivery of the United States mail had a distinct bearing on the maintenance of the inter-town roads. Somewhat indicative of this fact was the action of the Kentucky General Assembly forbidding the erection of gates across roads over which the mails were delivered.[102] In the case of Clark County, according to the postal map of 1878 only three Clark County roads fell into this category. These were the Lexington-Winchester-Mount Sterling road, the Winchester-Richmond road, and the Winchester-Irvine road.[103]

Throughout most of its history the Clark County population has been intensely agrarian and rural. It was distributed generally over the area of the county, gathering as indicated earlier, in tiny villages. This was true of Kentucky generally. Throughout the nineteenth century the state was said to have had the largest number of fourth class postoffices of any in the nation. No one, not even the statisticians of the postmaster general's office, seemed ever to have had an accurate account. There were known to have existed at least 4,000 offices between 1792 and 1900. Clark County had during that century twenty-seven offices, all, except Winchester, were located on county maintenance public roads.[104] Among the offices were Indian Fields, Becknerville, Ruckerville, Log Lick, Dunaways, Kiddville, Flanagan, Sycamore, and Arlen. Most of the offices had short life spans. The last survivor was Indian Fields, which according to the official postal directory, closed in 1970. The closing of the Indian Fields postoffice symbolized the closing of an age in Clark County. Rural free delivery and hard surfaced roads made the fourth class post office a relic of the age of rural isolation and muddy roads.

After an endless amount of crusading by the populist-agrarian senators and congressmen the Congress in 1896 enacted the law creating the rural free delivery service all across rural United States.[105] An experimental route was first established in West Virginia in 1902,[106] and in fast order literally hundreds of routes came into existence. Clark County was to share in this modernization of the United States postal service. Rural free delivery evolved through several stages. First carriers traveled horseback, in carts and buggies, and, maybe, sometimes, on foot.[107] They negotiated passage on the roads as best they could. Then came the era of hard surfaced roads and the use of automobiles and trucks. Country roads were lined with officially approved mail boxes,[108] and, in many ways, the rural mail carrier took the place of the country storekeeper-postmaster as a community "accomodater." Winchester is the lone post office survivor, and Kentucky stamp and cover collectors are overjoyed when they find an almost forgotten fourth class Clark County cancellation. The volume of mail which flows daily into the Winchester Postoffice no doubt equals that of a couple of decades, 1820-1840, and the great semi-trailer which brings it can outrun any fast express stage coach by a margin of forty to one, and not have become mired on a muddy road in the process.[109]

Whatever progress Clark County and its seat town made in the field of highway creation in the first two centuries of their existence, geography was a deciding fact. By the very physical nature of the county it came to be a significant middle area between the Inner Bluegrass Region and the Appalachian Highlands. Located well away from the route of the "grand tour" no domestic or foreign travelers came to criticize the institution of slavery, to quarrel about its crude taverns, or to cast an appraising eye on the advance of democracy. To enjoy notoriety in this area of Clark County and Winchester had to look to much less literate visitors.[110]

Four arterial public roads laced Clark County inextricably with the fortunes of the Appalachian Highlands. The historic highway which connected Lexington, Winchester, Mount Sterling, and Owingsville with the Big Sandy sliced through the northern shoulder of the highlands. The road which branched off at Mount Sterling and led up the Licking Valley to Paintsville and Prestonsburg was as much an integral part of the Clark County highway system as if it actually entered the county physically. The road which followed up the Red River Valley and across the ridges to the North Fork of the Kentucky River became a veritable funnel which carried travelers to and from the mountains. The fourth road wound down to the Red River, and up the Kentucky to Irvine and Beattyville, opening a direct line of travel and communication to highland communities almost as far away as Paintsville.[111]

Thus located at a geographical and highway apex, Clark County and Winchester enjoyed the trade and visitations parts of two of Kentucky's major geographical sections. To the west they developed a bluegrass culture, and to the east both economy and culture shaded off into those of the hills. For many a traveler trudging down over primitive roads from the highlands, Winchester was the first town he reached. Over the years the border position of Winchester has figured prominently in the history of Appalachia itself. For the courts the Clark County Courthouse was a legally and convenient neutral ground for the trial of change of venue cases which were too threatening to be tried on local home grounds.[112]

The opening of roads, and the continuing process of improving them was in fact an all but inerasable tracing of the progress of Euro-American civilization across the land. Clark County's history of road building, maintenance, and use might well be a microcosm of highway history across the Nation itself.

Grimes Mill, now the clubhouse of a hunt club, is representative of the mills which ground grain along the creeks of Clark County in earlier days. The mills converted Clark County grain into a profitable commodity to be shipped down river by flat boat. - *Photo courtesy of Jerry Schureman*

CHAPTER 6

The Agrarian Way

Tench Cox, a pioneer American statistician, in 1822 published a brief summary of the economic condition of the United States just as it was emerging from a biting depression. He described Kentucky as "agricultural," so could he have labeled Clark County.[1] For the first four decades of the county's agricultural history it is virtually impossible to uncover sound documentation so as to describe rapidly emerging fortunes of the area's economy. Only by resorting to anecdotal and inferential threads of information about agricultural developments can this basic chapter in Clark County's history be presented intelligibly.

It must be assumed at the outset, however, that within some definable parameters of acceptable data it is safe to describe the basic facts of agricultural beginnings. During two centuries of Clark County history the stamp of agrarianism was firmly impressed into the way of life. As indicated earlier, the availability of a rather large area of cheap virgin land became the irresistible magnet which brought droves of expectant settlers to the region north of the Kentucky River.[2]

Although lands within the bounds of Clark County have a wide diversity of qualities, historically they have been an impressive force in shaping social, economic, and political fortunes of their occupants. Over the more than two centuries the human population of the county has responded and adapted to strong geographical and environmental influences.[3] Basically, the land was suitable to the growing of a fairly generous variety of field crops. In fact, it is possible that few landed areas in North America have developed so successfully a combined agrarian and pastoral economy.[3] Too, few areas have sus-

tained so wide a diversity of farming economies within so confined a po-
litico-geographical entity. There has ever been a sharp division between farmers
who operated largely subsistent small farms and those who cultivated and
grazed farms ranging from three hundred to a thousand acres.[5]

From that all but forgotten moment when the first land claimant hacked
three tomahawk blazes on a corner tree and two chops on boundary trees,
and then declared a corn and cabin patch claim to the land, corn has been
Clark County's mainstay crop, if not in cash return, then in basic importance.[6] Though the statistics have seesawed up and down over the years, this
crop has clung steadfastly to its position of pre-eminence. Throughout all of
Kentucky history corn has been the sustaining ingredient of human and livestock consumption. From the beginning the pattern of Clark County agriculture was set. The four main crops have consistently been Indian corn (by
a preponderance of bushels or poundage), tobacco, wheat, and hemp, approximately in this order.[7]

Although the generous number of official estate inventories contains no
statistics as to crop production levels or other kindred data, they do reflect
vividly the overwhelming economic importance of farming in Clark County.
An examination of a rather full representation of the inventories of deceased
individuals who functioned at various economic levels produces a vivid revelation of farming as the central way of life in the county. The facts are impressive. The land was cleared and placed in cultivation by use of the most
elementary types of hand tools and implements. No matter the size of the
operation, basically all of the early Clark County farms were of a subsistence
nature.[8] No matter the number of acres, every farm had to be brought under
cultivation by the exercise of the most strenuous expenditure of human energy. No one possessed the labor-saving tools and machines. Breaking the
land and cultivating crops were done, in most cases, by generous use of work
oxen or steers. Most of the inventories indicate a varying number of black
slaves who were certainly important laborers in the early and primitive process of planting, cultivating, harvesting, and processing crops.[9]

Corn was cut, shocked, and shucked in many cases in earlier years by
common workings. Small grains were   threshed by hand and winnowed by
use of a device called a wheat fan.[10] Perhaps a visitor from ancient Babylonia
might not have been surprised to see this inefficient procedure of winnowing
grain still in use. Home-grown grain was converted to meal and flour by the
numerous gristmills located along the creeks of the county. The county court
was called upon on occasions to appoint viewing committees to inspect the
sites of proposed milldams to make certain they neither blocked streams nor

injured adjoining properties.[11] Much of the local grain was converted to whiskey. From the first settlements there were distilleries in Clark County. Whiskey could be transported to market without much loss from spoilage, and it was assured ready purchasers. There does not appear in either the county order books or the special distillery book any implication of moral resistance to the making of whiskey.[12]

For most Clark County farmers fields did not become fully productive prior to the adjudication of the feverish diplomatic issue over the free access to transportation on the Mississippi River and to a right of deposit of produce in New Orleans. The vital river economic lifeline was opened both by the ratification of the Pinckney Treaty with Spain in 1795 and the purchase of the Louisiana Territory nearly a decade later.[13]

As was true of so many events in Kentucky pioneer history there is not a clear record of when the first flatboats were drifted out of the Kentucky River headed for the gulf coastal market. What can be documented with certainty is the fact that the Kentucky General Assembly, at an early date, revealed a concern for the quality of Kentucky agricultural products shipped south, the conditions in the warehouses where they were stored and the establishment of systematic inspection of produce.[14] There no doubt was a sensitivity about the acceptance of Kentucky products by foreign consumers.

Well before Kentucky's separation from Virginia occurred and the state was admitted into the Union of states, there was concern with maintaining a market for agricultural products. In 1795 the General Assembly enacted the first of a rather extended series of laws regulating the packing and quality of flour, corn meal, cured meats, tobacco, and hemp. The responsibility for the approving of construction of warehouses and the appointment of inspectors of these products was placed squarely upon the shoulders of local officials.[15] Because Clark County was located on the Kentucky River, a direct channel of transportation to outside markets for farm products, and because its lands had become highly productive almost at the moment of making settlements, the Kentucky regulatory marketing laws had a high degree of pertinency.[16]

It is difficult to determine, because of the cursory notations of the legislative journals, precisely what motivated the enactment of the warehousing and inspection laws. The first of the series of laws applied specifically to the quality of corn meal, flour, cured meats, and hempen materials.[17] The law was amended in 1798 to include tobacco.[18] All these products were of primary importance to the farmers and millers of Clark County. They not only were commodities which could be converted to cash money, but most of them were vital to human subsistence. The law was drafted to be productive

of Kentuckians as well as foreign purchasers by providing not only for outgo-
ing products, but for the inspection of salt coming into the state.[19] It went
further by specifying the nature of the construction of barrels and hogsheads
in which farm produce was packed. Millers were required to brand each barrel of flour and meal with the net weight of the contents and to burn their
names in the head of the barrel.[20]

Inspectors were required to bore a half-inch hole in the barrel heading
and to extract samples of flour or meal to determine whiteness, fineness, and
freedom from trash. They were mandated to plug the inspection sampling
hole with a wooden bung. The inspectors also had to burn the name of the
place of origin in the head of the barrel. The law relating to the handling of
cured meats required packing in wooden casks and barrels, and the inspectors
were required to certify their qualities and soundness.[21]

Although an appreciable amount of tobacco had been shipped out of
Clark County and Kentucky prior to 1798, the General Assembly enacted
the first of what was to become a rather extensive volume of laws governing
the warehousing and marketing of this crop. It forbade both farmers and
boatmen to place aboard a boat a hogshead of tobacco destined for a foreign
market without having passed through a warehouse and undergone inspection. A master or captain of a boat who permitted uninspected tobacco to be
placed aboard his boat was subjected to a fine of fifty pounds. An offending
farmer was subjected to the loss of his tobacco, plus a fine of ten shillings per
pound for tobacco found to be uninspected. If a slave were found guilty of
violating the law he was subjected to drastic physical punishment. The law
was specific in prescribing, "And if any servant or other person employed in
navigating any such boat or other vessel, shall connive at or conceal the taking or receiving on board any tobacco in bulk or parcel as aforesaid, he shall
pay the sum of five (£) pounds, to be recovered as aforesaid; and if such
servant or any other person be unable to pay the sum, he or they, and every
slave so employed, shall, by order of such justice, receive on his bare back
thirty-nine lashes, well laid on."[22] If the master of the slave or of the boat or
other involved persons were unable to pay the fines, then they too were to be
subjected to a harsh penalty.[23] This law was of intense concern to Clark County
farmers because of the important points of flatboat debarkations on the Kentucky River.

No doubt receiving appointment as an inspector involved a certain amount
of political favoritism. The law set no qualifications for this job. The appointment was for a term of three years, and it produced an income from a specified rate per barrel, hogshead, or bundle inspected. Farmers paid the fee.

Nothing revealed the rurality of Clark County more clearly than the presence of twenty-three fourth class post offices which served rural patrons at every crossroads in the county. Long ago cancellations from these forgotten offices have become prized collectors' items.

Inspectors were required to be on hand six days a week from the first of November to the first of June each year. They not only were under orders of the county court to observe the law in the inspection of produce, but they also had to inspect and report on the condition of warehouses and on the inventory of tobacco carried over from one season to another, and to oversee the loading of boats and the incoming stocks of tobacco. The law also specified that hogsheads were to be constructed of well-seasoned and sound wooden staves four feet in length, and the barrels were to be thirty inches in diameter. If a farmer delivered tobacco in a larger hogshead he was required to unpack and repack the tobacco in legal-sized hogsheads; otherwise he was denied the privilege of shipping it. This law was of fundamental importance to the farmers of Clark County in that it attempted to safeguard the reputation of their farm products.[24]

On a broader base the Kentucky General Assembly demonstrated a responsible concern about the reputation of all Kentucky tobacco. Any Clark County farmer or master of a flatboat who attempted to ship uninspected tobacco was subjected to a fine of five pounds per hundredweight. A boat master undertaking to run uninspected tobacco downstream stood the chance of having his boat impounded.[25]

The 1820 amendment of the inspection law provided for the grading of tobacco into three classes; fine quality, good, and poor. In the latter classification the inspectors earlier were instructed to burn the tobacco.[26] The law of 1820, however, contained a proviso that a farmer could reclaim the inferior grade, or it could be turned over to warehouse scavengers called "pickers." These warehouse hangers-on were allowed to pick through the discarded tobacco, selecting the leaves of passable quality which could be repacked and sold.[27]

Major links in the preparation of grain products especially for the foreign market, were the millers, distillers, coopers, and warehouses. Clark County had a generous number of grainmills, distillers, and warehouses. There are no indications of many of the agricultural products from adjoining counties which were processed or stored by these facilities, but the volume must have been substantial. Perhaps the most important warehouse was that of William Bush, which was located on the Clark side of the Kentucky River near the mouth of Lower Howard's Creek.[28] Since the county had a fair boundary on this stream and its lands became highly productive at an early stage of bringing it under cultivation, warehouses came to have tremendous economic importance. This, of course, was true for all of Central Kentucky. On December 22, 1803, the General Assembly enacted a broad general law which was designed to control both the agricultural marketing process and the safety and security of warehouses. The law even designated the types of materials which could be used in the construction of warehouses, which included brick, stone, and wood.[29]

Pertinent to Clark County was the fact that the new law placed the responsibility on the county courts to oversee the construction of the warehouses, the appointment of commodities inspectors, and the appointment of viewing committee-inspectors to visit the warehouses and to make reports on the condition of both the structures and the products in storage. The warehouses were privately owned, but technically, at least, under the supposedly watchful eye of the county court.[30] Obviously the record is blurred as to the effectiveness of the inspections and operations of the warehouses, but surely

this was an area in which the partisan favoritism which so colored such matters in the "Little Kingdoms" had broad latitude.

Over the years warehouses were owned and operated by John Holder,
William and Thomas T. Bush, James Hampton, John Tuttle, Thomas Wells,
Samuel Howard, and others. From time to time complaints were made to the
county court about the condition and operation of a warehouse. In February
1806, Samuel R. Combs came to court to make a complaint against Robert
Richards, the tobacco inspector in John Holder's warehouse.[31] The court sustained the plaintiff's charges, and fired Richards, and appointed William
Tinsley to be inspector.[32] Almost immediately the court also appointed John
Price to the position. Over time some of the produce and warehouse inspectors included John V. Bush, appointed in November 1807 to be the inspector
of tobacco in Thomas Bush's warehouse; Roger Quisenberry, who was made
inspector in Eubank's warehouse; and John G. Allen, who was assigned to
Bush's warehouse.[33] There was in time to be a veritable procession of inspectors for tobacco, flour, cured meats, and hemp. Occasionally there appeared
in the Order Books notations critical of the conditions of the warehouses,
and on at least one occasion every warehouse in the county was brought
under criticism.[34]

Reflective of the public complaints was one made against the warehouse
of William Bush in October 1811. The minutes of the court noted that "A
return of the situation of the Bushes warehouse returned an assignment and
ordered to be rendered which is as follows to wit annual return of Bushes
warehouse we have since overseen return of October last inspected and received 101 new hogsheads of tobacco we have delivered 568 and have 101
now on hand with the warehouse large enough to hold about 450 hogsheads
more they are not in order to receive as the roof on one of them has several
bad leeks which not subjects the tobacco to considerable damage. The weight
and scale are particularly in need of adjustment and repair."[36] What the court
recorder, in his bumbling reports, meant was that Bush's warehouse was in
unsuitable condition to protect tobacco from serious damage. This may well
have been the case with all the Clark County warehouses.

Next to clearing the land and fallowing it for cultivation the greatest
need of the early Clark County farmers was a means of reasonably cheap and
efficient transportation for their products. As indicated above, there was from
the dawn of settlement an intimate connection between the spread of settlements and the Kentucky River. This stream from 1792 till 1840 was a vital
economic lifeline for farmers. Not one of the farm products of Clark County
in this era could pay its transportation costs overland, not even whiskey.[37]

Transportation to an outside market was a determining factor as to whether the county would progress or become stagnated by an overproduction of field crops. At the same time the distance between the boat landings at Boonesborough and New Orleans was awesome and challenging.[38]

A bill of lading of the principal Clark County farm products packed aboard flatboats headed for the lower Mississippi River market generally included flour, corn meal, distilled and fermented spirits, maple sugars, tobacco, and hempen fiber in the form of bale rope and cotton bagging. From the pasture and forest came cured meats and from the orchards dried fruits.[39] No statistician kept a record of the tonnages of these products shipped down river, or of the monetary wealth they returned to the farmers.

As vital as flatboats were to the early economy of Clark County, no local historian described the building of the boats or named the builders or the masters and crewmen who drifted them downstream. John Holder's boatyard on the Kentucky River was an important enough place to be one of the first connected by road to the internal Strode's Station and then to Lexington.[40] The ready availability of an abundance of boat building timbers was an important fact.[41]

Where there were cattle there had to be hay, and Clark County produced both in abundance. - *Photo courtesy of Jerry Schureman*

The spring and fall departures of flatboats constituted a near seasonal pageant. In these seasons there appeared in the *Kentucky Gazette* frequent appeals for boatmen to propel boats southward. Merchants in Lexington were highly dependent upon this service. They received their trade goods by boat from Pittsburgh and the Ohio River and then traded them for farm produce to be sold south.[42] This early mercantile trade embraced Clark County. Perhaps most of the manufactured items which appeared in the Clark County estate inventories were bought in Lexington.

Fortunately a foreign visitor observed the departure of flatboats on the Kentucky River. He described the nostalgic echoes of the boatmen's horns as they passed through the great limestone corridors of the Palisades. In 1802 he wrote, "That the merchants of Lexington nearly monopolizes the commerce of Kentucky. They receive their merchandise from Philadelphia and Baltimore, in thirty-five or forty days; the total charge for conveyance is from seven to eight dollars per quintal [hundred weight]. Seven tenths of the manufactured articles consumed in Kentucky as well as the rest of the United States, are imported from England; and principally consist of coarse and fine hardware, cutlery, nails, tinware, drapery, mercury, drugs, and china."[43] Many of these items appeared often in Clark County estate inventories. Merchandise was landed at Limestone (Maysville) and transferred to Lexington on wagons and packhorses.[44] Few if any farm implements were imported to Kentucky, but it was important that the hardware and tools necessary to create them were contained in the importations.[45]

Flatboatmen and their crude vessels were as necessary to the agrarian welfare and economy of Clark County as were the farmers and their bar share plows, reap hooks, and wheat fans. Flatboatmen, however, have almost fallen through the cracks in Kentucky history.[46] No doubt Benjamin Cassedy was correct in his *History of Louisville,* when he contended that the rough half-horse-half-alligator image of the boatmen was overdrawn. He wrote, "The bargemen were a distinct class of people whose fearlessness of character, recklessness of habits and laxity of morals rendered them a marked people. Their history will hereafter form the ground work of many a heroic romance or epic poem. In the earlier stages of this sort of navigation, their trips were dangerous, not only on account of the Indians whose hunting grounds bounded their track on either side, but also because the shores of both rivers were infested with organized banditti, who sought every occasion to rob and murder the owners of these boats. Besides all this, the Spanish Government had forbidden the navigation of the Mississippi by the Americans, and thus, hedged in every way by danger, it became these boatmen to cultivate hardi-

hood and wiliness of the pioneers...."[47] Many of the boatmen were also Clark
County farmers. Too, the products of the county's farmers figured significantly in raising the diplomatic pressure which broke the hold of the banditti
and the Spanish on the Mississippi, leaving this channel of commerce open
to the upriver farmers and merchants.[48]

Henry Bradshaw Fearon, a visiting Englishman, quoted a local Kentucky
estimate that there were shipped away from Kentucky at an earlier date a
million dollars worth of flour, three hundred and fifty thousand dollars worth
of pork, five hundred dollars worth of whiskey, a million and a half dollars
worth of tobacco, and five hundred thousand dollars worth of hempen cord-
age, baggage, and other fiber. This estimate coincided almost precisely with
the kinds of agricultural products shipped down river by the farmers of Clark
County.[49]

Although early agricultural statistics are sparse, available evidentiary
sources aid substantially in creating a basic general concept of the early pattern of farming in Clark County. The rather extensive number of estate appraisals comprises a significant documentary profile of agricultural procedures.
Depending upon the season in which inventories of estates were made, there
appears some material notion of the source of field crop seeds. Frequently
there were notations of corn, wheat, rye, flax, and hemp seeds. These were
selected and saved from one crop year to the next. Unfortunately the estate
appraisers gave no indication of the process by which these seeds were selected.[50] The most common filed crop seed was corn. The term "seed corn"
became a popular idiom in local folk speech. No doubt there survived through
numerous crop seasons corn crops which were seeded with descendants of
seeds brought across the mountains from Virginia and Pennsylvania, and year-
to-year selections of better ears were made in Clark County.[51] This was obviously true of all seedstocks for wheat, rye, tobacco, flax, and hemp. No one in
the age had much if any knowledge of the genetics of field crops. Nevertheless there went on a constant hunt for more productive varieties of corn.[52]

Again, the estate inventories revealed beyond contradiction that farming
in most of the nineteenth century was labor-intensive and physically arduous. As indicated elsewhere, farm tools and implements were of the black-
smith-home-made types. It seems mysterious that three generations of Clark
County farmers exploited so much land without the use of more sophisticated implements. Repeatedly, appraisers of estates listed hoes, mattock,
scythes, reaphooks, grubbing hoes, and axes as basic hand tools. Plows, harrows, and plow gear were of the simplest kind of construction. The fact that
cutting colters were frequently listed indicated that the breaking of land was

a vexing ordeal.[53]

Listed in many of the appraisals were scythes, cradles, and wheat fans. The small grains in the pre-McCormick reaper days, were harvested with cradles, implements which required both skill and physical endurance.[54] Harvesting occurred usually in the warm days of late spring and early summer. The methods of harvesting the grain, threshing it, and cleaning it differed little from the manner in which man from early ages had processed bread grains. Grain that was turned into flour in Clark County was processed in one of the water-powered mills.[55]

Frequent notations of hemp and flax breaks and flax spinning wheels and ropewalks reflected the fact that these crops were significant in the manufacture of textiles, cotton bagging, and rope. Over the years the fireside industry of spinning and weaving linen and hempen cloths became an important cottage industry. There existed in Clark County ropewalks which were used to wind hempen fibers into rope both for the rising steamboat trade and as bale rope to bind cotton bales.[56]

Repeatedly, kegs, casks, noggins, and tubs were listed in the estates of distillers. If any one estate inventory might be singled out as a prime example of the home distiller it would be that of Robert Clarke, Jr. His estate was inventoried by a court-appointed appraiser on February 23, 1807.[57] The report was highly revealing of the items which this founding farmer had accumulated. He died possessed of three stills of 120- 110- and 60-gallon capacities. He owned a 50-gallon boiler and a 41-gallon mash tub, three flake stands, and four doubling "cags," and a number of barrels and hogsheads. Distilling in the first half of the nineteenth century was a means by which a considerable volume of grains could be transported to an ever-flourishing market, in season and out.[58]

It is not until the decades of 1840 and 1850 that a dependable profile of Clark County agriculture can be produced statistically. In these decades the United States Census Bureau extended its schedules to collect data on agriculture and manufacturing. The census report of 1850 especially contained sufficient data to determine a long-time pattern of farming. By the opening of that decade there was the astonishing number of 794 farms listed as being in operation. These produced 1,213,007 bushels of Indian corn, which was an average of 26 bushels per acre. The small grains, though not producing so high a bushel rate, were of major importance to the overall Clark County farming economy. There were produced 84,682 bushels of rye and oats, 25,162 bushels of wheat, 650 bushels of flax seed, 18,215 pounds of flax fiber, and 450 tons of hemp.[59] Despite the major emphasis placed on the inspection of tobacco at the river port, this crop in 1850 totaled only 66,335 pounds.

Fascinating quasi-agricultural productions in Clark County before the Civil War were maple sugar and syrup and honey and bees wax. In 1856 there was produced 24,581 pounds of honey and wax. Beegums were listed in many estate holdings. For several decades the making of maple sugar and syrup was impressive. In 1850 the county produced 5,960 pounds of sugar, an indication that there still stood in Clark County a considerable number of hard, or sugar, maple trees.[60] This tree thrives in the Kentucky River Valley.

Apparently the census enumerators found it difficult to distinguish between agricultural activities and manufacturing. The two were so closely interrelated that there was actually little difference. Blacksmiths were at once repairmen and makers of plow and implements. Cottage spinners and weavers were wholly dependent upon field-grown raw materials. So were the operators of the numerous flour mills and gristmills in the county. Strangely, the census reporters listed no distillers or the quantity of whiskey they produced in Clark County. They did report eighty-one distillers in Kentucky who produced 366,896 gallons of whiskey and consumed 30,529 bushels of rye, 65,650 bushels of barley, and 551,350 bushels of corn.[61] From internal evidence and notations in the Clark County Distillery Book, the local distillers contributed generously to the general statistics for Kentucky.[62]

The process of farming in Clark County differed little from that employed all across the expanding nation. One year followed another with slight improvements bringing modest changes. The published statistical reports, the Clark County Court ordered estate inventories, and occasional brief articles in the *Franklin Farmer* and *Western Farmer and Gardener* collectively created a profile of the Clark County farm in general.[64] Fortunately there lies buried in the *Reports* of the United States Commissioner of Patents a ground-level view of things by a local farmer. Dr. Samuel D. Martin seems to have been as ready with his pen as with his stethoscope. In 1854 he informed the commissioner that "Corn is our main crop, and is probably worth more than all the others cultivated here. The average yield is about 60 bushels to the acre. Some fields produce double that amount per acre. The market price is usually about 25 cents a bushel; this year 75 cents."[65] It should be noted that Dr. Martin wrote from a highly fertile section of Clark County. The early winter freeze and extremely wet weather in the harvest season fermented the corn so that it had quickly to be turned into whiskey or fed to livestock, which accounted for the tripling of the price.[66]

Throughout the history of Clark County there have been changing patterns of crops produced. At best, for instance, hemp was far from being a

Though this cluster of four pictures of hemp growing were made in the 1920's on David S. Gay farm, they represent an important chapter in the agricultural history of Clark County. - *Photo courtesy of Ruth Gay Gaitskill and David S. Gay*

Corn was and is an agricultural mainstay in Clark County agricultural economy. So Dr. Samuel D. Martin proclaimed it. - *Photo courtesy of Jerry Schureman*

stable and profitable crop, and in 1854 local farmers were giving up its culti-vation. Dr. Martin wrote, "The yield of hemp is from 500 to 1000 pounds to the acre. This year it is worth $100 a ton. The price is so uncertain and fluctuating that many persons have stopped raising it."[67]

By the mid-nineteenth century many Clark County farmers, especially those once devoted to livestock production, turned to the culture of nonrow grasses and clovers. Dr. Samuel D. Martin declared in no uncertain terms that, "Our best grass in Kentucky is the `Kentucky Bluegrass' (poa pretensis). It forms a fine, thick sod, affords much grazing, and continues green all win-ter, so that stock will keep fat upon it throughout the year." The literature sage of Colbyville advanced an interesting explanation of the origin of this grass. He said, "The seed of this grass was brought from England by a family which accompanied Boone to Boonesborough, in the first settlement of Ken-tucky, and planted it in a garden at that place. It became troublesome and was dug up and thrown over the fence. But it could not be so easily rooted out, and in time spread over the state. It is the `Speargrass of England'."[68] The doctor may have been right, but there is a gaping hole in his historical fact, no family accompanied Daniel Boone to Boonesborough "in the first settle-ment."[69] This account of the origin of bluegrass in Kentucky is counter to the oft-repeated legend that it was introduced at the Indian Old Fields trading post. Maybe both Dr. Martin and the proponents of the Old Indian Fields legend had a grain of truth for each place. English trade goods had arrived in Kentucky packed in grass.[70]

The aesthetics of the early Kentucky farms were not of much refinement. The earlier settlers had dreamed of a western eden, but an unadorned one. Thomas Aflect, an associate editor of the *Western Farmer and Gardener,* visited Clark County in the spring of 1841. He reported in his journal that, "There seems to be a strange and unaccountable dislike, felt by the farmers in the West, to their wives and daughters displaying the slightest taste for gardening or the cultivation of flowers; and in Kentucky it is evident as elsewhere. What a cheap gratification if is! Why deny it them? One hand a few days each spring, would suffice to put the garden in order and keep it so. The garden! what do we generally find it? a poor, miserable, badly fenced, weed-overrun, smothered to death nook! We know some farmers otherwise men of taste and judgement, who would absolutely eradicate their wife or daughter's little bed of flowers, to stick in their parcel of cabbage or onion, for which abundance of room could be found elsewhere; but then ` they can see *no use* in such silly things as flowers; they would rather a precious sight, see a hill of potatoes or corn! Shame, gentlemen, shame!"[71]

The pattern of cultivation in Clark County varied little except for the introduction of improved implements and the increased production per acre of crops. The newly formed Bureau of Agriculture, Horticulture, and Statistics published its first report in 1878. The Clark County correspondent listed corn, wheat, rye, oats, barley, tobacco, hemp, and flax as the principal crops.[72] He might well have been reporting the order of production for 1820 with only slight exceptions. Two new crops were beginning to gain favor. These were white burley tobacco and bluegrass seed. Quickly, white burley was to become a main cash crop for the county after 1870.[73] The Civil War had stimulated an increased demand for tobacco products, and the rise of the cigarette industry further increased demands. The building of railroads across the county after 1870 shifted the location of tobacco warehouses away from their traditional locations on the Kentucky River to Winchester and Lexington, and after 1921 and the introduction of the open floor auction sales tobacco culture and sales underwent a second major revolution.[74]

The Clark County reporter noted that the area's soils were growing thinner, and it was becoming necessary to make generous applications of chemical fertilizers to maintain production. The agricultural land pattern of cultivation reflected only minor changes, with some of the poorer soil areas being turned back to pasturage or scrub timber growth, or what John Fox, Jr. in *Bluegrass and Rhododendron* called "brush country."[75]

In a contemporary summary of agricultural conditions in Clark County in 1878, the reporter to the Kentucky Bureau of Agriculture, Horticulture and Labor Statistics might well have turned to county history to review at least two major facts. Clark County farmers, like all their Kentucky neighbors, lived in a somewhat isolated and provincial world during the first sixty years of the nineteenth century.[76] They nevertheless were not so provincial that they did not sense the impulses of change which were occurring in American agriculture. Despite all the inventions and innovations of the 1830s and 1840s which wrought both a scientific and mechanical revolution on the nation's farms, none was greater than the improvements made on the plow. This was the age of Jethro Wood, John Deere, Cyrus McCormick, and Jeremy Newbold. All of them, plus an assortment of patent infringers, made improvements on the plow, and other implements that revolutionized the breaking of the land and cultivating crops. These improvements had a distinct influence on farming in Clark County.[77]

During the same decades farm journals began publication all across the country. They published numerous essays, publicized new inventions, discussed plant improvements, and agitated for the establishment of agricultural and mechanical institutes. The Kentucky agricultural societies followed their lead. *The Franklin Farmer,* for instance, was an organ of progress which enunciated the views of Kentucky's most progressive farmers.[78] For Clark County the mid-decades of the nineteenth century were both years of change and formative ones. In large measure the steamboat replaced the flatboat, making the Kentucky River a more important artery of commerce for the county than ever. The organization of the joint county-private investor turnpike companies vastly improved the farm-to-market road system, and the inception of the railway era wrought deep and fundamental changes in the transporting and marketing of farm products.

Both the Kentucky and Franklin farmers magazines publicized the tremendous changes which came by midnineteenth century in the field of agriculture.[79] Some of the agrarian leadership in Clark County responded to the changes. Chilton Allen, an ex-congressman and popular politician, was one of the group of central Kentucky farmers who met in Lexington in 1838 to form an agricultural society; Allen was selected president. The society had as its purpose the collecting and dispersing of recent scientific agricultural information to the state's farmers, to secure legislation to benefit farmers and stockraisers, and to agitate for the establishment of an agricultural and me-

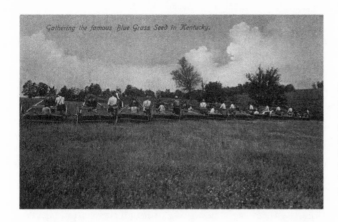

Gathering the famous Blue Grass Seed in Kentucky.

Stripping blue grass seed was once an important agricultural activity in Clark County. Seed from the county was sold on a widespread national market.

chanical institute. The Lexington group was well ahead of a laggard General Assembly in their thinking. Legislators refused to charter the society.[80]

Almost two decades elapsed before a second effort was made to organize a Kentucky Agricultural Society. On January 6, 1857, an assembly of central Kentucky farmers and businessmen gathered in the Franklin County Courthouse to effect an organization of farmers and to seek the passage of vital legislation.[81] Present from Clark County and active in committee assignments, were William R. Duncan, C. A. Preston, J. B. Huston, and Dr. S. D. Martin. In the organizational meeting J. B. Huston submitted a resolution requesting the General Assembly, in its 1857 session, to enact a law to determine the number of dogs in each county, and to report the number of sheep killed by dogs, wolves, and wildcats. Dr. Martin submitted the central resolution requesting that the legislators grant a charter to the society.[82]

The organizational meeting in Frankfort was well attended. A considerable number of people who had not become members of the society attended. A recess was declared so they could register their names. Present was an unusually large representation of Clark County farmers. Among them were I. Cunningham, Jr., Eli Bean, John R. Bush, W. R. Duncan, T. W. and H. C. Lewis, J. H. Moore, Washington Miller, C. A. Preston, James Price, Josiah Parker, Daniel Smith, S. G. Sudduth, Isaac Smith, and interestingly Mary Strode, and J. R. Worrell.[83] This was virtually a roll for the leaders of Clark County's pioneer families and its economic and political leaderships. The newly enrolled member, C. A. Preston, was active in the proceedings. He offered a progressive resolution seeking the establishment by the Kentucky General Assembly of an agricultural and mechanical institute for the education of farmers, to perform research, and to disseminate information.[84] Dr. S.

D. Martin of Colbyville was appointed a member of a special commission of the society, and afterwards he was quite active in the affairs of both the state and local organizations. William R. Duncan was a signer of the eloquent invitation to Kentucky farmers to attend the meeting.[85]

At home the Clark County agricultural leaders organized a local society either in 1856 or 1857, under the name, "Clarke County Stock Society."[86] The prime movers of this society were William R. Duncan, W. David Sutherland, Harrison Thompson, John Goff, Thomas W. Lewis, Daniel Smith, C. A. Preston, James Hodgkin, and John Clinkebeard.[87] At least one fair was held in the county, but no mention was made of farm produce in its program. This farmers's movement was disrupted by the outbreak of the Civil War.

The era of the Civil War, though disruptive of much of Kentucky's economic life, had little basic effect on the history of agriculture in Clark County. It was off the main north-south penetrative roads of Kentucky and had no railroad or manufacturing plant that produced the goods of war. Unquestionably its continued production of major food and feed crops was important; to the South they would have been vital if they could have been secured. No doubt the failure of the Confederate forces to establish a foothold in central Kentucky relieved Clark County from being caught up more actively in the conflict.[88] The county suffered no damage from warring raids across its area. Perhaps the greatest loss the county suffered was the artificial capital one it had in its relatively large number of slaves. This, however, may not have been an actual loss because an overwhelming number of the freedmen remained in the county as tenant farmers and cash wage hands.

If the statistics published in the Ninth United States Census Report in 1870 in a period of reconstructive political turmoil, can be trusted, there was significant continuity in Clark County farming from the antebellum decade to 1870. It was significant, however, that tremendous changes were taking place in all American agriculture. The farms of the expanding Old Northwest became America's bread and meat heartland. Kentucky's position in the national statistical tables was substantially reduced.[89]

Estate appraisals submitted to the county court during the latter half of the nineteenth century reflect the material holdings of selected families. These document the fact that Clark County farmers made only a minimal response to the mechanical and technological advances of the post-Civil War years. There still appeared in the inventories old-style plows, scythes, cradles, hoes, and wooden harrows. There were no hints that such things as mowing machines, reapers and binders, small grain threshing machines, corn shellers, riding cultivators, and disc harrows existed. Surely some farmers owned these modern implements. Along with the listing of the primitive tools were work steers or oxen. If the appraisals appearing in the court order books are representative of all farming in the county, then a "Cincinnatus" of 1820 would have been quite familiar with the implements which his Clark County grandsons were using to turn the soil and harvest the crops in 1880.[90]

The old pioneer, viewing the pattern of land ownership in 1900 would have been startled at the erosion caused by subdivision. The increase in the Clark County population, all of it of original residual parentage, during the nineteenth century bore decisively on the reshaping of the pioneer land pattern. In 1850 there were 12,884 persons living in the county, and one third of this number were slaves. Practically most of the population lived on farms, or a small number of tradesmen were employed outside the crop fields but were engaged in agriculturally related occupations.[91] As indicated, the Clark County population throughout the county's history has been predominantly rural and agrarian. A majority of them lived on 792 farms in 1,364 dwellings. Their farms in 1850 averaged 193 acres.[92]

By 1850 most of the old landholds of 400 and 1,000 acres had almost been erased by a series of subdivisions. This came about largely because of the fairly numerous members of families who shared in the divisions of estates.[93] The Clark County wills constitute an eloquent saga of this social and economic progress of human affairs in the county. With regularity there appeared in the quarterly sessions of the county court petitioners armed with land plats diagraming the subdivision of larger estates. Widows sought verifications of their dower rights in the division of real property. A clear example of the impact of the subdivision of landholds is mirrored in the fact that in 1850 there were 792 farms, and a half century later there were 1,773; and most in the latter period ranged from only three to 260 acres, with a majority of them falling into the 100-acre range. In 1920 there were 1,656 farms, 779 under 100 acres.[94] As the farms were reduced in acreage there came to exist in the population more subsistence farmers who lived on and off the lands products.

The decade 1850 to 1860 must be viewed as one of the golden eras in Clark County. The frontier had been conquered, families had established themselves on solidly settled homesteads. They had built even third-stage homes on affluent scales in the middle of the well-fallowed and productive farms and pastures. Estate inventories revealed much more refined collections of household furnishings, and the way of life in every manner was greatly improved. At that moment in the opening decade of midcentury there were no ominous political or economic crises to cloud the future. Nationally, however, and well outside the borders of provincial Clark County, there were political conflicts which in time would bring on a devastating sectional war and changes to all of America. The Civil War was to bring about both economic and social changes of monumental importance. The Clark County slaves were freed by the war and the amendments to the United States Constitution, but they remained in a remarkably large number on the land as tenants and day laborers. In Clark County in 1870 there were 4,647 freedmen out of a population of 4,762 former slaves.[95] In numerous other ways the era of the Civil War for Clark County was a watershed in history and fortune.

During the remaining half of the nineteenth century the crop routine remained largely intact. Hemp was still a cash crop, but its future was fading because of rising competition from foreign jute and other types of fibers.[96] Almost simultaneously with the declining importance of hemp was the spread in the planting of white burley tobacco.[97] This crop, which had a slightly romantic beginning, was to revolutionize in time the cultivation and marketing of tobacco. Burley was to crowd out the old and traditional variety of tobacco which had been grown in Clark County for almost a century and which had figured so prominently in the downriver commerce.

After the Civil War corn production leveled off, as did that of most of the grains.[98] As indicated, this was an era in when all of Kentucky began to feel the rising competition of farmers in the expanding northwestern grain belt. Fortunately Clark County farmers were able to turn to several alternative crops to stabilize their economy. There was an increase in tobacco and hay, in the gathering of bluegrass seed, and, of course, in the production of livestock.

Thomas G. Stuart, the Clark County reporter to the newly created Bu-

Once the harvest season in Clark County was celebrated by the shocking of the corn. This season was one of intensive labor. Grimes Mill, now a hunt club center, represents the numerous mills which line the creeks of Clark County. Repeatedly committees appointed by the county court went to inspect and approve the construction of mill dams across creeks. - *Photo courtesy of Betty Berryman*

reau of Agriculture, Horticulture and Labor Statistics, wrote in 1889 that the primary timber resource of the county was practically exhausted, and that, "The principal products of our county, of which there is a surplus produced for the market, are hemp, white burley tobacco, wheat, corn, rye, barley, oats, hay, bluegrass seed, fruits, and vegetables. Hemp, tobacco, hay, and bluegrass seed are especially profitable crops."[99] This was in fact largely a summary of a broad segment of Clark County field crop history, a chapter which extended well into the twentieth century.

The twentieth century, with its recurring worldwide upheavals and domestic crises, wrought significant changes in all American agriculture, and that of Clark County was no exception. Hemp ceased to be a crop, despite a brief revival during World War II, and white burley tobacco became the main cash crop.[100] The bluegrass seed harvest gave way to competition; and haying, with the introduction of mowing and bailing equipment, reflected both a profitable successor to row crops and a necessary source of forage for the livestock industry. The introduction of new types of grasses all but crowded the historic bluegrass off the Clark County farm.[101]

By the end of World War I the mechanization of the American farm had a distinct bearing on the farms of Clark County. The pickup truck and the tractor crowded the mule and the work ox off the land and out of the estate inventories.[102] In 1950 there were 1,356 farms which averaged 103 acres, and 84 percent of the land was either being cultivated or in hay and pasturage. A marked change had come to farm homes. Almost 100 percent of them had electricity, half had telephones and tractors.[103] The automobile and improved highways gave farm families a degree of mobility never conceived of in the past.[104] The old term "community" now assumed new dimensions and implications. Significantly, there was a near balance in cash income between crop and livestock production. The county boundaries in 1950 enclosed 259 square miles. There was a population of 18,898, with 78 individuals per square mile. The population was almost equally balanced between urban and rural dwellers, with 9.9 percent of the population classed as nonwhite.[105]

Internally the advances made in the twentieth century brought a reorganization of local institutions. The tractor, truck, and farm implements dealer replaced the traditional blacksmith, buggymaker, and wagonmaker. Both the truck and tractor, along with other mechanical farm implements, greatly reduced the need for farm labor. The use of power mowers and "round" hay bailers, for instance, cut the demand for human labor fully 80 percent.[106] Perhaps a reversion to nonrow crops had the same impact on farm labor. The ratio of the number of persons a single farmer could sustain showed a steady

Once some of the fields of Clark County gave the appearance of an Indian village of tepees. Harvest time of hemp gave an aura of romance to the land. - *Photo courtesy of Herbert and Carolyn Sledd*

increase in Clark County.

The Kentucky burley tobacco farmers during World War I received a considerable boost in the demand for their crop. Then they suffered an almost disastrous decline immediately after the end of the war. The 1920 crop was heavy in volume, but of less than prime quality, a season which brought disaster to large numbers of small farmers.[107] In order to stem the tide of disaster the old Burley Association was revived through the efforts of a number of Kentucky and Cincinnati leaders and the support of several banks. The actions of this crisis period were to have tremendous impact on the future of tobacco culture in Clark County. A far more sophisticated system of warehousing and the open floor auction system were a long leap away from the old days of the Kentucky River warehouses, the inspectors, and flatboat transportation.[108]

The Great Depression would severely affect all American farming, and that of Clark County was no exception. The county, however, suffered less from the depression than did those counties east of it. The Agricultural Adjustment Administration Act, 1933, the Soil Conservation Act, 1936, and the Agricultural Adjustment Act, 1938, all had an affect on farming in Clark County.[109] In fact many of the traditional ways of farm management and life were sharply revised. The Soil Conservation Act was in a way an answer in many respects to the reporter's statement to the Kentucky Bureau of Agriculture and Horticulture in 1878. "The farmers", he wrote, "want more light on the best method of fertilizing and preserving their lands, so as to keep them rich, so as to produce larger crops with less labor."[110] That was in large measure the intent of the federal legislation.

World War I introduced a new age of chemistry. The nitrate plant at Muscle Shoals, Alabama, was converted to the production of high-test chemical fertilizers; and in time, through the work of the University of Kentucky Agricultural Service and the experiment station the early reporter's statement to the Kentucky Bureau was confirmed by the application of the necessary chemical fertilizers to restore and enhance the productivity of the Clark County lands.[111]

Through two centuries of history, the social, cultural, and economic profile of Clark County was shaped by the twentieth century, and in the post-World War II years, Clark County had remained somewhat encapsulated within its boundaries. The impact of the war, with the building of Interstate Highway I-64, and the introduction of modern industrialization threatened the old agrarian system. Nevertheless, in the long draw of history, Clark County could easily be viewed as a microcosm of provincial, self-sufficient, rural America itself. There were years of rising prices and years of depression. Agricultural fortunes also were shaped in the latter years by the acceptance of modern agricultural research and the practical application of new findings. The age of the machine revolutionized the farming process.

The official records of Clark County reflect on most pages the very fibers of an agrarian society in the never-ending process of adapting to the challenges of a system of social and political responses to the land. Patriarchical names disappeared from the annals of the county. Often they left the most positive evidence of their having lived in their land deeds, wills, and order books of the county court, and that final official transaction, the inventories of their estates. One generation followed another, all in some way infected with the starry-eyed dream of the pioneers that their land was indeed the realization of an agrarian-pastoral Eden. One can only speculate at the reactions of William Sudduth, John Strode, William Bush, John Baker, C. A. Preston, and all the others if they could be released for one brief visit to Clark County's rolling hay fields, lush green pastures, and hundred-bushel-an-acre corn fields, fields never touched by the sweaty hands of the barshare plowman.[112] The types of crops grown would be somewhat the same as they had known, only rearranged in a modern order of farming.

Abram Renick, or his heirs, made sure that posterity would not forget this major short horn cattle breeder. The name "Renick" was synonymous with the rise and success of the short horn cattle breeding activity in Clark County. The stone marking his grave in the Winchester Cemetery is as much a historical testimonial as a memorial. - *Photo courtesy of Jerry Schureman*

CHAPTER 7

Lords of the Pasture

Historically the rolling hills of the Clark County pastures produced the proud symbols of excellent herds, flocks, and droves. Nature itself decreed the future course of the land. When Kentucky pioneers drifted downstream on the Ohio River in overcrowded arks or flatboats or struggled up the muddy Wilderness Trail, they brought into the land droves of domestic animals to found a new industry. Livestock animals, like their human counterparts, came west to produce future generations of offspring and to feed a thriving domestic economy in the primeval Eden.[1]

Obviously the Clark County lands skirting the Kentucky River, the Inner Bluegrass and the rising hills on the east proved highly adaptable to grazing and foraging. There were places already in Clark County with modestly spreading, grassy, meadow land. The growth of cane along the numerous streams furnished almost inexhaustible natural forage. The virgin forest annually dropped heavy mast falls of oak, hickory, black walnut, and chestnut. Here cattle, hogs, and sheep were fattened without much expenditure of human energy. Thus it was, on this fertile natural foundation, that the incoming settler farmers were within the next century to script a brilliant chapter in domestic animal husbandry.[2]

No domestic animal which fattened on the generous largess of the land was more contributory to the sustenance of human life and capital income than the cow. It furnished milk and butter, beef, leather, and work power. Like the pioneer mother herself, the milk cow made the long and grueling journey to Kentucky, furnished milk and butter on the trail, and was especially sensitive to Indian presence. Its offspring were butchered to supply fresh

Laced through the early history of Clark County is the name of the Scotsman Isaac Cunningham. He was road referee, volunteer in the War of 1812, a member of the Kentucky House of Representatives. Thomas Aflect, editor of the *Western Farmer and Gardener* wrote, "I have never seen a more beautiful situation than that on which Captain Cunningham's house is built." His short horn cattle were famous.

meat; its fat was rendered into tallow for the molding of candles and had a dozen other uses, including the greasing of aching parts of the body. Beef hides were tanned and turned into shoes and harness. Many estate inventories in later years noted the presence of cowhides among personal possessions. Even horns could be scraped and converted into gunpowder receptacles or sounding tocsins to warn of danger or urge on hunting dogs. Too, horns could be made into buttons to fasten linsey-woolsey shirts and pants.[3]

In more general fashion Clark County cattle could be rounded up from open range and pastures and driven overland to eastern and growing southern markets.[4] In calfhood work steers were selected and broken to yoke to draw everything from plows and ground slides to wagons and carts. These chosen animals were set apart regularly in estate appraisals as having special value. There were the partisans, like Dr. Samuel D. Martin, who declared the ox to be the superb plow animal. They could drag a plow at greater depth and at a more stable gait than horses.[5]

Characteristic of the entries made in an estate inventory were those on November 27, 1801, of the William Hays estate. Hays died possessed of three slaves, four horses, twenty fattening of cattle, among them four work steers. To feed all this livestock he left, already gathered from the field, 180 barrels of corn. The listing of William Hays' livestock and worldly goods might well have represented the majority of Clark County's farmers in this era.[6]

No doubt the twenty fattening hogs listed in the Hays inventory were of the native woods breed, which Dr. Samuel D. Martin characterized as "original backwoods, long-nosed, long-legged shadbacks."[7] Nevertheless, they were pioneers driven onto the Clark County frontier to fend for themselves under forest cover. This animal had strong, contrasting positive and negative traits. It was largely self-sustaining, bred frequently and generously, and could be managed in droves.[8] This "shadback" woods animal proved a vital link in the Clark County food chain. It supplied an abundance of meat both for its master's table and for exportation as cured pork and lard. This rangy hog was hardy enough to be driven long distances to outside markets, often foraging along the way.[9]

Pork, or some kind of pork product, was a standard dietary staple throughout the year on Clark County dining tables. It was consumed as fresh meat in season and as cured pork throughout the year. Lard was a basic shortening, and it served as grease for many lubrication purposes. Cured pork was the only kind of meat which could be transported the long and tedious flatboat journey to the lower South and tolerate the heat of the region after it reached the market.[10]

Marching in lockstep with the pioneering cattle and hogs were the flocks of sheep. They too were of the long-legged, rangy type adaptable to raw frontier environmental conditions. They produced a coarse type of wool, largely suitable for spinning and weaving into coarse linsey-woolsey fabric, for the knitting of stockings, sweaters, and coverlets.[11] The open range of early Clark County was well suited to sheep grazing, except for the fact that forest cover harbored wolves and wildcats, and the settlements were stocked with free-ranging dogs. As described earlier, the Clark County Court on numerous occasions paid bounties for wolf scalps.[12] Later importations into central Kentucky of the more refined and improved English and Spanish breeds of sheep, producing a longer-fibered and silkier fleece, have received more historical attention than the hardy old pioneers with their burr choked wool. But the rangy sheep had first clothed the earlier settlers of the county. They were the progenitors of an important chapter in the history of animal husbandry in Clark County.[13]

Almost as a matter of course, and historically, the horse and later mule were the primary animals throughout most of Clark County's past. The horse came west across the Appalachian Highlands as a dependable beasts of burden. It was a prime target of countless horse-stealing Indian raids, and always it was an essential means of transportation and travel.[14] There came in time the more romantic type of sporting horse. But the horses which figured so prominently in bringing the early long-hunters, land speculators, and settlers to the western country, like their contemporary cattle, hogs, and sheep, were rugged descendants of nondescript ancestry.[15] They were well suited to withstand the ardors of the rugged woodland trails burdened with the freight necessary for establishing a foothold on virgin lands. Once on the scene in Clark County, they drew the plows and the ground slides and the carts of the developing farmsteads. No doubt for all the county's pioneer settlers the horse was their beauty, their strength and prowess, and their speed. Once they raced their steeds up and down the primitive streets of Winchester and stood their stallions in public view until a combination of state law and city ordinance forbade the practice.[17] Universally, inventories of estates listed saddles, masculine and feminine, harness, and other horse-related accouterments. In many respects the bond between man and horse was closer in Clark County than with any other farm animal unless it be the dog. Horses were given names and also special attention to the supply and pricing of horse feed in the setting of annual price scales for the local taverns.[18] Horses were listed in the estates appraisals with descriptions of their colors and blaze markings, and sometimes by their hands' height. There not only were indications of pride of ownership of horses, but a distinct sense of dependence upon them for the making of livelihoods.[19] The sporting horses in Clark County never gained the importance of those in neighboring Fayette and Bourbon counties.[20]

The history of the mule in Clark County is somewhat veiled by the fog of poor description. Even as late as 1850 the United States Census lumped horses, mules, and asses in a single category without giving a hint of the numbers of each breed.[21] The history of the mule in Kentucky is fascinating. Henry Clay was among the first Kentuckians to import Spanish jacks and to begin the breeding of mules at his Ashland Farm.[22] Sometime after 1830 the mule became an animal of both work and trade. Dr. Samuel D. Martin wrote the United States commissioner of agriculture in December 1852 that, "The growing and fattening of mules is now considered the most profitable business of the farmer in Kentucky. So many persons are engaged in it that it has increased the demand for young mules so much that large numbers have been brought from Indiana, Illinois, and Missouri, to be prepared for in this region of Kentucky."[23] Dr. Martin owned mules, and surely he meant to include Clark County in the area his statement described.

The heart of Clark County's success in livestock growing was not in the mule stables, but in its meadows and pastures. For over two centuries the name of Clark County was all but synonymous with cattle and hog breed-

A good pair of mules, a cold dog, and an ice cutter at the Old Spurgeon Pond. This was a source of ice for Winchester.

ing.[24] Through this period there existed an almost equal balance between the income from field crops and that from the sale of livestock and livestock products. An unidentified, but certainly scripturally literate native son, boasted that only an eloquent passage plucked from the Old Testament adequately described his county's potential for cattle raising. He was inspired by the arrival in Kentucky of the Patton brothers, William and James, and their brother-in-law James Gay, driving before them some of the crossbred Patton cattle from the Shenandoah Valley of Virginia. Their coming, said the native son, was blissfully reminiscent of that moment in Gad when Moses spoke to the children of Reuben, saying, "Now the children of Reuben and of Gad had a very multitude of cattle, and when they saw the land of Gilead, that, behold, the place was the place for cattle." These first introducers of cattle of nobler breeding, might well have stood in Boone's Gap in Madison County in 1785 and exclaimed, "we have arrived in Gilead, the place for cattle."

The Pattons and Gay were the first to bring improved cattle to Kentucky. They emigrated west from the Shenandoah Valley and settled first in Jessamine County either in 1783 or 1785; there is some confusion in the record as to the specific date.[26] In 1790 the Pattons' father, Matthew, came with his cattle to settle in Clark County. In his herd he brought several head of the improved breed to write a record of cattle breeding in Kentucky in indelible imprint. No one knows how many times his name and the names of his cattle would be written in American livestock history. He had bought of Gough (Goff) and Miller several head of English cattle, including the famous herd sire Mars and the brag cow Venice (Venus).[27] Between 1790 and 1806 Mars sired an extensive number of progeny in both Kentucky and Ohio. When Matthew Patton died in 1803, Mars was sold to a cattle breeder in Mont-

With the exception of the boat this scene on the Kentucky River at the mouth of Lower Howard's Creek remains much as it appeared to Captain Billy Bush, John Holder, and other land claimants who settled near this place. - *Photo courtesy of Jerry Schureman*

gomery County; later he was sold to a breeder in Ohio, where he died in 1806. Lewis Allen described Mars and the cow Venice (Venus), saying "the shorthorn bull, red in color, with white face, rather heavy horns, yet smooth and round in form, was called Mars. He is recorded as number 1850, in the *American Herd Book*. The cow was called Venus, white in color, with red, small short horns, turning down. She bred two bull cows to Mars, and soon afterward died. Mars got many calves on the native cows in Kentucky, which were said by the old breeders to be both excellent milkers and good fattening animals."[31]

The year Matthew Patton died, (1803), his son James Patton, his son-in-law James Gay, and his grandson Daniel Harrison bought from the importer cattle dealer Miller of Virginia, a two-year-old bull which they named Pluto, a dark roan, milker, shorthorn sire. Like Mars before him, Pluto was a productive herd sire. He was bred mostly to Patton-type cows, and their progeny were "fine" milkers. He too was bought and taken in later years to Ohio, where he died in late 1812.[32]

Matthew Patton's grandson Daniel Harrison described the full-grown Pluto as the "largest bull I have ever seen." He said, "Pluto was bred to cows produced by the Patton bull Mars, which produced stock that has rarely been excelled in all the essential qualities of the cow kind. They were unquestionably the best milkers that have ever been in Kentucky, taken as a stock in the general, and but little inferior to point of form to the most approved stock of the present day, and of greater size."[33] Harrison wrote this estimate of the Patton importations in 1839, thirty-six years after the death of his grandfather.[34]

By 1803 Matthew Patton was no longer in the business of breeding and grazing cattle, or the record is obscure on the subject. Following his death, in 1803, in September of that year, the Clark County Court appointed John Davidson, Robert Cunningham, and J. P. Bean as appraisers of his estate. The inventory they produced was one of the more extensive ones of that period. Patton died possessed of an impressive number of black slaves, eighteen head of sheep, an extensive collection of household furnishings, numerous farming implements, a collection of books, and some money.[35] The appraisers recorded two stills with two worms and an assortment of distilling equipment consisting of a boiler and kegs. Patton had thirty-six hogs, four calves, and a yearling heifer. Surely there must have been other cattle kept from the appraisers' view, or perhaps Matthew Patton had turned over to his sons and son-in-law his herd of cows and other livestock.[36]

In a more personal context, Matthew Patton left behind a highly displeased wife. In February 1804, Ester Patton appeared before the county court to renounce the part of her husband's will which related to her dower interest. The court in turn appointed William Sudduth, Robert Cunningham, and Benjamin Radcliffe to estimate the value of Matthew Patton's estate at a time prior to his making his final will.[37]

The years 1806-1817 was a period of disruption of relations between the United States and Great Britain. The war of 1812 brought a complete cessation to American livestock breeders' cut going to the British Isles to purchase purebred beef and milker cattle.[38] The year 1817 becomes a significant date because of the opening of relations once again with the British cattle breeders. Almost as soon as the Treaty of Ghent was negotiated and finally ratified in both the United States and England, Americans were once again touring the pastures of Yorkshire, Kent, and other English counties in search of breeding stock. No less a person than Henry Clay himself stopped in Britain on his way from Ghent in Holland by way of Paris to London. He made the purchase of two bulls and two cows of the shorthorn breed to be shipped to Ashland.[39]

Politician and member of the Congress, Clay mixed the tying up of diplomatic ends in London with the inspecting of cattle in the Yorkshire countryside. His cattle, along with purchases made by Lewis Sanders of Lexington, were shipped from Liverpool aboard the vessel *Mohawk* bound for Baltimore. Sanders was in England, but it is not clear whether he and Henry Clay met. After a stormy sea passage the cattle arrived in Baltimore on April 30, 1817.[40] Sanders' allotment consisted of four bulls and four heifers of the shorthorn type. He bought also two bulls and two heifers of the longhorn breed. Not all of the Sanders cattle reached Kentucky. Because of Lewis Sanders precarious financial condition he lacked money enough to pay the passage for his cattle, and then to hire a drover to deliver them afoot to Kentucky. So he sold a third of the animals to Dr. William Teagarden, and a second third to James Munday.[41]

Owners took great pride in their imported cattle and gave them names, some of which became better known than most Kentucky legislators. They became the classic names of cattle breeding both in Kentucky and Ohio. There were *St. Martin* and *Comet,* bulls, and *Mrs. Mott Durham* Cow, *Rising Sun,* and *Georgia Ann,* the cows.[42] In time Dr. Samuel D. Martin brought *Den, de la Motte,* an offspring of the 1817 importation.[43] No one, including Henry Clay, Lewis Sanders, and Dr. Martin, could say with any degree of certainty what impact the imported breeding stock would have in the inception of a long and successful history of breeding a much higher type of cattle in Kentucky and Clark County.

Dr. Martin prepared seven tables listing the famous dams of the 1817 importation, and including the names of their owners. This roster reads almost like that of the leading farmers of the Bluegrass.[44] The saga of these cows very much resembles the "begats" of Old Testament fame. Dr. Martin observed, "Thus will be seen that the three imported cows produced thirteen heifers, besides sundry bulls, and that four of those heifers produced fifteen heifer calves, besides bulls; twenty-eight known females. Supposing the eight other heifers had produced three calves each, making twenty-four, three would be in the second generation of imported cows, including `Beauty by Prince Regent' forty breeding cows; and those well cultivated in their breeding faculties during their lives as their liberal proprietors, both in Kentucky and Ohio would be sure to do, we can well imagine that their numbers at the present time, would swell to an extent much beyond what the pages of the herd book represents." Indeed, Dr. Martin's excursion into the numerical progression of cattle in Kentucky and Clark County would all but overwhelm the compilers of the herd books.[45]

The mixed breed Patton-Durham cattle quickly established a fine reputation as milkers. Joseph Huffman of Cummingsville, New York owned a cow of such breeding which was said to produce well without extra feeding or "pushing." The editor of the *Western Farmer and Gardener* wrote that the production of this cow surpassed her rivals. He said the cow had "a promising appearance, and particularly the enormous size of her finely shaped udder, would indicate, giving, for a time, without pushing or any other food than grass, thirteen and a half pounds of butter a week."[46] This was enough butter to supply even the most extravagant family of six every week. In Kentucky Dr. Samuel D. Martin had a brag cow to match Mr. Huffman's prize producer. Dr. Martin's cow, said the editor, "was also of mixed Patton-Durham breeding, and produced, on `very little keep; forty-two quarts of milk a day two months after calving."[47]

The years 1817-1860 were seminal in the establishment of a well-stamped tradition of the breeding of fine livestock for both Clark County and its neighboring Bluegrass areas. Both Kentucky farmers and livestock breeders stirred to a high point of interest the importation of British cattle, horses, hogs, and sheep. This was a highly speculative age in the Bluegrass region during which some of its capital farmers were willing to spend considerable amounts of money to purchase blooded domestic animals. Too, this was an era when there existed a close linkage between the farmers and livestock breeders of southern Ohio and those of central Kentucky. In fact the periodic importations of purebred Hereford, Devon, Durham, and Ayrshire cattle became a near mutual enterprise between the farmers of the two states.[48]

The interests between the Kentucky and Ohio cattle breeders became so intimately intertwined that now it virtually requires the knowledge of a sophisticated pedigree registrar for the owners of imported bulls and cows to delineate the exchanges between owners and to trace the histories of their descendants. Dr. Samuel D. Martin undertook to do this in the preparation of a herd book which detailed the records of bulls, cows, and their descendants unto third and fourth generation. In this connection the names of the famous Clark County cattle almost rival those of the prominent citizens. Among them were *Mars, Venus, Gem, Rose of Sharon, Challenger, Fortunates, Yorkshire, Flattery, Pluto, Geneva, Lad,* and so on as endlessly as the generations themselves. So personified were many of the famous Durhams, shorthorns, and longhorns, that it led to some humorous comment on social conditions in Clark County upon the removal of Kentucky Wesleyan College from Millersburg to Winchester. John E. Garner observed in a whimsical speech that, "It has been remarked by an observing stranger from a neighboring state that the people in Kentucky educate their cattle and turn their boys out on grass. We are proud of our cattle, and when out of our bailiwick if asked where we are from, we reply in a manner as impressive as possible, 'from the county of Clark!' Should the questioner, however, not seem to realize the importance of that place, it is with pardonable pride that we enumerate to him our distinct attractions and advantages. We say to him, Sir, the county of Clark is the birthplace and the present residence of the Arkhoon of Swat, and the Chevalier de Montrose, two of the finest Poland China Pigs that ever made a track in the mud..."[50] John E. Garner failed to mention the real pigs, Dr. Martin's Bertha and Bernice, who became involved in a national breeds and feeding controversy, or W. R. Duncan's aristocratic *Young Tarista*, who was pictured in a popular agricultural journal. Young Tarista was sired by *Tam Hander*, descended from *Black Hawk* and Old Berk of England. Oftentimes cattle names were as impressive as those of local Clark County families.

Following the events of the cardinal year 1817 there were other importations which stocked the Clark County pastures in after years. Especially important were those made by the Ohio Importing Company and those by the Northern Kentucky Importing Company. Late in 1833 Felix Renick and two companions sailed for England to inspect cattle in the various breeding counties. They carried with them a letter of introduction from Henry Clay, who was well known to some of the British cattlemen because of his 1815 visit to their farms and because of his subsequent importations. On their visitations to the cattle breeders in Yorkshire, Devonshire, Kentshire, and some of the other counties, Renick and his companions selected milk-producing shorthorns. These cattle were shipped to the United States in two consignments and were landed in New York in June and July, 1834. From that city they were driven partly overland and then transported by steamboat to Ohio, where they were prepared for public sale.

At a public auction on October 26, 1836, Solomon Van Meter and Isaac Cunningham of Clark County bought a half interest with Felix Renick in two heifers, which after Renick's death were removed to Clark County.[51] Later some of the offsprings of Comet Halley and Rose of Sharon were also brought to the county by Abram Renick. In time other imported cows, or their immediate progeny, found their way south in the closing years of the 1830s and early 1840s.[52]

By 1839 Clark County breeders were making direct importations from the English cattle counties. Dr. Samuel D. Martin, Hubbard Taylor, and J. P. Taylor made importations which arrived in Clark County in October 1839.[53] One of the most fascinating importations, however, was that made by the

Northern Importing Company, an organization formed by farmers of Bourbon, Clark, and Fayette counties in March 1853. The company set a spending limit of $25,000 for its representatives. The buyers sent to England were C. T. Garrard of Bourbon, N. Dudley of Fayette, and Solomon Van Meter of Clark.[54] They departed Kentucky on March 10 for New York, traveling by stagecoach to Cincinnati, and then by railway car by way of Pittsburgh to New York. They sailed from that city to Liverpool. In many respects this was one of the most spectacular importation ventures and certainly was one of the best recorded. Charles T. Garrard kept a detailed diary of the inspecting and buying activities. These were not always pleasant. Tramping through the stone cattle barns of Yorkshire in March and April was often a wet and cold ordeal. The three Kentuckians visited Yorkshire, the Cotswold, and the farming area about London. They were highly discriminating in their selection of cattle, sheep, and the stallion they bought. They inspected numerous cattle herds and sheep flocks, some of which could not be bought. In the end Garrard, Van Meter, and Dudley purchased twenty-five head of cattle, a stallion, and eighteen head of Cotswold, Leicester, and Southdown ewes and bucks. These animals were shipped from Liverpool aboard the vessel *Crown*. The Kentuckians employed a ship carpenter to install in the hold of the vessel special stabling and mangers. They purchased a large volume of assorted feeds and employed experienced herdsmen to care for the animals on the voyage to

Dr. Samuel D. Martin, son of John Martin, was a scion of a leading founder of both Clark County and Winchester. Trained in medicine at Transylvania University he conducted a heavy practice in Winchester. Dr. Martin was truly Clark County's renaissance man. He was physician, cattle importer and breeder, a master hog raiser, a correspondent to the nation Commissioner of Agriculture, the originator of the Kentucky herd pedigree book, and chronicler of the daily weather conditions.

Samson and Cherry, Dr. Samuel D. Martin's prize Woburn pigs whom he defended with vigorous gusto.

Philadelphia.[55]

From Philadelphia the Northern Kentucky Importation Company's animals were transported by rail to Cincinnati by way of Pittsburgh. They were accompanied on the train by the English herdsmen. At Cincinnati they were driven to the Brutus Clay farm in Bourbon County. This perhaps was the most important shipment of English cattle and sheep to be brought directly to the Bluegrass.[56]

On August 18, 1853, a public auction was held on the Brutus Clay Farm near Paris. Four of the bulls were purchased by the Clark County breeders Van Meter, Goff, and Company. Robert S. Taylor and Isaac Van Meter also made purchases. So did Solomon Van Meter, who bought the two-year old cow Gem. W. R. Duncan bought the year-old heifer Flattery. The remainders of the imported herd were bought by Bourbon County and Fayette County breeders. The bulls ranged in prices from $601 to $1,000. The cows and heifers sold for prices ranging from $535 to $3,000, and the sheep brought $52 to $1,010 a head. The importing journey and animal purchases cost the Northern Kentucky Importing Company, including freight, $23,000. The auction sales yielded $55,976.00, a net profit of $32,000.00. Beyond this, however, was the much greater profit derived from the introduction of a significant core of cattle and sheep breeding stock, and from their future progeny. This expedition made an almost incalculable addition to the reputation of Clark County as a rich livestock producing region.

The era of the Civil War saw a disruption of almost every aspect of Kentucky life, but seems to have had minimal effect on the cattle breeding activities of Clark County, and to have caused no serious reduction in the number of animals. In 1860 there were 10,084 head of cattle, and in the more dependable United States Census report, for 1880 there were 17,931 head.[59] As a matter of fact the county was to experience the very pinnacle of its golden years of cattle breeding and production in the 1870s and 1890s. Nevertheless the opening of the Southwest and Great Plains cattle frontiers in time was to have a magnetic effect on the eastern cattle raising industry. Many Kentuckians moved west and opened a new market for blooded breeding stock. Negatively, of course, the west created a rising competition for the American beef market.[60]

In a generous dash of nostalgic hyperbole, Lucien Beckner, son of the famous Winchester editor William M. Beckner, exclaimed in 1952, that, "Where the shorthorn grazed, wealth showered upon the land life gifts from a fairy's wand; from their footsteps civilization sprang as did men from stones which Ducalien cast behind him; where their beeves went to market, new populations arose which could not have been fed without them. They did not make two blades of grass grow where one had grown before; they took the one blade and made two beeves grow, where one scrawny longhorn had all but starved before. They had been the glamour of the Eastern farms; they now became the glamour of the Western ranches; driving out the buffalo and wild Indian to make room for twenty-one new stars in the galaxy of our Union."[61] In this case Colonel Beckner must indeed have been pixilated by the great dream that had brought the Pattons, Gays, Martins, Van Meters, and Renicks to the vales of Clark County.

In 1871 there was organized the Clark County Importing Company. Lewis Hampton and William C. Van Meter went to England as the company's purchasing agents. These men represented a new generation of Clark County cattle breeders and grazers. Visiting the ancient barns and pastures of the pastoral English cattle producing counties, they purchased twenty-three shorthorn bulls and cows which were shipped to Kentucky. In a subsequent auction these animals were sold, bringing, even at 1870s depression prices, $19,685. The following year Abram Renick achieved a reputation by selling a consignment of breeding stock to Scottish Lord Dunmore, reversing the fields of cattle importations. Lord Dunmore, was the grandson of the colonial governor of Virginia for whom a border war was named.[62] From two head of descendants from the famous Rose of Sharon dam Renick realized $10,000. In 1873 he refused an offer of $20,000 for the bull Duke of Geneva, and in a New York Mills sales Renick and Van Meter refused an offer of $16,000 for their second herd sire Duke of Oneida.

Ben R. Groom of Clark County, who was once the agent for Robert Aithcheson Alexander, sold the second Grand Duchess of Airdrie, a suckling calf in 1875, for $17,000.[64] These were indeed the halcyon days when the rolling meadows of Clark County became a cattle breeding focal center in the era of the great American fervor to improve the breeds of all the nation's livestock.

The climatic moment for cattlemen in Clark County was surely the time in 1880 when Winchester was host to cattle breeders from all across the United States and Canada. The occasion was the gathering of the members of the American Shorthorn Association. The town was decked out in Japanese lanterns. There was a parade, people flocked to the railway station to greet incoming visitors; and every shorthorn bull and cow which made any claim to bovine aristocracy was sheared, clipped, and polished. Two thousand breeders were invited, and five hundred accepted. This was the kind of occasion, in the waning American gothic era when states and cities went to extravagant ends to create the "grande illusion." Kentucky towns like Winchester were used to entertaining campaigning politicians, church delegations, and annual circuses, but never so prestigious a multitude as the cattlemen.[65]

Visitations to the Renick, Van Meter, and other farms were preceded by a three-hour long banquet, the likes of which had never been seen along the Kentucky River. The banquet was held in Simpson's Music Hall, and the Schwartze and Roche Lexington Band added a soul-satisfying touch during the banquet. This feast must surely have rivaled even the Lucullan orgies. The banquet tables were laden with at least a dozen different kinds of meat, prepared in as many ways. Shorthorn beef was the central viand. There were varieties of pickles, relishes, ices, fruits, and nuts *ad infinitum.* The wine list was selective and generous. There was no mention of vegetables in the menu, and strangely none of bourbon whiskey. No doubt the latter had been consumed prior to seating at the banquet. All this culinary extravaganza cost the hosts $1,200, less than $3.00 per guest. By comparison, the general cost was about the price of a medium-grade shorthorn heifer calf.[67]

If any of the feasters survived the stupor of the afterfeast hour of 1:00 p.m., they were treated to a second bonanza of largess. The assembled horde was addressed by that old legendary roof-raising orator, the Democratic United States senator from the Mississippi Delta, John Sharp Williams. This golden-tongued orator of the Cotton Belt had the powers of eloquence to waft even a field full of cattlemen and their lowing herds past the Golden Gate without having to show their credentials. Present also were other powerhouses of the stump, J. C. S. Blackburn of Kentucky, J. H. Pickrell, speaker of the House of Representatives of Illinois, and the chief justice of the Kentucky Court of Appeals, B. J. Peters.[68]

Following the banquet and the great showering of oratory, a part of the ritual of every Kentucky gathering, the guests were taken out to the famous cattle farms to view the aristocrats of shorthorndom. The animals had been prepared to exhibit their most dominant virtues. This was the moment of high noon in the history of livestock breeding in Clark County to which future breeders would look back with deep nostalgia. This moment of triumph was highly reminiscent of those years when the Patton stock was being driven west to Kentucky from Virginia. There now stocked the Clark County pastures such distinguished herd sires and dams as Rose of Sharon, Desdemona, Geneva Lad, and Rose of Thorndale.[69]

By no means, however, did the noble shorthorns of the Gay, Renick, Hampton, Duncan, Van Meter, Martin, and Taylor pastures represent the majority of cattle in the county. In 1890 the United States Census reported there were in all 14,091 head of cattle, 530 of which were listed as "purebred," and the remainder were classed as half-bred plus.[70] In 1990 there were 52,000 head of cattle grazing in the Clark County meadows, where great half-ton round bales of hay and long-waisted cattle vans were now the monumental markings of the modern pastoral scene. Two centuries had wrought revolutionary changes in the cattle industry from the days when herds of range frontier woods animals were herded to Baltimore, Philadelphia, and Charleston. The old-line shorthorn nobles had been replaced by Herefords, Charolais, and Friesans.[71]

More dramatic interest, historically, has been concentrated on the importance, breeding, and raising of cattle than any other animal in Clark County livestock history; but cattle represented only one phase. In many respects the breeding of swine in Clark County was just as fundamental to the local economy and to the dietary needs of the people as the breeding of cattle. From the outset the ratio between the number of hogs and the human population was impressive. In 1850 the United States Seventh Census reported there were 30,484 hogs in the county and 12,683 people, or two and a half hogs to each individual.[72] The number of hogs grown on Clark County farms continued at a relatively high number. In 1840 there were 35,713, in 1860, 25,648; in 1880, 20,284, in 1890, 16132; and in 1900, 11,383, and in 1920,

Cattle grazing in a Clark County field. - *Photo courtesy of Jerry Schureman*

12,078.[73] The latter numbers are indicative of the sharply rising competition from the corn-growing states of the Old Northwest, and Great Plains.

Some emphasis was placed in an earlier chapter upon the importance of the hog as a hardy, self-sufficient Clark County pioneer and a consistent supplier of cured meats and lard. It can be assumed that the hog was a basic farm animal in the county for more than a century of its history. The earliest arrivals which trod through Cumberland Gap were descendants of early American Colonial stock. They could lay no claim to distinguished blood lines or brilliant ancestral names of breed. In fact, the Clark County pioneers were so many generations removed from the original old world breeding and British colonial importations that all traits of their earlier breeding and origins had been erased. Over fully two centuries they had made environmental adaptations, even to changing body contours, and had suffered the degenerative results of frequent in-breeding. The early arrivals in Kentucky were long-snouted and tusked, long-legged, heavy in the shoulders and slender in the hams. They were well equipped to crack the hard shells of the Kentucky forest mast, and they farrowed frequently, bearing large numbers of pigs. Their popular designation as "woods hogs" well suited them. These pioneers also enjoyed an added distinction in Kentucky pioneer history. In all the scores of accounts of Indian raid and horse stealing no mention is made of even a single hog theft.[74] No Clark County farm animal was a better traveler than the hog, as evidenced by the thousands of these animals driven back east to market. Finally, it was an unusual Clark County estate inventory which did not list hogs or pork products.

There is ample evidence that improved breeds of hogs were included in the historical livestock importations of 1817, and in the others down through the nineteenth century. W. P. Curd of Fayette County was one of the earliest central Kentuckians to import and breed the "new hog."[75] In time the major swine breeders were Dr. Samuel D. Martin of Colbyville, Richard Allen of Jessamine County, Edward Allen of Fayette County, Lewis Shirley of Jefferson County, James F. Taylor, Robert W. Scott of Franklin County, C. A. Preston of Clark County, and James E. Letton of Bourbon County.[76]

In the second quarter of the nineteenth century an active search was made among the livestock folds in Yorkshire, Berkshire, Ireland, and elsewhere for new types of heavy meat-yielding hogs which might adapt well to the climatic, feeding, and grazing conditions of Kentucky Bluegrass country. As a result of the searches there was formulated a list of promising breeds, among them Berkshires, Irish Graziers, Chinas, Woburns, and Neapolitans, or white Berkshires. In 1839 Dr. Samuel D. Martin reported that he owned several black Berkshires which he had either selected personally in England or had a trusted agent do so for him. He was also the importer and owner of several head of Neapolitans and of numerous Irish Graziers and Woburns.[77] The latter breed provoked some controversy and, maybe, some considerable argumentative heat among partisans of the various breeds. The Colbyville doctor became involved in 1840 in a rather heated argument with Editor Fanning of the *American Agriculturist*. The debate grew acrimonious and the contenders agreed to settle the issues, not with dueling pistols, as was the custom of the age, but with feeding troughs and "banner pigs." Dr. Martin's selections were pigged in September 1839 of an indifferent Woburn sow. They were given the very unmasculine names of Bernice and Bertha, perhaps indicating their barrow status, and were put on a special feeding routine. Editor Fanning selected two black Berkshire boars, and at it the New York editor and Colbyville doctor went. Dr. Martin, a master of record keeping, kept a precise journal on his pigs. After two months of feeding Bertha weighed 149 pounds, and Bernice 138. Fanning quickly conceded defeat, but Dr. Martin kept feeding his "banner pigs" until Bernice weighed 354 pounds and Bertha 345 at eight months of age. Dr. Martin was a determined competitor, whether it be in a contest with a New York agricultural journal editor or with his fellow Kentuckians, in the breeding of hogs, sheep, cattle, and a bit of dabbling with raising mules.[78]

Thomas Aflect, editor of the *Western Farmer and Gardener,* arrived in Winchester on Monday, January 25, 1840. He was met by Dr. Martin, who drove him out to Colbyville for an inspection of the farm and its livestock. He wrote, "And there met Dr. Martin with whom I returned home. That very evening I commenced a careful scrutiny of his noted stock, both hogs and cattle, continued it during my stay. His cattle are so well known, that I need not say more than they deserve the character they have earned for themselves. His importation of 1839 is a superior one in every respect, and their produce will be hard to beat. The Dr.'s knowledge of pedigrees and of their necessity of being pure, has led him to have a close eye to those of this own stock. Examine "Bernice Bernice the Fourth's and he is worthy of his pedigree. Dr. Martin's twin bull `Species'; is very fine, and Bertram are superior handlers. His large stock of heifers, of various grades, speak volumes to our farmers, in favor of breeding even their common cows to *thoroughbred* bulls but of this again. The various attacks made upon the Dr.'s hogs, many of which attacks were violent, uncalled for, and decidedly unjust and ungentlemanly; have given them, of late years a notoriety over almost any others, unless it be my friend Curd's, (to him I will pay a visit presently.) I myself am somewhat inclined to prejudice, and admiring the Black Berkshires even as I do, may scarce have done the Woburns and White Berkshires even-handed justice; and verify I have my reward; for though I cannot retract one word I have said respecting my still favored breed, I have brought myself into the unpleasant predicament of acknowledging I was *prejudiced,* but think I shall avoid it in the future. I was most agreeably disappointed in Dr. Martin's `Woburn' - I found him a very large, well formed hog with good hams, legs, and handling qualities; though excessively coarse of appearance. When full grown at two years he will weigh 600 or 700 lbs. net, and can be made to reach 1,000 at three! - The Dr. has a great number of brood sows, of the Woburn, Woburn-Berkshire capital cross; and of other breeds. I cannot speak of each individual. A large flock of superior sheep, in good order, a good many mules and horses, and a fine farm, not quite in the order it might be; brings me to the *banner pigs,* which the Dr. is feeding against Mr. Fanning, Editor of the *Agriculturist.* The banter arose out of a dispute about the said White Berkshires, and the Dr. ending the discussion by offering to bring the matter to what our friend Stevenson calls the `avoirdupois argument'; by feeding a pair of boars set against a pair of any other breed. Mr. Fanning chose the Black Berkshires, and at it they went."[79] As indicated Dr. Martin won the contest hands down, even though his two fattening boars were named Bernice and Bertha.

A pair of prime good mules of Clark County breeding. During the years 1830-1920 the mule was almost as important on the local farms as cattle and hogs. These animals enjoyed a ready market in the Lower Cotton South.

Editor Fanning published in the *American Agriculturist* a coy response to the contest, saying, "Whenever one advertises every kind of stock, merely to please the fancy of all, you may rest assured he breeds with no judgement, and it is doubtful if you get the animal you order from him. Always buy from a man who has independence enough to have an opinion of his own, and is not afraid to avow it."[80] The doctor in Colbyville had both independence and the courage to express an opinion. This vague compliment from New York was taken in stride, and his "banner pigs" continued to grow fat.

This was an age of fat hogs, fat cooking; there were no meddling dieticians around to wave the grim sickle over the eating of pork and lard. As an example, Courtenay, dam of the "banner pigs," was imported by Dr. Martin from Virginia. B. Savery of Colbyville purchased six pigs of Dr. Martin, five Woburns and a Bedford, in late winter 1830. When slaughtered they yielded 600 pounds of lard, the twelve hams weighed 600 pounds, and there were eight barrels of pickled pork.[81] There prevailed among Kentucky hog breeders great pride in their ability to produce hogs of great weight. For instance, Andrew Wilson of Maysville killed a barrow on January 8, 1860, which weighed 1340 pounds and was armed with fourteen-inch tusks.[82] The history of hog breeding lacked the romantic appeal of cattle and sheep breeding, but this industry nevertheless was as vital to the general economic welfare of Clark County as were the other animals.

In the golden decade, 1850 to 1860, there was great interest in both general agriculture and livestock breeding. The organized drive to initiate a new age, as described in the previous chapter on agriculture, had a definite impact in Clark County, except the emphasis was placed directly upon the improvement of breeds of farm animals.

Directly related to the thriving progress of the livestock industry in Clark County throughout the nineteenth century were the livestock and agricultural exhibitions of fairs. Lewis Sanders set a seminal precedent in the history of Kentucky fairs and exhibitions when he organized a cattle show at his Sandersville Estate near Lexington in 1817. A basic objective of the Sanders exhibition was to show the cattle he had purchased in England. Silver julep cups were awarded as premiums to such brag animals as Captain Smith's bull Buzzaed.[83]

With the ingenious Dr. Samuel D. Martin of Colbyville as a leader of the Clark County Agricultural Society, which was organized in 1838, success was almost certainly assured. This association held local fairs annually for the next four years. During the session in 1840 fifty cattle and fifty hogs were exhibited. In addition breeders exhibited eleven mules, ten of which stood sixteen and a half hands. One of the hogs in the show weighed 960 pounds and had the potential to produce enough lard in which to fry every chicken in the county.[84]

After the bright exhibition of prime animals in 1840 there occurred a hiatus between fairs from 1840 to 1856.[85] In the latter year the Clark County Horse and Mule Improving Association was formed with Judge James H. Bush as president; Colonel John H. Moore, A. C. Barrow, Thomas W. Lewis, vice presidents; William H. Winn, secretary; and the board of directors was composed of Daniel Smith, Robert S. Taylor, James H. Wornall, Tandy

Tippecanoe - a progenitor of the mule breeding industry in Clark County. This industry became important enough after 1830 to cause a mule breeders association to be formed. - *Artwork courtesy of Western Farmer*

Quisenberry, Dr. William B. Duncan, Harrison Thompson, Thomas G. Sudduth, James T. Locknane, Thomas H. Goff, Dr. William H. Cunningham, John Vivian, and John W. Hunt. Though primarily this was a society for the promotion of mule breeding in Clark County, the roster of officers and directors came close to being one of the important Inner Bluegrass families.[86]

The Horse and Mule Society held a three-day event in which a veritable herd of horses and mules were paraded before a board of judges. Breeders came from Fayette, Bourbon and Woodford counties. Locally, Mary Strode won a prize for the best stallion colt shown. Thomas Lewis won first awards for two year-old saddle mares and a year-old stallion, H. G. Bush exhibited the best "blooded" mare, William B. Duncan had the best pair of mules, and John H. Moore owned the best mare of any age.[87]

By the end of the ante-bellum decade in 1860 the traditional breeding and grazing of prime livestock in the three or four major categories was well established. Beyond this the pastoral way of life in the western half of the county had reached a high degree of maturity. Life centered around the animal husbandry of the region. In fact, this became a core element in it history.[88] In all the descriptions of entries in its various fairs and special society exhibitions, however, there appears no record of the exhibition of field and garden produce or any sort of culinary or handicraft art. Surprisingly, no proud hog breeder who boasted of slaughtering animals that yielded fifty-pound hams offered a prime specimen of this favorite viand.[89] Agriculture and the domestic arts had to await a future age when they would become central exhibits in the local fairs.

The fairs in the post-Civil War era became more than simply agriculture and animal oriented. They came to be annual social gatherings, with band concerts, harness and running horse races, nightly dances, and, always, a week of visiting, catching up on the local gossip, and listening to interminable political oratory.[90]

In every objectively measurable criterion the history of livestock breeding and grazing in Clark County demonstrated a remarkable continuity from one era to the next. Opening the great western cattle frontier beyond the Mississippi River drew off some of the glamour which had so vividly colored the earlier era, as importations of choice breeding stock were somewhat subdued by the drama of the long cattle drives with mounted cowboys, the rising cattle towns along the expanding railroads, and the contributions of the contemporary novelists and historians, such as Owen Wister, Zane Grey, Harold Bell Wright, Andy Adams, and Theodore Roosevelt. The opening of the western cattle country added a dimension of space and environment, and an aura

KIRKLEAVINGTON DUCHESS 18th.

Kirkleavington Duchess, a short horn cow advertised in the Ben B. Groom and Son's catalogue of 1875. This sale occurred at the height of short horn history in Clark County.

which a profoundly dedicated, family-centered community like Clark County could not match, but which in no way reduced the importance of its agriculture and animal husbandry or the powers of its rich rolling meadowlands.

The expansion of the corn-hog belt in the post-Civil War Old Northwest and the rise of the packinghouse centers in Cincinnati, St. Louis, and Chicago opened a highly competitive situation for the Clark County hog breeders who had contributed so brilliantly to improving the breeds and productivity of the American swine economy. There was no erasing of the fame of Dr. Samuel D. Martin, William B. Duncan, Robert S. Taylor, William A. Preston, Solomon and Isaac Van Meter, and Abram Renick. They were pioneers whose names were inscribed indelibly in the annals of American animal husbandry. But events occurring well beyond the boundary of the county had cardinal bearing on local history.[91] The Civil War marked a watershed in the annals of the livestock history of the region. In a sense it disrupted the pork trade between Kentucky and the Lower South which was never restored. Emphasis on the breeding of hogs shifted to the Old Northwest. Too, the rise of the agricultural colleges with their experiment stations and extension services assumed cut many of the functions which had been so effectively performed by private breeders. To a considerable extent the formal scientific agricultural services, for which the Kentucky Agricultural Society had earlier campaigned, replaced the county fairs in the fields of both agricultural crop improvements and the breeding of livestock.[92] The Kentucky College of Agriculture and its associated agencies marked a new and more scientific era in the history of Clark County.

Throughout the decades 1840-1990, and despite all of the changes and historical events which occurred in that interval of time, Clark County has maintained a remarkable degree of productivity in at least three categories of livestock. From the time the first pioneer cleared a cornpatch in the future Clark County area sheep raising was an indispensable part of human domesticity itself. Throughout the latter decades of the eighteenth century, all of the nineteenth, and half of the twentieth century sheep breeding and flocking maintained a steady statistical level of production.[93] In 1850 there were 8,015 animals in the local pastures.[94] The number increased to 11,942 in 1870,[95] a decade later there was a phenomenal increase to 25,931. It is quite possible that the defective 1870 count was in grave error. In the latter year there were still being used on the Clark County farms 774 work oxen.[96] This was the last census report which showed a major number of these animals. Mules had replaced them.

Just as purebred cattle had brought fame and fortune to Clark County, so did sheep. During the decades 1930-1960 it led the nation in the production of spring lambs and ranked first in the exhibition of Southdown sheep in various categories. Henry Besuden of Vinewood Farm won thirteen grand championships at the International livestock Exposition in Chicago.[97] He specialized in the breeding and raising of the Southdown sheep; many single animals and pens of four or more were recipients of rich national awards. One of Besuden's Southdown lambs was sold for $1,125.00. For Clark County in more recent years the traditional sheep growing has been threatened by feral dogs, and only recently by the invasion of coyotes.

The age of the mule was largely the last three quarters of the nineteenth century and the first quarter of the twentieth. In 1987 the United States Census reported that there were still seventy-eight mules on twenty-one farms which it sampled, a radical drop from the 1,558 on all farms in 1895.[98] In 1840 there was the impressive number of 32,891 mules.[99] In all of the Kentucky fairs and exhibitions there were mule breeders on hand with their "brag" animals. Two world wars and the introduction of motorized vehicles and farm implements sent the mule into oblivion just as the mule had earlier supplanted the work oxen.

The production of livestock by no means ceased or was slackened in two main categories. On January 1, 1892 and 1893 agricultural statisticians estimated there were more cattle of all classes in Clark County than in any previous year.[100] They said there were 52,000 head at the beginning of each of the years. Hogs, however, showed a drastic reduction from 6,000 a head on December 1891 to 3,000 in 1892.[101]

From the beginning of the first settlement in the county there persisted a high ratio of the average number of cows per farm. In 1850 the ratio was fourteen cows per farm, and in 1950 there was a twenty cow average per farm. The number of farms during the century had changed from 792 to 1338. Because of the more than two centuries of cattle production, and, especially, that of the early importers and breeders, the Clark County Court might well have ordered the casting of a golden calf to be erected before the front portal of the courthouse.

None of the modern statistics dim in any way the dramatic history of men and their families settling in the fertile meadow lands of Clark County and developing a pastoral history as exciting and romantic as any the famous cattle counties of England produced. Spotted about the Inner Bluegrass plateau are the Georgian homes of the early cattle barons, within themselves are monuments to a way of domestic life peculiar to Bluegrass Kentucky. Those stylized homes, so reminiscent of attachment to upper valley Virginia origins, in fact symbolized family roots in the virgin country beyond the mountains. These were the homes of the Taylors, Goffs, Sphars, Sudduths, Van Meters, Martins, Cunninghams, Renicks, and their neighbors. Equally important, they stand today as aged monuments to a day when the importation of blooded livestock from English pastures brought the Clark County meadows to a full realization of their potential. These family estates located atop their tree clustered knolls, and almost near a bubbling spring, became veritable microcosms of the way of life which had enticed so many eighteenth century emigrants to undergo the ordeals of planting a close-knit society in a new land. Perhaps the old homesteads document in a highly tangible fashion the fact that the migrating Virginians brought with them that invisible piece of baggage, a shrewd eye for fertile land. Today their landmarks stand out as boldly in central Kentucky as did those ancient ones in the plain of Gad and Gilead.

The master livestock breeders of nineteenth century Clark County gave greater heed to the validity of the pedigrees of their cattle, hogs, and sheep then they did to those of their families. None of the old livestock patriarchs took more seriously his role in livestock than did Abram Renick. Even in death he perpetuated his fame in stone. The obelisk limestone shaft which towers over his grave in the Winchester Cemetery has deeply carved into it a cameo likeness of his bearded face. Above it are the heads of a bull and a cow.

2d LORD COMPTON WILDEYE.

Short horn bull of the type which Clark County breeders established their herds. This bull was included in the Ben B. Groom and Son sale in 1875.

A crown tops off the figures, indicative of the fact that one of the "royal dukes" of the Clark County meadowland lies beneath, but documenting the fact that he and his neighbors gave the local heath a greater era of glory in the field of animal husbandry, a glory which in time was to be noted wherever purebred domestic animals trod.

The arrival in Kentucky of the Black Angus, white faced Hereford, Charolais, Brahmas, Sana Gertrudis, and Friesans marked the opening of a new era in the history of Clark County as a center of prime cattle breeding. No doubt Dr. Samuel D. Martin, Abram Renick, Robert Taylor, and Solomon Van Meter would be startled today to see herds of black Angus, many of them with white faces, grazing where once royal Kentucky shorthorns had reigned.

The great majority of farmers in Clark County never aspired to the fame enjoyed by their Inner Bluegrass neighbors who became widely known importers and breeders. Nevertheless, the yeoman farmers contributed significantly to the economic fortunes of the area. Decade by decade their herds of grade cattle contributed materially to maintaining the statistical level of cattle production in their county.

The Winchester stalwarts with their great pitcher Fred Toney, fourth from the right in the back row. - *Photo courtesy of George S. Brooks' Scrap Book, The Winchester Public Library*

CHAPTER 8

Winchester, County Town

The history of Clark County and Winchester, the county town, are inseparably intertwined. Since the chartering of the town in 1793 the centrifugal center of the county has been its official seat clustered, earlier, around an ever free-flowing spring, and the rising courthouse square. Throughout more than two centuries Winchester has remained the only town of appreciable size in Clark County. It has expanded over the decades as a center of population, of commerce, legal, public, and social activities. From modest beginnings the trading area surrounding Winchester has widened, thrusting its tentacles of commerce and service into a broader area. Located some distance from the Kentucky River shipping points, the town historically from its beginnings was dependent solely upon primitive road connections. Fortunately the county, over several decades, busied its officials with the opening of a network of rural roads leading out in all directions from Winchester.[1]

Like every rural American courthouse-market town, the dividing lines between rural Clark County and the rising town of Winchester were at best highly blurred. Often surveyors were commissioned to establish new outward municipal boundaries to accommodate a growing population and the addition of new properties. Located centrally in the new county and on land proffered by the enterprising John Baker, Winchester was literally to spring from the loins of the ever-generous spring. Aside from this vital fountain there were no other natural landmarks such as a sheltering mountain, a navigable stream, nor rich mineral deposits, but the town was located in the center of a highly fertile Inner Bluegrass countryside.

Winchester was born and swaddled in the cradle of Kentucky agrarian-

ism. Commercially the town was dependent upon the countryside's rich farming and livestock productivity for its future growth as a trading community.
It, however, had competition from its older neighbors, Lexington and Paris.[2]
Nevertheless, the large geographically insulated village of Winchester, located
in a thoroughly insular situation away from the historic Kentucky pioneer
trails and roads, responded vigorously to the demand for the opening of connecting highways leading to the other trade centers, and with the emerging
communities in outlying Clark County.[3]

    In the authorization for the creation of a county seat for Clark County,
the Kentucky General Assembly followed its established policy of mandating
a local governing board of town trustees. The legislation named Richard
Hickman, David Bulloch, Josiah Bullock, William Bush, Josiah Hart, John
Elliot, Benjamin Combs, and John Strode trustees.[4] The charter required the
governing body to administer the platting of the sixty-six acres of Baker land
into town lots, giving special attention to the location of the courthouse square
and the site of the big spring. In 1793 ten and a half acres were added by a
transfer from Josiah Hart, expanding the town site to seventy-six and a half
acres.[5] The form of government prescribed by the General Assembly for Winchester was the simplest type for early Kentucky village or town administration. There was not in Winchester for almost a century, a central town hall or
permanent official center. The trustees met in stores, in private homes, and in
the circuit clerk's office in the courthouse. They were empowered with the
authority to lay out streets, to protect the big spring from pollution, to operate a central town market, to make rules for fire protection, and to adopt
ordinances regulating the use of streets and alleys. From the beginning the
trustees had to deal with certain matters of public decorum, such as standing
stud horses openly on the streets, controlling wayward slaves, silencing bark-
ing dogs, and curbing rowdy horsemen who tore through the streets at breakneck speed.[6]

    When one examines the trustees' minute books and statistical tables it is
obvious that Winchester made slow progress up until 1870 in its advancing
beyond the status of being a rural Kentucky village. The population of the
town in 1830 was 5,16; in 1840, 1,647; in 1860, 1,144; and in 1870, 1,400.[7]
In terms of population growth the village remained rather static over the
decades. Sometime between 1820 and 1830 much of the old frontier dynamics was lost.[8] When the first wave of householders moved into the town and
the earlier stores and shops were established there was a process of leveling
off. Few, if any, of the early inhabitants of Winchester had background experiences in living in a close and cohesive community. They were inexperi-

enced in managing such things as protecting a public water supply; fire danger; building of streets and sidewalks; setting tax rates; maintaining a public market; and controlling weights, measures, and public scales. The early buildings in Winchester were highly vulnerable to fires. Wood structures and poorly constructed chimneys were open threats to safety.[9] In a series of ordinances over the decades the town trustees sought to enact protective measures to control and combat fires. They ordained the possession of fire buckets and ladders by householders, bought such equipment for the town, and undertook to see that fire ordinances were enforced.[10]

As mentioned elsewhere in this text, the public spring flowing in the heart of the village was a constant matter of concern. Amazingly this vital source of the town's water supply was threatened with pollution by slovenly users.[11] Perhaps no one in Winchester during the earlier years had any knowledge of bacteria or of chemical contamination. The current sense of pollution related to watering horses in the spring, the presence of manure, the emptying of laundry water, the throwing of trash in and about the spring, and muddying the waters was unknown.

Amazingly, as late as 1808 the Winchester spring was still being imperiled by willful pollution. John Ward, John Bruner, James Spillman, and George Webb were commissioned by the town trustees to erect a post and rail fence around a quarter of an acre of land about the spring.[12] In that year the authoritarian finger of angry trustees was waggled under the noses of the collective and slovenly citizens who continued to wash their clothes in or near the spring, hitch their horses within the thirty-foot off-limits, and otherwise defile the public water supply. Three years earlier, March 1805, trustees James Simpson, James Spillman, James Clark, and Peter Flannigan met at Captain John Martin's house and dealt with the issues of protecting the town's spring. They forbade individuals to take liquor, horses, cakes, or other pollutants inside the railed off area. Violators were to be fined three dollars for each offense.[13]

As a matter of fact, the populace of Winchester was subjected to the ordeals of muddy streets during the winter months and stiflingly dusty ones during the summers. For decades the trustees wrestled with the problems of opening new streets and surfacing older ones. They enacted ordinances regulating the building of sidewalks and bridges over drainage ditches. John Bruner was appointed to keep streets clear of rubbish, to bury the carcasses of dead animals, and to remove all other obstructions.[14] He was also directed to oversee the walkways, and the block landings for carriages and horses and to make other repairs. To finance the street work all white males above twenty-one

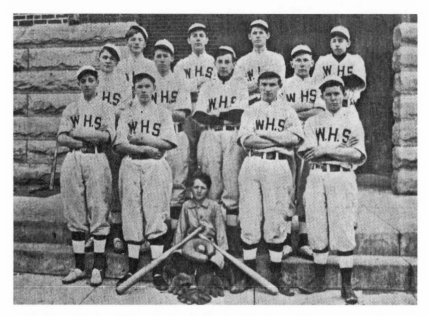

The Winchester High School basebal team circa 1908, and in an age when baseball was every boy's sport. - *Photo courtesy of Winchester Sun*

years of age were required to contribute three days' labor on the streets, alleys, and walkways. This "tithing" practice was the same one required of rural Clark County white males to work on the country roads.[15]

The Winchester Board of Trustees managed the affairs of the town on the slenderest budget imaginable. In January 1819 there was reported in the trustees' minute book a revealing profile of the white male population in a listing and assessment of their property holdings in six or seven categories. There appeared the names of 105 individuals who were subject to the payment of the poll tax; there were 131 slaves and 117 horses listed. Six individuals held licenses to conduct mercantile businesses, there were five tavern-keepers and fourteen taxable residents owned carriages with four wheels. Taxes collected from these sources amounted to $14,767, a fact which explains why so many entries made in the trustees' minute book were for less than one dollar.[16]

The secretary of the Winchester board of trustees in 1826 listed persons liable for town taxes. There were 129 householders and 158 white males over sixteen years of age. The clerk of the town listed all the town lots and the numbers of slaves and wheeled carriages. In that year the Winchester town slaves were valued at the impressive figure of $581,520, even at the fractionally low assessment rate. Heading the tax list was Chilton Allen, who possessed lots worth $3,000. Seventeen merchants were said to own assessable merchandise. W. J. Garner, E. Ferguson, James Daniel, Thomas P. Dudley, William Irvin, Robert Kennedy, Micah Taul, Richard Vallandingham, and Robert Tolliver were among the holders of larger numbers of slaves in Winchester, although none of them exceeded $3,500 in assessed value.[17]

The impress of the Kentucky frontier bore heavily upon Winchester for the first half century of its history. Many of the houses of the town were more or less of primitive log construction. Chimneys of the town ranged from crude mud and grass batten to wood and stone or brick construction. Fireplaces were a necessity, but at the same time they were a fire menace, especially during the winter months. Firefighting was done strictly by volunteer householders using limited and primitive types of equipment. On July 20, 1819, the trustees enacted and published an ordinance requiring every householder to provide fire buckets in proportion to the number of chimneys in his residence. Everyone was required to have at least one bucket. The number required of families, however, was based upon the number of chimneys in a house; up to six buckets for those having twelve chimneys. Strangely, the trustees, in enacting the bucket ordinance, failed to specify either the type of fire bucket or its capacity, or whether the householder should keep buckets filled with water at all times.[18]

The fire bucket plan was never fully completed. Too, there were, as always, some individuals who failed to obey the ordinance. A town sergeant was directed to make inspection visitations to each house in Winchester to determine whether the fire bucket ordinance was being observed and to see if the buckets were placed conveniently for emergency use. Along with the placement of fire buckets there was the matter of making available long and short ladders, some of which were bought by the trustees.[19]

Meetings of the trustees seemed to have been more or less informal; some of them seemed to have been little more than a discussion around a store stove or in the county clerk's office. Meetings were called when problems arose. During the first half century of Winchester's history the trustees dealt with the weighty matters of keeping the streets cleared of all sorts of carelessly placed obstructions, with licensing itinerate peddlers, forcing stud horse owners to breed their animals out of public sight, fining spring polluters, and dealing with other nuisances. None of these, however, struck a tender public nerve than the attempt by the Winchester trustees to curb the dog menace. The town clerk recorded a note in the trustees' minute book that the dog population, which appeared to be equal to if not greater than that of the human race, was, "A nuisance in said town to such an extent, as to make it dangerous through the negligence of its citizens, and for the love many of them have for the canine race that the numbers are insufferable.[20] To curb the menace the trustees voted a tax on every dog in excess of one per owner. The town fathers ordained further that there "Be levied and laid on every dog or bitch, large or small," a tax. They added further that no slave could own a dog unless expressly permitted to do so by his or her master. In an attempt to bring order to their town the trustees trod on tender toes. Kentuckians of the era laid great store by their dogs. They might even have been more tolerant of a tax on every child in a family in excess of one.[21]

No doubt the dog tax was both a major and highly emotional issue in politics. In the election of town trustees on June 1, 1830, only John Ward was returned to office. The new board of trustees meeting in George Frye, Jr.s' store on June 12 reconsidered the dog tax. Francis B. Moss and George Frederick favored retention of the dog ordinance, but A. Bowen and Elisha Dickerson opposed it.[22] This left the decision up to the board's president, John Ward. He voted for repeal.[23]

Dogs were left to wander freely about the Winchester haven without let or hindrance. No one seems to have known how many there were or to whom, if anybody, most of them belonged. Five years later the trustees were impelled once again to consider the unpalatable issue of levying a dog tax. This time there was a new board consisting of Jim Turner, Samuel Berry, William Hampton, and Henry G. Poston. All of them except William Hampton favored the levy of a tax on the towns' runaway dog population. William Hernden was instructed to make a count of the dog population. He reported, in what was obviously a casual counting, that there were sixty-two animals subject to taxation.[24]

The decade of the 1830s was an era of the coming of the modern age for Winchester. The limits of the town set by the original sixty-six acres of land had become too constrictive. Now many residences had been constructed outside the borders of the old town that enjoyed many of the advantages of the corporation without paying taxes. The Kentucky General Assembly in 1831 authorized extension of the Winchester town boundaries so as to include a square mile, or 640 acres. East and west base lines were surveyed parallel to Main Street, as were north and south lines of the quadrangle.[25] By that date, 1831, the population of Winchester had sprawled out beyond the town's ancient boundaries in an amoebalike pattern from the courthouse square westward along the Winchester-Lexington Turnpike. Trustees assured the legislators that the householders, then outside town limits, were quite willing to be annexed into the new boundaries. The trustees and legislators, however, issued a caveat that forbade the opening of new streets and alleys in the added area. This privilege was reserved to the occupying property-holders.[26] On this point the law was specific: "That said trustees, or their successors shall have no power of authority, to open or lay off streets or alleys, in or through so much of said town, as is included in this act, and that did not heretofore belong to it; but the proprietors of the real property within said boundary, shall have the right to use and enjoy said property, in any manner they please." The new town limits were surveyed by Thomas Hart on November 2-10, 1831. The legislation extending the Winchester town area left town planning in the hands of individual property-holders. Streets and alleys were now laid off along the courses of wandering farm roads.[27]

Expansion of the town boundaries thrust Winchester into a new era of urban expansion and maturity, with all the problems this implied. This was an era when the town made the most remarkable transition from being a semifrontier village to becoming an established farmer-courthouse town having to adopt more precise rules of governing the more intensively settled community. It became necessary to appoint both a night and day watch to ensure security. It was now necessary to have someone alert around the clock in case of an emergency, such as a street disturbance or a fire. This was made even more necessary by the expansion of the commercial area.[28]

As the town grew the danger of both fires and lawbreaking increased. Repeatedly, the trustees adopted ordinances requiring householders to have fire buckets placed strategically. Sometime in the past either the town or county officials had authorized the creation of a public cistern on the courthouse square. By 1831, however, this receptacle had fallen into a state of disrepair. A. L. Ferguson and James B. Duncan were appointed commissioners to repair this facility with the implication that it would once again supplement the town's water supply.[29]

Of almost as great concern to the trustees as fire prevention was the operation of the public market. This institution seems to have had its origin in 1794 or 1795. Although there are no inventory reports, the market appears to have been operated largely for the sale of fresh meats, meal, flour, dry grains, and some types of vegetables. Unhappily, the official records are vague about the trade of the market and its purpose as a public institution.[30] The position of market master was one of importance, even if the pay was minimal. The master was saddled with a multiplicity of responsibilities, including the testing of scales and weights, the policing of the market to make sure rules were followed and the place was kept clean and that it was opened on time.

At day-break on market days the master proclaimed the market open for trade at the break of day by sounding a bell.[31] There were always the skinflints who attempted to avoid paying market fees by slaughtering their animals on the grounds. These were to be driven away, as were those who brought tainted meat to market for sale. The master had to be on watch for speculators who came to buy produce to be sold on other county markets. Finally he was the custodian of the town's fire ladders and buckets. The master was required to perform all these services for twenty-five dollars a year.[32]

The office of market master no doubt was a sideline for individuals holding the title. As early as 1817 the town trustees instructed James Spillman, market master, to perform the duties of collecting a twenty-five cents tax for every $100 worth of real property in the town, and in addition he was to collect a dollar poll tax on every white male over sixteen years of age.[33]

The challenge of lifting the central part of the town of Winchester out of the mud and dust by hard-surfacing the streets and boarding or paving walkways was an ever-present one. Every new house raised in the village, every new street or alley opened, demanded serious official attention. Following the year 1815 there was put under way a plan to improve the main streets, and to have constructed ten-foot-wide walkways in the heart of the business area. Owners of fronting property were held responsible for this street and walkways work.[34]

Streets and sidewalks, however, were not the only issues to confront the town trustees. Christmas seasons in Winchester must have been a time of wild expressions of jubilance. Too, snowfalls stimulated excessive expressions of joy. Throwing snowballs got out of hand at times, and the trustees sought to curb this sport by lashing out at free white persons, twenty-one years of age or older, who felt impelled to throw snowballs. Offenders, when caught, were fined $5.00 for each offense. If a slave, however, was found guilty of the act he laid his master liable to pay the fine, or to feel the town sergeant's thirty-nine lashes on his bare back.[35]

At Christmas time the citizens were harassed by overly exuberant celebrators "hollowing" in the streets, banging on barrels and boxes, blocking passageways, and strewing buckets in the streets. To check the practice the trustees ordained that persons who in that manner, "Or in any other manner make any unusual noise in the town limits to the disturbance of the citizens thereof," were to be subjected to fines of ten to fifteen dollars, the highest recorded to date in the trustees' journal. An additional dollar a day was to be paid, slaves were to receive the traditional thirty-nine lashes on their bare backs.[36]

To enforce the noise ordinance, Peter Frye, William Jones, and Thomas C. Barr were appointed to be night and day watchmen. On December 21, 1833, the trustees amplified their action against the peace disturbers by stipulating that "hollorers," if they attempted to avoid arrest by running into a house, and if the householder refused to name or deliver them, then he or she became liable for a fine.[37]

While the Winchester trustees were angrily lambasting the rowdy noisemakers, they considered another, but well-removed, issue. They paid William Flannigan $1.75 to survey a Winchester public burying ground, and to prepare a deed for its purchase. William Herndon was employed to construct eighty-one panels of fence around the cemetery tract at a dollar a panel.[38]

There seems to have been an obsession of fear that slaves in Winchester would get out of hand. Repeatedly slave violators of town ordinances were subjected to harsh penalties; penalties which seem to have been far too severe and brutal for the crimes committed. One might well read into the sentences an uneasiness on the part of the white citizens of Winchester about their slaves. The slaves were prohibited from going into one of the four or five town taverns to buy a drink of liquor without incriminating themselves. If he or she did so they incurred a penalty of a severe lashing by the town marshall. No slave, in fact, could be caught with a jug of liquor, own a dog, or go into the public market to buy something without his or her master's written permission.[39]

If a white person was caught drinking liquor or playing cards with a slave, "Or doing any other illegal act," he was to be fined at least two dollars and no more than three. On February 25, 1843, the Kentucky General Assembly enacted a rather extensive piece of legislation which reinforced the Winchester trustees' ordinance against slaves patronizing the local tippling places.[40]

In another piece of legislation the General Assembly in February 1843 all but rechartered the town of Winchester. Under the prevailing Kentucky corporate laws it granted the town's trustees rather broad powers. Trustees were to be elected annually, elections to be held on June 1 succeeding years in the Clark County courthouse. Entitled to vote was every free white male over the age of twenty-one years, who had resided in the town for at least six months and who had paid both *ad valorem* and poll taxes. Under the law the Winchester trustees were entrusted with the power to adopt ordinances or by-laws and to adjudicate cases where the possible fines would be less than twenty dollars. Cases involving a greater amount were still to be tried before county justices of the peace. All arrest warrants were to be served by the sheriff. In a broader area the trustees were made responsible. "For the governing of the said town as will tend to the safety and well-being of the same, and for the preservation of the peace, and good order and morality therein and also for preventing, and removing nuisances, and prohibiting the retailing of spirituous liquors contrary to law, or the giving, selling, or otherwise disposing of spirituous liquors of any sort or description, either directly or indirectly, to any slave, or slaves; except as authorized by law."[41]

There was an obsession in both Frankfort and Winchester concerning the sale of whiskey to slaves. Repeatedly this issue was discussed by the General Assembly and by the town trustees. The law of 1840 went further by prohibiting slaves from loitering in the town or otherwise creating disturbances. In midsentence the law turned from laying lashes on the bare backs of liquor-drinking slaves to admonishing the trustees to keep the streets, alleys, sidewalks, and passways clear of obstructions, to grade and maintain the streets, and to perform all the other acts necessary to the promotion of good government.[42]

As indicated in another chapter, Winchester was most reluctantly hospitable to the roving proprietors "Of any theatrical performance, show or exhibition of any kind." No doubt they had reason to be. Many a showman of the early years was as much a sharpie as were the river boat gamblers. The trustees levied a tax or license fee, and if a showman tried to avoid the tax the town fathers stood ready to levy a fine. Court day crowds were prime pickings for the pitchnen who traveled across Kentucky.[43]

Winchester went through many of its metamorphic stages in the decades 1830-1860. This fact was especially discernible in an incident which appeared to mark an awareness that it needed an institution stronger than the Winchester Academy to smooth its rough intellectual and cultural edges. In a fairly explicit law the Kentucky General Assembly granted a charter to the Winchester Lyceum in February 1841. The organizers of this institution were authorized to accept gifts, including estates, to sustain the Lyceum in "perpetual being," and to order its activities. The purpose of the institution was to promote interest in the sciences, in literature, and in the general dissemination of knowledge. Charter members of the lyceum were Charles Eginton, John B. Houston, Edwin Poston, James J. Winams, and Henry Jones. Membership in the lyceum was to be by selection and election.[44]

The Winchester town trustees, however, had their minds focused on more immediate and mundane problems. No matter how many fire buckets, long and short ladders, and cisterns were in place, the menace of building fires was ever-present. There possibly was never written a report on the effectiveness of

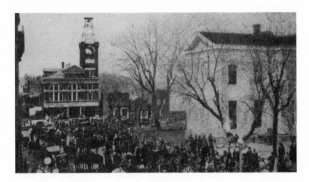

Winchester and the courthouse square were to become the centralizing spots on Clark County. Court day in the 1920's took place near John Baker's big spring. This was "mule day."

the use of fire buckets in the hands of a milling band of excited citizens. By 1838 the trustees had come to realize that inadequate firefighting equipment and undisciplined volunteer firemen were no longer adequate to protect the growing town. In February that year the Kentucky General Assembly authorized the Winchester trustees to take a citizens vote on the levying of an *ad valorem* and poll tax to finance the purchase of a fire engine. To make the proposition more palatable to voters it was provided the cost could be spread over several years. Obviously at that point the new engine was to be operated by inexperienced volunteer firemen.[45]

A decade later, February 22, 1848, the Kentucky General Assembly again considered Winchester's need for more adequate fire protection. It chartered the Rough and Ready Fire Company of Winchester to operate in the town. Petitioning members were Charles Eginton, Henry W. Holhass, Charles A. Algier, James Allen, Henry Louba, William S. Downey, A. M. Preston, and John Waldridge. This was a fairly regimented body which operated under strict rules of conduct in the whole process of firefighting. The law made clear it was the "Indisputable duty of each officer and member of said company, when alarms of fire are given, to meet promptly, with their engine, buckets, and other apparatus, the same; and shall, in all cases, render obedience to the officers of said company."[46] The engine referred to in the act was the one which had been bought by the town in 1838. The trustees turned use of it over to the Rough and Ready Company along with all the other firefighting equipment owned by them with the understanding that they could reclaim it at any time in the future.[47]

In the stirring American decades after 1840, Winchester underwent significant changes of both institutions and expansion. The population of Clark County had grown to 12,683, a gain of 2,000 souls since 1840, and of this number 4,840 were slaves. Winchester's population had grown from 516 in 1830 to 1,040 in 1850.[48] In March 1851 a rather colorful, if not nagging, chapter in the history of both the county and the town drew to a close. The General Assembly granted the town trustees legal authorization to dispose of the public spring lot at auction. This did indeed close the saga of use and abuse. James Flannigan bid in the spring lot on the behalf of Mrs. L. Flannigan, but through some unbelievable oversight the trustees failed to transmit a deed to the property. On June 25, 1860, James Flannigan appeared before the board of trustees and requested that a deed be made in his name, a request which was granted.[49]

The hammer of change rang frequently in this era. A second ancient institution passed into oblivion. Both Clark County and the town of Winchester were granted legislative approval to sell the stray pen to the best advantage for county and town. Both governments were relieved of the responsibility of maintaining this outmoded institution, even though the streets of Winchester a that moment were not entirely clear of animals wandering at large. Stray animals were to be held at some designated place and brought forward on court days to be sold at auction.[50]

In the same 1851 session of the General Assembly the Winchester roster of officers was modified slightly. Election of trustees, town attorney, town sergeant (or marshall) and market master was to be an annual event. The tax assessor was denied the privilege of collecting taxes for a year after he left office. Once more the legislators took up the question of loitering in the streets of Winchester. The new law granted the town trustees the right to "prohibit slaves from living within said town, or from owning a horse or mule. If they violated the law they were subjected to a back lashing, and their masters had to pay fines. If by chance a slave owned a horse or a mule, the animal was to be sold and the funds turned over to the town.[51]

In another way the trustees of Winchester were involved with slaves. In 1851 they hired from the estate of William Herndon the slaves Gilbert and Billy; they paid $75.33 for Gilbert's labors and $25.33 for Billy's. Slaves were frequently subjects of concern with the Winchester trustees. On the eve of the outbreak of the Civil War in 1860, they ordered a curfew forbidding slaves to be on the streets after 9:00 p.m. Offenders were jailed or subjected to the standard bareback lashing of thirty-nine licks.[52]

In 1866 two events occurred which may have not shaken the foundations of Winchester all the way to Strode's Station, but they were historical changes nevertheless. The trustees on April 2, 1856, ordained that the famous old town marketplace be closed for good. On that day the final master, Robert Oliver, reported that he had collected only ten dollars that year in stall rent, a sum which paid less than half of Oliver's $25.00 salary. The town marshall was instructed to try and rent the stalls and to pay over to the town treasurer any rental funds he might collect.[53] The town perhaps needed the money because earlier that year the trustees had spent $3.00 to buy a desk from Christopher H. Parrish for use of the town clerk-attorney. They then bought a lock for the drawer to insure the safety of the Winchester town papers and minute book.[54]

Joel Storm, town marshall, presented the trustees a fascinating list of persons he had arrested and kept in jail. For instance, he was paid $1.13 for taking John Whitehead into custody. John Hart got caught in the sergeant's net and languished in jail, running up a board bill of $9.40. John Huxley was incarcerated for twenty-four days at a cost of $9.30. Other citizens of parts on Joel Storm's invoice were Thomas Harding, George Henry, Richard Crouch, and Thomas Strong. John Whitehead, John Huxley, and John Hart seemed to be the star boarders.[55]

In the hot and humid days of August 1854, Winchester, according to the official record, seemed to be aglow with effluvia. Earlier, July 28, the trustees ordered the town sergeant to notify property holders that they must clean the street in front of their holdings and quick lime their cellars, privies, and back-yards in, "A thoroughly sanitary manner." In their session four years later, 1858, the trustees sought to erase the last trace of the town's frontier background. In a by-law which almost smacked of anger, they decreed that officials no longer would tolerate hogs running at large in the streets and alleys. The town's marshall was instructed to capture and impound the animals. He was to advertise the fact he was holding the hogs by placing a three-day notice in the courthouse and in two other public places. If no claimants came forward he was to sell the animals, keeping five percent of the money for his troubles and turning over the rest of the money to the town bearer, who was instructed to search out the hogs' owners and pay them. He was paid ten cents a head for bearing the bad news.[56] After 1860 one reads the minutes of the Winchester town trustees and is almost oblivious to the fact that the Civil War was occurring. There, however, appear two intriguing notes indicating deep changes were occurring in the area of racial relations. On December 7, 1864, a "woman of color," Judy Whitaker, petitioned the trustees for permission to have an oyster supper at Brucy's Old Tavern. She sought the trustees to recognize the fact that the "Colored people in town and vicinity," be allowed to attend the supper unhindered, a permission which was granted.[57]

Three weeks after granting Judy Whitaker's request the Winchester trustees reflected anxiety that Winchester would be overrun by Negroes escaping the yoke of slavery. For the first time in the official town records there appeared the term "Negro" instead of "slave."[58] In a vain effort to stave off the threat of congregating "freedmen" the Winchester trustees adopted an ordinance in a futile effort to stem the tide of history. The ordinance threatened to fine the owners of offending "freedmen-slaves" if they did not get their people out of the town within ten days after its publication. This tide, however, ran too high and swift to be controlled. Within the year both Clark County and Winchester were set on new courses of racial relations, and with the change went the sergeant's lashings of thirty and thirty-nine licks on bared backs.

It is remarkable, in fact, miraculous that the Civil War had so little visible impact on Winchester and Clark County, aside from the freeing of slaves. No skirmishes or battles were fought in the vicinity, no property was burned or otherwise injured, no homes were raided by soldiers of the Union or Confederate armies, and no guerrillas beset the area. The importance of the war to the region lay in the aftereffects. There occurred during the immediate postwar years a veritable cultural, social, and economic revolution, and in no place did this become more evident than in the town of Winchester. Major portions of the town ordinances were nullified by political and social changes. Consigned to the historic past were the sentences of bareback lashings of slaves, of curfews on the movements of persons of color, and of other petty restrictions. Ex-slaves, now termed, "Negroes," were free to move about, to engage in businesses and trades, and to seek an eduction. The latter prospect, however, hinged upon whether the colored people were able to generate enough taxes to finance schools. Remarkably, there were few disruptive racial incidents. On December 4, 1869, the Lexington *Observer and Reporter* published a story that "Mrs. Col. Wickliffe Cooper, while walking upon a Winchester street several days ago, and just in front of three villainous Negro soldiers, was fired at with a pistol by one of the scoundrels who was drunk, the ball just passing her head. As soon as the shot was fired the Negroes ran off."[59] No doubt the prevailing sentiment in Clark County in 1866 was heavily pro-Confederate. In essence, however, one would never detect this fact from the documents created by the central power structure.

On March 18, 1870, the Kentucky General Assembly essentially revised and broadened the Winchester town charter. In that extensive bit of legislation the thought was expresses, "To further Amend the Statutes in Relation to the Town of Winchester." This act was little short of being a blueprint of progress for the future decades of the nineteenth century. The taxing powers of the trustees were broadened in order to finance the rising demands for urban services. The trustees were empowered to ordain both an *ad valorem* and a poll tax. The new law contained the inclusive phrases relating to taxes, "on each free male inhabitant." The ancient racial limitation "white" was removed. Once again for the third or fourth time the General Assembly mandated that all theatrical performers, circuses, concert artists, and every other kind of public exhibition would be required to pay a license fee. Local property owners and merchants were also caught in the new revenue net. Penalties for no payment of fees and taxes were drastically increased.[60]

Ushering in a modern phase of Clark County-Winchester history, the revised statutes were specific in requiring town lots. Failure to conform would result in the seizure and sale of property after an order had been obtained from the Clark County Circuit Court. The Winchester trustees were instructed by law to keep streets and alleys of the town free of obstruction. They were required to construct cisterns and dig wells to ensure sufficient water to combat fires. All combustible materials, including gunpowder and dynamite, were to be moved outside the town limits. For the first time since 1793 the law of 1870 made the town of Winchester the owner of its streets and alleys. Along with the combustibles, there went the public stocks and whipping post. In their place there was established a public workhouse, where persons who were unable to pay fines were forced to work them out at a minimal daily wage.[61]

The General Assembly went further in drafting the 1870 law by prescribing the protection of the public decorum for Winchester. The law frowned on almost every act a rowdy country bumpkin could commit in town. Stern penalties were placed on those who fought in the streets and alleys or disturbed public worship, or were charged for drunkenness, loud swearing, racing horses and mules up and down the streets, driving carriages in a reckless fashion, firing off guns, shooting firecrackers, blowing horns, screaming and yelling at night, or exposing themselves.[62] The law was stringent in its inveighing against indiscretions, but after all one could become intoxicated and stumble up and down the Winchester streets for the price of a five-dollar fine or commit any of the other forbidden acts at the same price. The trustees were empowered to deal sternly with all miscreants who violated ordinances or offended the Commonwealth of Kentucky by their acts.[63]

Surely there must have been reckless horsemen in Clark County and Winchester. For about the fifth time they were admonished by law not to race their horses and mules along the streets or break in horses and mules there. Once again the law recognized the fact that cattle and hogs ranged the streets, laying their owners open to the possibility of having their animals sold to pay fines.[64]

Strangely, the law of 1870 contained a section authorizing the Winches-

Clark County High School's state champion basketball team. This team defeated the Cuba high school team to win the state championship in 1951. - *Photo courtesy of Winchester Sun*

ter town trustees to, once again, open and oversee the operation of a public market. The town records, however, do not make clear whether the law was observed by the building of a new market or by reactivating the old one. A market master was to be appointed, and he was to rent stalls to patrons for the purposes of selling, "Meats and other articles."[65]

By 1870 the old ways of life in Winchester were rapidly slipping away. The modernization of almost every aspect of life in the United States was being reflected in some fashion in the town in those seminal decades 1870-1900. No phase of life and change in this era was greater than that in the field of transportation. The history of building railroads across Clark County is one of confusing complexities. As early as 1852 promoters were granted a charter to build a railroad from Lexington to the mouth of the Big Sandy River by way of Winchester, Mount Sterling, and Owingsville. Though none of the commissioners mentioned in the charter were from Clark County, its citizens were asked to subscribe $200,000 to finance building the railroad. Two years later, March 1, 1854, the officials of Clark, Bath, Montgomery, and Carter counties were asked to purchase bonds to pay for construction and to levy special taxes to pay for the interest.[66]

As was true all across the ante bellum South, legislators, railroad promoters, and local public officials had more enthusiasm than cash in the matter of building railroads. Thus the ambitious project to connect Elizabethtown with the mouth of the Big Sandy River involved too much faith and money for it to be built. By the opening decade, 1880-1890, Clark County and Winchester were to be caught up in the rash of railway building. By 1880 the old Elizabethtown, Lexington, and Big Sandy road was constructed to become ultimately a part of the Chesapeake and Ohio railway system. Trains in this decade were to make Winchester a thriving railway hub: the building of the Chesapeake and Ohio Railroad by Collis P. Huntington, and the opening of the Appalachian coal fields.[67] Nevertheless, the passing trains were in some measure life-threatening. One danger was the jumping on and off of the moving trains by local daredevils. Too, the crossings of the railroads on Main Street constituted a hazard. The Winchester town council ordered the railroads to construct gates across the street and to hire "A competent and reliable gatekeeper" to man the gates. This must be done by February 1, 1889, or the railway companies would be fined ten dollars a day until the gates were erected and being tended by a gatekeeper.[68]

Hardly had the council crossed the last "T" on insuring safety at the railway crossings before it became involved in a frustrating proposition to have streetcar tracks laid along some of the main streets. At their October 10, 1889, meeting councilmen reviewed a proposal from T. G. Stuart of Boston, Massachusetts, to build tracks and operate street cars. The council approved the yankee proposal. Minutes detailing their action, however, do not indicate whether the cars were to be horse-drawn or electrically propelled. By no means did the town council treat the Stuart proposal casually. The city attorney drafted a lengthy and detailed agreement which covered every possible aspect of streetcar operation which the lawyer could conceive. He absolved the town of liability for personal injuries and property damage; he even prescribed the type of rails to be used and set the fare at five cents a ride. In addition, Stuart promised to operate the cars on a set schedule.[69]

The dream of operating street cars in Winchester within a short time turned into disappointment. Stuart and Associates were back before the town council asking that they be given until March 1, 1890, to put the cars in operation. This time the council demanded that Stuart and Associates put up $500 in good faith money; in the end, however, the Boston contractors quit the project and forfeited their deposit. Two local men, J. D. Simpson and C. Lisle, representing, "A company of gentlemen of Winchester," appeared before the council seeking the street car franchise. Their petition was approved June 19, 1894, on the same basis as the Stuart contract. The "company of gentlemen" was given the $500 Stuart forfeited. Directors of the new company were T. G. Stuart, J. D. Simpson, H. P. Thomas, John E. Garner, C. E. Stuart, and W. M. Beckner.[70]

At the moment adjustments were being made in the streetcar contracts a second Boston company appeared in Winchester seeking a franchise to build and operate a public waterworks. It promised to lay four and a half miles of pipeline and to construct a pumping and tank system. William Wheeler and Charles T. Parks, operating under the company name Wheeler and Parks, were granted a franchise on the condition that the company would furnish 2,000,000 gallons of water a day to the town and would deposit $10,000 as a good faith bond. The company would have water flowing in the pipes at the earliest possible date. This meant the Wheeler and Parks company would create a waterworks of sufficient capacity to serve a town of 10,000 population and would insure the availability of sufficient water to quench fires.[71] A year later the town council entered into a second contract to install fireplugs and to extend the originally planned pipeline.

There was a distinct atmosphere of "booming" in all the progress being made along the streets and alleys. The councilmen, however, were not too involved in modern progress to ignore the morals and public behavior of the town. They enacted an ordinance threatening fines for saloonkeepers who served females either inside their saloons or in siderooms. For such an indiscretion they would be under duress to pay fifty dollars for each offense. The councilmen also poured scorn upon the heads of able-bodied persons who loitered along the streets with no visible means of support and owned no property nor worked at a steady job. Such wretches were sunk lower in their misery by being fined up to a hundred dollars. The public workhouse was always ready to welcome penniless loiterers.

The Kentucky General Assembly enacted a law, framed by William M. Beckner, which initiated distinct changes in the way fourth-class Kentucky towns were governed. This was the act which truly changed the status of Winchester from "town" to "city" as provided in the law of 1882. After April 1883 Winchester was to be governed by a mayor and council. Town meetings were to be held on the first Friday of each month and in established council chambers. A temporary mayor was to be appointed by the council to serve until an election could be held. There was a realignment of town officials. A chief of police was to be appointed along with a city attorney, a police judge, a city engineer, and a treasurer. The mayor was to receive a salary of $250; councilmen, $3.00 for each meeting attended. Surely the treasurer much have served largely *pro bono publico* because his annual pay was $25.00.[73]

Once settled into the routine of their respective offices, the mayor and council on March 8, 1894 opened a veritable Pandora's box of legal wrangling when they asked the city attorney to open correspondence with other

Kentucky towns relating to a case then pending before the Kentucky Court of Appeals. This case involved the dispute over the power of towns to tax banks. At that time there were the Clark County National Bank, established in 1864, the Citizens National Bank, established in 1872, and the Winchester National Bank, established in 1885. Kentucky banks were generally plaintiffs in the case, and those in Winchester were no exception. The issue strained relations between the city government and the banks. In March 1894 the city attorney was asked to prepare a rearrangement of the Winchester by-laws so as to permit the assessment of special licensing fees. This he did, and his revisions were adopted unanimously.[79]

If the decision to tax the banks stirred controversy, there was no audible protest when the council voted to tax peddlers and all other types of "hawker" salesmen and itinerate merchants. The council was wide-ranging in its definitions of the term "peddlar." It included, "Anyone selling any goods, wares, or merchandise, or any clocks, watches, jewelry, gold or silver plated wares, spectacles, drugs, medicines, nostrums, or any wagon, carriage, or buggies or any wheeled vehicles, or any saddles, saddlery, harness, gear, or bridles, or any mechanical agricultural tools, as implements, or other things within the limits of the said town.[75] About the only thing not mentioned in this ordinance were pocketknives and pistols.

After all the verbiage pertaining to peddling of goods and wares, the fine for violating the ordinance was only five dollars, a sum less then the license fees in some cases. No doubt the antipeddler ordinance was adopted largely to protect court day crowds and merchants. A part of the excitement of court days was the appearance of the hawkers of goods. Court day crowds were open sesame to the sharpies who preyed upon unsophisticated countrymen with their dazzling arrays of "cheap john" wares and medical fakeries.[76]

Like every other Kentucky courthouse town, Winchester was included in the circuits of some kind of circus or tent show. There were moments when elephants trumpeted, lions roared, and monkeys chattered in cages. There were always the scantily clad ladies who draped themselves with boa constrictors, rode horses bareback, and performed trapeze acts. Then there were the seductive dolls of the sideshow "for men only." There were the accompanying pitchmen selling everything from sparkling diamonds mined fresh from the inexhaustible King Solomon lodes to bottles of the elixir of life dipped fresh from the fountain of youth. The Winchester fathers taxed the shows fifty dollars a day for the privilege of fleecing the local citizenry.[77] On the local scene there were more stable sources of revenue, the billiard halls and tenpin alleys; they yielded ten dollars weekly. Those centers of leisure and liquid stimulation which violated the Sunday blue law were forced to contribute twenty-five dollar fines and have their licenses to operate canceled. All merchants, druggists, and saloonkeepers were required to purchase permits to operate six days a week, but never on Sundays. Livery stable operators, transfer wagoners, coal dealers, and express company agents were required to obtain licenses which cost from five to fifty dollars.[78]

Throughout the latter quarter of the nineteenth century the town of Winchester and its population experienced impressive territorial and commercial expansion. Its main streets were lined with a generous mixture of stores, banks, and professional offices. The residential part of the town was constantly being thrust outward, necessitating an extension of streets and public services. In 1881 the town trustees requested J. C. Tuttle to make a map showing the town limits, including the urban islets known as Haggardsville, Kohlhasville, and Bowmanville. The trustees ordered this action not so much for revenue purposes, but more likely to extend the town's police jurisdiction.[79] One of the town's problems was putting a quietus on the indiscriminate shooting of fireworks on the Fourth of July. The trustees enacted an ordinance which forbade sending up balloons, firing Roman candles, shooting firecrackers, and "sounding" anvils. The firecracker ordinance may have been adopted somewhat in keeping with the southern taboo on the shooting of fireworks on the Fourth of July because that was the date General Ulysses S. Grant's army captured Vicksburg. Southerners touched off their fireworks at Christmas time.[80]

In many respects the summer of 1881 was a troubled one for Americans, locally and nationally. It was exceptionally hot, and politics bubbled over in partisan rivalry. On July 2 Charles J. Guiteau, a mentally unbalanced and disappointed political appointee, shot and mortally wounded President James Garfield as the President was preparing to board a train in the Washington railway station. For eleven dreary weeks the President lingered on the verge of death until September 19. During the traumatic weeks both the national and local newspaper press reported the details of Garfield's suffering, both from his wounds and from bungling medical care. On news of his death, the Winchester Town Trustees adopted a resolution of respect and sympathy which was dispatched to the Garfield family. They asked that all Winchester businesses close their doors from 1:00 to 5:00 p.m. on September 23, that local church bells be tolled from 2:00 to 3:00 p.m., the time of the funeral, that homes be draped in mourning, and that clergymen of the various churches hold special memorial services. Finally, the trustees resolved that they would wear mourning badges for thirty days. They also ordered that the minutes relating to the presidential tragedy be inscribed on a separate page in the trustees' minute book.[81]

Still draped in their presidential mourning badges, the Winchester trustees on October 19, 1881, turned to another but more mundane death issue. There was the urgent matter of removing the carcasses of dead hogs and dogs from the streets. They paid Ab Taylor fifty cents a head for removing the animals.[82] More life-threatening, however, was the revelation that Jeff Thomson had in store a large quantity of black powder on his lot near the railway depot, and that elsewhere there was a considerable amount of dynamite stored in Warren and Company's store, awaiting an explosive accident. In direct terms the trustees ordered the explosives removed to some place beyond the town limits *FORTHWITH*. If the owners failed to act, then the town marshall was to remove the explosives, again *FORTHWITH*.[83]

Thus it was in sessions held at various places in Winchester that the trustees, month after month, gathered to deal with the housekeeping chores of their town. Fortunately for them the population of the town was relatively small, and they "pinched" by on a severely limited tax base and a minimal amount of tax money. They were not burdened in 1881 with any great service costs or the regulation and management of projects. Life progressed in Winchester at the leisurely pace of a rural agrarian community. There were, however, signs of changes in the condition of local society. There remained, however, the nagging problems created by communal living. This was still an era when dead dogs and hogs lying in the streets demanded official attention, and the live ones wandering about at will created even more concern.

Constantly streets were being extended and the town boundaries were being thrust outward. Reluctant property owners had to be officially nudged to build and maintain sidewalks across the fronts of their lots. Town cisterns were a nagging everyday concern and always in need of repair. Sanitary needs expanded more rapidly than did the population. No longer would old-fashioned privies ensure the safety of health in the town. Every month there were problems, serious and foolish, needed the attention of the trustees. The railway age dragged into Winchester a somewhat amusing but aggravating custom of men and boys proving their macho by jumping on and off moving trains, and endangering life and limb. The trustees adopted a stern ordinance making this sporting venture a crime subject to the levying of a heavy fine.

There was some symbolic meaning to men and boys sporting with the trains. In a way they were making adjustment to the new age which was dawning in industrial and commercial America, an age which was rapidly creeping into Clark County and its county seat, Winchester.

Providence church (Old Stone Church). - *Photo courtesy of Jerry Schureman*

CHAPTER 9

The Seeds of Religious Faith

A motivating force behind the creation of Clark County in 1792 was the pressure exerted by the rising inrush of settlers. New settlers arrived in the area faster than social and political institutions could be established and matured to serve their needs. Too, there was a distinctly growing element of wildness, if not in fact a streak of animalistic behavior among the population which beckoned mightily to missionaries.[1] Back of the spread of religion onto the Kentucky frontier there had been an earlier period of emotional revivalism which had been stirred by several forces.[2] Many of the early settlers who came to the new Clark County brought overland in their cultural baggage the seeds of a devout but simplistically literal religious faith. In some cases emigrating parties were led by ministers.[3]

No single religious group which reached Clark County had a greater impact on the region than the "Separatist," or (later) "Regular", Baptists. The history of this sect shades off into a blurred and thinly documented past. There are traces in their beliefs of the theological and philosophical traditions of the New England Theocrats.[4]

Whatever the origins of their religious beliefs and tenets, no religious faith was more portable than that of the post-revolutionary War, Virginia and Carolina Baptists. Paradoxically, the truly faithful among them comprised a relatively small but adhesive core which held congregations together with considerable success.[5] Yet there prevailed a rigid sense of rule and order in the congregations. Every congregation set its own rules of faith and decorum, adopted its rules of governance, elected its deacons, chose its minister, and administered its own discipline.[6]

The Baptist cultural baggage did not contain a dedication to the importance of education. Separatist Baptist ministers were drawn from laymen ranks,
served without pay in money or kind, and looked down upon theologically
trained ministers as a distracting force of the true faith.[7] The timing for the
transfer of the separatists from Virginia to Clark County was propitious. Separatist Baptist congregations back in some of the Virginia counties had been
subjected to harsh prosecution and imprisonment at the hands of the Established Church.[8]

On June 4, 1768, Lewis Craig, John Waller, James Childs, and William
Marsh were brought to trial in Fredericksburg, Virginia, on charges of having
preached without having been licensed to do so. An assembled crowd attended the trial, unified in its support of the ministers. On that occasion the
spirit of the "great Revival" which had stirred the backcountry of Virginia
and the Carolinas was vigorously aroused. When the five ministers refused to
submit to the British Crown's rule and were marched off to jail, the cause and
the will of the Baptists were greatly strengthened.[9]

There is an open question and an intriguing interlude in the relationships of the various traveling Baptist groups which were organized in Virginia
in the closing months of the American Revolutionary War. This was a moment of high excitement, when strong personalities came to the fore in connection with the great migrations to the opening Kentucky country. One
such individual whose name appeared prominently on both sides of the mountains was Captain William Bush. Bush, perhaps, has never received his just
historical dues as a trail-breaking pioneer, land speculator, and leader of a
socio-religious colony. He was with Daniel Boone in the opening of the trail
northward to Boonesborough, was a member of the rescue party in the famous Boone-Calloway girls' capture, and was at Fortress Boonesborough
during the Blackfish-Dequindre siege.[10]

By clear documentary evidence William Bush had mixed motives in the
organization of a special religious colony in 1780-84. He was a perceptive
land scout and laid claim to a small empire north of the Kentucky River and
along Howard's Creek. It matters little whether the Bush emigrant colony
was a party of traveling church groups, as it was devoted to the same objectives. What is historically clear, William Bush planted a hierarchy of kith and
kin in early Clark County where the name "Bush" was as well known as the
name of the county.[11]

The Bush colony began its laborious journey west in the early fall of
1780 but was held up at the Wolfe Hills (Abingdon, Virginia) during the
"starving winter of that year, and by the ominous threats of surprise Indian

attacks along the Wilderness Trail, 1775-1795. Once underway in 1784 the "Bush Colony" traveled across the Holston, Clinch, and Powell valleys to Cumberland Gap, and then over the Wilderness Trail to the Rockcastle River[12], where they followed the Skagg's Trace to Gilbert Creek in present-day Garrard County. They then moved to "Cragg's Station," where they experienced "a badness of the weather." Finally on November 27, 1784, the colony reached the lands north of the Kentucky River from Boonesborough which had been located by Captain Bush.[13]

On lower Howard's Creek, "Through a turn of God's providence, a church was established, later to be called Providence." Here, the congregational clerk wrote, "For the health and prosperity of Sion we have constituted a church meeting at brother William Bushes." The membership role of the new "Sion" in a major part contained some of the more prominent early settlers of Clark County. It included the names of the numerous Bush family, the Vivians, Johnsons, Dozers, Bledsoes, Bakers, and Duncans.[14]

Though the coming of the Bush emigrants to Lower Howard's Creek was a landmark event in the religious history of early Clark County, it had far more significance in a social, political, and economic sense. The impact of establishing the rather compact, but stable settlement on Howard's Creek created a safe anchorage for future settlements. Too, the time spent on the laborious and storm threatened journey and along a stretch of wilderness trails constantly under the surveillance of resistant Cherokee Indians was a seasoning experience of the first order. The added experience at "Cragg's Station" with the "badness of the weather and scattered situation," prepared the colonists for the ordeal of making settlement north of the Kentucky River and on virgin lands. By the time the Bush emigrants planted their religion at the Howard's Creek Meeting House their faith and spiritual tenacity had been thoroughly tested.[15]

The religious beliefs and faith of the Separatist Baptists were anchored firmly in the Scriptures, especially the Old Testament. To be admitted to full membership the supplicant had to give evidence of having been spiritually born again, to submit to baptism by immersion, and to attend regularly the monthly Saturday church meetings.[16] So thoroughly were the Virginia Separatist Baptists angered by the persecution of the Established Church and by the perfidy of the Crown government that they made sharp departures in their rules. They chose their ministers from their own laymen ranks, "constituted" their own rules, and operated as free and independent congregations.[17] It may have been possible that some of the Separatist Baptist ministers were totally illiterate and unable to read the Scriptures.[18] Yet there came to exist

among the Clark County congregations some leading elders such as Robert
Elkin, Andrew Tribble, John Vivien, and James Quisenberry.[19]

Though strict fundamentalists and literalists so far as their spiritual beliefs and interpretations of the Scriptures were concerned, and patriarchal in
the governance of the flock, there was also a streak of liberalism. The Separatist Baptists, like the congregation at Providence, seems to have tolerated a
certain amount of consumption of alcohol; they accepted women somewhat
freely into membership, but not into governance, and in time admitted some
slaves to membership with the approval of their masters.[20] There was an expression of tolerance toward the yet spiritually unwashed, and "unreborn."
The Baptists adhered to a dedicated work ethic, as evidenced by the rapidity
with which they laid out claims and opened the land to cultivation. It may
even be said that in the respect accorded the elders there was a leadership
generated which reached well beyond the church grounds. It would be difficult to envision a historian of Clark County being unaware of the presence
and influence of the numerous Bush tribe or the Quisenberries, Martins,
Johnsons, Viviens, and Frenches, all drawn from the Lower Howard's Creek
and subsequently the Providence church rolls.[21]

The proceedings of the Providence Church recorded by a semi-literate
clerk were for the most part as drab and colorless as an elder's coat and hat.
Occasionally there flared up some excitement. On August 13, 1790, and in a
spread of the settlements, some doctrinal contention, and, no doubt some
personal egos, arose some dissension at Howard's Creek, and the congregation was split into Providence and Unity. No religious split ever occurred
without friction, and this one was no exception. Some members were threatened with excommunication but were saved by the appointment of referees
to make peace.[22]

It was only a matter of time until the serpent of physical sensuality slith-
ered into the garden of Providence and led Sister Martha Bush down the
primrose path. She was forced to stand before the deacons on June 13, 1792,
and be charged for, "Her suffering a young men to lie the chief part of a night
with her on a bed, & has contradicted herself in her own relation of the
matter." Martha was cast into the outer darkness of excommunication.[23] A
month later the deacons adopted a resolution, "Ordered that no male shall go
out of the meeting house in time of business without leave of the modera-
tor."[24] Administration of the sacrament of communion was a fundamental
tenet of the Separatist Baptists. A member at Providence asked, "Whether it
is becoming in a church after the communion to take the remainder of the
wine and eat or drink it before the congregation?" The answer was a resound-

ing, "No."[25]

The Providence congregation admitted the black slave woman Cisly to membership in June 1793.[26] Two years later it appointed William Bush, Robert Elkin, William O'Rear, and David Ramsey to purchase a new church book. At the same time Edward Kindred was driven out of the congregation for having bought a lottery ticket.[27]

In essence, the Primitive Baptists who broke their way onto the raw Clark County frontier appeared to have had a mission to tame the rowdy, take the land, and spread the gospel of their narrowly conceived theocratic doctrine. The years the Baptists arrived were years in which the great flood of emigrants came to the Kentucky frontier from the post-Revolutionary war disruptions in Virginia, Maryland, and the Carolinas.[28] The very disruptive force of the incoming emigrants created social problems. Thus the disciplining of brothers and sisters of the Baptist faith became more taxing. For instance, John Lisle drank too much "likker." Elizabeth French became involved in an incident of vague gossip which landed her before the deacons for questioning. In a spirit of anger she and her husband William withdrew from the congregation, but within a month Elizabeth was back, having repented from whatever indiscretion she had committed.[29] Dollie Conkwright committed the absolute and unpardonable sin. She strayed away from the fold to be embraced in the welcoming arms of Methodism.[30] The deacons literally cast Dollie out into the outer darkness of apostasy.

Thus the sands of religious life filtered down slowly in the glass of Separatist Baptist Saturday church meetings from 1783 to 1850. The Separatist Baptists, by the very course of events, were to undergo divisions and dot Clark County with their rural church houses. Yearly, new members came to the mourners' benches and baptismal holes in the creeks were often riffled by confirmation of the sacrament of immersion. Still Satan was often around. Some members drank too much to be waited upon by special committees. Women became pregnant out of wedlock. Black slaves were admitted to membership on the approval of their masters as well as by confessions of faith, some of them strayed away into disorderly activities or were charged with rowdiness and thievery.[31]

Satan invaded the boundaries of Clark County in various forms. There came to Winchester showmen and pitchmen to aggravate both the Baptist deacons and the magistrates and town trustees. When Brother Robert Elkin raised the question of whether it was "right" to attend theatrical performances, the deacons were direct in their opinion that communicants should not attend shows.[32]

As the population grew and new Baptist congregations came into existence there was a growing need for some form of interfaith communication
and the establishment of orders of faith. By 1810 there were at least four or
five Baptist congregations in Clark County. Because of the lack of some central documentary statistical source the number is necessarily vague. Likewise,
it is difficult to assess the repercussions on the Baptist congregations caused
by the Great Revival at Cane Ridge in nearby Bourbon County, which appears to have had only a minimal direct effect on the Baptists.[33] Their religious approaches were less emotional than were the outpourings of emotion
in the Great Revival. Changing times, however, made it difficult to maintain
an insulation from more expressive youthful populations that reacted to the
sociological and psychological energies released in the great folk gathering.
Responding to the need for some form of interfaith communication, in October 1787, members of several congregations undertook to project an association. This group gathered in the Tate's Creek Meeting House in Madison
County and there devised a loose association of the nearby congregations.[34]

As the Kentucky population expanded after the creation of the Commonwealth of Kentucky this move for organizing an association of the Baptist congregations in Clark County gained momentum. There took place on
the first Friday in October 1802 one of the most remarkable gatherings of
people in the county's history to date. Assembled in and about the Unity
Meeting House were said to be 1,929 messengers and attending members
from twenty-four neighboring Regular Baptist congregations. Messengers
representing the Clark County churches came from the Red River, Providence, Unity, Howard's Creek, and East Fork churches. Among the local
preachers were Robert Elkin, James Quisenberry, Moses Bledsoe, and James
Haggard. This assembly resulted in the formation of the North Association,
which included all of the Clark County constituted churches.[35]

At the turn into the nineteenth century, there appeared on the Kentucky
and Clark County scenes some impressive competitors to the near monopo-
listic hold the Regular Baptists held on the western country. These competitors were a growing number of Methodist circuit riders, the organization of
Methodist conferences, and the rise of a new denomination with leaders fired
with the intense emotional zeal of the Cane Ridge Revival.[36] Too, there existed within the ranks of the Baptist faith itself irritative if not divisive elements. The strict rules of the various congregations and the narrow literalness
of the orders of faith almost inevitably kindled a state of strife.[37] Too, as the
raw frontier came under exploitation and the Indian menace was erased the
opening of new social, political, and economic eras destroyed much of the

magnetism of the close-knit faith which had brought the traveling congregations west. Congregations found themselves involved in issues over slavery, the admission of black slaves as members, the buying of lottery tickets in an age when Kentuckians were trying to finance public enterprises, a question about Free Masonry, the eternal presence of drunkenness, personal morals, and enforcing the rule of regular church attendance. Congregations held different views about the administering of the sacraments of communion and of baptism.[38]

The Regular or Primitive Baptists of Clark County reached their zenith in the history of the area in the year 1811-1812, when twenty-eight congregations were said to have had a combined membership of 2,835 souls. A decline set in after that date which in time all but destroyed the old orders of the churches.[39] An issue which strew the virus of discord among the congregations in 1814 was that of supporting foreign missions.[40] Providence, for instance, appears to have supported the idea for only a year and then abandoned it. By 1829 there arose debates and discussions on the forms of the churches' spiritual vitality or the waning of it. As an example, Lulbegrud Creek and Cane Spring churches took offense at the mode of administering the communion and the manner in which baptisms were being conducted by some of the churches. No matter what aberrations occurred in performing the services, the real erosions of the old Baptist faith arose from the growing sophistication of the Clark County population and the competition offered by other faiths.[41]

Only a slender historical cord still linked the Clark County Baptists to their beginnings at the outbreak of the Civil War. Membership dwindled before threatening laws, Regular Baptist ministers made poor showings in the frequent challenges to debate those of other faiths, other denominations offered a considerably less austere achievement of grace, the holding of harvest season revival camp meetings met both a deep-felt social and spiritual need for the rural people, and, finally, the dull sermonizing of many of the semiliterate preachers repelled uninhibited youthful and potential communicants. It is not hard to imagine the contrast between lay Baptist literalist ministers and more eloquent clergy like Barton W. Stone, Bishop Francis Asbury, Alexander Campbell, "Raccoon" John Smith, and, later, Robert Jefferson Breckingridge.[42]

Strangely, there does not seem to exist in the documentary materials of Clark County religious congregations a copy of an early Separatist Baptist sermon. The sermons which have survived in print are from other areas or are more humorous caricatures than serious ministerial homiletics. No doubt it

This surely has to be a world record Sunday School Class for a rural county seat community. There are represented in the photograph 121 members of D.L. Pendleton's Pendleton Bible Class of the First Christian Church. - *Photo courtesy of Winchester Sun*

was true that most of the sermons delivered in the early Clark County Baptist churches were extemporaneous rather than created from inscribed notes or full sermon texts. Comments were made about the powerful preachings of such ministers as James Quisenberry and Robert Elkin, but these comments give no hint of the contents of their sermons. Somewhat tragically, the patriarchical Baptist leaders had undertaken to control their people by congregational orders rather than by gauging the rapidly changing conditions in the society about them. This was especially true where youth were concerned.[43]

Despite the limiting bonds of their faith, the Separatist or Primitive Baptists cut deep grooves in the tablet of Clark County history. Many of their members were influential founders and servants of Clark County. Some of their leading men served in county offices, as overseers of roads, judges in elections, estate appraisers, and rural school trustees. Perhaps the most fundamental contribution the Primitive Baptists made to Clark County was planting on the face of the land tight family clusters and communities which evinced from the start rugged wills and powers of survival.[44] Culturally and intellectually they contributed materially to the shaping and conditioning of a rural-agrarian turn of mind which continued through almost two centuries in the fields of politics, education, and slave and race relations, in the shaping and support of public institutions, and, always, in the exertion of a rugged spirit of individualism. The membership roll of the Providence Church alone is also in good measure that of Clark County's early settlers and leaders.[45]

If those strong-willed Regular or Primitive Baptists who sat in stern judgment of their fellow men and women at Providence, Unity, Howard's Creek, and Lulbegrud were hardy pioneers of the forest era, and bearers of the simple faith of post-Revolutionary War revivalism, so were the Methodist circuit riders who invaded the domain. The Wesleyan Cavaliers who rode the lonely forest trails, endured the harsh environment, and survived, were intrepid hunters of hungry souls receptive to spiritual enlightenment.[46] Though Clark County was located well off the beaten path of the early Methodist circuit riders, it in time was discovered as a virgin field ripe for the harvest. The dark-suited horsemen of the sprawling Kentucky frontier Methodist circuit were inveterate crusaders. Most of them gave a year of their lives on the lonely ridings and then retired to recuperate their health. As one historian of the denomination wrote, they had to fight for every inch of ground and then fight to hold it.[47] They did oral combats with the Regular and Separatist Baptist and Anabaptists from one end of Clark County to the other. On April 30, 1792, in the year Clark County was chartered, the Methodist held their great landmark conference at Masterson's Station just west of Lexington on the Leestown Road. During that gathering the Hinkston Circuit was designated as covering Clark, Montgomery, Harrison, Bath, and Nicholas counties.[48] This large and thinly populated circuit was assigned to Richard Bird, newly arrived in Kentucky. At the time there was not a Methodist meeting-house in the region, and few converts to the faith. The rising tide of incoming emigrants kept the region astir with locating lands, building cabins, and clearing fields and meadows. Preachings, or "love feasts," were held in cramped smoke-stained, living-dining-bedrooms or out under the stars and under the timber.[49]

Here on an emerging settler frontier saddle-worn Richard Bird tested his zeal, eloquence, and health to stir his tiny congregations to a high pitch of emotional fervor. One year riding across the vast region between the Licking and Kentucky rivers on the Hinkston Circuit exhausted Bird.[50] He was succeeded by Thomas Wilkerson of Amelia County, Virginia.[51] Aside from competing with the Baptists and assembling the emotionally and spiritually hungry in crowded cabins, Wilkerson left behind an intriguing account of life in the early Clark County settlements. In 1795 he wrote, "We kept up with the frontier settlements, preached to the people in their forts and blockhouses. Here I met no D. D.'s to discuss doctrine, or to make out reports about moral wastes. We had nothing to contend with from without but Indians, the wild beasts, and smaller vermin. We thought ourselves well accommodated if we had a half-faced camp or cabin to shelter us, and some wild meat to eat. It has been a matter of enquiry how we found much ready access to the frontier settlements. We followed the openings of providence, as did Mr. Wesley. Owing to the uncertainty of land titles, emigrants would squat down on the frontiers, where they could get permission. Our brethren, moving from the old settlements together, would settle in the same neighborhood. As soon as they could build some cabins, they would go in search of a preacher; and there would be a society raised. As soon as they became acquainted with the country, they would seek homes of their own, and, as lands were always cheapest on the frontiers, the class would scatter in different directions, and, as before, search out the preachers and invite them to their houses; so we had not to go in search of preaching places, but the people searched out the Preachers."[52] This condition of life in Clark County was far removed from the fairly comfortable environment of Lincoln College in Oxford University, where John Wesley conceived the philosophy of Methodism. His disciple Thomas Wilkerson rode the Hinkston Circuit a year, and, like his predecessor, went away to recuperate and raise a family.[53]

The most notable landmark of Methodism in Clark County is Ebenezer

Church located six miles west of Winchester on the Todd's Mill Road. This was possibly the first Methodist church house built in the county, and up to 1824 it was the focal center of the faith. In the latter year the Methodists established a church in Winchester.[54] There were societies, and, later, churches located about the county, but they did not enjoy the degree of stability of Ebenezer. Drawing from contemporary ministerial sources, W. E. Arnold, in his *History of Methodism in Kentucky*, wrote, "Stores were few and small, and trade was meager. So far removed from the older settlements, with such limited means of transportation, and with so little money in circulation, neither barter nor sale was possible beyond a very limited extent. The people produced and manufactured in their homes nearly everything they used. They carded and spun their own clothing. The spinning wheel and loom were indispensable in the home. The wild life of the forest supplied the meat for their tables, while garden and field yielded the other staple foods. Maple trees and sorghum patches furnished the sweets used by the family, and one preacher testified that he did not smell coffee in ten years! There was little inducement to live in town, and the wealth of the country was in the rural sections. It was much easier for a body of people to feel entertainment in the country than in the towns."[55]

That the wealth of Clark County was in the countryside rather than the tiny village of Winchester was true so far as the community about the founding congregation of Ebenezer Church was concerned. The founders of this church were among some of the ablest people in Clark County at the time. They were Dr. Thomas Hinde, the English physician and doctor to Patrick Henry, Mary Todd Hinde, Martha Hinde, William Kavanaugh, John Martin, a Mr. Summers, and Elizabeth Heironymus, mother of Julia Tevis.[56]

In 1798 a log meetinghouse was constructed on land owned jointly by Dr. Thomas Hinde and John Martin. Among the tiny flock of Ebenezer were four members who were to contribute substantially to the organization of Clark County, to Kentucky, and to Methodist history. These were John Martin, the first sheriff of the new county; William Kavanaugh, father of the famous Bishop H. H. Kavanaugh; and Mary Todd Hinde, a woman of strong will and mind who contributed to the movement to establish schools in the county. Among other members of the Ebenezer congregation were the Scobees, Owens, Landrums, Stampers, and Harbers.[57] Physically the Ebenezer Church meeting place was to go through an extended metamorphosis of buildings as the years passed.[58] By 1824 a Methodist Church was established in Winchester, documenting the fact that the arduous ridings of the impoverished old circuit riders had succeeded in planting a firm foothold of their faith on the lands of Clark County. By the latter date the Methodist Church had been transferred from being a society to being an efficiently formed full church body.[59] The old fashioned, highly emotional love feasts of frontier cabin days were past, and circuit riders, like Indian raiders themselves, had disappeared from the backwoods trails.

As indicated above, the history of the various Baptist faiths and that of Clark County from the outset of settlement of the area became so intertwined that at times it is difficult to determine which is religiously doctrinal and which is secular. For two centuries members of the Baptist congregations have numbered more than half the church membership of the county. In 1870 there were twenty-three churches in Clark County, twelve of which were of a Baptist faith.[60] Two decades later there were three Primitive, nine Regular, and eight New Conference Baptist congregations with a collective membership of 4,900 members. By 1906 the population of Clark County had expanded to an estimated 16,694 individuals, of whom 7,774 were church members, and 3,032 were Baptists.[61]

In 1980 there were located in Winchester the three larger congregations, Broadway, First Baptist, and Central. In the rural areas of the county the Baptists continued to be the prevailing faith. Dealing with church statistics is at best an act of wavering faith, and because of this there is an ever-present need for caution. There perhaps exist no dependable criteria by which a full judgment of the impact various Baptist orders have had upon the collective mind of Clark County, on social issues, politics, and local folk mores. It is reasonable, however, to surmise that the influence has been of major importance.

Surprisingly, Clark County did not receive from the inflow of emigrants to its frontier a strong Calvinistic group, as did Danville, Lexington, Louisville, and, possibly, Paris. The cluster of Presbyterians who were influential in the formation of the commonwealth and the development of a rich Bluegrass economy stayed within the Inner Bluegrass area. Among the predominant protestant faiths Presbyterians remained a numerically minor one. In mid-nineteenth century there were four Presbyterian congregations in Clark County with a combined seating capacity of 1,300 "sittings," but there was no documentation of the membership.[62] In 1890 the number had been increased to five congregations, the most important of which was the first Presbyterian Church of Winchester. This church was organized in 1813, and in time it was to absorb the dwindling flocks of several faltering churches.[63]

No part of Clark County church history has so involved a social and theological background as does the Christian Church. This was made so by the fact that so many strands of events, doctrines, and strong ministerial personalities were involved in its creation. Obviously the intense religious emotions generated by the Cane Ridge Revival, the doctrinal differences raised by the principle minister on that scene, and the subsequent debates all in some way contributed the foundation history of the Christian Church.[64]

Reflective of the separateness of many of the formative congregations in Clark County, one group had little or no knowledge of what another was doing. In the case of the founding of the Christian Church there arose a "restoration" movement to restore the "New Testament" Church compliance with the Bible. This movement started in several congregations, with none being informed of what was happening. The restoration movement was led by more than half a dozen strong-willed pastors, among them Alexander and Thomas Campbell, Barton W. Stone, "Raccoon" John Smith, James Kelly, and Abner Jones.[65] In time these men constituted a virtual debating society, contending among themselves and with ministers of other churches. The points of internal contention were considerably reduced in 1832 when unification began in various areas. Dr. Alonzo W. Fortune delineated in his book *The Disciples in Kentucky* both the strands of doctrinal differences and the processes by with congregations were melded into unified beliefs in the Christian Church.[66]

The Christian Church of Winchester dates its founding from 1791. Obviously at this early date the bedrock congregation was Separatist Baptist, and in 1801 it came under the emotional influence of the Cane Ridge Revival and its aftereffects. Dr. Fortune wrote, "The most important result of the Cane Ridge revival was not the spiritual awakening which it produced, although it was significant. It led to an ecclesiastical revolt which spread through the churches of Kentucky. Mr. Stone and the other preachers who were associated with him in the revival preached a doctrine of salvation which was in opposition to Calvinism."[67]

The history of the Christian-Disciples denomination was further complicated by the theological and ecclesiastical beliefs of Barton W. Stone and Alexander Campbell as central figures in the creation of the "New Testament" Church. Added to the doctrinal differences of the two men was the delicate matter of separating from the Baptists. Sectional meetings took place to discuss this matter. One of the meetings was held at Mount Zion Church in Clark County in October 1829. At this meeting also some progress was made in reconciling the points of differences of the Disciples-Christian faiths.[68] Dr. Fortune took serious notice of the points of differences in the Christian Church. He wrote, "As a result of these controversies The Disciples have divided into two bodies, the one designated as Disciples of Christ, and the other designated as Churches of Christ. Each published its own yearbook and has its own report in the governing publications. There are two quite different parent stems among the Disciples, and at times it looked as though there would be another division, but much of the controversial spirit has disappeared...."[69]

All the crosscurrents of beliefs and controversy surely must have been felt directly in the emerging Christian churches of Clark County. Like its neighboring congregations of other faiths, the Winchester Christian Church underwent chrysalis stages of transformation. On February 17, 1846, the Kentucky General Assembly authorized Samuel Wheeler to act as a commissioner and sell lot number 94 of the old Winchester city plat, where earlier the Christian Church congregation had established its first house. This half acre lot had been conveyed to the church by John Hampton and his wife by deed, dated July 11, 1827. Funds derived from the sale, the General Assembly directed, were to be invested in a more suitable site for the church.[70] Later, February 1, 1858, the Winchester Church was again empowered by law to sell a part of its church site and to apply the funds to finance other church purposes.[71]

There was a second phase to the rise of the Christian Church to such a prominent position among the Kentucky church bodies. The federal publication *Religious Bodies in the United States* reported in 1901 there existed 1,103 colored churches in Kentucky, but only 51 of them were of the Disciples faith.[72] At least one of these was the Broadway Christian Church in Winchester. This congregation was organized in 1868, a peak year in the post-Civil War era of Reconstruction.[73] Like its white neighbors, this colored church has survived years of stringent financial conditions, the evolution of church house structures, and interfaith competition. For some doctrinal, racial, or social reason during the years 1853-1927 the Christian Church in Kentucky failed either to appeal to colored parishioners or to assume leadership in assisting the organization of colored churches. No doubt the fact that the antebellum Separatist Baptists had admitted blacks in attitudes toward serving some of the spiritual needs of slaves gave these denominations a historical advantage and appeal.[74]

In his eightieth year Edward S. Jouett, a Clark County native, wandered through vicariously and down memory's lane, recalling in tender nostalgia what surely must have been the experience of a host of youth who grew up in the Christian Church. He became a member of the First Church of Winchester at the age of twelve years. From a perspective of years and sentimental memories Jouett wrote, "In those early days Winchester was a small place, about the size of its population rivals, Paris, Mount Sterling, and Richmond, and from every viewpoint amongst the best of the Bluegrass towns.[75] There was, he reflected, a strait-laced austerity about Winchester society and the town's church congregations, and the First Christian Church in particular. Jouett wrote that in relationship to the Methodists, Baptists, and Presbyterians, "The Christian was probably the most pronounced in the field of discipline. For example, the waltz and other round dances were strongly condemned, and in some Bluegrass churches indulgence in them was grounds for expulsion. Card playing with ordinary cards, with no money at stake, was frowned on but other games with different cards, such as Flinch and Rook, were in common use by the best church members."[76] Times changed, said Jouett, and churches began providing recreation facilities for social gatherings. Even the morally innocuous games of Flinch and Rook passed into oblivion, and in time some of the decks of these games became collector's items. With the sociological, religious, and economic changes which swept over the Clark County borders after 1915 many of the old disciplines had become badly eroded. More sophisticated church members played bridge, and bingo, and no doubt bought Kentucky lottery tickets. The more supple ones even danced the tango, Charleston, boogie-woogie, and all the other forms of dancing. Edward Jouett's youthful days were indeed far back in both the chronological past and accepted mores.

As indicated above, there remained like a shadow of guilt a concern on the part of Clark County slaveholders for the spiritual welfare of some of their people. In some instances, as that of the Providence Regular Baptist Church, a limited number of slaves were admitted to membership in the predominantly white master congregation.[77] In some other churches, prior to the Emancipation Proclamation in 1863, there were slave balconies, and in a few instances slave ministers were permitted to exhort congregations of joint whites and blacks.[78]

Sometime around 1830 William and Philip Landrum held services for slaves and free persons of color in the basement of the New Winchester Methodist Church.[79] Four years later Landrum returned to the Hinkston Circuit as a presiding elder; he reported finding 591 white members and 198 slaves and free persons of color as members of churches in the circuit or conference.[80]

Once slavery was abolished there seemed to be preferences among blacks for the Methodist and Baptist denominations. There was organized in New York City as early as 1796 an African Methodist Episcopal Church, and after

1863 this body became active across the South, especially in North Carolina, Florida, and Louisiana.[81] By 1890 the African Union Methodist Protestant Church had 2,131 church houses worth $4,833,207. This body claimed there were 184,542 members. In 1906 the southern Ohio and Kentucky Conference of the Colored Methodist Episcopal Church had fifty-four churches with the extremely low valuation of $114,925.[82]

Supplementing the numerical and spiritual strength of the Clark County Baptist's history were the rise of the colored congregations. Epitomizing this chapter in the local religious history, the First Baptist Highland and the Corinth churches of Winchester became anchor congregations. The First Baptist Highland was organized in 1867, and in an age when new freedom exerted the verity of their escape beyond the portals of their own churches. The church and access to the Kentucky political polls were indeed havens of freedom and independence. Documentary evidence, however, describing the number and location of the colored Baptist congregations is skimpy. Undoubtedly some colored congregations were offsprings of white ones like the ancient Providence Church or the Methodist Church in Winchester.

The history and fortunes of the First Baptist Highland Church closely paralleled those of many of the local white churches. There were struggles to gather membership, to retain ministers with leadership capabilities, and, most important of all, to raising enough capital to construct and maintain a suitable church house.[83] Accomplishing this objective constituted a major victory of persistence and faith. Many persons, first and last, were involved in building the modern First Baptist Highland Church, some of whom were Charles Sloan, E. D. Taylor, and C. O. Givens. The latter served as minister of the church for twenty-six years. It was he who worked so persistently to pay off the mortgage, which was done in 1944. The much younger Corinthian Church was organized as a mission congregation in 1825, and that year it was raised to full status as a Missionary Baptist Church.[84]

There arrived in Clark County in the 1840s a new wave of immigration, this time largely from Ireland. The newcomers were mostly Catholics but were too few in numbers to build and maintain a church. Among the early communicants were the Pender, Madigan, Kenan, McGarth, and Connor families. Priests from Lexington and, later, from Covington served these families. It was not until 1871, and through the leadership of Father Thomas Moore, that a church was constructed and christened St. Joseph as a mission church of St. Patrick's in Mount Sterling.[85] Later, 1887, St. Joseph attained full parish status with Father Edward Healy as its priest. The Census Bureau *Report of Religious Bodies in the United States* in 1906 indicated there were

280 Catholic communicants in Clark County. In the surge of modern industrial expansion in the counties in the latter half of the twentieth century this church has grown from the influx of new families.[86]

Every local church congregation in Clark County for the past two centuries generated a history and shared the fortunes of changing times. No institution, except the family, touched so large a portion of the population.[87] The catalog of ministers, church leaders, and mainstay individuals includes the names of almost every family that made any sort of a mark in the county's history. Too, the issues which beset the religious congregations were the same ones which concerned the secular community.[88] Inevitably the Clark County religious congregations were drawn into the realm of local politics. There were always issues which bore as much on the fortunes of the churches as upon the community as a whole. There were the questions of acquiring and holding land and property under the corporate laws of the commonwealth, support for public education, regulation of public taverns and traveling theatricals, and dealing with the intricate human issues of slavery, serving the needs of youth for recreation, the regulation of public morals, and, after 1830, the burning issue of temperance.[89]

Spiritually, there arose among the church congregations of Clark County the divisive circumstances of differing scriptural interpretations, formalities of footwashings, administering the sacraments, uses of musical instruments in church services, conflicts of ministerial personalities, and, always, interdenominational relationships. All of these problems assumed the colorations of the times and the prevailing conditions of life in Clark County and the town of Winchester.[60]

As the county seat town grew in population and the modernization of its public services in the latter decades of the twentieth century country churches suffered the losses of communicants and financial support. Some disappeared altogether. At the same time congregations in town grew, and so did church plants and recreational facilities. The vast improvement of highways after 1920 and the rapid expansion of use of the automobile greatly facilitated the movement of human beings. Added to this the vastly improved means of communication and increased social intercourse brought about some radical revisions of moral attitudes. In numerous ways the conditions of national and international society are in some way in the most isolated and struggling congregation to survive in Clark County. Whatever changes have transpired during the past two centuries, one fact remained crystal clear: the temporal and religious histories of Clark County have remained inseparately entwined. Too, the harvest of members for the various denominations has ever been fruitful. Throughout two centuries approximately half of the county's population has remained consistently outside the pale of an organized church congregation.[91]

Dealing historically with the statistics of church bodies opens some pitfalls. Some congregations seem to have been rather casual in keeping statistics and in recording full minutes of proceedings. Official statistics are seldom enlightening of more than mere numbers, and even they are open to question. The United States Bureau of the Census never really set a standard schedule for gathering such data. It largely abandoned gathering religious organizational data, leaving this task to central religious fact gatherers. Despite the difficulties in determining dependable statistical information about the development of churches in Clark County, it is possible to produce a fairly definite profile of church activities.

Earlier the Regular Baptists and later the Missionary Southern Baptists have consistently garnered more than half the church membership in Clark County.[92] The number of "sittings" in their church houses, however, has consistently exceeded the actual number of active communicants. Finally, the estimated worth of church houses and auxiliary properties remained extremely low in the early decades of this century; this was so even when the money standards are taken into consideration. Their rural churches in many instances reflected the qualities of the homes of communicants.[93] In some cases isolated country churches and schools in Clark County came near being institutional outcasts. For most of the churches preaching occurred monthly, and there were seasonal revival meetings which had as much a social meaning as a religious one.

Remarkably, the level of organized religious membership, 1792-1995, maintained a fairly consistent co-relationship with population numbers.[94] There always was a fertile field of unchurched to be corralled into the membership folds of the churches.[95] There prevailed an unwavering optimism that some day the gap would be filled between members and nonmembers. For example, by 1850 eleven county Baptist congregations had built enough housing to accommodate 4,400 "sittings," with the general church enrollment falling well below this capacity.[96] The local Methodist congregations gathered in eight churches containing 2,500 "sittings."[97] The midcentury census report made no mention of the physical properties of the Christian-Disciples congregations.

Immediately following the Civil War there were thirty-four church houses in Clark County with seating accommodations for 9,700 persons. Approximately a third of these were Baptist, and a third Methodist; the rest were

Presbyterian and Christian.[98] Thus the churches in Clark County history have prospered within the past two centuries. In 1980 the population of Clark County was 29,100, and there were fifty-one churches with 15,281 members.[99] With the consolidation of the public schools, the closing of fourth-class post offices, and the great reduction of the number and quality of the country stores, the churches in the local communities have become both the focal centers and the cohesive institutions which still give identity to communities which otherwise would have long ago disappeared both in name and in fact.[100]

Throughout its history Clark County has been family oriented. Family reunions, holiday celebrations, and personal pride of not only belonging in the larger communities of Clark County and Winchester, but within the comfortable bonds of a family. This Prewitt-Vanmeter gathering stands surrogate for all the families of the areas. - *Photo courtesy of Herbert and Caroline Sledd*

CHAPTER 10

The "Three R's"

The educational history of Clark County, along with that of scores of Kentucky counties, may have been best characterized by Winchester's humorous and iconoclastic mayor John E. Garner, who wrote, "Sir, the county of Clark is the birthplace and the present residence of the Arkhoon of Swat and the Chevalier de Montrose, two of the finest Poland China pigs that ever made a track in the mud. It is there that you will find the great purebred cattle interests. Within a radius of six miles of Winchester you see the animals with blood as blue as a Virginian's, whose tabulated pedigrees are as extensive as the Plantagenets and whose ancestry traces back to the white cow Mr. Bates rescued from the butcher.... Why is it that our cattle have reputations and our men none? The reason is obvious to anyone familiar with this locality, who has contrasted our schoolhouses with our cattle barns. The most eligible site is chosen for the barn. It is a great three story building as big as half outdoors, with windows and door frames trimmed in red; ventilated at the top, a lightning rod running up at each end with a brass rooster on it, and herdsmen employed to care for the cattle at a salary of a thousand dollars a year. The most out-of-the-way place on the farm is selected for schoolhouse, where the land is valueless for any other purpose. No lightning rod on that building. No one ever feared that lightning would strike a boy. It is a one-story structure with a leaky roof, broken window panes replaced with the backs of school atlases, and chinking fallen from between logs through which a small boy could be thrown."[1]

Much of the early history of education in Clark County is shrouded in a mist of meager documentation. Though there are frequent references to schools having been taught, the process of teaching in the various pioneer communities must have been of a desultory and informal nature. There was a total lack of official recognition of the fact that the organization and support of schools was a vital part of the pioneering social and economic facts of life. One searches through the Order Books of Clark County in vain for some documentary evidence of public concern for the creation of a system of common schools. At few times was the word "education" recorded on the pages of the official transactions. In this case the historian is left to draw heavily upon inferences.

At the outset of Clark County's educational history two facts were pronounced. A large proportion of the early population was of school age.[2] Families in most cases were numerous, sometimes astonishingly so. Then the process of clearing away the forest, building houses and barns, breaking the land, cultivating crops, and attending to livestock required intensive physical labor. Farming in pioneer Clark County involved little practical need for learning nor were there present exemplars of the advantages of education. Concerns for elementary learning in Clark County in the early years were related to the activities of surveying wild lands, keeping elementary warehouse records, reading the Scriptures, and conducting the simplest forms of business transactions. Paradoxically, there were among the early population individuals who wrote relatively clear English in a highly legible hand. The public records of the county, in many cases, are highly reflective of this fact.[3] Three areas of public documentary creation demanded considerable clarity of expression: the writing of land deed descriptions, the drafting of wills, and the reports of estate inventories. There of course was a considerable mass of the Clark County population which went unrecorded because it could neither read nor write. This group left behind no written record of its existence except as a digit in the United States Census reports, frequently as a "tithe" subject to paying a poll tax, occasionally, as being present before the court, or as collectors of wolf scalp bounties.

Despite the emphasis on the democratizing process of settling the frontier, creation of the basic institution of the common school was not considered as a primary concern. Surely those early emigrants who came west from Virginia must have brought some glimmer of knowledge of the quasi-public academy, not for the masses, but at least for a privileged few. This approach to providing elementary education prevailed in most of Kentucky until 1988.[4] The concept of universal public common school education went through an almost interminable period of intellectual and legal gestation.

In 1800, the first time the census taker made a population count of Clark County as a political entity, there were 5,968 white persons.[5] A major portion

The home of James Clark, Governor of Kentucky 1836-1839. It was from this home that James Clark went forth to challenge the Relief forces in the Kentucky General Assembly in the monumental case Williams v. Blair, then to the governorship of the Commonwealth. This house had moments being threatened with serious damage if not destruction. Presently it is a well preserved monument to one of Clark County's most notable citizens. - *Photo courtesy of Jerry Schureman*

of this population was under sixteen years of age. This was an impressive number of potential school-age children living in an area which to date had only the vaguest history of any sort of even informal schools having been taught. The census enumerators gathered no social or cultural information, and the local official records are silent on the subject. Much of the information about the earliest teachers and schools in the county comes largely from personal reminiscences. The census count in 1799 does establish the fact that among the youthful population there were 1,706 boys and 1,698 girls; only the males were the primary candidates for potential education. [6] Within the social and political context of the period's male-dominant society this was true. The girls of school age were automatically looked upon as apprentices to being housekeepers and mothers. There no doubt prevailed the thought that domestic wisdom for them would come by gaining practical experience.

Although a considerable body of primary and secondary sources is available for the writing of the history of education in the Commonwealth of Kentucky, there is lacking much basic data explaining the facts of educational origins in given localities. One of the strange anomalies of Kentucky is that when delegates sat in ten conventions in Danville, 1785-1792, debating the processes of establishing an independent state, there was no discussion of the role that education might play in its welfare. Someone in the numerous meetings of the conventions in a committee of the whole might have brought up the subject, but, the proceedings of these sessions were not recorded. This despite the fact that there were several highly sophisticated delegates present in the ten constitutional conventions. In this instance the negatives of history have a broader meaning than do the positives.[7]

Within the context of the first half century of the existence of the Clark County government the cause of education at no time was put forward as a pressing issue. Exploitation of heavily wooded forest land made strong demands on strong backs, willing hands, and some gumption. Tools for performing the laborious tasks of the Kentucky frontier were of the simplest design, and all of them were fitted predominantly for hand use. This was also true, as explained earlier, of farm implements.[8] With few exceptions, the planning and erecting of houses and outbuildings required little or no architectural sophistication. Skill in the use of the axe, broadaxe, foot adz, and whipsaw,

The Winchester High School baseball team in the days when the game was still the great American sport, and every athletically inclined boy dreamed of breaking Ty Cobb's record.

Winchester ushered in the age of football in 1907 with contesting teams of merchants versus the professionals. To a large extent the names of the players were representative of the pioneer families who settled Clark County. Among the players there Bush, Massie, Ecton, Clark, Hodgkin, Kidwell, Hampton, Jouett and Strode. No Baker made the team.

however, was a necessity. There survive in Clark County some well-preserved artifacts of early handicraft skills. One has only to examine the hewn logs in the cabin on the Hubbard Taylor premises or the sawn boards in the Taylor and Samuel D. Martin houses to find tangible proof of the pioneer work-men. For the mass of the Clark County population prior to 1830 there no doubt prevailed the feeling that mastering the physical skills was far more important in everyday life than mastering the "three R's." Even for the fortu-nate few who had access to any form of education the fourth grade was the pyramid of learning.[9]

Developing a system of common schools in early Clark County had an-tecedents which reached far beyond both the physical and chronological boundaries of the region. Central to almost every undertaking in pioneer Kentucky was the overweening influence of the land. Public land down until the moment of final occupation was in a major fashion the form of currency which enabled both state and counties to meet their fiscal responsibilities without levying taxes. The unclaimed wild lands were made available for the organization and support of schools. In May 1780 the Virginia General As-sembly, no doubt as a result of the prodding of the Reverend John Todd and his nephew John, granted to Kentucky County 1,800 acres of escheated lands belonging to the tories of Robert McKenzie, Henry Collins, and Alexander

The Belmont School, 1967, formerly the Winchester High School. The City School System was merged with the County School System after an appeal by the City School Board of Education, July 1, 1960.

McKie with the belief that "it being the best interest of this commonwealth always to promote and encourage every design which may tend to the improvement of the mind and the diffusion of useful knowledge, even among the most remote citizens, whose situation a barbarous neighborhood and a savage intercourse might otherwise render unfriendly to science.[10] Inherent in this grandiose statement was the unspoken notion of the Virginia legislators that the commonwealth's subject might be more difficult to subdue than the Indians if they were left in ignorance.

The grant of the escheated tory lands set a modest precedent for making no more than a public gesture at the support of public academics. Its General Assembly enacted the famous academy act of 1794 creating the Kentucky Academy at Pisgah in Woodford County.[11] There followed in rather quick order the chartering of other land-grant academies, all of them receiving grants of 6,000 acres of land located in the largely unsettled areas of the state where land could be found, but not always easily for claiming. No doubt legislators perceived of these grants simply as "seed money" because there was not 6,000 acres of wild land anywhere in Kentucky in 1798 which would produce enough money to erect a crude log schoolhouse and operate a school for more than a year or two.[12]

Though chartered by the General Assembly and subsidized as public educational facilities, the land-grant academies were controlled exclusively by the chartering petitioners or trustees. Thus the charter granted in December 1798 for the establishment of the Winchester Academy had behind it an established official and historical precedent.[13] The legislative act chartering the academy named Robert Clarke, Sr., Hubbard Taylor, John Lyles, Robert Clarke, Jr., Richard Hickman, William Kavenaugh, Jacob Fishback, Daniel Bullock, Dillard Collins, John Irwin, Patterson Bullock, and Robert Evans as trustees. This list of names almost replicated the persons who had been influential in establishing the county itself. They formed an unusually large board of trustees for such a tentative institution. As time soon proved, only some of the original trustees continued to be active in the affairs of the academy.[14]

The Winchester Academy was vested with the authority which would enable it "from time to time, to establish by-laws and regulations, rules and ordinances not contrary to the constitution or law of the state, as they [trustees] deem necessary for the government of said academy.[15] Though the list of trustees included representatives of the most prominent families in Clark County in 1798, and the academy was created as an officially chartered institution, it by no stretch of the imagination was a public common school that anticipated the later concept of the universal public school. Despite the fact historians of the westward movement in American history have devoted extensive attention to the democratizing influence latent in the process of territorial and population expansion, there prevailed on the Kentucky frontier, either by force of circumstance or will, no early zeal for universal education. Occasionally there was an outburst of philosophical oratory that learning was a prime attribute in the ongoing processes of civilization, but there was little or no action. One reads the pages of the *Kentucky Gazette* after 1787 and the inscribed proceedings of the various separation convention in Danville without seeing education discussed as an integral responsibility of the body politic. This is also true of the numerous discourses published by the *Gazette* from individuals who presented their views of the kind of government the western district should establish. No one made a plea for the education of the masses of the population.[16]

The first two Kentucky constitutions ignored education altogether.[17] In the convention which met in Frankfort on August 17, 1799, Robert Clarke, Richard Hickman, and William Sudduth represented Clark County and signed the revised draft of the new constitution.[18] One can only surmise that both delegates of the General Assembly shifted the responsibility of education almost by the code of unwritten law onto the shoulders of private individuals and the counties.

The 6,000 acres of wild lands granted to Clark County in 1798 were located generally on "the south side of Green River" Christian County.[19] In the case of the Cumberland River boundary it took either some geographic acrobatics or an invasion of the sovereignty of Tennessee to locate the land. In making the land grant to Clark County the General Assembly was more concerned with the administration of the grant than with its purpose.[20]

Development of the academic program of the Winchester Academy was left entirely up to planning by the trustees and by itinerant teachers who came to Kentucky during the first decades of the nineteenth century. The law creating the Winchester Academy was specific as to the duties of the trustees but made no provision for them to file reports with any central state official. Not even the location, survey, and sale of the land was controlled by the state. No minimum price was established for the land. Basically, the trustees were supposed to work through the county court, but, again, one searches in vain for any notation in the county Order Books for references to the academy or disposition of the grant lands. As indicated, the land was in Christian County; however, a part of the grant was placed in the Caldwell County in 1809 when that county was created.[21]

There are gaps in the history of the Winchester Academy when little or nothing was done to hold classes. Even the date of beginning instruction seems to be foggy. It is certain that there was a lessening of interest on the part of some of the trustees. In September 1809 trustees John Ward, Thomas Pickett, Peter Evans, John Irwin, Thomas Scott, Chilton Allen, Thomas Irwin, and Samuel Taylor signed an indenture transferring a hundred acres to James Sympson. He paid $750 for the land, and the money became the first funds which could be used for obtaining a schoolhouse and offering instruction.[22]

Trustees Samuel M. Taylor, Benjamin A. Buckner, John Ward, Samuel D. Martin, Thomas B. Moore, and Chilton Allen sold to James Sympson 728 acres of land in Caldwell County in 1811 for an unstated amount of money. In the meantime James Sympson died, but not before he had sold the land to Chilton Allen, though the deed was not recorded.[23] The trustees then revised the deed in Allen's name, and he paid $596.00, or slightly over seventy cents an acre. Thus in all the Winchester Academy realized $1,346 for its land in the two sales.[24]

There appears in Clark County Deed Book Number 7, April 20, 1810, an indenture made among Hubbard Taylor, Peter Evans, John Ward, Thomas Pickett, Samuel Taylor, John Wallace, David Dodge, John Irwin, Chilton Allen, James Sympson and James Clark transferring a parcel of land adjoining the town of Winchester to be used as the site of the Winchester Academy.[25] This deed carried out one of the commitments by John Baker, Sr. when he sought the location of the county seat on his land. The plot described in a deed, made in 1810 by John Baker, Jr., was "to be applied to use of said seminary of learning by trustees aforesaid, and whereas the trustees have on the faith of John Baker's subscriptions aforesaid erected on said lot or parcel of ground a house for the aforesaid seminary, the said John Baker in consideration of the promises and earnest solicitude to the cause of learning, and for the consideration of one dollar to the said John Baker in hand paid."[26] The land parcel's boundaries were described as not being in the original area but along the Four Mile Road. The Baker grant was involved in some disagreement and legal complications because of the reluctance of the son to honor his father's commitment. The deed to the property was not executed until 1810, twelve years after the General Assembly had chartered the Winchester Academy, and eighteen years after John Baker had made the offer of the plot near the big spring on his land.[27] The county record is not clear as to whether school sessions had been held prior to 1810; perhaps not.[28]

William W. Martin advertised on April 6, 1813, that he had selected able assistance in the superintendence of the academy, and he was prepared to offer instruction in reading, writing, arithmetic, English grammar, geography, rhetoric, logic, and dead languages, natural philosophy, astronomy, mathematics, and ethics. Charges for the teaching of these subjects ranged from five to ten dollars a session. The academy would begin its first session on the first Monday in May 1814 in a building on the Baker lot. Professor Martin made the commitments that great care would be taken in the teaching of the English language and close attention would be given to the moral conduct of both sexes. He assured prospective patrons that a private room would be set apart for "the exclusive accommodation of young ladies, where they will be instructed in all the necessary and useful arts of a complete education."[29] This meant that a small number of Clark County girls would receive instruction in social manners and graces and in domestic responsibilities for taking care of a husband, children, and a home, with a dash of the aesthetic arts.[30]

Boys were to be instructed in the more rugged and masculine of the arts, such as the sciences, mathematics, astronomy, and the English language. For an added fee they could be drilled in the dead languages. No aspect of the academy's instructional program was free. Prices for instruction varied with the subjects taught. Payment of the fees was a matter between parents and the "professor."[31] This was not a trustee duty.

As "A" or Amzi Lewis, late of New York, advertised in 1814 that he would hold classes in spelling, reading, writing, arithmetic, English grammar, Latin, and Greek; all of these subjects for a fee of eight dollars. This indeed was a full curriculum of learning for one instructor to deliver in so brief a school term of three months. Lewis informed his prospective patrons that there would be an added fee to pay for "fuel, etc."[32]

The history of Winchester Academy is badly veiled by friction among trustees and a discontinuity of sessions. It seems clear that there was no academic action prior to 1808, if not 1813. In the former year the Kentucky General Assembly authorized the issuance of warrants or land patents to the trustees of the academy.[33] This legislation was largely of a general nature applying to all the academies that held warrants to unlocated and unsold lands. As indicated earlier, two tracts of land, one in Christian County and the other in Caldwell County were sold to James Sympson and in turn to Chilton Allen.[34] The disposition of the academy lands seems, from surface evidence at least, to have been an inside, no-bid transaction. Certainly it was one which yielded very modest cash returns. The fortunes of the Winchester Academy ebbed and flowed with the changing times down to 1844, when it was merged with the Winchester municipal schools and came under the control of the town trustees.[35] Later, in 1874, the academy was turned over to the Winchester school trustees to become a part of the city's public school system. Never in its history did the Winchester Academy, despite state grants, become a truly public school.[36]

The history of public education in both Kentucky and Clark County pursued an uncertain path before it became a part of the fabric of the political and social systems.[37] A negative fact in Kentucky history must have been those moments when the commonwealth failed to take advantage of promising opportunities. Tragically, this was true in 1820, when much of the rest of the country was organizing public school systems. At that date the commonwealth was beset by a devastating financial crisis; its people were seriously, if not violently, divided politically; property values were greatly reduced; and the levying and collecting of taxes was a near impossibility.[38] This condition in Kentucky prevailed in what for many other states was a seminal period of growth and institutional expansion. This was especially true in the neighboring Old Northwest, where states were organizing public school systems.[39]

Kentucky's legislators in this moment of financial crisis undertook to shunt public social and fiscal responsibilities for the organization of common schools into as painless a groove as possible. The General Assembly enacted legislation setting aside half of the "clear profits" earned by the Bank of the Commonwealth as a literary fund.[40] This law was fraught with failure at the very moment it was being enacted. In order to facilitate the law a special committee was formed, with William T. Barry, the lieutenant governor, as chairman, to make a national survey of public education and to solicit opinions and advice from national leaders. The committee made its report in 1822, and it was blithely filed away with perhaps only a few of the legislators having read it. Certainly, in the political climate prevailing in Kentucky, public education was not a subject of prime interest.[41]

In the decade 1820-1830 other reports were produced which revealed the low state of learning in the commonwealth and advocated the creation of a system of common schools. A group of private individuals kept alive the spark for public schools. In a somewhat less politically emotional moment the General Assembly enacted a basic public school law. The law of 1838 outlined a system of common schools for the state, but did little more. County courts were instructed to organize each county into school districts and to create boards of school commissioners (school boards). A poll tax of fifty

Graduates of the St. Agatha Academy, 1930. This was near the end of the era of the "Sweet Girl Graduate." In dress, facial expressions, and bridal-like wreaths, the young women have more the appearance of being bride's maids, than academics.

cents was to be levied against every white male over twenty-one years of age, and the general property tax levy was to be set at six and a quarter cents of each hundred dollars of assessed property.[42]

In an area quite aside from education, the act of 1830 set a notable social and historical precedent in that it mandated that widows, feme sole, and property-owning infants subject to taxation could vote, "in person or by written proxy; and any infant, residing and owning property, [in Clark County,] subject to taxation for school purposes, shall have the right to vote by his or her guardian." This law, so far as the counties were concerned, was in essence a bit of piety if not sham which was devoid of enforcement authority and left the matter of establishing and financing common schools up to local politically minded politicians to levy taxes on resistant voters.[43]

There is no substantial documentary evidence that the education law of 1838 really had any discernible bearing on the organization of public schools in Clark County.[44] Again, the Clark County Order Books contain no mention of the law or of public schools in the period. The law made no provision for the election of a state superintendent of public education; its application and enforcement were left up to the discretion of the county courts; and no mention was made of any sort of a school curriculum or of teacher qualifications. There was absent from the law the usual pietistic tribute to the taming of the savage heart through education which was such a standard part of the most early nineteenth century education laws.

In Kentucky every aspect of the school law of 1830 was centered upon the tender subject of taxes, and upon the collection and accounting for funds. As the proceedings of the Clark County Court during the decade and a half 1830-1846 reveal, the magistrates were primarily concerned with regulating the erection of gates across the public roads, granting licenses to prospective tavern keepers, locating mill dams, relocating rights-of-way of crooked public roads, occasionally manumitting a slave, naturalizing immigrant citizens, and making improvements to the courthouse and jail.[45]

There may have been some educational implications in the fact that W. Simmons, L. Evans, and Lewis R. Grigsby were ordered by the County Court in October 1843, to present lists of taxable property and to collect the poll tax levy. A year later the sheriff reported that he had collected poll taxes from white males over twenty-one years of age in the sum of $638.50, hardly an amount to build many one-room school houses and employ teachers to staff them.[46]

Annually James Bullock, county clerk, reported that he had collected funds from the sale of "seals" and licenses. In January 1846 he reported that

For many older residents the Washington Street School had profound nostalgic meaning. More important it symbolized advancement in the educational efforts of the City of Winchester. A storm demolished one side of the building forcing a major reorganization of classes in the town.

he had collected $115.00 from the recording of 230 land deeds, $20.00 from imprinting the county seal on notarized documents, $80.00 from the issuance of tavern licenses, an unspecified sum from peddlers and yankee clock salesmen, and fifty-five receipts from owners of stud horses and jacks in the sum of $61.00. It appears on the face of the record that the levying of taxes and the management of fiscal affairs in Clark County in this era were administered in a modest if not casual manner. At the October 1846 term of court the county clerk devoted a full paragraph to noting the fact that it was "ordered by the shff [sheriff] or treasurer of this county to pay to John Williams the sum of 65 cts, the amount of one county levy wrongfully charged to him by the commissioners of tax for the year 1846 as guardian of Ann Williams." Such transactions were reflective of the fact that Clark County, like every other county in the commonwealth, was hardly in a fiscal condition to finance any sizable public undertaking, including a system of universal common school education. Before the counties could embark upon a program of public schools it was necessary to make drastic revisions in the state's educational laws.

A major fact in Kentucky's social history was the crusading effort of a relatively small number of people to bring about the institution of a universal system of common schools. They sought to raise the office of superintendent of schools to the status of a state official, to set minimum standards of teacher qualification, and to devise a rather fluid but standardized curriculum.[49] There

The Hunt School in this photograph of 1904 is of the building which supplanted a log structure on the Winchester and Muddy Run Turnpike. The land on which the building stood was donated by Mrs. David Hampton. It took ingenuity on the part of the two or three teachers to crowd such a large number of children into the small building. This photograph was made more than a decade before Clark County schools were consolidated.

occurred in the closing year of the Jackson presidential administration one of those incidents in American history which had far-reaching influence. The United States Treasury had accumulated a substantial surplus which was turned back to the states. In 1837 Kentucky was a recipient of this windfall in the sum of #1,433,736.[50] The General Assembly agreed that approximately a million dollars of this sum was to be distributed to the counties on the basis of children enrolled in school and as the county courts made request for it. Not only was it Kentucky's good fortune to receive the federal surplus funds, but it was a landmark incident in the state's educational history. Actually the amount of the surplus funds set aside for schools was $850,000. James Clark of Clark County was governor. Measured by several criteria, he perhaps was the most liberal and far-sighted governor to date. His messages to the General Assembly revealed a clear perception of the state's social and cultural needs, and of many of its fundamentally underlying problems. He advocated the creation of a system of public common schools, and figured prominently in the formulation of the major public school law of 1838.[51] Up to this date masses of Kentuckians lived in an abject state of illiteracy. No one at the time had a truly objective notion of this condition. Historically, the old academy approach and the legislative gesture of creating a self-perpetuating literary fund were failures. Neither of these did anything for the masses of Kentuckians.

James Clark was a Virginian by both birth and legal training. He was brought to Kentucky by his parents as an infant. He read law in the office of a Virginia brother, served in the Kentucky General Assembly and in the United States Congress, and was a member of the Kentucky Court of Appeals. Then he served as a judge in the Clark-Bourbon County District. As judge of the latter court he created a major furor in Kentucky politics in the rendering of his decision in the case of *Williams v. Blair*. This case pertained to an attempted breach of contract in the infamous Kentucky Replevin Law. This law was enacted by a headless General Assembly yielding to the presence of suffering debtors rather than observing the constitutional sanctity of contract. In his decision James Clark wrote himself into a footnote at least of American constitutional history.[52] His decision at the state court level sustained the sanctity of contract.

As Governor of Kentucky James Clark's messages were both perceptive of the state of affairs in the commonwealth and literate. On the subject of public education he wrote, "There is another subject; dear to the philanthropist, and more intimately connected with public virtue, and the durability of our form of government, than the superficial observer on the first reflection is aware. It is the subject of Education through the medium of public schools. The dissemination of knowledge, and useful information to all, is demanded by a monitor, that ought not to be disobeyed, or disregarded. The history of all past time proves that ignorance leads to anarchy, and anarchy to despotism. Education is necessary to form the citizen for either military or civil affairs. To maintain and preserve our rights, it is necessary that we should understand them. To appreciate the blessing and advantages of a good government, we should be able to contrast it with those, where licentiousness on the one hand, or oppression on the other, are found to predominate. The best plan for the general diffusion of knowledge, is a matter for your deliberation, if it be deemed advisable to you, to act at this time upon this subject. It is not expected that a great deal can be effected at once, but when a commencement is made, and some regular system is adopted, the benefits resulting from it, will manifest themselves so clearly, that the friends of the measure will have no cause to despair of its success. It is true that a great many schools are scattered over the country [Kentucky], and opportunities offered to a large majority of our citizens to educate their children, but it is at the same time to be remembered, that either through the improvidence or the misfortunes of parents, they are frequently found destitute of the means necessary to send their children to school. It is this class of our population that requires your aid. To the children in this situation, the State ought to stand in the place of a parent, and take them her protecting care."[53]

Governor Clark addressed the House of Representatives on December 4, 1838 giving that body an eloquent analysis of the importance of public education. He told the representatives that in the decade of 1810-1840 there were 146,000 to 175,000 children in the commonwealth who were denied any form of educational instruction. He reported that by competent computation a third of the Kentucky adult population could not read and write. He saw as "the great obstacle to the establishment of common schools, however, not so much the defects of the law as the apathy of the people. No law can be efficient unless the people are impressed with the importance of its execution...."[54] He might well have been standing on the front steps of his home in Winchester talking to his neighbors when he delivered his address.

No historian can say precisely what immediate influence the common

Log jam near Ford in 1906. Literally millions of feet of virgin timber from up the Kentucky River were landed before the Burt-Brabb Mill. - *Photo courtesy of Marjorie F. Lisle*

school law of 1838 had on Clark County. The County Court Order Books do not even mention the word "education," let alone some plan for the creation of school districts, the erection of school houses, and the holding of classes. The magistrates, in the records of their proceedings at least, seemed to have been unaware of the enactment of the school law of 1838. In that year Clark County had a heavy responsibility. Its families were in considerable numbers unusually fecund, some of them having ten to fourteen children. In 1838 the United States Census reported that there were 4,386 white children of school age, or a third of the white population of 12,031 individuals, and the same proportionate numbers prevailed in 1840. Consistently in the decades prior to 1860 more than a third of the population was of school age.[55] No doubt the reports of the Kentucky auditor are grossly unreliable, but for the years 1844-1852 the number of school districts established in Clark County ranged from a low of fourteen in 1844 to a high of thirty-five in 1852. School terms varied, but indications are that they averaged three months. There were, however, school districts which reported sessions ranging up to eleven months. The number of children reported as being enrolled in schools rose from 137 in 1844 to 911 in 1850, and the state distributed money from the sinking fund which ranged from eighty-four dollars to a high in 1850 of $1,450.20.[56] There, however, is a sharp variance between the Kentucky auditor's report and that of the United States Census, with neither being precisely correct. For instance, in 1850 the census reported there were 833 pupils in school in Clark County, and the school fund was reported to be $1,850.[57]

The school law of 1838 gave heed to the philosophical contention that the masses of children in the commonwealth were entitled to a common school education through the lower grades at least. The law corrected the fundamental gap in Kentucky's educational program to date by providing for the appointment by the governor of a superintendent of public instruction. The county courts were mandated to organize school districts "in a convenient number of schools containing not less than thirty or more than 100 children between the ages of seven and seventeen."[58] The courts were also instructed to assess the value of real property in each district for the purposes of levying a school tax. A county school commission consisting of five members was to be created, and this body was to exercise oversight of all funds. The commissioners were to prescribe the length of school terms and to report the number of children enrolled in school. The only mention the law made of teachers was that they were to be appointed at the discretion of the local district trustees. No district was to share in the distribution of funds until a school was organized and a house was provided. District trustees were given the power to select sites for school houses, to erect buildings, and to see after other needs. They were entrusted with setting the pay of teachers, and they were required to take a census and report the number of children living in a district and the number enrolled in school. The mandate contained a potentially self-destructive provision in that taxes were to be voted upon by districts. A poll tax of fifty cents was to be levied on each white male over twenty-one years of age.[59] On the point of taxation Charles A. Wickliffe of Nelson County spoke for the great mass of Kentuckians when he said in the Constitutional Convention of 1849, "I offer no hostility to education in my amendment but I appeal to the zeal I manifested originally in setting apart the sum of $850,000. But I am unwilling to impose the taxation which must be imposed to put this [public education system] in operation in five years."[60]

Clark County conformed with the law of 1838, as documented in the Kentucky auditor's report and the report of the superintendent of public instruction. The first county education commissioners were Dr. Samuel D. Martin, Samuel Wheeler, and R. Cox. Succeeding them was a long list of commissioners who served terms of varying lengths ranging from two to nine years.

The first common schools taught in Clark County were opened in four districts containing 343 children.[61] They were open for one to two months. The first official state superintendent of public instruction to serve under the provisions of the law of 1838 was the Baptist minister Ryland T. Dillard.[62] His reports to the General Assembly were perceptive and comprehensive. He summarized the state of mind which prevailed in both Clark County and Kentucky when he wrote, "that to extend the blessings of popular education over all the mountains, hills and plains of the state is not the work of a day or a year. In the very nature of things, it must be a gradual and progressive work. Ignorance has to be enlightened, prejudice subdued, and the public mind brought up to see the incalculable benefits of such a plan."[63] Dr. Samuel D. Martin, a commissioner of public education in Clark County, could not have spoken more pointedly or eloquently in describing the local attitudes. This fact was borne out in Clark County in 1843-1844, when there were only four school districts containing 343 children, but only 137 children maintained a semblance of school attendance.[64]

At the outbreak of the Civil War the number of school districts in Clark County had been expanded phenomenally to forty-one, with 2,099 children who attended school for varying periods from three to eleven months. However, only 707, or a third of the school-age children, really maintained a reasonably stable period of time in school.[65]

Progress in establishing common schools in Clark County was identical with that for the commonwealth as a whole. The process was handicapped by lack of central county administration of schools; a dependance on the transient and, too often, inadequately prepared teachers; and, always, an inadequacy of physical equipment and financial support. No doubt the most deterrent fact was either resistance or indifference to education on the part of parents. They were products of an age when too many people looked upon education as a waste of time for living in a workaday world. For the county the organization of public schools in conformity to the law of 1838 was a setting of new social and cultural precedents.[66]

The Commonwealth of Kentucky, despite the enactment of three basic educational laws, did not give constitutional sanction to education until 1849, when delegates to a constitutional convention wrote an inadequate section into the new constitution. On December 10, 1849, delegates to the convention engaged in a rather bizarre debate on the subject of common schools. John D. Taylor, delegate from Mason County, reported for the committee on education. The members declared that the commitment on the subject should be, "The diffusion of knowledge and learning among men being essential to the preservation of liberty and free government, and the promotion of hu-

Main building, Kentucky Wesleyan College. This structure was designed by Crapsy and Brown, 1888-1889. It burned in 1905 causing serious damage to the fortunes of the College.

man virtue and happiness, it shall not be the duty of the General Assembly to establish within _____ years next after the adoption of this constitution, and *forever* hereafter keep in existence an efficient system of common schools throughout this Commonwealth, which shall be open to all white children thereof." Taylor advised filling in the blank with "two years," but William E. Preston of Jefferson County suggested "five," a move to kill the report."[68]

Clark County was poorly represented in the Constitutional Convention of 1849 by Dr. Andrew Hood.[69] His name appeared in two instances, one as a member of the committee on the public debt and the other as favoring limiting the power of the state to amass an indebtedness of more than $500,000. He took a leave of absence and only twice more appeared in the record. Dr. Hood took no part in the debate on education, and it is doubtful that he was present in Frankfort in December 1849.[70]

While legislators and delegates to the Constitutional Convention of 1849 debated issues of founding in the Commonwealth of Kentucky a system of commons schools, officials in Clark County were laying out school districts. In 1843-1844 the had established four, and six years later there were thirty-four districts.[71] The number of children within the districts rose from 343 to 2,282. School terms varied, but generally they were of three months duration.[72] In the school year 1850 only 911 children maintained a record of attendance. [73] Quickly the face of Clark County was literally plastered over with the boundaries of local school districts, most of which, perhaps, were indifferently administered by semiliterate trustees. Classes were held in inadequate buildings, and teachers presided over them who were not properly prepared for the task. Many a thoughtful citizen of the county must have agreed with the fiery, crusading Robert Jefferson Breckinridge, who wrote in 1850, "One of the greatest hindrances to the steady improvement of our school system has been its lack of stability. There have been frequent changes in the laws in the past that even the lawyer could not keep up with them. Every new representative in the legislature wants to `introduce a bill', and what is so easy as a school bill? This has been bad, very bad for the schools which of all things needs a steady persistent policy."[74]

The crusading Presbyterian minister and state superintendent of public instruction had abundant reason on his side. There were in neither the state nor the county set policies either as to precedent or history for attaining stated educational objectives. This despite the growing volume of school laws which dodged central issues more so than setting guidelines for an effective educational system. Nevertheless, plans were under way in 1850-1860 for at last establishing a system of universal common schools within the reach of most

The all male Winchester School Board circa 1910. This group was highly representative of the ante-female voting era. As a group they virtually presented a personal facade of the town's business and professional community. - *Photo courtesy of the Winchester Sun*

school-age children.[75]

There reared up great barriers which had to be penetrated, laws or no laws. Teachers were almost universally unprepared for their tasks, schools were ungraded, textbooks were few in number and often unsuitable. Aside from the philosophical attachment to the "three R's," there was no prescribed curriculum beyond reading, writing, and arithmetic. For the most part local district school houses were small, inadequately lighted and heated, and aesthetically shabby.[76] Seating and other equipment was of a "home-made" variety. Dr. Breckinridge was right. In all the enactment of school laws, 1830-1860, there appeared no mature definition of educational objectives beyond a few hackneyed oratorical flights. Legislative and constitutional attention was focused on almost entirely upon the husbanding of school funds and upon not adding fiscal burdens to the tender shoulders of property holders. Above all no law began even to penetrate parental resistance to the enrolling of their children in school and seeing that they maintained suitable daily attendance, even during the short span of three months out of the year.[77]

There is no lack of statistics of sorts, or laws relating to schools in Clark County, but one hunts in vain for first-hand descriptions of what actually went on in the schoolhouses. Perhaps there is tucked away in some obscure attic or trunk a diary or other form of record detailing school experiences prior to the Civil War; if so, none has come to light. The nearest thing to a contemporary observation on the rural common school experience is contained in Julia A. Tevis' *Sixty Years in a School Room: an Autobiography*. She said she walked two miles daily to attend school in a Clark County log school house. She wrote, "The stentorian voice of the master calling out, `Books! Books!' at the sound of which all ran eagerly to their seats, beginning to con over their A. B. C.: to spell, A bit-sel-fa (Aby itself-a), bel, Abel; b-a, ba, k-e-r, baker; c-d-e-r-, der, cider; while class read aloud, `An old man found rude boy' etc; the teacher, meantime passing around the room, rod in hand, encouraging all to `say out' which was done with a will, and without any apparent confusion, because each one minded his own business and not that of another; and it certainly taught the power of abstraction if nothing else."[78]

What Julia Tevis, later to become headmistress of the Science Hill Academy for Girls in Shelbyville, observed in her mellow years was in fact a "blab" cut school. She described a teacher who was part stern disciplinarian, rod in hand, and part instructor in the "three R's." Perhaps at times the scene she pictured occurred at thirty-four district schools across Clark County.

At the outbreak of the Civil War Clark County had embraced the public school concept after a fashion, but with considerable reluctance. There was still a sharp divergence between children reading in a given school district, those enrolled, and those maintaining in a satisfactory daily attendance record. The numerous school districts permitted parents to keep children near home. Financial responsibilities for a three-month school taught in a shabby building employing teachers at poverty level salaries were within the parameters of local control. Despite the meager beginnings and the undefined missions of the rural common schools, the seeds of a mild social and cultural revolution had been planted in both the Kentucky statutes and the minds of its citizens.[79]

Had Robert Richardson, a former Kentucky legislator, in 1869 as superintendent of public instruction reported on the educational progress in Clark County instead of in the commonwealth, he could not have been more precise in describing the status of common school education in the area. he wrote, in his annual report, "Kentucky is prolific, in certain localities. Although due importance is to be attached to it [the differences between the number of children in school districts as reported by county commissioners and those reported by local tax assessors], still this whole number of children reported to the Superintendent is not of itself, a sufficient evidence of our educational advancements. If the idea exists that it is, let us reject it at once, as shallow and delusive. A better proof of the propensity of the schools is to be found in the whole number attending; a better system still than that, in the length of time these schools were taught, and the average number attending throughout the that time. More knowledge is imparted to fifty scholars who have regularly attended six months' school than to three times fifty who have gone, about a fortnight each, to a three months' school."[80] Thus the hand of experience and of prophecy wrote on the tablet, not only of Kentucky educational history but that of Clark County, in the watershed eras between the ante-bellum decades and the rather turbulent ones which closed out the nineteenth century. Clark County in those decades was to experience along with the commonwealth moments of drastic changes and ever raising expectations.[81]

L. C. ROBARDS,

DEALER IN NEGROES,

LEXINGTON, KY.

PERSONS wishing to Buy or Sell Negroes, will, at all times, find a market for them by calling at my *NEW JAIL* a few doors below the "Bruen House" on Short street.

N. B. The highest cash price will be paid for Young and Likely Negroes.

july 2-81-y

Negroes Wanted.

THE undersigned wish to purchased a large number of NEGROES, of both sexes, for which they will

Pay the Highest Prices in Cash.

Office on Main-street, opposite the Phœnix Hotel, and 2d door above the Statesman Office, Lexington.

SILAS MARSHALL & BRO.

March 15, 1859–50–tf

Although Lewis Robards, the notorious slave trader was located in Lexington, he plied his trade in all the bluegrass counties. - *Photo courtesy of J. Winston Coleman*

CHAPTER 11

Life In Thraldom

Clark County prior to 1792 was not only geographically and politically a part of Fayette and Bourbon counties, but also institutionally. During the decades 1792-1865 slavery was inseparably a part of Clark County's human history. The extensive and clear documentary record of this phase of the county's social history is highly descriptive. Human slavery was as relevant to the society and economy of the region as were livestock and field crops. In the matter of numbers Clark County owners had fewer slaves than did those of the mother counties of Fayette and Bourbon.[1]

There possibly exists no note of who brought north of the Kentucky River or up the Wilderness Road or down the Ohio River slaves from older states of Virginia and Maryland. It is an established fact that there were slaves at Boonesborough from the beginning. In fact, there were slaves in Daniel Boone's trailblazing party in 1775; one of them was killed in the surprise Indian raid known as Twetty's Defeat.[2] A more clearly defined historical note of the role of slaves on the Kentucky River frontier were their labors as frontiersmen. Slaves in the unfolding region of Clark County contributed generously to the labors of building cabins and outbuildings, minding livestock, and even helping ward off Indian raids. Historically, the institution of slavery became as firmly rooted in the future Clark County region as homes, Regular Baptist churches, and water driven grain mills.[3]

In a number of instances of Indian attacks against the settlements slaves played significant roles.[4] Historically, Clark County shared the glory of the famous slave Monk of Boonesborough who proved to be an all but indestructible man. There occurred one of those incidents so common on the Kentucky frontier. A war party of approximately twenty-five Wyandottes attacked Strode's Station, killing two men, and they went on to the Kentucky River at a point upstream from Boonesborough. Apparently they accidentally let a canoe get loose, and it floated by the fort as a warning of their presence. In some way the Indians captured Monk and took him with them back to across the woodlands to Little Mount. In the skirmish at that place between Indians and white, Monk cried out to Captain James Estill that there were only twenty-five warriors present, and for the whites to stand their ground. Estill was killed, and James Berry suffered a thigh wound and was unable to travel. The Indians had spooked the settlers' horses, and Monk carried Berry the twenty-five miles through the wilderness to Estill's Station.[5]

In the post-Indian raiding days Monk enjoyed a heroic reputation. He extracted nitre from the guano in Payton's Cave for making of gunpowder, a tremendously important material to the settlers. Wallace Estill, the deceased James' son, manumitted Monk, with a promise of food, clothing, and lodging for life. Later Brown Lee Yates, a member of the Estill family, described Monk as being, "Five feet five inches in height, and weighed about two hundred pounds. He was the husband of three wives, by whom he had thirty children. He was the father of the first colored child, Jerry, born at Boone's Fort. Afterward [Monk was] a preacher in the Baptist church at Shelbyville. He was a respected member, when white and colored lived in the same church together, and broke bread at the same ceremonial table. He was my neighbor for twenty-four years, and died about 1835."[6]

In writing about slavery in Clark County emphasis must be placed on the fact that, first, a definite majority of slave owners in the region owned relatively small numbers. In fact, they owned only one or two family groups. Seldom in the inventories of estates were there listed more than eight or ten slaves at most. The Eighth United States Census Report, 1860, indicated there were the relatively large number of 757 slaveholders in the county. The great majority of these (561) owned from one to eight slaves, 202 owned eight to thirty, and the largest slaveholder owned seventy or fewer.[7]

It is historically significant that surviving buildings in Clark County which are said to have been slave quarters are in close proximity to owner's residences and barns, indicating small numbers of slaves.[8] There are not any hints in the documentary sources that any slaves in Clark County were worked in gangs in a comparable manner to those in the Old Cotton Lower South. There is, however, plenty of evidence that master and slave worked alongside each other at all the tasks associated with farming. Unlike the Cotton South there was not grown in Clark County a single labor-intensive crop such as

cotton, rice, or sugar cane. Even Clark County's major crops of corn, tobacco, hemp, and small grains made variable seasonable demands on field
laborers.[9] In the case of livestock production, slave labor was not of pressing
importance to achieve success. Nevertheless, many Clark County slaves proved
unusually valuable both as caretakers and as herdsmen for the premium-bred
cattle, hogs, sheep, and mules. Dr. Samuel D. Martin of Colbyville operated
his notable livestock and crop production farm by use of slaves. Dr. Martin,
however, was, relatively speaking, a rather small slaveholder.[10]

By inference if not by sound documentation, the black slave was ideally
adaptable to the navigation of produce-laden flatboats. A Kentucky law, however, prevented their use for the specific reason that they might throw off the
shackles of bondage in the interstate travel along the rivers.[11] Always there
was a direct connection between the slaves and the land of Clark County.
With the passage of time, and the passing of original land grant holders, the
landholds grew progressively smaller through the process of estate subdivision among numerous family members. In 1860 there were remarkably few
landholders in the county who owned more than the traditional Virginia
land law basic grant of 400 acres allotted in 1776. From the outset the ownership of a large acreage of land did not necessarily indicate that the owner
had any appreciable part of it in cultivation or really operated it in a true
plantation style of management.[12]

Statistically, at least, it almost seems that there was a competition between whites and blacks as to who could produce the most children. There
was a close correlation between the races in this social area.[13] The ratio of
slaves to whites during the years 1800-1860 remained fairly constant. Phenomenally, there were 1,535 slaves in Clark County in 1800 as compared
with 6,212 whites. A decade later the number of slaves had more than doubled
to 3,768 as compared with 4,550 whites. [14] The subdivision of Clark County
from parts of Fayette and Bourbon counties initially has some bearing on
these numbers. Subsequently, the subdivision of Clark County to form a part
of Estill and Powell counties had a bearing on population numbers.[15] Too,
after 1810, there was appreciable immigration from Kentucky into Indiana,
Illinois, and Missouri, plus some to the expanding Cotton Belt in the Lower
South.[16] Unfortunately there is no documentary evidence of how many immigrants from Clark County were involved in this out-movement. In 1850
there were 7,709 whites and 4,840 slaves.[17] A decade later, and on the eve of
the Civil War, the county's white population numbered 6,598 individuals,
and the slave population was 4,782, a loss of only 78 individuals during the
decade.[18] This latter figure seems to indicate that the interstate slave trade

made only a limited inroad upon the slave population.

At least 95 percent of the slaves in Clark County were engaged in agricultural pursuits. Slaves in the first half century history of the region performed prodigious tasks of hard physical labor in clearing away the forest, building cabins and other structures, and fallowing the land. This is most eloquently revealed in the rapidity with which the woods were cleared away.[19] Too, there is some definitive evidence that a considerable number of slaves were occupied in performing domestic services which consisted of cooking, housekeeping, laundering, gardening, spinning, weaving, knitting, shoemaking, butchering, and child care. The Clark County Order Books contain abundant entries revealing that slaves were often sent in the place of their masters to open and maintain roads. Under the tithe system of managing roads slaves proved exceedingly useful as laborers.[20]

As indicated elsewhere, and in connection with other phases of Clark County's history, the local government operated under the official mandates of the commonwealth's ever-expanding volume of statutory laws regulating slavery. Running through the various legislative acts of the General Assembly there is more than a trace of defensiveness regarding the slave system against a varied assortment of external influences and incidents. This is also true for Clark County. At the state level the issue of chattel slavery was set forth in a law which required local slaveholders to equate their slaves with their real property in the appraisal of estate assets and in the administration of wills. This was done, no doubt, to direct the descent of property. The wording of the law itself has a provocative overtone. It provided that, "All negro, mullato, or Indian slaves, in all court jurisdictions and other places in the Commonwealth, shall be held, taken and adjudged to be real estate, and shall descend to the heirs and widows of persons, departing this life, as lands are directed to descend in and by act of the general assembly entitled, `An Act Directing the Course of Descent.'"[21]

Both the wills and estate inventories in Clark County, up to 1860, reflected the force of the descent and other laws.[22] One other statute relating to the descent of slaves as property or real estate ordered that slaves devised as property in an estate left to a single female heir were to receive special handling. In the instances where a feme sole inherited or owned slaves, they became the absolute property of her husband, who under the law became a feme covert. Fathers making wills in Clark County frequently designated that slaves should be bequeathed to their unmarried daughters and to their widows. In filing reports on estates, court-appointed appraisers listed slaves almost always early in their reports along with the livestock of the estates. They

This is perhaps one of the few if not the only illustration of a Kentucky rope walk. There were rope walks in Clark County. This industry was intimately associated with slavery.

generally described the slaves by sex, age, and, sometimes, physical condition. In many instances the appraisers listed values, or in the cases where they supervised the sale of property they indicated prices paid.[23]

On the surface relationships between the free white population and the black slaves in Clark County appeared to be amicable, with a marked degree of social and spiritual compatibility even though it was a highly patriarchal system. Though the record of slave religious life and church affiliation is hazy, possibly it was an established practice that many slaves followed the religious leadership and convictions of their masters. It seems clear, from the limited documentary information on the subject, that slaves belonged to the same churches, though they sat in galleries or other specially designated spaces.

There exists a highly revealing period of slave church affiliations and decorum in the minutes of the board of deacons of the Regular Baptist Providence Church. This congregation was an offspring of the famous Traveling Church, led across the mountains from Virginia in 1781 by Lewis and Elijah Craig and Captain William Ellis.[24] The Providence contingent was strict in its concepts of moral and social behavior and decorum. The members were reigned up before the board of deacons, charged with their moral and spiritual lapses, and separated from the faith. Nevertheless. there seems to be clear evidence that the congregation was concerned with the spiritual welfare of slaves.

The Providence congregation on June 12, 1792, received in fellowship a black woman named Cisly.[25] Six years later Napper and Dinah, slaves belonging to a Mr. Neales, were received into membership.26 Member Amy, a black woman belonging to Captain William Bush was charged with lying to her mistress.[27] Slave Ambrose was charged with, "Sinful conduct shush (sic) as being concerned with theft," and was separated from the church.[28] It is clear that the Providence congregation misread the statutes of the commonwealth when it concluded that it was illegal for them to allow a slave to preach to the congregation. What the statutes provided were benefits of clergy for slave preachers comparable to those granted white ministers.[29] Later the Providence Baptists consented for George, George G. Taylor's slave, to exercise his gift of exhortation "Among his bretheren as far & as long as is consistent with the master's will & of this state."[30]

In 1808 Joseph Steven's slave Lucy was charged with disorderly conduct and was dismissed from membership in the church. The charge was adultery and other sinful acts.[31] Finally the Providence deacons dealt harshly with Brother Coulter's man Bob when the slave sought a letter of transfer to enable him to join the newly organized Friendship Church. The deacons contended that Bob was seeking to enter spiritual outer darkness because Providence had no religious communication with that congregation.[32] Thus Bob was left suspended spiritually between his master's church and one of his own liking.

Relative to slave associations with white churches there appeared a somewhat puzzling entry in the minutes of the Winchester Town Trustees for November 13, 1835. Without giving an explanation for its action, the town's governing noted that it, "Respectfully suggests that the city's council clerk communicate with each `Denomination of Christians' in the town that when they may devise and authorize the negroes of the said town to occupy either (sic) church for religious purposes, that the board will request the favour of the Elders to select some member of said church to superintend & control such meeting of said negroes."[33] This ordinance was either poorly stated or it may have been enacted because some churches were allowing slaves to use their buildings for holding their own meetings. Some Clark County slaveholders demonstrated genuine interest in the religious development of their people. Some provided in their wills that their slaves be taught well enough to be able to read the Scriptures.[34] There is evidence that master and slave often worshipped in the same service, being separated only in seating arrangements.

Despite some sharing of religious affiliations and spiritual experiences, and much of the general way of life, there runs through the documentary records of Clark County which pertain to slavery a trace of fear and suspicion manifested in such practices as monitoring slave religious services held in white churches, as suggested by the Winchester Town Trustees in 1835. There occurred a public incident in the town which stirred suspicion, if not downright fear. Perhaps there may have been an African folk tradition arising out of some hazy past or just a slave response to some imagined incident. Workers in one of the Winchester ropewalks indulged in an annual celebration of a folk goddess. Each November 23 they went on a holiday honoring "Queen Katharine," a lady apparently of mystic powers. She was revered as the inventor of the art of rope weaving. On the annual November holiday the Winchester slaves paraded through the streets shouting and making other noises. Following the Queen Katharine celebration in 1835 the town trustees adopted an ordinance forbidding future celebrations. The town marshall was ordered to prevent future parades and noisemaking. The ordinance was attested by George Smith, chairman of the board of trustees, and John Ward, town clerk.[35]

The gathering of slaves for any purpose appears to have aroused a certain amount of suspicion and uneasiness. It was feared that if slaves were allowed to parade or assemble they would get out of control. Under the Kentucky statute laws of 1799 and 1814, the county was to lay off the area in as many districts as were necessary and to appoint patrollers. The patrollers were to go through the districts at least twelve hours in each month. "And negro quarters and other suspected places of unlawful assembly of slaves."[36]

Both the city of Winchester and the county of Clark employed patrollers to keep a vigilant eye on slave activities. These officials, of less than prime social standing or warmth of humanity, often resorted to excesses in the performance of their duties. In June 1896, George Washington Brown, an exslave, was interviewed by a reporter from the *Clark County Democrat*. This interview was revealing in that it gave the slave's view of the patroller excesses. Referring to Lieutenant Roger Hanson, Brown told the reporter, "And how I remember when under the Black laws of Kentucky when more than two negroes were considered an unlawful assembly unless they were on their master's premises, and the `Patterrolers' was a holy terror to the black people in and about Winchester, who could not have a dance, party, or picnic or any entertainment without the presence of a white man, presumably to see that such assembly was not for insurrection purposes or to advance the causes of the underground railroad; however, the `patterrolers' claimed their best services was rendered to [what was whimsically called] the Hen Roost Protective Association. [This was a derogatory term concerning the belief that slaves were genetically chicken thieves].

About this time Mr. Roger Hanson made himself very dear to the blacks of Winchester, for whenever they desired to have an entertainment and could get a suitable place to have it that was not a trespass on some gentleman's premises, upon their promises to be orderly, he would chaperon the party, closing in good season. Many was the `possum' and chitterling supper he took with them and always paid for what he got. They begged the honor of treating him, but he would never consent to it, saying it would look too much like receiving pay for his services. He rendered such service when called upon and expressed pleasure in so doing....`Roger Hanson' the Winchester elders delighted in calling him, was a typical Sunday School youth, but as a young man he prevented the `patterroller's from interfering with colored people attending religious services when Moses Martin preached. Moses Martin was a gifted, unlettered preacher, perhaps eloquent beyond his own knowledge. He was a slave in Dr. Martin's farm a few miles west of Winchester. The colored people had no church in town, but by the kindness of Mr. Frank Moss and John Lampton they obtained the basement of the Methodist church and Moses Martin to grace the pulpit. Mr. Hanson was invited to be present as they expected trouble with the `patterollers'. Mr. Roman was filling the office at that time. Mr. Hanson met Mr. Roman near the church and said to him, `Mr. Roman, I wish to speak to you,' and stepping outside, he

The idea of stocks on the public square was a direct Virginia importation and was associated almost altogether with the punishment of slaves, or with their public whipping by the town sargent. There seems to be no record of the Clark County public stocks being used.

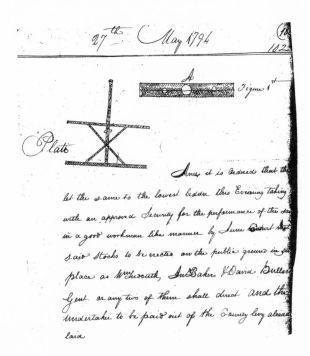

continued, 'I tried to speak to you this afternoon. I wanted to talk to you about your practice of disturbing negroes at their religious meeting. You know you are mistaken in regard to your duties in the premises. The law does not require you to do it, and the trustees did not contemplate it in your own employment, about which I tried to see them this afternoon but failed.' Mr. Roman contended it was his duty to whip any negro he caught after 9 o'clock without a pass which he intended to do after church let up, to which Mr. Hanson replied in these words: 'As you do bear, it in mind one thing my father has twelve servants in there. If you touch one of them I will make you personally responsible as though you had struck me or my little brother.' By prearrangement Roger Hanson and the churchgoers schemed to distract Roman. They pretended a row at Fairfax and Main streets where they would cry: 'Thief! He's got my watch! There he goes.' and Roman broke for the scene and the thief ran over the hill and a half dozen joined Roman in the chase toward the public pond, and the signal for dismissal was given and they all got home safe."[37]

The Winchester Trustees forbade white persons to gamble, play cards, or drink in association with slaves. Kentucky state law, however, permitted master-owners to share liquor with their chattel slaves if they chose to do so. Tavernkeepers and others, however, were not allowed to sell liquor to slaves. If they violated the law, tavernkeepers would have their licenses revoked. They also were subject to fines, and in some cases to jail terms.[38]

Kentucky criminal law was harsh in its application to slaves. No provisions were made for slave offenders to be confined in the state penitentiary. A slave found guilty of murder, arson, rape of a white female, robbery, or burglary was to be put to death. For the commission of, or being accessory to, other and lesser crimes, he or she was to be beaten on the bare back at the public whipping post with up to thirty-nine lashes.[39] Clark County official records make no mention of a rape of a white woman by a slave.

Without doubt the most humanely insensitive and guilt-arousing incidents in the history of Kentucky slavery were the public auctions and sales of slaves. Figuratively at least, "The door of the Clark County Courthouse" was at times an auction block. The interstate slave trade which prevailed in Kentucky during 1815-1864 cast a deep stain of inhumanity on all Kentucky slaveholders. The breakup of families, the presence of slave jails or places of detention, and the physical and psychological indignities imposed on the defenseless victims of many of the sales were in essence insults to the dignity of all Kentucky humanity.[40]

If slavery in a final and objective analysis had any basic economic importance in Kentucky, it ceased to have central importance after 1820.[41] By that date most Clark County lands had been cleared of timber and were in cultivation or pastures. As indicated in connection with the history of agriculture, the pattern of farming was irreversibly formed, and demands for many labor-intensive tasks underwent significant changes. Some Clark County slaveholders found themselves in possession of more slaves, added by family increases, than they could employ usefully.[42] Too, there was in the livestock producing area in the western part of the county need for more responsible types of labor than most slaves could render. Responsive to both internal and external pressures, the institution of slavery for Clark County was never stable.

Though the veil of obscurity on much of the slave history was never fully drawn in Clark County, there remains some historical difficulty in penetrating many phases of the institution. Fortunately, both the basic United States Census schedules and the published statistical data of the Commonwealth of Kentucky do present a revealing perspective of the subject.[43] In contemporary advertisements of the slave traders who operated in Lexington and Paris the name of Clark County does not appear. There may have been an exception to this fact in some obscure journal or lost files of the county's newspapers. Certainly the auctioneers and traders did not announce for publication the names of owners and sellers. The seller of slaves was protected under the law of the commonwealth, a law of long standing, which provided that, "No person selling or alienating any such slave otherwise than by gift, marriage, settlement, deed of trust, or mortgage, shall be obliged to cause such sale or alienation to be recorded.[44]

As the Lower South staple crop areas expanded slave traders became quite active throughout the Kentucky Bluegrass area. No doubt they were able to acquire slaves through private transactions in Clark County or through sales in Lexington. There are early accounts of slave traders driving coffles of slaves along highways. One case in particular received publicity and criticism. Edward Stone of Bourbon County, owner of the famous Greek revival house the Grange on the Maysville Road just outside of Millersburg, ran an advertisement in the Paris newspaper in 1818 that he wished to purchase twenty slave boys and girls, ten to twenty years of age. His classic home was sullied by becoming a symbol of the opening Kentucky slave trade.[45] In September 1822, a contemporary traveler and antislavery proponent saw, "Between seventy-five and one hundred miserable wretches galling under the yoke of despots, doomed to leave their homes, their country and loved ones, rendered dear to them by the strongest ties of nature, from the earliest dawn of life."[46] This was an impressively large number of traded slaves for this early period. Edward

Stone had collected them from a larger surrounding area than Bourbon County. So many times incidents of this nature were cited, and the Lexington papers were read in Clark County.

In his thinly veiled account of life and personalities in Clark County, Thomas N. Allen described two slave incidents which he said he witnessed. He described a mounting block opposite the courthouse which was also used as an auction block for selling slaves. He stood by and saw a slave boy put up for sale in order to settle an estate. Next the boy's mother was placed on the block for the auctioneer to cry her off to the highest bidder. A daughter of the deceased owner bought the mother but exhausted her capital in doing so. In the proceedings the slave mother displayed such intense anguish at the sale of her son that she was able to stir the emotions of a savior. The attending slave traders ran the price for the boy up to twelve hundred and fifty dollars. At this point a benevolent local citizen, called by Allen "The Squire," put up the purchase money. The successful final bidder, no doubt, a front for the squire was "Obe Crewes", maybe Flannigan. Allen wrote, "The auction began and the bids were lively from the start. Those hard-faced `negro traders,' as we call them, contended with one another in the offers, first one of then another bidding on the boy, and at last they ran him up to twelve hundred and fifty. I turned and saw, somewhat to my surprise, that it was Obe Crewes, for I supposed Obe already had all the servants he needed at his tavern. The negro traders quit bidding and the boy was knocked down to him.

"That night he told me how he came to attend the sale and make the bid. He said that for years he had bought butter and eggs from the old mother, who marketed them from her master's little farm in the country, and that she was such a kindly, good old negro he couldn't resist her appeal to him to buy her boy when she hurried down to the tavern and told him her troubles. He also said the Squire was present when he came and heard what she said and immediately became interested.

`Go Obe,' said he, `and buy him in. If you need any money let me know.'

`Spose,' replied Obe, `them dam nigger traders run him on me out of all reason?'

`You buy him,' said the Squire, `if you have to pay more for him than you think him worth. I'll take him off your hands."[47]

Thomas N. Sanders described a second slave sale when a grown slave man was put up for sale on the courthouse mounting block. In this case he was being sold by the county itself because he had become a chronic community rogue and general nuisance. "George," said Allen, "had such a notorious reputation that no local slaveholder would buy him. He was left a sure victim of the slave traders to be bought and sent to the southern cotton fields, this `George' knew." The slave was able to simulate a violent fit by rolling his eyes and slobbering. When a trader asked him what was wrong, George told him that he had fits. This ended the auction, and Allen said Winchester's notorious rogue was led off to live a far more comfortable life in the Clark County jail than in a steamy Mississippi Delta cottonfield.[48]

For most Clark County slaves their fortunes were intertwined almost inseparably with those of their masters, in both their health and their fortune. When an owner died his slaves were left largely at the mercies of the court-appointed estate appraisers, provisions of wills, the whims of heirs, and the state law of the commonwealth.[49] As decades transpired the Kentucky laws pertaining to slavery grew more voluminous. From 1792 to 1865 all of the laws pertaining to the institution had some kind of bearing upon Clark County. As indicated earlier, much of the sale of slaves was obscured in secrecy by force of the law.[50]

Not only were there anxieties and a generous trace of guilt about the slave trade, but there was the matter of dealing with the freedmen. By the latter years of the first decade of the nineteenth century there arose a fear in Kentucky that freed slaves from Pennsylvania, Maryland, and Virginia were being encouraged to go to Kentucky. There was concern that they would stir unrest among the state's slaves. This was especially true of freedmen who came from Pennsylvania and its Quaker spirit of opposition to slavery. In legislating against the entry of freedmen to Kentucky the General Assembly seemed to be incensed by the notion that the state was being abused as an escape region for freedmen. The preamble to the rather extensive law enacted on February 23, 1808 decreed, "Whereas it is represented to the present general assembly, that a very serious evil is likely to be produced by the emigration of emancipated slaves from different parts of the Union to this state, and that many of the states have passed laws compelling slaves when emancipated by citizens of their respective states to remove out of such state within a given time." The given time was twenty days. The freedmen had to raise a $500 bond to insure his departure. If he failed to do so he could be ordered to be sold into one year of slavery by the county court.[51]

One of the first cases, if not actually the first, was brought against Samuel Oats, a Virginia freedman who had migrated to Clark County. He was detected and brought before the county court on the charge he had overstayed the period of grace. Charges had been brought against him by jailer John

The celebration of the mythical queen Katherine's day no doubt raised fears of an organized slave uprising.

McMeacham. When Oats was unable to raise the $500 bond, he was ordered sold back into slavery for a period of one year.[52]

In February 1860 there occurred in Clark County one of those heart-rending incidents which so bitterly damned slavery. There came into the county court Adam Abbott, a free man of color who sought authority to emancipate his wife and children. He was supported in his petition by Dr. Thomas H. Robinson, "A gentleman of honestly, probity, and well known as such by this court." They sought the emancipation or manumission of Harriett Abbott, the slave wife purchased by Andrew Taul. Harriett was described as being forty years of age, of bright yellow complexion, good looking, having a scar above her left eye, and missing a front tooth. Adam Abbott also brought into court his son Bazil, the child of Harriett, for judicial inspection. The boy was described by the court clerk as being four years old, of a bright yellow complexion, and with a scar on the right side of his upper lip. There was also a three-year-old daughter, Evaline, who also had a bright yellow complexion, was good looking, and possessed gray eyes. There was a fourth person, Anthony, apparently Adam Abbott's son by another woman, who had been purchased from Mrs. Evaline Abbott. He was described as being twenty years of age, standing five feet six inches tall, of a dark color, and badly crippled. The Clark County Court granted Adam Abbott certificates of manumission for the four members of his family.[53]

Possibly the last slave sold in Clark County of record was a man named Mat who had belonged to George W. Razor, then deceased. Mat was detected as a fugitive by William P. Allen and turned over to Sheriff Samuel M. Stuart to be sold as a slave at the courthouse door to the highest bidder. This was in May 1865, when an investment in a slave was a serious aberration of judgement. John H. Boone bought Max for $66.66. When no one came to the sheriff's office to claim the money, the county clerk, after subtracting court costs, turned over to William P. Allen $40.33 for spotting Mat and his keep. Time, however, in that late day in 1865 was on Mat's side. The Thirteenth Amendment to the United States Constitution set him free. He was placed beyond the reach of Sheriff Stuart and the county court. John H. Boone made a bad investment, and Mat could wander the roads of Clark County without fear of being apprehended.[54]

Inscribed in the Clark County Court order books is a veritable litany of slave affairs. Regularly there came before that body persons of color either seeking certificates of manumission or being awarded their freedom by their masters. The clerks of court were punctilious in recording the physical appearances, scars, and physical defects of the supplicants. None of the entries, however, give much if any hint of the backgrounds of individuals being emancipated or make notations of their future plans to fit into the county's social and economic system. There is more than a suggestion in many of the physical descriptions of miscegenation. Almost a majority of the physical descriptions bear a notation "bright yellow" of color.[55]

Occasionally masters of Clark County slaves expressed warm affection for particular slaves in their wills. Masters facing the inevitable termination of their lives wrote into their final legal testaments that certain of their slaves were to be granted freedom. In some instances Clark County slaveholders sought freedom for slaves for a variety of reason, most important of which was tender and attentive service.[56] The historian is obligated to note the fact that in many instances there was emphasis placed upon the descriptive adjective "bright yellow," which may have had important bearing on the reason for seeking from the county court certificates of manumission. The county court all but confirmed this fact in its entries in the official order book.[57]

In 1841, John Strode appeared in court and sought certificates of emancipation for his slave Frank. The clerk described Frank as being thirty-six years of age, five feet and six inches tall, of "common" size, with a scar on his left chin, and of a bright yellow color.[58]

Seven years later John Randolph, a man of color, was granted a certificate of manumission from Isaac Stepp and Ed H. Parrish. John was six feet and one inch tall, weighed 160 pounds, and was a bright-colored mulatto. An unusual petition for freedom was made by Matilda Wornall in May 1850.

She sought certificates of freedom for five light-colored mulatto children who were said to have been born of free parents. In order to issue the necessary certificates of freedom, the court required that their physical descriptions, ages, and color be made a matter of formal records. These children were said to be both the children and grandchildren of Matilda Wornall.[59]

In 1853, James Lewis, a free man of color, came to court bringing with him a pillar of security, Dr. Samuel D. Martin. The court clerk noted that Dr. Martin was "Especially known to this court." James Lewis' free status was affirmed by certification.[60] There were other cases, many of them. Some were of an unusual nature. Moses Robinson, a free man of color, came before the court seeking the emancipation of his enslaved wife Emily and their children, Sarah and Dickenson. Emily was described as black, standing about five feet eight inches tall, twenty-seven years of age, and above a common size. Her daughter Sarah was of light color, three feet four inches tall, about six years of age. The son Dickenson was said to be about three months of age, bright yellow color, healthy looking, and of common size. At the same time John Bristow sought emancipation for Sarah Jane, a "Girl of color." She was described as being nineteen months of age, light black of color, not very short, two feet four inches tall. For some unstated reason this infant was granted a certificate of emancipation before she had reached an age of realization.[61]

One of the most dramatic instances of the humane aspect of slave fortunes was that involved in the management of the estate of the underage Mary C. Wilhoit in 1861 and 1862. She was under the guardianship of Jacob Hughes. Mary was a lady of material substance; she owned 359 acres of land and sixty-three slaves. Most of the latter were hired by various persons, including Charles French, Isaac Stipp, James M. Sphar [sic], John T. Webb, and others. Hughes retained for Mary's personal use her slave Bob and his wife and children. The appraisers of her property noted that after the hiring out of slaves there was a residue of individuals. There were Caroline and four children, Harriett with six children, Charles, Linny, and Charity; in all sixteen individuals whom the appraisers listed as worthless. A creditor, Colonel John L. Wilhoit, maybe an uncle, laid claim to a man named Littleton, a claim which was disputed. In all the hirings and other disposals of her slaves, Mary Wilhoit received only $160.00. The majority of her able-bodied slaves were hired to neighboring people at less than a hundred dollars each per year.[62]

It was an astonishing if not unrealistic fact in the social and economic history of Clark County that there were people in the middle of the Civil War, and on the eve of Abraham Lincoln's Emancipation Proclamation, still willing to pay anywhere from $200 to $800 for slaves. This was the case in the appraisal of James Thomson's slaves on September 24, 1864. A year earlier Hugh McDonald, Isaac Stipp, and William R. Duncan appraised the slaves held by underage William I. Risk.[63]

The end of the Civil War left Clark County with approximately 4,000 ex-slaves. This fate was predicated after 1863 by the issuance by President Abraham Lincoln of the Emancipation Proclamation and by the successes of the Union Army. The record does not indicate that the political and public leadership recognized that it was only a matter of brief time before their source of slave labor would be disrupted. When general emancipation occurred no phase of the county's social and economic life was left untouched by the fact. During most of the latter war years it seems certain some local slaves were recruited into the Union Army.[63] There appeared a note in the court order book of a slaveholder who sought pay for the services of his recruited slave.[64] Approximately 29,000 Kentucky slaves were said to have enrolled in the military service, and as late as 1866 there were complaints that black soldiers were committing criminal acts. Statistical information about the presence of slavery in Clark County is abundant in will and order books, reports of the Kentucky auditor, and the schedules of the various decennial censuses. Even the minutes of the Winchester Town Council reflect many of the facts of local slavery. Lacking, however, is descriptive information about the day-to-day lives of slaves. Exactly what routine of labors did they live by? Did it vary from that of their masters' families? Some substantial physical documentation has survived in the form of slave quarters which stand near some of the older homes in the western part of Clark County.

Fortunately some material information seeps through in the meticulous accounts of the ubiquitous Dr. Samuel D. Martin. He seems to have been obsessed with the matter of keeping records. His "Sundry Accounts" book contains a mixture of medical, livestock, farming, financial, and slave notations. Frequently he noted making medical calls to treat slaves who were suffering from various diseases. He may even have performed dental extractions and obstetrical services for them. In the case of his own slaves he bought books and shoes for them in October 1861, and he paid tavern bills for Negroes.[65]

In August 1862 Dr. Martin drove to Lexington, where he bought materials to make slave clothing. He purchased fifty-eight yards of jeans, twenty-seven yards of linsey, and forty-three yards of broad cloth for which he paid a total of $69.63. In July 1864, and near the legal end of slavery, Dr. Martin purchased in Lexington shoes and boots for both men and women. He also bought linsey for woman and children, and jeans and coarse cotton cloth to make clothing for men. In all he spent $354.00.[66]

There seems to linger a tradition that Dr. Martin freed his slaves. Nothing in his "Sundry Accounts," his will, or the census schedules sustains this belief. In May 1862, he received a slave named Fanny and her children in payment of a mortgage by J. A. Jackson which he in turn gave to his daughter Elizabeth. This transaction was flawed by the confusion that Jackson thought he owned the slaves, when in fact they were owned by his wife. In December that year in a mortgage foreclosure by a man named Nelson and wife, Dr. Martin acquired John, valued at $489; Lewis, $350; Frederick, $300; Ann and children, $325; and Dicey, $1.00. In November and December that year he paid two dollars for handbills advertising the foreclosure of a mortgage and paid Bush ten dollars for the sale of Negroes. He also paid to the *Lexington Observer and Reporter* and three other printers two dollars for slave handbills.[67]

Dr. Martin made no mention of slave diet, a subject which is so prominently noted in the treatment of slavery in the Lower South. In none of the sources is this subject mentioned. Thus it surely must be assumed that slaves, like their rural Clark County masters, depended for food almost altogether on the products of the land and pastures.[68]

In the absence of specific documentation of the fact, many Clark County slaves no doubt achieved their release from servitude by being granted Palmer's Passes to travel anywhere they chose, principally out of the state. An almost overwhelming number of blacks descended upon the military post at Camp Nelson on the Kentucky River. General J. M. Palmer, a native of Scott County and an immigrant to Illinois, was in command of the Kentucky District. He was deeply opposed to slavery and undertook to hasten its end by his generous distribution of passes. Camp Nelson was a center of the black military contingent. In 1864 there were 1,500 colored troops stationed there. At the end of the war the number of black troops had expanded to 5,000.[69]

Camp Nelson at the end of the war not only was a major black military base, but it was overrun by women and children refugees, many of them no doubt from Clark County. In November 1864 General Speed Fry had attempted to deal with the camp follower problem by sending the women away, and, in some cases, having women whipped. By April 1865 there were in the camp 1,600 newly freed women and children, and it was predicted that 6,000 would soon arrive.[70]

Back in Clark County there was not only the problem of freedom but also a political problem which developed around the polling places. There was an interference with white voting in some of the precincts. Among these

There were no provisions for the imprisonment of slaves. Their punishment was physical as indicated in this Winchester City Ordinance running horses up and down the town's streets.

were the Germantown, Gordes, Princeton, and Blue Ball voting places.[71] In all of these precincts elections were declared void because the radicals and ex-slaves had proscribed names of traditional voters. A reporter for the *Lexington Observer and Reporter,* November 8, 1865, summed up perhaps with some dependable insight when he wrote of the Bluegrass area as a whole. he said that labor had become scarce and wages were increased. "Few ex-slaves," he wrote, "were left at home and farmers generally, and many residents of cities and towns were suddenly left without their accustomed and necessary help, the long established system of labor terribly disturbed, and citizens excited almost to revolution."[72]

Well could the white population of Clark County, in 1865-1866, have joined Governor Thomas E. Bramlette in his lament over the problems of racial readjustments. The governor, in his address to the General Assembly on December 5, 1865, asked pleadingly, "What is to become of the Negro?" He answered his Socratic question by saying, "This will be solved by time and the natural laws of governing population and labor. The question if let alone, will solve itself; or, rather, the future will suggest a proper solution. The question of what shall become of him, constitutes neither an objection nor an argument against the proposed Thirteenth Amendment. He will be free; what more, the future must develop." [73] This was a master statement of ambivalence in the face of a biting social, political, and economic challenge. The people of Clark County were soon to discover this fact when they came to deal with the aftereffects of emancipation of the slaves and the presence of freedmen in the area.

In keeping with the shape of the problem which Governor Bramlette so skillfully dodged, the courts, the school system, and the labor demands had to make some realistic readjustments after 1865. This fact was eloquently documented by the entries in both the order books of the Clark County Court and the journal of the Winchester Town Council. There came into the county court, sitting in its capacity in chancery, in 1866 a considerable number of cases of colored children almost in their infancy who had been abandoned. Such a predicament was that of Alice, a child of color, who was three years of age in June 1866. She was bound out to Miss Alice Thomas until she reached the age of eighteen years. Miss Thomas was obligated by the court to instruct the child in the art of housework.[74]

The 1866 terms of the county court saw a veritable procession of children who were left abandoned by the act of freeing the slaves. There came Wood, Ish, Jane, Miles, Jesse, Sam, and Ruth, younger children of color whom the court bound out to Benjamin B. Groom. The girls were apprenticed to Groom to be taught the art of housekeeping until they were eighteen years of age. The boys were to be taught the art of farming, were to be bound out to their guardian until they were twenty-one years old. Thus the court in numerous other cases solved the problem of child desertion, but no doubt created a new form of involuntary servitude in doing so.[75]

For Clark County the end of the Civil War, the freeing of the slaves, and the high emotions created by radical opportunistic politicians created a historical watershed. This moment in national history opened up a new era in American bi-racial relationships in a free and open society. True to Governor Thomas Elliott Bramlette's murky predictions, the future created new problems and prompted responsible solutions in the fields of education, labor relations, political realignments, and every other area of bi-racial human relationships. In some respects the history of slavery in Clark County was a mixed one which was balance between being a form of benevolent patriarchialism and the elements of the harshness of chattel slavery within the context of a local cultural, labor, and economic agrarian society.

Joel Tanner Hart, sculptor of a bust of Cassius M. Clay, busts of Henry Clay, John
Jordan Crittenden, Andrew Jackson and others. His masterpiece was Woman
Triumphant which was destroyed in a Fayette County courthouse fire. - *Photo courtesy
of the Winchester Sun*

CHAPTER 12

The Golden Harvest

In all of Kentucky's numerous counties none has woven a tighter web of provincialism and sentimental attachment about its people than has Clark County. For two centuries its people have reflected the impacts of physical environment, of economy, and sociological forces stemming up from the land. Here in this fertile region of such wide human diversities, authors, artists, and poets should have been inspired to creation. The province of Clark County has ever been hospitable to its inhabitants; generation after generation the natural setting has exerted strong sentimental influences in the shaping of the human psyche, destinies, and fortunes.

There lie, largely dormant, a veritable informative mine of historical materials which portray the mores of a developing rural-agrarian society. Consistently official statisticians have revealed that Clark County has ever been populated by American born ancestral stock.[1] Since that date when the Bush colony was planted in the domain-sized land claim along Lower Howard's Creek native-born families have thrived and extended themselves in succeeding generations. Out of this matrix of kinships have sprung creative men and women who escaped the shell of provincialism to make significant contributions in the field of the refining arts. Among them have come artists, writers, historians, poets, and educational leaders. Just as the sprawling bluegrass pastures of western Clark County offered up livestock animals of proud ancestry and worth, the same region has sent forth sons and daughters who made brilliant contributions to American civilization itself.

In its more than two centuries of existence the "Little Kingdom" of Clark County became the birthplaces, and, in a few cases, the homes of individuals who were imaginative and creative in the fields of the arts and letters. It must, however, be observed at the outset that more emphases should be attached to birthplace than to residences of creation.[2] Doubtless there were fundamental underlying reasons why this was so. The county never spawned a prominent portrait painter of the stature of Matthew Harris Jouett, or a novelist of the caliber of James Lane Allen, or a major poet such as Robert Penn Warren, with the exception of Allen Tate. No journalist comparable to Albert Gallatin Hodges came from the region. In several capital instances artists, authors, and poets who were born in the county left in their infant or adolescent years to become productive elsewhere.

The Clark County system of common schools, like those all across Kentucky, was too slow in maturing to inspire authorship or artistic talents in the earlier decades of regional history.[3] The various religious faiths, in the earlier years, were highly conservative, often frowning upon some of the arts such as the theatricals, and, no doubt upon the novel. It seems reasonable to assume from the various documentary records that life in Clark County flowed on from day-to-day with a high degree of complacency with the productivity of the land, and with the sobering tempo of rurality itself. The land presented altogether different challenges from those of the creative arts.

In search for primary sources of information about Clark County there did not come forth personal diaries, bundles of family letters, and other materials which would give an insight into the history of the county in various periods. Dr. Samuel D. Martin did keep an account of weather conditions, farming activities, and medical records of his patients, all mixed in together.[4] There are a few first-hand biographical vignettes, but few or no full scale biographies. No local historians wrote and published books comparable with Robert Peter's *History of Fayette County*, or Benjamin Cassedy's early *History of Louisville*.[5] When Richard H. Collins revised his father's *History of Kentucky*, and added a second volume containing county sketches, Judge William M. Beckner, D. J. Pendleton, and James Flannagan submitted the Clark County entry which was made up largely with a biographical sketch of George Rogers Clark. There were two notations about James Flannagan's family. The text contained a brief geographical reference, and a listing of legislators from the county. One could read this historical note and be almost oblivious as to the rich history of the region.[6]

Clark County and the town of Winchester were off the routes of the "grand tours" of the eighteenth and first half of the nineteenth centuries.[7] As described elsewhere, no domestic or foreign visitor came this way to make observations, take notes, and go away and publish a travelogue. No prospector who came west to seek out a landhold on which to plant an immigrant settlement visited the area east of Lexington. In some ways this was a loss even though most of the travel accounts of the era were thin and superficial. No foreign observer figuratively held up a literary mirror for the natives to view themselves as seen through alien eyes.

Few if any of the local ministers kept and published journals describing the social and religious condition of their congregations. Those who did publish something were nearly always concerned with doctrinal and theological matters rather than their parishioners. Of all the contemporary figures who might have recorded exciting personal journals were the flatboatmen who drifted south from Boonesborough and the mouth of Lower Howard's Creek. Some flatboatmen from other areas did keep such a journal.[8] An account of the return of the Clark County boatmen over the Natchex Trace through two Indian nations, and on the road north from Nashville would have been one of high adventure. If there was published a novel with a Clark County setting it did not find its way into the listings of the several books dealing with Kentucky's literary history.

A cardinal source of pride among Clark County people has been the proud fact of their pioneering forbears, and of the exciting experience of their entering into the "Western Eden" which held for them both unbridled joys and tragedies. To claim descent from one of the early pioneering family has long been akin to claiming royal descent itself.[9]

If there ever was a local spot in North America where artists, writers, poets, musicians, and historians could find ample grist for their creative mills it surely would have to include Clark County. If this area of diverse geography, social strata and relationships, and self-containment did not yield the raw but rich materials, none in Kentucky did so. After all is said about literary and artistic development of Clark County, or a lack of development, there was a positive side. Clark County produced some highly skilled artists, writers, and craftsmen. In the case of many of the native sons and daughters who achieved eminence in their fields, they went outside the county to do so. Some of the more notable ones had humble beginnings, but in time overcame, if they did not capitalize, on the fact. In nearly every instance the creative men and women had direct ancestral connections with one or several of the earliest pioneering families who reached the county before the close of the eighteenth century.[10]

One of the first truly talented native born Clark County sons to gain fame as an artist was Joel Tanner Hart. Like most of the subsequent creative sons and daughters, Hart developed his art and spent his mature years outside the county. For a budding sculptor there was not available an instructor in the art of stone carving, or the quality of stone needed to create a finished piece of sculpture. Even so there did exist some contributory advantages, one being an attachment to the land.[11]

Joel Tanner Hart was born February 10, 1810, into a family living on the raw frontier. He arrived in this world in an era when Henry Clay, Richard M. Johnson, and hosts of other Kentuckians were agitating for a war with Great Britain.[12] Too, 1810, was a year of booming prosperity for many Kentuckians, but not for the Hart family. Joel Tanner Hart's father was Josiah and his mother was Judith Tanner Hart. Both were members of the earliest pioneering families in the area. The Harts were settled on Constant Creek in a three-room log cabin, the birthplace of their son. Like his pioneering neighbors Josiah Hart was engaged in land surveying, farming, and engaging in the flatboat trade in farm produce and slaves down river to the Lower South. He operated in partnership with a man named Rochester, and as a member of the Hart, Rochester, and Company. In 1803 Hart and Rochester loaded a flatboat with tobacco, flour, and other farm products, and several slaves to be sold south. When the ladened boat drifted out of the Mouth of the Lower Howard's Creek with Rochester in command, it embarked on a voyage of no return. Neither Rochester nor the boat and its cargo were ever heard from again. Rochester may have fallen victim to boat wreckers and river pirates, to storm, or some other disaster. More probably, however, he reached New Orleans and sold the cargo and slaves and vanished into obscurity at the moment of the high political situation in that country. He arrived in New Orleans no doubt at approximately the moment the United States completed negotiations for the purchase of Spanish Louisiana. Whatever Rochester's fate was the loss of income from the shipment left Josiah Hart bankrupted, and left his family in dire economic straitened circumstances.[13] In time the family moved to various places to live, once to a place on Ecton Road, then to one on Morris Pike. The fortunes of the Hart family were further straitened, 1800-1820, not only by the loss of the flatboat cargo, but by the inflation which preceded the War of 1812, and the great panic of 1819.[14]

During Joel Tanner Hart's formative years educational development in Clark County was in a primitive foundling stage. Hart received only three months formal schooling, hardly enough for him even to learn the alphabet and numbers to say nothing of learning to read and write.[15] Such information and education as he acquired came from exercising an active mind and self-study and disciplining. By good fortune Hart was given access to some books owned by Phillip B. Winn of Clark County, and later, when he moved

Homer Ledford, teacher, folk musician, and expert dulcimer maker. Ledford has earned a national reputation as a master craftsman and musician. - *Photo courtesy of the Winchester Sun*

to Bourbon County to board in the home of F. W. Houston, there were books available to him.[16]

Whatever Joel T. Hart's interest in books might have been, early in his life he exhibited a talent for carving figures from wood, and in stone work. He also developed an aptitude for drawing. Early in his life he began working with stone, mostly in the business of building chimneys, rock fences, and laying structural foundations. In Hart's Bourbon County interlude he learned something of cabinet-making.[17]

Almost ironically Joel T. Hart, at the age of twenty-two years, was employed to teach school in Nicholas County. Because of ardent self-study and practical experience he doubtless was as well, or maybe better prepared, than were other teachers in that county. It was not the classroom, however, which captivated the young teacher. He was spurred on by the urge to work with stone and develop the art of carving or sculpturing. In Clark, Bourbon, and Nicholas counties he had no opportunity to associate with more creative stone workers. Using his own imagination, Hart carved wood likenesses of George Washington, Andrew Jackson, and Henry Clay.[18] Clay especially caught his eye and imagination, and throughout the rest of his life he engaged in creating images of the Kentucky statesman.[19]

Joel T. Hart moved to Lexington in the panic-stricken year of 1833 when asiatic cholera raged in the town, taking a considerable number of lives.[20] That November Henry Clay had returned to Washington and Congress after being defeated for the presidency the year before. Nevertheless his presence was deeply felt in Lexington. Joel T. Hart found employment with Patrick Doyle who operated a marble yard. Later it became the property of M. Pruden. This marble yard filled orders for all sorts of stone work ranging from the fashioning of door sills, marble mantels, down spout drains to tombstones. Here Hart learned something of carving images into stone, of designing, and the nature and texture of marble.[21]

Fortunately when Joel T. Hart arrived in Lexington there was present Shobal Vail Clevenger the Cincinnati sculptor. Clevenger was there to make a cast for the sculpturing of a bust of Henry Clay. Clevenger was the first true stone sculptor who Hart came to know. He was inspired by Clevenger's technique and methods of design and work.[22] As a result he tried his own hand at creative sculpturing, creating a bust of young Richard Farthing of Winchester. Encouraged by the favorable comment this bust engendered Hart was inspired to adventure into even more challenging areas of the art. He was commissioned to create a bust of Cassius Marcellus Clay. In 1838 Clay had only recently moved from Madison County to Lexington, and at the moment was in a hiatus in his political career. He had been defeated in a rowdy campaign for the office of legislator from Madison County. The issue of the campaign centered around Clay's attitude toward slavery. In Lexington he was on the eve of a campaign to return to the Kentucky General Assembly.[23] Hart's bust of the young and vigorous Cassius M. Clay established the fact that he did in fact have genuine creative talent. This work was to have opened a broad career vista to future success as a sculptor. The Clay bust fortunately has survived changes in ownership, and is now on display in the special collections division of the Margaret I. King Library in the University of Kentucky. It portrays a man of strong will power, as well as a handsome face.[24]

The Clay bust was to launch Joel T. Hart's artistic career. Cassius M. Clay paid him $500 for the bust, and a generous commendation for his art.[25] The popular Kentucky portrait painter Oliver Frazer gave Hart substantial encouragement. As a result of his initial success Hart was commissioned by the Kentucky Friends of General-President Andrew Jackson to create a bust of the aged hero. Jackson had just retired from the presidency of the United States and was in ill health. He agreed to sit for Hart, and welcomed him to the Hermitage in Nashville. The bust turned out well and it pleased the ancient Jackson. He wrote, "Mr. Hart may be ranked with the best artists of the age."

Other commissions followed in somewhat rapid succession. Hart executed busts of local Kentuckians, among them Judge Thomas Hickey of the Fayette Circuit Court, John Jordan Crittenden, Robert Wickliffe, James Taylor, Henry Clay, and Alexander Campbell.[26] By 1845 he had achieved sufficient experience, confidence, and local fame to prompt him to venture out into the more sophisticated realm of American art. That year he set out from Lexington to exhibit his bust of Cassius M. Clay to be exhibited in the National Academy of Design display in Philadelphia, then the American Art Center. Hart and the Clay bust arrived in Philadelphia too late to be entered in the Academy's regular exhibit program. The influential John Sartain engraver, publisher, and editor of *Sartain's Magazine* interceded and the Clay bust was placed on exhibit.[27]

Joel T. Hart's visit to the East Coast and his meeting with artists in the influential art center of Philadelphia and in New York, Baltimore, and Richmond forged yet another link in his burgeoning career. There prevails a certainty that this journey marked a turning point in his career. In Richmond, Virginia, the Ladies Henry Clay Association commissioned him to execute a full length statue of Henry Clay, a commission which led to others.[28]

In keeping with a nineteenth century American artistic tradition, Joel T. Hart planned a visit to Italy where he would come into association with both the ancient art of sculpturing, and with contemporary artists then in residence in Florence. Too, in the latter city he would be near a source of virgin Carraran marble, so necessary to the creation of finished sculpturing.[29]

Joel Tanner Hart departed Lexington, bound for Florence, Italy on September 20, 1847, a date which essentially marked the end of his Kentucky phase of development.[30] Unhappily his model casting of the Clay statue, one of two, was lost at sea, causing for Hart an agonizing delay until the second model could be shipped from Kentucky.[31] In the meantime he worked at inventing a pantograph type of instrument which promised to greatly reduce the time required of a sculptor to measure and reproduce the contours and other features of a subject. Basically the instrument was designed to enable a sculptor to execute with greater exactitude of features.[32]

In Florence Hart had an opportunity to form a friendship with Hiram Powers, the American sculptor of the "Greek Slave." They had much in common. They both grew up poor in their childhoods, both had been influenced by Shobal Vail Clevenger of Cincinnati, and both were self-made artists.[33] When the second Henry Clay model arrived in Florence Hart set to work creating the statue for the Virginia Ladies Association. The statue was finished in 1859 and was shipped to Richmond to be placed in front of the Virginia Statehouse. Hart came home to be present at the dedicatory ceremony in Richmond, and later to visit his family and friends in Clark County.[34] He was warmly welcomed back in Kentucky. Governor Beriah Magoffin gave a state dinner in his honor in Lexington at which Cassius M. Clay was the after dinner speaker.[35]

Officials of Jefferson County commissioned Joel T. Hart to execute a copy of the Richmond Clay statue to be placed in their courthouse.[36] In 1874 the Kentucky General Assembly commissioned him to create busts of Henry Clay and Andrew Jackson to be placed in the statehouse.[37] Hart's crowning achievements, however, were the graceful statues of *Il Pensorosa* and *Woman Triumphant*. *Il Pensorosa* has survived and is on display in the Special Collections division of the Margaret I King Library in the University of Kentucky.

Joel Tanner Hart died in Florence, Italy, March 4, 1877, leaving his masterpiece *Woman Triumphant* not quite finished. His assistant George H. Saul finished the piece and it was sold to Tiffany and Company of New York City. Later it was purchased for $5,000 by an association of Lexington women and it was placed in the rotunda of the Fayette County Courthouse.[38] A fire that destroyed that structure also crushed and destroyed *Woman Triumphant*, on May 14, 1887.[39]

The Commonwealth of Kentucky, at the instigation of Thomas G. Stuart, a legislator from Clark County, appropriated $12,000 to exhume and bring Joel Tanner Hart's remains home from Italy.[40] In June 1887 in an elaborate internment ceremony in the Frankfort Cemetery Hart was buried in a place of honor. Judge William M. Beckner of Winchester delivered the memorial address, and James Flannigan of Clark County was an honorary pall bearer.[41] From the plebeiaan trade of building rock chimneys, laying door sills, and carving tombstones, Joel Tanner Hart developed into a master sculptor. He as much as any pioneer in Clark County realized the great American dream of success.

Contemporary with Joel Tanner Hart and progress to achieving an artistic career, Julia Hieronymous Tevis on Lower Howard's Creek laid the intellectual groundwork for a lifetime of intellectual achievements. Buried in the

pages of her voluminous autobiography is the account of the colorful beginnings in the pioneering era of Clark County.[42] She spent her early years amongst
her Hieronymous and Bush kinsmen. She was born December 9, 1799 in the
Bush settlement of Lower Howard's Creek, and in an era when the region had
been freed of the Indian menace.[43] Much of the forest had been felled to open
farms and grazing meadows.

Looking back from the perspective of nearly eighty years Julia
Hieronymous Tevis recorded her recollections of life in early Clark County as
she and her kinsmen had experienced it. Growing up in two ancestral fami-

lies with four grandparents and a
host of aunts, uncles, and cousins
Julia Tevis absorbed in full measure
their experiences. She heard the
older members of the family describe their experience in settling the
land, and hacking a livelihood from
it.[44] Her ancestral Bush family
members were staunch Regular Baptists while her Hieronymous kinsmen were equally as devout
Methodists.[45] The Bush family had
in its history the tradition of the
traveling religious colony which had
followed Captain Billy Bush across
the mountains in a grueling move.[46]
They were major founders of the
Lower Howard Baptist Church, and
subsequently the Providence
Church. Her grandmother
Hieronymous was a founding member of the Ebernezer Methodist
Church.[47]

Allan Tate, native son, literary critic, author,
poet, and a member of the famous Vanderbilt
University Agrarians. - *Photo courtesy of the
Winchester Sun*

Ironically Julia Hieronymous separated herself from the Bush faith when she married John Tevis, a Methodist minister. When she moved away to Washington as a young girl she had left behind immediate family relationships with the Vivians, Elkins, Embrys, and the Quisenberrys. She recorded in her memoirs all were, "Uncles, aunts, or cousins; and at one time you might travel for miles without being outside the family circle."[48] She no doubt carried away a special memory of her aged uncle, the patriarch of the settlement. She wrote, "My old Uncle Billy, the famous old Indian fighter, after having suffered, in common with the rest of the settlers, many privations, and having endured much, found himself with but a few hundred acres of that domain he fought to defend. He had munificently given away much, and was, probably, bereft of some by defective titles. He spent his latter years in the visionary pursuit of silver mines, which he never found. Like the mirage in the desert they eluded his grasp—forever and forever vanishing as the spot neared.[50] This is an interesting allusion to the search for the mythical silver mine. Perhaps Julia Tevis had never heard of Swift's silver mine for which her Uncle Billy searched so expectantly to find. This activity of William Bush may have been the first in the pursuit of the Swift will-'o-the-wisp which has persisted so passionately in eastern Kentucky. The legend of Swift's silver mine is a bit of the folklore in all the counties east of Clark.[51] Surely the legend was bandied about among the Kentucky River Valley settlers after 1775, and Billy Bush who had so boldly led a colony of settlers to the "New Eden" believed the story of John Swift had buried a mountain of silver at some undesignated spot.

Of all the bits and pieces written about early Clark County none is more intimately personal or informative than Julia Tevis' recollections.[52] From infancy to early girlhood she grew up in the environment of the raw frontier. She was on close speaking terms with the settlers who settled on the Bush lands, she was quite conversant with the furnishings of their cabins, their way of life, and their aspirations. As a beginner she attended a primitive "blab" school where she learned her letters, and to read.[53] She visited frequently with her Bush and Hieronymous grandparents, always receiving diametrically opposite religious views. Her German grandparents still clung to the old world customs.[54]

Julia Tevis wrote one of the clearest contemporary accounts describing the conditions of life along Lower Howard's Creek. She wrote, "In the early part of the present century, [nineteenth], the cotton fields in Clarke County yielded enough of the best quality of cotton to supply the wants of every family; and while tobacco was the staple of the state, rich harvests of wheat, extensive cornfield, and every variety of cereal gladdened the happy farmer with the consciousness of a beautiful provision for his family. Sugar was made in abundance from the maple, whole groves of which were found in Kentucky before the utilitarian axe of the woodsman laid them prostrate, to give place to the more useful bluegrass. One of these groves, on my grandfather's place contained a thousand trees, many of which are still standing [in 1878]. The sugar-making time in February, when the rich sap began to flow abundantly, was a glorious time, and looked forward to with as much delight as Christmas. A regular encampment on the ground made a pleasant home for two weeks devoted to this gypsy life. The children, including the little negroes—and there were swarms of them—to use their own words, 'toted' sugar in their tiny pails, hour after hour, and were amply rewarded when the sugar was in the transition stage of waxy consistency with as much as they could eat. My grandmother's sugar chest was every year filled with grained sugar, whiter and purer than that made from cane; while a great quantity was put up in cakes for eating—like candy; and much molasses was reserved would abundantly supply the family until sugar-making time came around again."[55]

Adopting the strong denominational loyalties of her grandmother Hieronymous, Julia married John Tevis, a Methodist preacher and moved away to Nashville, Tennessee from her parents' home in Washington.[56] In 1825 her husband was assigned to the Shelbyville charge of his faith. In that Kentucky town Julia and her husband founded the famous Science Hill School for girls. In time this institution was to gain a wide reputation in the South.[57]

In the founding of Science Hill, John and Julia Tevis may have had in mind the operation of a school for the religious training of its students, but under Julia Hieronymous Tevis' direction it became an important institution for the liberation and training of southern girls to be something more than housewives and mothers. From 1825-1880, the year of her death, Julia Tevis was an important Kentucky educational leader.[58] It may have been true that few people in Clark County knew of her work, but as the bride of a Methodist she created an important educational career for herself which old great Uncle Billy Bush would have approved. Her book, *Sixty Years in a Schoolroom*, is an important documentation not only of the education of girls in Kentucky and the South, but her early chapters describe life as it was lived in early nineteenth century Clark County.

There surely prevailed among the pioneering families who settled Clark County a creative yearning. Along with their boundless human endurance of physical hardships, there was also a toughness of mind and determination to grow intellectually. Those who clung so assiduously to the tenets of the Regular Baptist faith of exhibited other virtues. This seems to have been true in the personality of Pleasant Jefferson Conkwright, Sr. who became a minister of that faith, and moved on westward with the expanding frontier.[59] He served several churches in and around Sapulpa, Oklahoma, the era when that Indian country was filling up with new settlers. The German Conkwrights were among the early pioneer families of Clark County. P. J. Conkwright, Sr., courted and married Mildred Fox. She was a member of the numerous Fox family which included John W. Fox, principal of Stony Point Academy, and the father of John Fox, Jr., the novelist who gained national literary fame writing about the people and life in Appalachia.[60] The Conkwrights lived on Pretty Run Creek. It was there that their son, P. J., Jr., and two daughters were born. Pleasant Jefferson Conkwright, Jr. was born 1906.[61], and in mature manhood became one of the most respected book designers and typographers.[62] In 1923 he returned to Kentucky to enter the University. He graduated from that institution in 1928 with a bachelor of arts degree.[63] He then attended the Chicago National Academy of Commercial Art. Returning to Oklahoma he worked briefly in a print shop before becoming the book designer and typographer for the University of Oklahoma Press in Norman. At that press he was to be associated with the much respected director Joseph Brandt. In 1938 Brandt became the director of the prestigious Princeton University Press, and he employed P. J. Conkwright to be the designer of that press' books.[64]

At the Princeton University Press P. J. Conkwright had a generous range of books treating a multitude of subjects which required textual designs and typographical arrangements. He produced the design for the monumental collection of the *Papers of Thomas Jefferson* which were being edited by the erudite Julian Boyd. He also designed the format for the collected *Papers of Woodrow Wilson*. It was the multi volume *Jefferson Papers*, however, which set the high standard for the publication of all the other papers of public men and women, which were supported by the National Historical Commission.[65]

Almost with annual regularity books designed by P. J. Conkwright won major awards. Forty of his books in the annual fifty best designed books of the year, contests conducted by the International Type Design Competition.[66] A generous number of Conkwright designed books were placed on exhibit in the American Designer Series of the prestigious New York Metropolitan Museum of Arts.[67]

P. J. Conkwright was a recipient of a Guggenheim Fellowship to travel abroad and visit with famous European book designers and typographers. At Princeton University he held an associate professorship, an institution which

John Jacob Niles
folksinger-folk
lorist-lecturer-and
colorful Clark
County resident.
This striking
photograph was of
a man who had
become a bit of
folklore in his
times. - *Photo
courtesy of the
Winchester Sun*

awarded him an honorary doctorate of Letters in 1966. The University of Kentucky also honored him with an honorary degree in literature, in 1964, and the following year he was awarded a centennial medallion, an honor recognizing the accomplishments of a hundred of the University's graduates.[68] The following year Conkwright designed the centennial symbol of the University's first hundred years.[69]

P. J. Conkwright returned to Kentucky often to visit in Winchester and Lexington. He was married to Hazel Boone who had family connections with Clark County. Conkwright died on January 21, 1986, eighty years after his birth in Winchester.[70] During the years, 1994-1995, funds were subscribed by fellow book designers, publishers, and authors to collect his design materials, and to publish a book of superior design in his honor. On March 20, 1995, a thirty-two page copies of Conkwright design was published, and Mark Argetsinger published a lengthy essay detailing with P. J. Conkwright's career and accomplishments.[71]

In many respects this younger native of Clark County was the equal if not the superior to Joel Tanner Hart. The two men worked in different mediums, and both achieved reputations of high orders. Both Hart and Conkwright had roots in somewhat the same area of Clark County, both were descendants of pioneer families. P. J. Conkwright had the advantages of a twentieth century education, yet Hart and Conkwright would have found many experiences to share between them, and both would have admired the other's artistic achievements. If ever there was a place where youth were born and inspired to realize the great American dream of success, it was that microcosmic region enclosed within the Clark County boundaries.

Jack Kennedy Hodgkin, a member of an early Clark County family in the Kiddville neighborhood is one of the few, if not the only portrait painter, from the county. His heroic portrait of the youthful Daniel Boone is on display in the Boonesborough State Park Museum. In this upright portrait the great Kentucky trailbreaker is portrayed as a young man with anticipation imprinted in his face. Jack Kennedy Hodgkin has combined an interest in portrait art with one in music. His grandfather, John Kidd Hodgkin, set an artistic precedent. In 1920 he wrote a nostalgic poem of place and life in the Kiddville Lulbegrud area. This poem has essence of family attachment and love of place which essentially characterized much of the personal history of Clark County.

The writing of history is an art, if it is an art, unto itself. At times it is difficult to isolate the history of the Kentucky Valley area relating specifically to Clark County. There are a few anecdotal incidents which give color and insight into the dawning of civilization in the region. There is a fascinating literary allusion to what is now Clark County in Boone-Finley narrative. Some member of that long-hunting party lugged along a copy of Jonathan Swift's *History of the Travels of Samuel Gulliver* which was read in camp.[72] They established a temporary camp in the wilderness north of the Kentucky River where they read, maybe fittingly, Jonathan Swift's famous satire on the adventures of Samuel Gulliver. On one occasion Alexander Neely returned to camp and told his companions that he had been hunting in Lulbegrud (Lorbrugrud), and that he had killed two Bordernags (Brobdingnags). Thus the creek near Log Lick where Neely had hunted was named Lulbegrud.[73] This surely must be one of the most unusual literary allusions in Kentucky history.

There prevailed among those earliest individuals who trudged over the Boone Trace to reach the Kentucky River a vague sense that they were sharing an important historical moment. Of the three contemporary journals kept by travelers making the wilderness passage that of William Calk is most fascinating. Spelling phonetically, and writing in terse sentences, Calk clearly conveyed a sense of the ordeals of breaking trail into virgin country. This journal has been quoted many times by historians of the westward movement. While William Calk was only tangentially associated with Clark County, he did at one time technically live within its borders prior to the creation of Montgomery County. The Calk Journal might well be the earliest bit of primitive quasi literature produced by a resident.[74]

More than a century and three quarters later William Stuart Lester produced a solid scholarly history of the movement west by the Transylvania Company. Dr. Lester, a professor of history in the Kentucky Wesleyan College, did intensive and careful research among the contemporary manuscripts and documents.[75] This book, *The Transylvania Company*, has genuine pertinency for the history of early Clark County. Though Professor Lester's text is enlightening, the fact that he inserted generous excerpts from the original diaries, journals, and other source materials adds substantially to the value of the study. This book has direct bearings of the history of Clark County; also, it might well be regarded as one of the most scholarly works produced in the county.[78]

Other historians have fathomed Clark County's past. In the concluding chapter in volume two of *The Proud Land*, Dr. Goff Bedford added a brief epilogue telling his reader that, "Knowing who one's ancestors are is often not enough. The fulfillment comes when one knows what their ancestors did for a living, what they dreamed, what they hoped for, what they feared, and what their sins and goodnesses were."[77] He might have added what environmental and outside economic and social forces bore down upon them. His observation is a sound formula for the writing of local history. In his two volume History of Clark County, (1977,1983) Dr. Bedford gathered and presented a phenomenal collection of personal, social, and political materials. In fact his volumes may well be considered encyclopedic for the decades down to 1860. In the writing of his history he wisely interrelated that of the county with that of the Commonwealth. He did meticulous research in the country's official records, dredging from them an impressive amount of primary documentary information.[78]

In the writing of his history Dr. Bedford seems to have been guided by the ancient historical adage that, "The closer the historian comes to the treatment of a circumscribed local area, and to people at the grass roots of human affairs, the more anecdotes and incidents become important." The provincial demesne of locality revolves, always, within the orbit of the larger spheres of state, nation, and the world. No local region is an island unto itself.

It appears that in the preparation of his *History* Dr. Goff was faced with making the decision of whether to cast his narrative in a chronological mold, or in a topographical order. The indexes to the two volumes reveal in essence how important families and individuals have been as actors on the broad chronological stage of two centuries. As a matter of fact family borders on being the central theme of Clark County history. In a brief epilogue or concluding sentence Dr. Goff makes an age-old observation which every historian has had to heed. He wrote, "However, there is only so much that can be put in a book and only so many pages."[79]

Always in use of the broad term history, it must be recognized that there is more than a single vein to be mined. There is a multiplicity of approaches which may be used to describe the human experiences within a geographical region. R. Gerald Alvey of Winchester has made at least three significant book length contributions in the field, of local folklore. His *Kentucky Folklore, Kentucky Bluegrass Country,* and *Dulcimer Maker, the Craft of Homer Ledford* add a substantial dimension to an understanding of the basic culture of a broad spectrum of the Kentucky people. Strangely, to date, no author had followed the local colorist precedent set by the novelist James Lane Allen until now. Alvey, in *Kentucky Bluegrass Country,* presented revealing glimpses into the many facets of every day and commonplace incidents and myths which, historically has given the Kentucky Bluegrass Region a specific identification on the American Continent. The plumbed the social and local dynamics which colored the history of the region, some of which were positive while others contrasted sharply with the conservative mores of bluegrass society in general. Alvey dissected with craftsmen like skill the anatomy from which so many central Kentucky myths and traditions have sprung.[80]

F. Gerald Alvey has observed and written about Kentuckians who have gone about their commonplace roles of being themselves, of being both virtuous and sinful. He kept in mind those incidents, human mores, and anecdotes which from the beginning have given the Bluegrass Region a distinct historical personality.[81]

Moving from the consideration of a socio-geographical region to that of a single personality, R. Gerald Alvey adds a distinct folk dimension to *Dulcimer Maker.* He has described the progress upward of Winchester resident since 1955, Homer C. Ledford has had a colorful career, growing up in rural eastern Tennessee then gaining a perspective on the field of folk music and instruments at the John C. Campbell Folk School in Brass Town, North Carolina.[82] In the latter place he was inspired to cultivate his talents for repairing and making folk musical instruments, and in the singing of folk songs.[83]

Ledford came to Winchester in 1955 as a teacher of industrial arts in the Clark County Public School system. He had attended classes in Berea College and had graduated from the Eastern Kentucky Teachers College. In Winchester Homer Ledford gained national fame as the maker of dulcimers and other musical instruments, and as a folk singer. In time the name of Ledford on a dulcimer became a hall mark of originality and superior quality. He elevated the simple folk musical instrument, the dulcimer, to the status of being both a symbol of folk music sophistication, and of folk craftsmanship. Ledford gained fame as a folk craftsman when a dulcimer and a dulcitar were placed on permanent exhibition in the Smithsonian Institution.[84] Alvey wrote, "His [Ledford's] dulcitar was also placed in a traveling exhibit to illustrate innovation within traditional folk craftsmanship."[85] By 1960 Ledford had created 4,700 dulcimers plus a number of banjos, guitars, and violins.[86] Within the context of Clark County history, Ledford must be added to the names of Joel Tanner Hart and Pleasant Jefferson Conkwright, Jr. as an artist who has given the county and Winchester a significant niche in three creative artistic areas.

There were other Clark County natives who achieved some degree of fame. Among them was Allen Tate. He was a biographer, novelist, poet, and respected literary critic. Tate was born near Winchester, November 19, 1899,[87] the son of John Orley and Eleanor Varnell Custis Tate. His father was engaged in the mountain lumber and tool timber handling business. It would be difficult to define any impact which Clark County had on Allen Tate except for the fact where biographical mention is made to Tate his birthplace is named. Tate's family moved to Ashland, and then to Washington, D.C.[88]

In his formative years Allen Tate was exposed to a badly disrupted elementary school education. It was not until his admission in Vanderbilt University in September 1918 that he was to receive a challenging exposure to learning. In Nashville the eighteen year-old Tate became associated with John Crowe Ransom, Donald Davidson, Frank L. Owsley, and fellow student Robert Penn Warren.[89] A literary group called the Fugitives had been formed by townsmen and Vanderbilt faculty members which in time was to have a strong influence on Allen Tate. He was first of the Fugitives to move away from Nashville when he went to New York to embark upon a writing career.[90] Later he became one of the staunchest members of the Nashville Agrarians, a group of defenders of the southern way of life consisting of Donald Davidson, Herman Nixon, Frank L. Owsley, and John Crowe Ransom. By 1930 the Agrarians had generated a considerable body of writings which appeared in newspapers and magazines, but it was their collective essays published in a

Pleasant Jefferson Conkwright, no doubt was conceived in Clark County, and was a descendant of a distinguished pioneer family. He came home often and visited in the county almos anonymously. "P.J." was a truly distinguished artist with a highly honored international reputation. - *Portrait by Ulli Stelzer, 1970. Photo courtesy of Princeton University Archives, Rare Books and Special Collection.*

book entitled *I'll Take My Stand* (1930), that attracted the most attention regionally and nationally.[91]

For the rest of his life Allen Tate remained a confirmed agrarian as set forth by the Vanderbilt group. He, however, is remembered as the biographer of Jefferson Davis and General Stonewall Jackson. His fame will also rest firmly upon his poetry, literary criticism, and teaching. He could lay claim to the fact that his place of birth was a fully confirmed agrarian region which inoculated many of the folkways and philosophies set forth in *I'll Take My Stand.*[92]

Possibly the most prolific author to spring from the land of Clark County was Anderson Chenault Quisenberry, a descendant of the famous pioneer German family which settled in that part of the county about the Lower Howard's Creek drainage area. He was born October 26, 1850, the son of James Francis Quisenberry. He was related in some form of kinship with members of several other early settler families. Quisenberry graduated from Georgetown College, and after a somewhat brief career as a journalist, he moved to Washington, D.C. to hold a position with the United States War Department, a position he held throughout the rest of his life. In time he wrote and published six books and several essays pertaining to local and Kentucky history. Quisenberry wrote as a biographer, genealogist, and historian. He was the author of *The Life and Times of Hon. Humphrey Marshall* (1902), a book which was published in Winchester. He produced two books in the field of genealogy which related to the Quisenberry and related families. In *The Memorials of the Quisenberry Family and Other Families*, he included an account of the old Providence Church and its members. In 1906 Quisenberry ventured into the field of history, writing of the quixotic Lopez Expedition to Cub, 1850-1851. This book was published as a part of the distinguished Filson Club Series.

Though he spent most of his mature life away from Clark County and Kentucky, Anderson C. Quisenberry never lost a deep nostalgic attachment to place and his home people. He was one of the few Clark County natives whose biographical sketch appeared in the prestigious *Who's Who in America*, and later in *Who Was Who*.[93] His writings have had a lasting value in the field of Kentuckiana, and they have the added value of being partially contemporary in nature.[94]

In more recent years Robert Collins, a former Forest Supervisor of the Cumberland National Forest, wrote and published an extensive *History of the Daniel Boone National Forest, 1770-1970*.[95] His book covers a broad scope of time and contains a veritable source of details of the land and its past. Beginning with the opening of the area designated as forest preserve down to the establishment of the National Forest Administration of the area, the author traces step by step the historical changes which had occurred, including the official creation of the Daniel Boone National Forest.

None of the area of the Daniel Boone National Forest lies within Clark County, yet the region is intimately associated geographically and administratively with the forest. The central administration offices are located in Winchester. Robert Collins outlines the operation of the large federal forest preservation area in Kentucky, and the return of the land to its natural wood state. By 1937 the Federal Government had acquired 408,567 acres of a gross projected area of approximately a million and a half acres.[96] Robert Collins' *A History of the Daniel Boone National Forest* is the first major book relating to such a large natural portion of Kentucky.

The cultural and literary development in Clark County over the past two centuries embraced more than artists and authors. Despite the fact the titles of very few books appeared in estate inventories during the early years, there was an spark of literary interest. A small group of men, including William N. Lane, James Simpson, James Clark, Chilton Allen, Samuel Hanson petitioned the Kentucky General Assembly for a library company, a request which was granted in a formal act on December 27, 1810.[97] The petitioner proposed creating a depository for books, maps, charts and drawings. The legislative act outlined the procedures of organizing and administering the company.

Only sparse bits of information have survived to indicate the fate of the Winchester Library Company. Anderson Chenault Quisenberry, writing more than a century later, about the publication of the Winchester *Advertiser* said, "There seems to have been a literary awakening in Winchester in 1814, or thereabouts; for it was about that time that the 'Winchester Library,' chartered by the Legislature in 1810, was fully established—a concern which had a comparatively large number of standard books and which not only survived, but throve and prospered during an existence of more than forty years." The fact that Winchester's public library and first newspaper were contemporaneous, suggest that one impelled the other.[98]

If Quisenberry was correct in his chronology the library company went out of existence at mid-nineteenth century, perhaps for lack of funds and of support. As the century advanced there appeared listings of greater number of books in private hands. Whatever caused the dissolution of the first public library, there was a century-wide gap in the public library history in Clark County and Winchester.[99]

Strangely, in all the documentary materials about the establishment of churches and their activities there is little or no evidence that they maintained collections of religious books to accommodate their communicants. The Bible, as a matter of course, found its way into most homes. There were small accumulations of school textbooks such as Webster's Blue Back Speller and McGuffey's and Butler's readers. Some of the more progressive livestock breeders such as Dr. Samuel D. Martin, subscribed to farm journals, especially the *Kentucky* and *Franklin Farmer*.[100] Dr. Martin contributed articles and notes to these journals, and in the agricultural section of the United States *Patent Office Reports*. It is doubtful, however, that there were many subscribers to such national or regional periodicals as *Niles Weekly Register* or *DeBow's Review*, or one of the literary magazines published in the East. There may have been a few subscribers to Godey's and Graham's lady books. No inventory revealed library holdings which began to equal those owned by the Franklin County farmer, Robert Wilmot Scott.

No doubt the promoters for the removal of Kentucky Wesleyan College from Millersburg to Winchester in the latter part of the nineteenth century believed its library would also be available to the town. This did not prove to be a substitute for a public library, and it was not until the closing years of the post World War II decade that there was a revival of an effort to establish a public library.[101] For Kentucky as a whole this was an era approaching the creation of libraries first by organizing bookmobile projects. In the early 1950's the organization of a children's library in Winchester was undertaken by a group of interested citizens. This library was housed in a room in the courthouse. In 1953 the collection was moved into a converted railway car contributed by the Codell Construction Company.[102] This car-library was located on Maple Street. Five years later the library was again moved, this time into the former Presbyterian church house.[103] This structure was built in 1857, and was used by the Presbyterians until 1892, and between that date and 1920 the building was occupied by a fruit market, a skating rink, by the printing plant of the *Winchester Sun*. The library supporters owned a lot on Belmont Street alongside one owned by the Church of Christ, the last tenant of the Main Street building. A trade was made with the Church of Christ, and the library again moved. The former church was converted to library use.[104] In February 1995 the structure and the library collection were threatened with destruction when workmen on the roof accidentally started a fire.

The Winchester Public Library is the result of the efforts of the Fine Arts Club. As the collection and patronage have grown the shelf and service areas have been enlarged, financed by a tax levied in 1974 and again in 1994. The latter levy was approved to permit the planning and construction of a modern library building to house the current collection of 42,000 books, and to permit its expansion.[105]

The art of editing and publishing a newspaper must be regarded as an art within a circumscribed sense. In the early years of Clark County history newspapers seemed not to have been a pressing necessity. This may be accounted for by the fact that as a part of Fayette County and the *Kentucky Gazette* served the pre Clark County era. The Gazette began publication in August 1787, and became a main source of news and the publication of advertisement and notices of all sorts. No doubt in pioneer Clark County there was only limited interest in a newspaper. Perhaps the most important subscribers were the numerous tavern-keepers. There were few or no commercial businesses which conducted a sufficient volume of trade to justify advertising. With the exception of the Virginian, Thomas Parvin, a schoolteacher at Strode's Station, no printer had settled in the county.[106]

In 1807 William W. Worsely and Samuel M. Overton began publication of the Kentucky Observer in Lexington.[107] This paper became a regional one carrying both news, legal notices, and advertising of local interests. It was not until 1814 that a newspaper, the Advertiser, was published in Winchester. Copies of this paper are preserved in the Durrett Collection in the University of Chicago, and they indicate that in the war years of its founding advertisements of names of recipients of letters held in the local postoffice, notices that merchants had sold their stock of goods and asked their debtors to pay their bills, and listing of stray animals were the major contents of the paper.

The name of the paper was changed to the *Kentucky Advertiser* in 1816, and four years later to the Kentucky Advertisers and *Farmer's Magazine*. A fourth change of name was made in 1830 to the *Winchester Republican*, subscribing editorially to the principles of Jeffersonian republicanism. In 1831 Nimrod L. Finnell moved *Republican* printing equipment to Lexington to be used in the production of the Observer. During the years 1814-1831 the Republican had as editors number of local professional and business men.

There appears to have been a gap in the publication of newspapers in Winchester during the years 1831 to 1850. Anderson Chenault Quisenberry wrote that a paper of some unspecified title was published in this era, but he could not be certain of the fact. It seems clear that Clark County newspaper readers patronized first, the *Lexington Observer*, then the *Lexington Observer and Reporter*, the *Kentucky Gazette*, and the *Kentucky Statesman*.[108] In 1852 Richard W. Clayton, a Virginian, published the short-lived *Winchester Review*. There followed the *Winchester Chronicle*, published by Robert S. and John Williams.[109] The editors of this paper seems to have been anyone who came by the printing office and had something he wanted to write about, among them were James Flannagan, Wallace and John Gruelle, and Dr. J. M. Riffe.[110] This paper ceased publication in 1861 and on the eve of the Civil War. A second was the National Union, 1859 to 1861, and was edited by George M. Jackson. Winchester was without a newspaper during the Civil War years. Quite obviously ante bellum Clark County and Winchester were not the most productive places in which to publish newspapers, and receive local support from advertisers. It must be noted that often the County Court would instruct the county clerk to run legal advertisements in the Lexington papers.

During the post-Civil War years there was a repetition of the history of the ante bellum period. In 1867 the printing equipment of the defunct *National Union* was taken out of storage by Captain James M. Parrish to print the *Clark County Democrat*. William M. Beckner was the editor of this paper in the era when post-Civil War Kentucky was in a state of political upheaval over the excesses of radical reconstruction. There were also other issues which demanded public attention, among them public education, rapidly changing economic conditions, the building of railroads, and the rise of the Democratic Party. There occurred a series of transfers which blurred the history of the *Democrat*.[111] At one time Benjamin F. Turner, a Winchester merchant, owned a half interest in the paper, then Parris bought back Turner's interest. In April 1870, Anderson Chenault Quisenberry bought half interest in the Democrat, and the next year became its sole owner. He in turn sold an interest to John E. Garner and William M. Beckner. Judge Beckner then bought the paper and continued a its editor and publisher until 1878 when he was joined by Thomas G. Stuart as a partner. D. G. Lisle and former postmaster Walter B. Nicholson bought the Democrat in 1883, and between the latter date and 1890 it appears that almost half the male population of Winchester had a hand in editing and publishing the *Democrat*. There were other short-lived newspapers published in Winchester, including the *Chronicle*, a six month trial balloon, and there was the jocular printer's offering, *The Smooth Coon*.[112] The *Coon* was edited and published by James J. Adams. This whimsical little publication proved to be a seminal one out of which grew the *Winchester Sun* which became Kentucky's first semi-weekly paper. Anderson C. Quisenberry edited the Sun until 1881 when he became editor of the *Lexington Daily Transcript*. Chenault took the Sun's printing equipment to Lexington where the *Sun* was printed.[113]

During the years 1881 to 1903, *The Winchester Sun* underwent a series of changes of owners and editors, and political persuasions. The Weekly Sun was discontinued in the latter year, but the semi-weekly *Sun* was published until 1912.[114] The first issue of the *Winchester Daily Sun* appeared on March 1, 1912. To date the files of this paper remain incomplete, making it difficult to traces its full history. Perhaps there other areas in Kentucky history where there was an equally complex newspaper history as in Clark County, but it is to be doubted that so many individuals were involved in publishing and editing. No doubt the numerous newspapers published and perished in Clark County, 1814 to 1912, had some sporadic effect in the fields of politics, social affairs, public opinion, and in advertising, but there were no strong and consistent editorial voices which spoke out for any length of time.

Though native sons and daughters made magnificent contributions in the various fields of arts and literature, few of the newspaper editors were to make lasting contributions. All of these creative individuals added degrees of luster to the land of their origins. Their accomplishments were indeed a golden harvest of prestige for the places of their nativity.

A "V" of ante derby hat era dudes before the paint store of S.H. Templeman and Company's door. There was nothing casual about this sidewalk assembly.

CHAPTER 13

In the Shadow of the Courthouse

.

For two centuries Clark County has been a politically classic example of a "Little Kingdom." It would be difficult to find among Kentucky's other 119 counties one which has lived and functioned more completely within its own borders or one which is more oriented to its courthouse center. Winchester sits almost as a perfect center geographically in the county with all the web-work of roads branching out from the courthouse square. The political history of the county, however, also may be viewed from within the parameters of the state and national governmental systems.[1] From that moment in 1792 when the county fathers gathered at John Strode's house to begin the organization of the county's government an inner "courthouse ring," in some fashion, has steered the course of county politics. In the broad chronological sweep of Clark County's history there have always been the necessities of conforming with the statutory actions of the commonwealth, with three constitutional revisions plus numerous amendments, with federal statutes, and ultimately with court decisions.[2]

No American politicians have been more acutely aware of the whims, demands, and angers of grassroots voters than county officials. They have functioned nearest their constituents, and two centuries of experience in this area is eloquently reflected in Clark County.[3] Significantly, local government was being instituted in the newly created Clark County simultaneously with the organization of the commonwealth itself.[4] The two entities of government historically made comparable responses to the people, and to the rapid transition from being a frontier to becoming settled and progressing communities. Again, the political history of Clark County has been an inextricable part of the much broader one of all the numerous counties of Kentucky; all have had to operate under the common umbrella of statutory regulations and limitations.[5]

Dealing with issues at the courthouse level of government, constituent personalities have always been more highly visible in the day-to-day functioning and application of the rules of government. It was this rudimentary fact which brought about the formation of the new county in the first place. In line with the Jeffersonian philosophy of the cardinal role of government, it was basic that citizens be more aware of what was going on in the courthouse than in the state capital and in Washington. In the more precise political implications of the democratic process, the courthouse must at all times be fully accessible to citizens who ride into the county seat on horseback, transact business, and return home by sundown. No clearer physical example of this axiom could be found in all of Kentucky than in Winchester and Clark County.[6]

The details, many of them minuscule, of the political history of Clark County are all but overwhelming. One reads through the pages of order, will, trustee, and town council books with a realization that literally hundreds of personalities, incidents, social situations, and administrations of some political implication fill the page of ponderous volumes of records. The order books of the county court alone reveal preoccupation with locating and maintaining roads, inspecting the sites of mill dams to insure water impoundments so they would not injure adjoining properties, laying off the county in road and voting districts, adjudicating issues arising after widows' dower rights, adjusting property boundaries and those of the county, granting the rights of citizenship to immigrants, appointing guardians of dependent children, manumitting slaves, and scores of other problems.[7] The Clark County public records are helpful even in their terseness. Clerks wasted no ink and paper in describing backgrounds of the problems presented in county court sessions and in town trustee meetings. Surely there were constant background pullings and haulings and the granting of political favors.

The very act of presenting a petition to the Kentucky General Assembly seeking the creation of Clark County was a political one. Representing the areas of Fayette and Bourbon counties, which were to be pinched off to form the new county, were two influential political figures, Hubbard Taylor and James McMillan. Public records generated during the formative year of 1792 are mostly silent about the maneuverings in both the area and the newly designated state capital, Frankfort.[8] Was there a ground swell drive on the part of local settlers in the area, or was it a desire on the part of the more far-sighted settlers, or was it simply giving in to that old frontier urge to create a county in which a power structure could be formed to the glory of the politically ambitious?[9] As far as the new state itself was concerned there was a fair number of potential leaders to be drawn upon. When Isaac Shelby was chosen as the first governor, much of the western constituency felt comfortable with him as a trustworthy and down-to-earth leader. In his first, and severely abbreviated, speech to the newly organized General Assembly, he observed that "The happiness and welfare of this country, depends so much on the speedy settlement of our land disputes: that I cannot forbear my hope, that you will adopt every measure to give full operation to the most pointed out by the constitution for that purpose."[10] This plea of Governor Shelby would have been just as appropriate for Clark County had he stood before John Strode's hearth to deliver it.

How well the new state and the new county of Clark would succeed hinged heavily upon leadership. There was a potential and capable leadership resident in Clark County. Despite a lack of documentary information as to the maneuverings which brought about the creation of Clark County, one fact is crystal clear. Two of the political leaders of the annexed area of Fayette and Bourbon counties were adept at managing political matters. Hubbard Taylor is mentioned elsewhere in this text, but it is pertinent to discuss him further in this connection.[11] He surely deserves more attention than historians have devoted to him. James Madison on one occasion said that Taylor was a distant relative, but more precisely he was Madison's advisor on Kentucky land matters one of his ablest western correspondents, and a shrewd political analyst. In midyear 1791, Madison wrote Thomas Jefferson that he had received news of the political situation in Kentucky, at the time when Virginia's western counties were moving rapidly toward independent statehood. Madison told Jefferson, "I have this letter from a Mr. Taylor a pretty intelligent man engaged in their public affairs."[12] Despite his offhand reference to a "Mr. Taylor," Madison knew of Taylor quite well; if not in person, then through correspondence; as a highly observant commentator on Kentucky affairs.[13]

Taylor was quite frank in his appraisals of the leadership capabilities of his neighbors. He wrote James Madison, December 17, 1791, "Nothing material has transpired here lately except the late unlucky affair of Genl. St. Claires defeat, wherein it is said he lost between 900 & 1000 men killed. The election for the members to the convention is now on hand in this place, the people were pleased to nominate me among the rest & it is probably I shall succeed the others are more doubtful. I have you a list of the members from the counties where the elections are over and flatter myself I shall at a future day to acquaint you of Colo. Nicholas's election as it is a matter sent James Madison of the utmost importance in this district; for I fear the letter above mentioned should not come to hand, if your leisure will admit—shall be glad to have one similar thereto. Great doubts seems to prevail respecting two houses in the legislature & elections of all kinds whether they shall not be solely in the hands of the people or partly so."[14]

When it became clear that a Kentucky constitution would finally be placed in draft, and then in final form, Hubbard Taylor conveyed to Madison a cynical observation about his doubts as to whether there then resided in Kentucky men of adequate capability and experience to staff the courts. He said, "I must confess I feel some uneasiness on this head, not so much on account of a disposition not contrary to the interest of the Community, as for the real capacity to do so in a regular, proper & equitable manner. You probably will be informed by your Brothers Ambrose, of want of men of abilities in this country. Colo. Nicholas has utterly declared never to serve in the Legislature, we must have Six Judges, two Senators for the Federal Gov't, two members of Congress and a Governor & several other inferior officers, which ought to be such that after taking the best we can furnish, they cannot be admired."[15] Taylor possibly had the same idea about the prospective officers of the new county of Clark.

Once the commonwealth was made a member of the Union and the General Assembly met in its first session, Hubbard Taylor sent James Madison a supplementary report in which he explained that central issues before it were the raising of revenue and the establishment of courts. The debate over revenue struck close to the hearts of Taylor and Madison. Both were major landholders in Kentucky. Legislators in their first session debated the question of whether the tax assessments on land should be per acre or in multiple lots of 100 acres. The levy as finally set was 219 shillings.[16] Again, Hubbard Taylor regarded many of his legislative colleagues as unfit to serve in a capacity where laws governing the commonwealth were being drafted and enacted.

Hubbard Taylor's colleague to form the new county was William McMillan.[17] Both men wielded considerable influence in social, economic, and political affairs. Few Kentucky counties formed after 1792 had such able representation at the outset in Frankfort as did Clark County.

Though there are no documentary sources which would reveal the background of Hubbard Taylor and William McMillan's actions prior to the legislation creating the seven new counties in 1792, it must be inferred that they planned carefully and effectively.[18] No doubt they contended, as was com-

Cooking burgoo for Judge Ruby Laffoon of Madisonville just prior to the election in 1931 when the Democrats recovered the Governor's office from the Republican Flem D. Sampson of Barbourville - *Photo courtesy of Mrs. Nellie F. Adams*

mon for all promoters of new counties, that every citizen must have access to a courthouse and county officers within a day's horseback ride to and return from the county seat.[19] The historian, however, is left to wonder what trades and compromises were made outside of the legislative halls in Frankfort to bring about the creation of the cluster of seven new counties. Specifically, in the case of Clark County, new political agencies came into being in the area, and the seat of government was located near at hand for every individual in the region. Politically central in the area were the courthouse, the jail, the twelve magistrates, the circuit court, and the sheriff. The magistrates wielded the most power; they sat as a county court and as presiding magistrates over minor district courts, and they made all policy decisions. In line of importance after the magistrates were the sheriff, the county surveyor, the clerks, the coroner, the constables, and the slave patrols.[20]

As prescribed by charter, Clark County in 1792 was a broad area governed by the above coterie of officials, with prominent landholders always in the background but powerful. The geography of power in the years 1792 to 1800 was along the creeks which emptied into the Kentucky River and on the rolling western slopes next to Fayette and Bourbon counties.[21] The population was sparse in all the region, but more so among the eastern forested ridges. In 1793 there was no concentrated knotting of population in a town or village, no settled central area in which to plant a county seat. A rural road system had to be opened mile by mile, and the land had to be cleared and fallowed for cultivation. Thus the newborn county grew literally out of the raw opening frontier, a fact which was to have an important bearing on the political process for a half century.[22] The location and expansion of the county seat Winchester generated one of the earliest internal political incidents. There were three possibilities for the location of the county town: Strode's Station; a location on the Kentucky River and along the artery of trade and travel; or one, as mandated by the legislative charter, near the center of the ceded Fayette-Bourbon County region and the settlements.[23] The matter of the location of the county seat was not designated in the act of charter but came the next year in the chartering of Winchester.[24]

A fascinating political interlude was the appearance of the name of Enoch Smith among the founders and those attending the initial meeting at John Strode's house. Smith was a large landholder in the Little Mount area to the east. He in fact was a somewhat shadowy figure. He was present in Boonesborough and then was engaged in claiming land and surveying.[25] He was Clark County's first surveyor.[26] Following chartering of Montgomery County, Enoch Smith's name no longer appeared among legislators or in other official capacities, though he was still alive in 1822 and no doubt enjoying some fortune. Along with other promoters, he initiated the chartering of Mount Sterling with the hope that it would become the Clark County seat; this despite the fact he was one of the viewers of the Baker lands about the big spring.[27]

The meeting of the charter officials at John Strode's house on December 20, 1792 to formally organize Clark County must surely have been one of the most interesting political gatherings in Clark County's history. James McMillan administered the oath of office to Enoch Smith and John Holder.[28] Also present in that meeting, obviously, was John Strode, who engaged actively in the discussions. Also on hand was the ubiquitous John Baker, who was lobbying heavily for the location of the county seat about his big spring and on his land.[29] John Strode met with the magistrates once more and then disappeared from the political scene after viewing the Baker site.[30] Political control of the new county rested firmly in the hands of Hubbard Taylor, Robert Clarke, William Sudduth, John Martin, John McGuire, and, possibly, William Bush. Taylor, Clarke, and McGuire were the chief magistrates.[31]

Certainly in the years 1792 to 1800 Clark County had only severely limited funds. Officials influenced voters and granted favors in the locating and opening of new roads; settling land boundary disputes; refereeing deed conflicts; licensing of taverns; annually setting the rates charged for board, lodging, and horse feed; paying bounties for wolf scalps; registering livestock brands; dealing with complaints of widows over their being shortchanged by deceased husbands in regard to dower rights; selecting guardians for orphaned and indigent children; manumitting slaves; administering oaths of fealty and newly naturalized citizens; exercising oversight of warehouses, milldams, and the stray pen and markethouse; and licensing of ministers, lawyers, and doctors. Quarterly the court dockets were filled with the domestic issues of a new county.[32]

Clerks of the county court were diligent up to a point in recording the court proceedings, but they gave little notice to the background of incidents before the court or to the discussions preceding the making of decision. Nevertheless, the order, will, and deed books constitute a virtual annalistic recording of the social, economic, and political happenings in Clark County. Spread across their pages are literally hundreds of personal names of politicians and of humble everyday citizens who filed through courthouse doors to transact business, both trivial and important. The will books in many ways constitute a worldly book of life. The masculine ordainers all but opened the secrets of their hearts, their coffers, and accumulations of worldly goods. They expressed love and affection for their prospective widows, favored some children, and sent messages of disapproval to others. In the round many of the wills were also confessionals prefatory to answering the Great Roll Call itself.[33]

The recorded wills and estate inventory records, along with the adjustment of dower rights, are the weavings of the very fabric of life itself in Clark County. Perhaps the only time many individuals ever appeared in the public records, aside from being called upon to work the roads and pay taxes, was in one of the county record books. Citizens came to court for a great variety of reasons, besides seeing and being seen. They sought adjustments downward of tax levys; fees for officiating at elections and guarding prisoners; to defend themselves against charges of bastardy, thievery, and mayhem; or authority for keeping ferries, whipping slaves, and inspecting products stored in public warehouses.[34] Political tentacles in some fashion or other reached out from the courthouse to all parts of the county. Clark County, like most all English and American counties, was indeed a political world encapsulated within a set of arbitrary geopolitical boundaries.

There, however, was a flowing outward of representation in the Kentucky General Assembly, in Congress, and in the governor's office. In 1792 Hubbard Taylor was a delegate to the tenth separation and constitutional convention in Danville.[35] On May 5, 1792, Taylor wrote James Madison that he had reservations on initiating state government at that date, "Not so much on account of a disposition to act contrary to the interest of the Community, as for the real Capacity to do things in a regular, proper & equitable manner," because he felt there was a lack of talent. The reason for his reservation was, "Our want of men of abilities, in this country."[36] Taylor also expressed a willingness to James Madison to abolish slavery from Kentucky by a constitutional mandate, but George Nicholas refused to support the idea. By 1792 Taylor had made rapid advances from being a land surveyor and speculator to becoming a statesman-politician. He served in the Kentucky General Assembly as a representative in 1792 and was a presidential elector from 1800 to 1825, voting for Thomas Jefferson, James Madison, James Monroe, and John Quincy Adams. He was also a member of the Board of Trustees of Transylvania University, appointed by action of the Kentucky General Assembly in 1818. This was in the golden period of the Horace Holley administration at that institution.[37]

Clark County sent William Sudduth, Robert Clarke, and Richard Hickman to Frankfort as delegates to the constitutional convention of 1799,

Excursion boat on the Kentucky River circa 1900. The gravel road down to the landing is still in place, except it is now a concrete boat ramp. Riding the excursion boat was a popular Clark County past time.

when the first constitution was revised. Interestingly the new document provided for the office of lieutenant governor, an office which Richard Hickman
was to hold during the War of 1812. The county was to be represented in the
United States Congress by three of its citizens, two of whom achieved enough
reputation to be included in the *Dictionary of American Biography*.[38] James
Clark was, perhaps, the most notable of the three. He was born January 16,
1770, almost under the shadow of the famous natural landmark, the Peaks of
Otter near Lynchburg.[39] When he was fourteen years of age his parents emigrated to Kentucky, settling in Clark County. James Clark was educated at
the famous Kentucky Academy at Pisgah in Woodford County and at
Transylvania University. After graduating from that institution he returned
to Virginia to read law in the office of his brother Christian. When he was
given a license to practice he set out to establish a practice somewhere on the
expanding western frontier. Finally he located his office in Winchester. By
the time he was twenty-seven years of age Clark had become an established
attorney, and he entered upon a long and distinguished political career. He
was elected to the house of representatives in the Kentucky General Assembly
in 1807 and 1808. In 1810 he was appointed judge on the bench of the
Kentucky Court of Appeals. He was elected a member of the Thirteenth and
Fourteenth Congresses, 1813-1816, when he resigned to become circuit judge
in the Bourbon-Clark circuit. Clark returned to Congress in 1825 to fill out
Henry Clay's unexpired term. Clay had been appointed secretary of state in
the John Quincy Adams cabinet. Clark served in the twentieth and Twenty-
first Congresses, 1825-1831.[40] Once more Clark returned to Clark County
when he was elected to the Kentucky state senate, 1831-1836. In this latter
office he was made chairman of the important internal improvements committee. This was a major appointment at a time when Kentucky was placing
unusual emphasis on the improvement of the state's rivers and streams for
steamboat transportation, and in the dawning of the railroad era. Clark also
became president of the Kentucky senate, 1831-1836. In the latter year he
was elected governor of the commonwealth.[41]

In politics James Clark was a confirmed opponent of Andrew Jackson
and was one of the organizers of the Whig party in Kentucky. As the circuit
judge of the Clark-Bourbon court, he was to stamp his name indelibly on the
pages of both Kentucky and national constitution history. He served as judge
in one of the most confused and complicated moments in the state's history.
During the years, 1810-1818 there occurred a period of runaway currency
inflation and land prices, an era which ended abruptly in the panic of 1819.[42]
Foolishly, the Kentucky General Assembly chartered banks almost on the

whim of every promoter. By 1819 there were somewhere in the neighborhood of fifty-four branch banks, known as the "Forty Thieves," of the Bank
of Kentucky. The branches issued paper money without sufficient collateral
backing. By 1818 there was afloat in Kentucky a large number of branch
bank notes; perhaps no one knew their total value in dollar terms. At the
same time there was no certainty about how many counterfeit bills were being circulated. The financial panic of 1819 brought about the destruction of
the branch banks and a sharp revision of Kentucky's banking history.[43] Large
numbers of Kentuckians were bankrupted because they had speculated in the
purchase of land, in buildings, and in other capital expenditures. The bank-
rupts immediately appealed to the General Assembly to enact some kind of
relief legislation which would save them from their follies. The legislature
obliged debtors by enacting two relief laws which ostensibly stayed execution
of debtors' notes.[44]

    Thus it was in a time of blinding trouble that James Clark was to gain
notoriety, not as a legislator, but as a circuit judge sitting in the trial of relief
cases. The timing was right for him. The United States Supreme Court had
rendered two major decisions involving the issues of contracts and the sanctity of charters. The cases were *Dartmouth College v. Woodward*, (1819) and
McCulloch v. Maryland (1819).[45] Both cases sustained the defendants and
upheld the charter and contract guarantee under the Constitution of the
United States.

    The two relief legislative acts in Kentucky violated the sanctity of con-
tract and undertook to tax the Bank of the United States. A creditor named
Blair brought suit against a debtor named Williams in Judge James Clark's
Bourbon County Circuit Court. In a penetrating constitutional decision James
Clark held the relief legislative acts unconstitutional.[46] This decision flew in
the face of an intensive desire to escape the losses caused by overinflation and
the panic. Clark found himself immediately involved in a raging controversy
with the General Assembly and the public. The legislators attempted to summons the judge before the bar of the house to censure him. He refused to
honor the peremptory summons in person; instead he defended his decision
in writing. He had sustaining him the powerful precedential decisions of the
United States Supreme Court and of the Kentucky Court of Appeals, which
upheld the lower court decision. The General Assembly compounded its folly
by an attempt to destroy the established court and creating a new one of
dependable relief partisans. This resulted in what came to known as the "Old
Court-New Court" contest. In time the "New Court" was declared unconstitutional, and Judge Clark became a political hero to the more stable conser-

vative element in Kentucky.[47]

In 1832 the voters of Clark County elected James Clark, for the second time, to the Kentucky senate, and from that position he was to become a Whig leader.[48] The Whig candidate for the Kentucky governorship in 1836, Clark was elected over the Van Buren Democratic candidate Matthew Flournoy by a vote of 38,387 to 30,491. Clark was to serve three years as governor before he died in office in 1839. During his three-year administration he was to make what must be considered one of the strongest governors. For the times he was well educated and had broad political experience at the judicial, state legislative, and congressional levels.[49]

James Clark's messages to the Kentucky General Assembly were carefully prepared and incisive in nature. He dealt with the ever-gnawing Kentucky problems of public financing and curbing violence. His most solid achievement was ushering through the General Assembly legislation which specifically laid the foundation for a system of common schools.[50] Possibly the education law of 1838 was one of the most significant pieces of legislation enacted during the first half of the nineteenth century. Prior to that date no other governor, unless it be Gabriel Slaughter, enunciated so clear a concept of the meaning of education. During the decade of the 1830s Kentucky faced major problems of violence ranging from horse thievery to murder. A burning criminal issue was the ridiculous practice of dueling, so prevalent in Kentucky. Governor Clark spoke out pointedly against this practice of settling personal slights and wrongs.[51]

Ironically, Governor James Clark left behind a family which was in poor financial circumstances. His home in Winchester passed out of the ownership of his heirs and was to suffer ill care by future owners and tenants, until it was rescued and restored as a public monument and landmark. As a fitting epitaph to this talented man, Victor B. Howard said in his sketch of James Clark in the *Dictionary of American Biography*, "Clark was a man of culture, refinement, and constructive philosophy, but he was courageous and completely independent."[52] Clark demonstrated in abundance both his "constructive philosophy" and his "courageousness." Perhaps few other judges in Kentucky's judicial history faced such a stern challenge to both his integrity and courage as did Judge Clark in the *Williams v. Blair* decision. The education act of 1838 stands as a permanent monument to his "culture and refinement."

A younger contemporary of Chilton Allen and Clark was Richard Hawes. Hawes was born in Caroline County, Virginia, February 8, 1797.[53] His parents brought him to Kentucky at the age of three years. He grew up near

Lexington and graduated from Transylvania University. Hawes studied law with Charles Humphrey and Robert Wickliffe, one of the largest slaveholders in Kentucky. He was admitted to the Fayette bar in 1818, and six years later he located a law office in Winchester, where he quickly developed a successful law practice.[54] He also engaged in the hemp processing business. Richard Hewes was a volunteer in the Black Hawk War, where he came into association with General Zachary Taylor and Jefferson Davis.[55]

Richard Hawes represented Clark County in the Kentucky General Assembly during the sessions 1827, 1829, and 1834.[56] He was an unsuccessful candidate for a congressional seat in 1834, but three years later he was elected to that office on the Whig ticket, and served in the twenty-fifth and twenty-sixth sessions. At the adjournment of the latter session Hawes returned to Kentucky and moved to Paris in Bourbon County, where he opened a law office and again became involved in politics.[57] In 1862 Richard Hawes was chosen to become the Confederate governor of Kentucky, and he had just taken the oath of office when General Joshua Sill's federal forces closed in on that city. The new Confederate governor had hardly entered the governor's mansion when he was forced to vacate it. As Lewis Collins wrote, "The Confederate Governor of Kentucky, four hours later, and the new government left Frankfort in dignified haste, never to return."[58] At the end of the war Richard Hawes returned to Paris to resume his law practice, and a year prior to his death in 1877 he served as circuit judge of the county.[59]

Down into the mid-1830s Clark County's central political leadership was almost altogether of Virginia origins, men who had followed the great edenesque land dream westward. The end of the Virginia era can almost be dated from the death of James Clark.[60] There, however, was one Virginian in Kentucky who went marching on to midcentury. Although Henry Clay had only tenuous connection with Clark County, he was very much a figure in its political history. Young Clay arrived in Kentucky late in 1797 with a brand new Virginia license to practice law.[61] On March 20, 1798, he appeared before the Fayette County Court seeking a Kentucky license to practice his profession.[62] Clay immediately became engrossed in public debate and politics. He entered into discussion of the issue of taxation pending in the constitutional convention of 1799. Writing to the editor of the *Kentucky Gazette* over the pseudonym of "Scaveola," he made passionate pleas for changes, including a bold speaking out on the subject of slavery.[63] In a second letter the young "Scaveola" was equally forthright. he criticized the conservative land-slaveholders who met in a session at Bryan's Station to discuss issues to come before the constitutional convention. Earlier Clay had stirred the enmity of the conservatives of central Kentucky by his address to a private club in which he expressed the Jeffersonian and Madisonian view of slavery.[64] He, however, recovered his favor in the rousing anti-Alien and Sedition Acts speech at Maxwell Spring.[65]

In none of the dependable documentary sources is there the slightest evidence that Henry Clay made either his first or last speech in Winchester. There, however, did appear an intriguing notice from him in the *Kentucky Gazette* on August 29, 1798, saying: "Lost, some short time past, between Winchester and this place, a *Red Morocco Pocket Book*, containing sundry papers, which can only be useful to the subscriber. It is unnecessary to describe them particularly, as any of them will shew to whom the book belongs; I will give Five Dollars to any person who will deliver the book to me, or secure it so that I can get it again."[66] No doubt the contents of the morocco case contained legal papers.

In his active political years Henry Clay was to enjoy a warm and cordial association with the people of Clark County. He appeared in the circuit court of the county in legal cases and as candidate for the presidency of the United States. It appears that his last appearance at court in the county was as an attorney involved in the famous Quisenberry Will Case. Clay's health was so poor that the court permitted him to remain seated while he presented his argument.[67]

Unequivocally, Henry Clay's last speech was delivered in the United States Senate, December 1, 1851. He spoke on the occasion of the election conflict between Stephen R. Mallory and David L. Yulee of Florida. Clay had a grievance against David Yulee and moved the seating of Stephen R. Mallory, which the Senate agreed to do. This was Henry Clay's final speech, and his final day in the United States Senate.[68]

There appears in several printed sources, and in the popular legend of Clark County, that Clay made his last speech in the county. It almost seems sinful to scotch this cherished legend. Editors of *The Papers of Henry Clay* are positive in their documentation of Clay's last speech.[69] The quaint legend of Henry Clay's last speech perhaps adds some color to a popular concept of history: however viewed, it is of no real historical significance.

What is of historical importance is the fact that over more than two centuries literally hundreds of individuals have served Clark County in some political capacity. A mere listing of their names would make a sizable publications. At the base level of local politics the fundamental interests have been centered upon four or five principal subjects. At all times the adjudication of confused land entitlements, conflicting property boundaries, dower rights and the descent of property, education, and maintenance of civil order, and, earlier, slavery were sensitive and challenging. Prior to 1865 the issue of slavery generated a kind of legal and social virus which infected the whole political system in the county.[70]

The names of the most prominent individuals in the county appear frequently in all of the documentary records of the county.[71] One can only surmise from this evidence that there was some continuity of the leadership and control of public affairs in the county. After 1824 there arose in the West, and in the nation, a new political leadership enunciating a new philosophy of politics and government. After 1824 there occurred a split between the Jackson-Van Buren Democrats and the more conservative Whigs, which James Clark was so instrumental in organizing into a party.[72] This new political era was to be reflected in elections in Clark County. Nevertheless, there remained a rather tight and conservative control of public affairs. At the grassroots level of the county's political roster new faces began to appear in the courthouse and in the magisterial districts. There are sprinkled on the pages of the order books of the county court, in the circuit court records, and in the minutes of the Winchester trustees, and, later, the town council a veritable litany of names of persons serving in some public political capacity. Among some of the earlier and more prominent were Dr. Samuel D. Martin, son of early sheriff John Martin; P. Bush, a member of the numerous Bush clan; John P. Bulloch; John Clinkenbeard; John Randolph; Robert John Williams; Aylet Buckner; Stephen Eubank; P. B. Winn; Richard Duncan; James M. Wood; and numerous others with names reminiscent of the early settlement of the county.[73] Every election brought changes in much of the official personnel of the county. With the advent of Jacksonian Democracy the elective process in Clark County showed new and more robust partisanship. But no one took time to write a contemporary description of what actually happened about the polling places in the nineteenth century.

Some concept of the electoral procedures is to be gained from a perusal of the list of expenses incurred in the holding of elections. There appeared in the statements of public expenditures the names of persons who served as judges and bailiffs of elections. Most of the claims were for two days' service in the polling places.[74] Voters expressed their choices in earlier years vive voce and in later years by telling clerks their choices, which were recorded for all to see. Without the benefit of clear documentation of precisely what went on around the Clark County precincts on election day, no doubt there was considerable drinking as candidates treated voters and, as sometimes happened, partisan tempers flared. There was rather heavy solicitation for votes, and both by the vive voce mode of voting or the clerks recorded ballots candidates knew how individuals voted. Often shrewd candidates held off their own rich rewards for serving the cause of democracy until votes were cast and accounted for. Caleb Bingham in his two marvelous engravings *Casting the Vote*, and in *Soliciting Voters*, portrayed the voting process in general.[75]

There arose considerable debate over the mode of voting which occurred in the constitutional convention of 1849. William Preston of Garrard County presented a proposal to maintain the vive voce process. William Bullitt of Jefferson County, in a highly revealing discussion, announced that he was opposed to the system of voting by ballot because "It would be said emancipation, as well as agrarianism, in all it's forms. He had as much confidence in the honor, integrity, and virtue of the people of Kentucky as any other people in the world; he would not yield the Kentucky character, but it was a fact well known, that there were bad men in all communities. If all men were perfect and invulnerable, why would we be sent here to make a constitution? A perfect man requires no law to restrain him, but they found it necessary in all governments, to impose restraints upon the wicked. What would be the effect of the ballot system? It would be this. There were bad men, it was admitted; men who would deprive their neighbors of their property if they could

High fashion late nineteenth century style. This church bound group might well have posed for a fashion magazine when derby and feathered lady's hats, and tight fitting corsets created hour glass figures of women.

have an opportunity of doing it by sneaking up to the ballot box, like *a sheep killing dog*, without being responsible to the influences around them. Where was the necessity for adopting the system of ballot voting?"[76]

The vive voce system of voting prevailed in Kentucky until 1890. However, the secret, or Australian, ballot was first used in the United States in Louisville, Kentucky, in a municipal election in 1888.[77] This was to have a distinct influence on the mode of voting in Clark County.

There were assumed to be 1,652 eligible voters in Clark County in 1824, an assumption which was far shy of the mark of persons interested in voting. In the presidential election of that year only 21.9 percent of the voters went to the polls. Seventy-nine of them voted for Andrew Jackson, and 274 favored Henry Clay.[78] Though only a fractional number of the potential voters supported Clay, he, nevertheless, throughout his political life had the loyalty of the voters of Clark County. Clay supporters that year frowned upon the rowdy tactics of the Jacksonian partisans.

Two years after the election of 1824, and half way through Henry Clay's administration as the United States secretary of state, Clay was invited to be the honored guest at a banquet in Winchester. A committee made up of Hubbard Taylor, Thomas R. Moore, Hay Battaile, John Mills, John T. Woodford, Benjamin H. Buckner, William McMillan, Chilton Allen, James Simpson, Richard Hawes, Jr., Richard French, and Isaac Cunningham assured Clay, "Your fellow citizens feel a pride in this triumph of political rectitude, which they wish not to suppress. On all occasions they sympathize [sic] with the victim of calumny. But when they view the arrows of distraction levelled at the breast of him, who has grown up among them, and upon whom they rely, as upon their own right arm, his cause is their cause, and his success is their success."[79] The men on this committee virtually represented the entire power structure of Clark County.

Two days after the invitation reached Lexington, Henry Clay responded to Hubbard Taylor and his colleagues, "Expressing the friendly congratulations of my fellow citizens of Clark County and Winchester, in consequence of my recent return to Kentucky, and inviting me to a public dinner which they propose on the 29th inst. Such an honorable testimony of esteem and confidence emanating from any portion of the public would be highly gratifying, but proceeding as it does from a respectable community, with many of whose members I have been intimately associated with in public and private life, for more than a quarter of a century, it has a value which no language can adequately express."[80] Clay said he was forced by the pressure of private business affairs to decline the invitation.

Despite the fact Henry Clay was forced to reject the Clark County invitation to a public dinner in 1824, voters remained loyal. Out of respect for him they supported John Quincy Adams for reelection in 1828. In the general election a remarkable 75.3 percent of the registered voters went to the polls to cast 537 votes for Andrew Jackson and 784 for Adams.[81] Four years later Henry Clay entered the race for the presidency for the second time and received in Clark County the impressive support of 1,470 votes out of the potential registered voters; Andrew Jackson received 409 votes.[82] In that year the Clark County voters gave Henry Clay the most support of any of the Inner Bluegrass counties.[83]

Whig party support remained steady for Henry Clay in Clark County when he offered for national office. In 1840 the Whigs supported William Henry Harrison, hero of the war of 1812 and the "Log Cabin Hard Cider" candidate. Harrison received three-fourths of the votes cast that year.[84] By 1840 the Whig registration has increased, largely because of the work of James Clark and Chilton Allen. Too, there lingered some dedication to the philosophy of Jeffersonian Republicanism. In time, however, this influence waned and the remaining Republicans had to make the decision to support one of the rising new parties.

The period 1840-1860 was a largely quiescent one in Clark County. The voters consistently supported the Whig ticket down to 1860. The turnout of voters at the polls in some of the elections was relatively light. This was a remarkable fact in the context of the great debates over national expansion and the extension of slavery, including the Kansas-Nebraska Bill and the Dred Scott decision. Neither Franklin Pierce nor James Buchanan excited the local electorate.[85]

The presidential election of 1860 was perhaps the most reflective of Clark County responses to the strong political crosscurrents of the times. That year local voters became responsive to the strong political currents which agitated Americans during the decade of the 1850s. Clark County voters appear to have been sensitized by the issues which faced the nation. In the presidential election in November, 83.7 percent of the registered voters went to the poll; 49 percent of them were slaveholders.[86] By election time the old Whig party which James Clark, Hubbard Taylor, Chilton Allen, and other prominent land-slaveholders had helped to organize had practically vanished from the political scene. The Democrat John C. Breckinridge polled 391 votes. John Bell, the constitutional union party candidate, received 959 votes, and one lone citizen cast a vote for Abraham Lincoln and the Republican party.[87]

During the Civil War years there was a distinct voter apathy, created partly by the confusion which existed in the Kentucky state government because of federal interference.[88] In the 1864 election less than half the registered voters cast a ballot; this time the majority of 636 favored George B. McClellan while 136 voted for President Lincoln.[89] In this election it was clearly evident that Clark County voters had shed the last vestige of Whiggism. Slavery was well on the road to extinction, and already Clark County was faced with the necessity of embracing a new era of social and economic reconstruction. This fact was most impressively reflected in the presidential election of 1872. By the latter year the number of voters in Clark County had increased a hundred-fold, rising from 1,742 in 1868 to 2,579 in 1872.[90] The potential voter rolls in the latter year reflected the appearance of the new freedmen at the polls. There widened a great political chasm between the days when the Whigs controlled political affairs in Clark County and the year 1872, when the ex-slave voters carried the county by a 51.1 percent vote for the Republican party. The Democrats, however, regained the lead in 1876, when there was an unusually heavy voter turnout. They voted for Samuel J. Tilden, the Democrat, by a majority of 56.6 percent over Rutherford B. Hayes, the Republican.

In the hotly contested election of 1900, when D. B. Redwine of Clark County was an active Democratic leader and Democrat William Goebel opposed Republican candidate for governor William S. Taylor, 90.1 percent of the potential voters went to the polls. Clark County gave William Goebel a 2,302-vote majority over Taylor's 1,900 votes.[91] Down to 1928 the county remained staunchly Democratic. The election of 1920 reflected a second moment of radically increased numbers of voters. In the presidential election of 1916 there had been 5,652 potential voters who gave Woodrow Wilson a 59.2 percent majority over Charles Evans Hughes.[92] By 1920 the number of registered voters had increased to 10,476. Adoption of the Nineteenth Amendment to the United States Constitution on January 9, 1918, when it was signed by President Wilson, had resulted in a heavy registration of women voters.[93] The heavy registration in Clark County would reflect the fact that women had political interests extending well beyond serving on school boards or as superintendent of the county's public schools. Despite all the publicity and local excitement in the anticipation that President Harry Truman would visit Winchester on his famous 1948 campaign swing across the country, only 44 percent of the registered voters showed up at the voting precincts in November to give Truman a decisive majority of 3,272 votes over 1,505 for Thomas Dewey.[94]

In the field of Kentucky politics since 1890 three Clark County citizens played active roles. Judge William M. Beckner was elected a delegate to the constitutional convention in 1890 and became a major voice in the debates. Unlike Dr. Andrew Hood in the constitutional convention of 1849, Judge Beckner was on hand and attentive to the proceedings of the convention. He became a leading advocate for change and progressiveness in nearly every instance. He frequently entered spirited discussions on the import of many areas of constitutional government. His most direct influence, however, was his strong advocacy of a more effective educational system for the common-wealth. Although he was not the originator of the central point expressed in Section 183 of the new constitution, it was his strong advocacy which got it included in the new document. There still remained in Kentucky in 1890 and in the constitutional convention some leadership with a Neanderthal cast of mind so far as education was concerned.[95]

The famous Section 183 became the constitutional foundation of public education, notwithstanding the fact that its mandate went largely unfulfilled for almost a century. The failure to provide an equal educational opportunity for every child in the commonwealth became the point at issue in legal pro-ceedings in 1989 and 1990, when both the Franklin Circuit Court and the Kentucky Supreme Courts declared Kentucky's public school system uncon-stitutional. No doubt this decision would have been heartily approved by Judge Beckner. Beckner's name appeared often in the proceedings of the 1890 constitutional convention, and he frequently revealed the fact that he was well prepared to enter into the debates.[96]

Boswell B. Hodgkin was elected state superintendent of public instruc-tion on 1948, in a period when public education was being called upon to meet the challenges of the highly fluid post-World War II years. His four years in office were transitional ones. He left behind a ten-point blueprint for the future of advancement of public education. In his valedictory he wrote, "This program is not the work of starry-eyes dreamers. It is practical. It is based on modern educational concepts with full regard to its implications for sound fiscal policy. It gives full regard to our resources as well as to our re-sponsibilities. When its full portent is understood by the citizens of Ken-tucky, they will demand that it be incorporated in order that no Kentucky child be denied his educational birthright."[97] This blueprint presaged the Kentucky Educational Reform Act of 1990.

One other Clark County native rose to the ranks of leadership power in Kentucky. John Alexander Rose was elected senator from the twenty eighth Senatorial District in 1987 and was reelected in 1990 and 1994. He was elected president pro tem of the senate in 1987, and president in 1993. Rose shared this honor with James Clark, who was president of the Senate in 1835-1836.[98]

Clark County voters have generally supported Democratic party candidates since 1872 in national general elections. Locally, however, the party label was not of primary consideration in the face of personalities, factionism, and parochial issues. At the county level political responses have centered upon immediate county problems and future projections. Always there has been that yeasty element, the strength and power of the "courthouse ring." This third entity of local government has ever been a salient fact in the outcome of the elections. From time to time the basis of operation of the "courthouse hierarchy" has undergone both constitutional and statutory changes, but none so far-reaching as that of 1975. There was a complete revision of the judiciary article of the Kentucky Constitution that year.[99] In the background research by the Legislative Research Commission and in the debates an inordinate amount of attention was given to the office of county judge. The title of this office was changed to "Judge Executive," with the strong constitutional implication that all matters pertaining to court trials were removed from that office. No longer did the county judge/executive have the duty of holding court to try petty cases at law. Also, the county court and judge/executive were held responsible for many of the ancient social duties of the county. In a eight-point section defining the "Powers and Duties" of the judge/executive this officer was made the enforcer of state and county laws, organizer of the fiscal budget, and controller of the county employees personnel and was charged with informing the county court on fiscal conditions and preparing and submitting an annual operational budget. The voter approval of the omnibus reworking of the judicial article of the constitution, however, had minimal bearing on the everyday political mores of Clark County, or upon any other county in Kentucky.[100] For two centuries there has ever been a kaleidescopelike changing of political personalities. Every election has the potential of sweeping out one set of officials and sweeping in another. The listing of office holders has progressively grown longer with the passing decades. Some elected officials have served with distinction while others lingered in office for four-year terms and passed into oblivion, leaving little more record behind than their names and the dates of their terms.

Two historical facts have been ineradically embedded in the annals of Clark County; some of its political stars have swept across the public horizon of history leaving behind a record of constructive achievement, while others fizzled into oblivion as nothing more than political aberrations. Whatever the merits or lack of merits of the great parade of county officials, one fact stands out clear and unimpeachable. The courthouses which have risen in the past near John Baker's great fresh water spring have been the magnetic centers of a practical and grassroots system of democratic government within a horseback ride for every citizen, no matter his social, economic, or political status.

A touring group lined up before the Brown-Proctor Hotel in July 1907. This was a day when the town fathers had prescribed strict driving rules for motorist using the public streets. - *Photo courtesy of Mrs. Carl A. Norton*

CHAPTER 14

Winchester, an Emerging City

On February 2, 1882, legally at least, by legislative fiat Winchester was thrust across the dividing line from being a rural county seat to becoming a fourth-class city. On that date the Kentucky General Assembly raised Winchester up a notch in status, but thrust upon it all the responsibilities yet few of the glories which the promotion implied.[1] The old designations of "town" and "trustee" were relegated to archival memory. Now the "city" was to be governed by a mayor and a board of council. In noting this fact the sitting town clerk, James Flannigan, wrote in the trustee book that a city council had been elected and its members were on hand to take the oath of office. Almost in an obituary tone Clerk Flannigan wrote, "The books, papers and sixty dollars $ .27 cents now in the hands of the treasurer will be turned over to the board of councilmen aforesaid, and this Board now adjourns *sine die*." It did indeed adjourn, never again to draft an ordinance or bemoan the pollution of the town's water source.[2]

F. H. Dudley, J. H. Jefferies, and Stephen G. Hays signed the "death certificate" of the old informal manner of governing Winchester. A new age of governance was begun under the watch-care of a mayor-councilmen dispensation. M. G. Taylor, V. W. Bush, J. H. Holloway, S. S. Hayes, and J. E. Garner took the oath of office as councilmen, an oath administered by Judge J. S. Allen.[3] In the first session J. D. Simpson was elected mayor over former town clerk James Flannigan in a divided council vote.[4]

In the daily course of life in Winchester the legalistic transition from the designation of "town" to the that of "city" made little, if any, perceptible difference. Hogs and dogs still wandered the streets, many of them dying there. Loud and rowdy loafers still congregated before the numerous saloons, at the livery stables, and at the railway depot. In the mid-1880s they congregated in such numbers at the depot as to block the movement of passengers getting on and off the trains. Early in their administration the councilmen attempted to thin the ranks of loafers by prescribing the assessment of fines of five to twenty dollars for the offense of crowding about the railway depot.[5] These were sums sufficient to finance a trip to Indianapolis, or even to Chicago. No doubt the city council had ample precedence for their actions. There had been enacted an earlier ordinance on the subject of loafing. The board of the council also frowned heavily upon the offense of indecent personal exposure by mandating a fifty dollar fine.

Throughout the latter decades of the nineteenth century the actions of the council were about evenly balanced between the upholding of earlier ordinances and devising new ones to meet the demands of an emerging city. Never before had the town's governing body had to deal with so many nagging and complex problems at the same time, problems which ranged from opening new streets and alleys, to building sidewalks, to insuring public health and safety.[6]

The threats and prices of progress in Winchester sometimes assumed life-threatening proportions. The building of the railroads and the opening of the eastern Kentucky coal mines were welcomed advances, but they carried with them the potential for capital danger. Channeling a railway roadbed through mountainous eastern Kentucky necessitated the use of large amounts of dynamite and black powder. This was also true for the opening of the mines. Considerable amounts of both types of explosives were stored in Winchester either in siding sheds or aboard freight cars, or they passed through the town aboard trains. On August 17, 1883, through a switching error a Chesapeake and Ohio train rambled into a car loaded with 800 kegs of black powder. The ensuing explosion killed a flagman, Charlie McMichael, and shattered windows. This explosion exemplified the danger to having explosives in the town.[7]

Now that Winchester had attained the status of being a city its councilmen had to live up to the connotations of the title. They were pressed to establish permanent offices of the urban government. No longer did a table with a locked drawer meet the needs of a more active governing body. The council purchased of Peasless and Gaulbert of Louisville a fireproof safe for $100 free on board in Louisville.[8] One thing the onrushing modern age did not accomplish was the legibility of the handwriting of the city clerks.

The Winchester city council dealt monthly with a multiplicity of prob-

Bradley's Grocery circa 1918. Some staple food items still came packed in barrels, and there were stylishly dressed clerks to run the shelves to fill customers' orders. - *Photo courtesy of Mrs. Gladys Tucker*

lems, great and small, spending about as much time on one problem as another. For instance, the chief of police was ordered to display in public places a notice as a stubborn reminder to free-willed citizens that after June 9, 1866, the law forbidding the free ranging of hogs on the city streets would be emphatically enforced.[9] Need for the notice implied that earlier ordinances forbidding this custom had been highly honored by their being ignored by the town-dwelling hog raisers. In the same session when the strident outburst of authority against free-ranging hogs occurred, the council authorized the employment of H. M. March as health officer.[10] He was to be paid an annual salary of $75.00. Other salaries and fees were on a comparable scale. Alma Johnson was paid two dollars and a quarter for feeding a destitute family; James Ecton, jailor, received twenty-four dollars a month; and D. T. Buckner was paid a salary of thirty-five dollars for unspecified services.[11]

At the December 3, 1886 meeting of the city council there came forward S. Solomon proposing to erect a gas plant and to lay pipelines in the city. A committee composed of J. W. Parrish, J. H. W. Spahn, and J. T. Conway was appointed to examine Solomon's proposal.[12] Earlier, Frankfort and then Lexington had installed naphtha gas works to generate what coughing and gagging citizens called "pole cat gas" because of its acrid odor. The proposition

Solomon was to install comparable gas works and pipelines for Winchester. The council approved and granted the promoter and franchise.[13]

Despite the fact the council approved the gas franchise there seems to have been considerable uncertainty about all the public services. Though the council approved the Solomon proposal in December 1886, it was not until May 1887, and following considerable discussion, that a second ordinance was devised and adopted granting Solomon an exclusive right to provide the city gas for twenty-five years. This ordinance authorized the placing of the pipelines along the streets and alleys.[14]

Though there were long drawn-out discussions of the granting of a gas franchise, those relating to providing adequate water to the city were more involved. In many respects a public water supply to Winchester came close to being a central theme in the town's history. The various town "fire" cisterns were under the care of a special committee of the council. It reported to the full council on December 3, 1886, that although the cisterns had been repaired, they were still too inadequate to furnish an ample supply of water to the growing town population and to ensure public safety from fires.[15] Two

This St. George Hotel bar may not have "healed the sick or helped the poor," but it did make a gesture to temperance groups by featuring buttermilk on its back bar mirror.

years later, December 1888, the city council was informed that there were still a number of cisterns about the town. Again, nobody really knew how many times the water supply problem had been discussed or how many committees had been appointed to seek answers to the need for stabilizing the town's water supply. Historically, it may not have been the most fortunate decision to locate the town near a large natural spring rather than a more abundant body of water. The new commission was instructed to solicit proposals from various outside waterworks companies. Strangely, no local entrepreneur stepped forward with a plan, nor was there ever recorded in the minutes of the trustees or the council a serious hint of finding water, with the exception of one suggestion that a pipeline be extended to the Kentucky River.[16]

It was not until 1888 that the Winchester City Council finally came to grips with the water problems. A franchise to establish a waterworks and necessary pipelines was granted the Boston, Massachusetts, firm of Wheeler and Parkes. Aside from establishing a waterworks and laying pipelines, Wheeler and Parkes was asked to install at strategic sites a number of fireplugs. In some measure the granting of this franchise was the death knell to the old fire bucket, short ladder, and fire cistern ordinances, but not the end of the water supply problems.[17]

Finding a dependable water supply and tapping it with a modern pumping and pipeline facility was in a sense an albatross about the necks of city councilmen. In the intervening years, 1888 to 1904, there does not appear in the minutes of the council the necessary data to describe with much detail the need for water in Winchester. On December 15, 1904, well after the establishment of the waterworks, Winchester was said still to be short of water. To confront this need J. L. Webber presented the council a forthright resolution in which he declared, "The water supply for this city is inadequate and unsatisfactory, and we feel that we now owe it to the various interests of the city to remedy this condition as speedily as possible." In response to this direct admonition, a committee composed of J. D. Ramsey, William Harding, J. D. Simpson, and W. F. Kens was directed to make a survey of potential water resources and to report their finding to a later council meeting.[18]

The committee surveyed the water supply for the town and reported to the council on June 2, 1905, saying that Winchester Waterworks Company had agreed to lay 12,000 feet of pipeline and to install a suitable number of fire hydrants. The council approved this report, apparently without discussion of the basic problem of the source of the town's water.[19] Perhaps this riddle was left to the waterworks company to solve as best it could.

In the somewhat feverish era of granting public services franchises the city clerk was kept busy drafting and recording the blueprints for the new-age Winchester. For instance, at the city council's June 18, 1886 meeting there was approved an inordinately detailed ordinance granting the Winchester Light Company the privilege of locating power lines along the various streets and alleys. Upon the entrance to the electrical age there arose an interesting folk contention, as published in central Kentucky newspapers, that the use of electric lights could only lead to blindness.[20]

Contemporary with building an electrical generating station, a gas works, and a waterworks, Winchester was sufficiently prepared to take a further long step into the electronic future. In 1883 the telephone had reached central Kentucky, and people in Lexington were entranced by its wizardry.[21] Alexander Graham Bell had demonstrated his wonderful instrument at the Centennial Exposition in Philadelphia in 1876.[22] From that date on the move to make the instrument both a domestic and commercial necessity gained momentum. For the southern region the Bell Company organized its subsidiary the East Tennessee Telephone Company. By 1880 phone lines had been strung to Frankfort, the three years later they reached Lexington. A crude telephone exchange was established on Cheapside in Lexington to serve twenty-two subscribers.[23]

The wonder of transmitting the sound of the human voice by wire bordered on sorcery itself. Among those doubters who had to be convinced that Dr. Alexander Graham Bell was not another county court day faker was Mrs. D. C. McClure of Clark County. In the summer of 1888 she drove to Lexington to hear with her own ear the sound of a human voice being emitted from a soulless metallic instrument.[24]

The East Tennessee Telephone Company strung a line from Lexington to Richmond and sometime in 1890 one to Winchester, where the company had been granted a franchise.[25] Once the telephone had been proved a reality to the people of Clark County and Winchester there ensued a veritable rash of telephone companies seeking a Winchester franchise. On May 4, 1894, the city council granted a firm begun by a local attorney, E. S. Jouett, Jr. and Associates, a franchise, but not before council members had extracted a promise from the company that it would place phones in the council's office and in that of the chief of police without cost.[26]

The Winchester City Council set rates for the companies at two dollars a month for residences and three dollars for other patrons.[27] A year later the council awarded a franchise to J. W. McDaniel and Associates, thus making either the third or fourth franchise granted for Winchester. On November 11, 1898, J. M. Benton, an attorney representing the East Tennessee Telephone Company sought for that company a petition which was granted. At the end of the nineteenth century, Winchester and Clark County were being served by at least three or four telephone systems. This multiplicity of systems must have complicated the use of the telephone locally. The county and town must have been one of the most overserved telephone districts in the commonwealth in 1900.[28]

A partial solution to the telephone dilemma occurred when, on June 2, 1905, the Old Kentucky Telephone and Telegraph Company made a bid to establish an exchange which would serve 750 subscribers. The company would string the necessary lines to serve all prospective patrons. It would install the new type of telephone capable of transmitting long-distance messages. The city government would be given, free of cost, special police signal wires, and three long-distance telephones would be installed in such places as the mayor

Harry Truman "whistle stopping" in Winchester in the famous presidential campaign in 1948. Truman hardly remained in the town long enough to throw a kiss to the ladies who worked so diligently to make his visit a triumphant one.

GUERRANT MISSION CLINIC AND HOSPITAL—WINCHESTER, KENTUCKY
EDWARD P. GUERRANT, M. D., MEDICAL SUPERVISOR OF ASSEMBLY'S HOME MISSIONS
MOUNTAIN DEPARTMENT.   PRESBYTERIAN CHURCH. U. S.

The famous Guerrant Medical Center in Winchester had a distinguished history in the era of emerging public health services. The elder Guerrant had served in the Confederate Army, was a medical missionary in Eastern Kentucky, and author of *Galax Gatherers*. The Clinic's mission was declared to be "heal the sick and help the poor."

and council designated. All other services would be rendered at the rate of twenty-seven dollars per annum for residential phones and thirty-six dollars for business and commercial phones. The contract with the Old Kentucky Telephone Company was signed by Mayor R. P. Scobee for the city and by D. L. Pendleton for the company, on June 2, 1905. This simplified the local telephone service.[29]

Next to finding a dependable source of water, the problem of generating adequate revenue was a chronic century-old challenge. Throughout its history there ran through Winchester's fiscal travails a thread of anxiety. If the trustees, and later the councilmen, ever prepared an annual budget, the fact cannot be documented in the public record. It seems clear that the town's expenses were paid by the treasurer out of such funds as he had in hand. It was also clear there persisted a strong resistance to paying taxes. At times a financial stringency caused a serious disruption of public services, none so serious, however, as the necessity to close the town's schools halfway through their session in 1883 because of a lack of funds.[30]

Remarkably, the town of Winchester was able to operate even its meager public services during its first century without an annual budget or a stable system of revenue. Certainly the various license fees charged various groups doing business in the town were far from being a certain source of revenues. Once Winchester achieved the status of being a city, with all that the title implied, one of the town's biggest challenges was the creation of a revenue system generating sufficient ensured income to sustain the public services in an age of growth and population expansion.

A possible source of revenue was the imposing of a tax on the three Winchester banks. Winchester was not alone in its attempts to tax these institutions. Kentucky banks generally resisted the move to tax them, and in 189_ they took their case to court. Finally in 1897 the Kentucky Court of Appeals handed down the decision in the bank tax case favoring the Kentucky towns.[31] This decision had a special meaning for Winchester. It came at a time, said Dr. Hart when its finances were "diminished." Dr. Hart drafted a resolution authorizing the collection of bank taxes back to 1893. The resolution and the tax involved the Clark County National Bank, the National Bank of Winchester, and the Citizens National Bank. Responding to the resolution, Beckner and Jouett, attorneys for the banks, filed a bill of exceptions on the part of the banks which sought exemption from the tax for the years 1893-1897. There is little doubt that the proposals to tax the banks and the railroads were the most perplexing ever to face the governing body of the city of Winchester before 1900. The town desperately needed the revenue, but to collect it involved litigation and costly delays. The bank tax issue was finally resolved on December 27, 1897.[32] At a called meeting of the council attorneys representing the city and the banks presented what was said to be a just compromise.[33] The council approved the compromise proposal, thus ending a long dispute between the town and its banks.

At the moment the nineteenth century closed and the twentieth opened the citizens of Clark County and Winchester could look back on an era of maturing, meeting pioneering challenges, and the emergence of a more sophisticated society. Winchester, the epitome of a rural Kentucky county seat town, had throughout the century operated on a slender budget and an even more modest tax rate. Only in the closing two decades of the old century had town officials been called upon to create the public services.

In an entirely different context, Winchester by 1900 had become a key town in sectionally Kentucky. Centered almost squarely between the Bluegrass and the Appalachian Highlands, it was the first town of any size that highlanders reached on their travels to the "outside" from a broad scope of hill country. Too, it was a politically and judicially neutral town in which some of the highly emotional Breathitt County feudists cases could be tried without an outbreak of violence.[34] A key to Winchester's growing importance was the fact that both the highway and railway systems were in an advancing stage of completion. Thus the town became a hub of both travel and commercial transportation.

Nevertheless, there remained tremendously demanding challenges for both county and city as they entered the twentieth century. As indicated earlier, many of the basic public services were in their early stages of development. Now the age of consolidating and improving them was upon councilmen and citizens alike. In September 1904 attorney E. S. Jouett, Jr. and J. M. Benton, representing Holbrook and Associates of Wilkes-Barre, Pennsylvania, came before the city council seeking a franchise to consolidate the Winchester Waterworks, the Winchester Street Railway Company, and Martin Construction Company, the ice plant and the Winchester Lighting Company into one body that would be put up at public auction.[35]

A contract to achieve unification of the local public service units was granted. A franchise was granted to Holbrook and Pinkress on October 12, 1901.[36] Left out of this drive to improve public services in Winchester were

The new post office, (1913), the pride and joy of the local Postal Service.

provisions for dealing with a century-old menace, the disposition of increasing amounts of sewerage. At the turn of the century the public health of the city was in danger of an outbreak of an endemic disease.

The ink had hardly dried on the consolidation of public services franchise before Winchester was thrown into a state of concern. It was reported there was a case of small pox in the town, at a time when a major portion of the population has not been vaccinated against the disease. The city council enacted an ordinance mandating that every resident be vaccinated, and that special care be taken that all children were afforded immunity against smallpox. The ordinance made parents and guardians responsible for the immunization of their children, and the town paid a physician to vaccinate the indigents.[37]

In March 1901, the Lexington Interurban Company, requested a subsidiary franchise for an interurban railway line between Lexington and Mount Sterling by way of Winchester. The petitioner was the Blue Grass Interurban Traction Company of which Louis Descoqne was president. This company sought permission to build its lines through selected streets of Winchester. The council turned the proposal down in a split four-to-three vote. Officers of the traction company were determined. They again presented a modified proposal on March 25, 1902, to a called session of the council; this time a franchise was approved. No doubt this approval came about after members of the council had read the long and detailed outline of the franchise and some inside persuasion. It was approved by a vote of five to two, and Mayor R. P. Scobee signed the ordinance. The franchise provided that the Lexington-Mount Sterling interurban line would pass through Winchester over Maple and Washington streets and Winn Avenue.[38]

A month later the city council was in a more pleasant frame of mind when it voted on April 4, 1902, to petition Andrew Carnegie to finance the building of a library for the town. Members argued that Winchester was centrally located and served a broad area of central and eastern Kentucky. Some member or members of the council undertook to seduce the Scotch philanthropist with a sales promotional statement. Carnegie was told, "Winchester is at the crossing of three independent railroads, has had a phenomenal growth of late years, is the gateway city for eastern Kentucky, where there is such an abundance of coal, timber and other materials for manufacturing. It is in the Blue Grass region with rich agricultural resources, and has an intelligent enterprising body of citizens who have by their own energy, enterprise and liberality, secured five graded pubic schools, waterworks, electric lights, street cars and other improvements and would appreciate a good library."[39] Whether or not this booster petition impressed Andrew Carnegie may be open to question, but the statement constituted an enticing summary of Winchester's state of development in that year.

Though there is no documentation of Andrew Carnegie's reply to the Winchester application, it seems clear it was negative. Undaunted, the city council made a second request. On March 3, 1905, that body adopted a

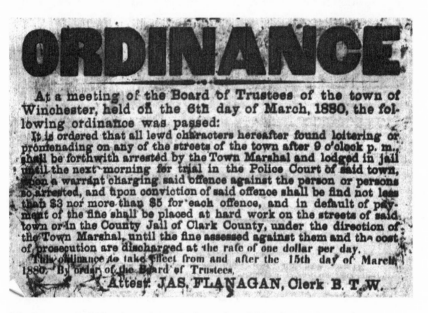

ORDINANCE

At a meeting of the Board of Trustees of the town of Winchester, held on the 6th day of March, 1880, the following ordinance was passed:

It is ordered that all lewd characters hereafter found loitering or promenading on any of the streets of the town after 9 o'clock p. m., shall be forthwith arrested by the Town Marshal and lodged in jail until the next morning for trial in the Police Court of said town, upon a warrant charging said offence against the person or persons so arrested, and upon conviction of said offence shall be find not less than $3 nor more than $5 for each offence, and in default of payment of the fine shall be placed at hard work on the streets of said town or in the County Jail of Clark County, under the direction of the Town Marshal, until the fine assessed against them and the cost of prosecution are discharged at the rate of one dollar per day. This ordinance to take effect from and after the 15th day of March 1880. By order of the Board of Trustees,

Attest: JAS. FLANAGAN, Clerk B. T. W.

John Garner no doubt found some humor in the wording of this ordinance. Apparently it was perfectly legal to cavort on the streets of Winchester provided one did so before 9:00 p.m. After that time there was the modest fee of three to five dollars.

resolution submitted by C. L. Van Meter, asking the council to join with the Winchester Commercial Club in seeking a library gift from Andrew Carnegie for the subsidization of a library in the Kentucky Wesleyan College. In this instance the council voted to appropriate up to $150.00 to pay the expenses of a special envoy to go to New York and try and urge Andrew Carnegie to look with favor on the Winchester supplication.[40]

In the opening decade of the twentieth century there was a distinct victory in Winchester's progressive advances to the future. There was an almost headlong rush by the citizens to modernize their town and to meet the demands of a modern urban society. As the population of the town increased; in 1900 it was 5,964, or almost exactly a third of that of Clark County; so did

John Edwin Garner, newspaper editor, Winchester businessman, mayor extraordinary, humorist, iconoclast, and superb after dinner speaker. - *Photo courtesy of Ogden*

the urgent demand for modern health-protecting services. Living in a fast-growing urban society required the setting and observation of more stringent controls. It would now challenge a vivid imagination to reconstruct a full concept of that turn-of-the-century era when old patterns and practices of social and commercial life in Winchester were required to adapt to new ways of life and intersocial relationships. As mentioned, Winchester from the days of its founding was intermittently threatened with the outbreak of endemic diseases. There, however, was no more threatening menace to health and happiness than the primitive means of managing sewerages. This fact was firmly brought to public consideration when Mayor R. P. Scobee, R. A. Perry, and J. A. Ramsey were asked to investigate and report on the pressing need for creating a modern sewerage disposal system. No longer were privies an answer, nor was the spreading of spats of quicklime as an antiseptic to prevent the spread of health-threatening contaminants and pollution.[41]

By early 1905 the ominous day of reckoning had arrived for the populace of Winchester; positive measures were mandatory to protect public health. The committee on sewerage made this fact crystal clear in their report. They said, "We find there is need for a safe and adequate system of sewerage in Winchester. So imperative has this become that a considerable proportion of our citizens have subcumbed [sic] the private expense of construction of various lines of so-called sewers. This has been done and with no provision for disposing of the sewerage, except to conduct it to some area of the town branch by which it is carried through the city."[41]

Reacting to the explosive sewerage situation, which was becoming more threatening almost by the month, the city council proposed the floating of $40,000 worth of revenue bonds to finance the planning and construction of an adequate sewerage disposal plant. To date this was the largest expenditure any political body in Clark County history had undertaken, certainly for the support of a single public facility. All of the former franchised projects were financed by private companies or by individuals for profit. The council was unanimous in approving this proposal. It was necessary, however, to conduct an election to secure voter approval of the bond issue. The bonds were to bear a 4 percent per annum interest and were to be liquated through annual installments of $2,800.[42]

Coupled with the move to sell $40,000 worth of coupon bonds in denominations of $1,000, the council introduced a second project to be financed by floating revenue bonds. There was considerable delay, much of it no doubt caused by local political in-fighting, in making a realistic response to changing times. In the November 1909 election substantial changes were made in the membership of the city council. New members were C. G. Bush, George [Hon.?], J. W. Wheeler, J. E. Botkins, John J. Allen, J. T. Stokely and M.A. Browne. J. A. Hughes was reelected mayor. There developed some difference of opinion early in the new administration between some members of the council and the mayor over the subject of bond issues.[43]

By October 1909, the pressure for developing the necessary public services to accommodate a growing population was an urgent matter. By this date Winchester had grown well beyond the stage when a casual governing body could deal with the complex issues of establishing and maintaining public services. On October 15, 1909, Mayor Hughes called a special meeting of the council to consider submitting to the voters at the November election the question of floating a bond issue to finance the construction of a city hall. The night before a mass meeting of citizens had occurred in the courthouse. It was reported that "A large crowd of citizens" had gathered to express a strong desire for the city council to have prepared a proposition to be voted upon in the forthcoming election. Interestingly, the citizens' petition was signed by two former council members, J. O. Simpson, a former mayor, and

A truck load of Eastern Kentucky patients awaiting to be admitted to the Guerrant Clinic in Winchester.

William Harding, both of whom knew intimately the affairs of urban government.[44]

In the November election voters gave substantial support to the issuance of bonds to finance both the sewerage system and to build a city hall. A new issue was raised when the new council took office which had a political bearing on the current management of the city and upon the potential sale of future bonds. Browne introduced a resolution that an auditor from the outside, but one approved of by the local banks, be appointed to audit the books of every agency of the city government. This resolution was to lead to an interesting conflict of views with the mayor and in the council. At a meeting on May 13, 1910, eight members of the city council approved a resolution which in essence declared moribund the issuance of $40,000 worth of bonds for the city hall and $65,000 for the sewerage system. This action came as a surprise to the mayor, who said the first he saw of it was when councilmen Browne drew a slip of paper from his pocket. The resolution apparently was drafted by a junta of tax resisters. The mayor vetoed the resolution.[45] Later, M. A. Browne made an extensive report to the council on the sale of the sewerage and city hall bonds. A partial sale had been made to a Mr. McEldowney, who represented an insurance company. The company had thought to use the bonds as the required deposit with the Kentucky state

Nancy S. Stevenson, elected County Superintendent of Schools in 1918. Miss Stevenson was active in the consolidation of the Clark County schools. - *Photo courtesy of the Winchester Sun*

treasurer to permit it to do business in the state. The treasurer refused to accept the bonds. Then a sale was attempted with a Chicago company, but because Winchester had an archaic records management system and no sinking fund the company refused to buy the bonds. Browne expressed the belief the bonds were good and proposed that a bounty system be adopted to pay commissions to individuals who might sell debentures.[46]

As M. A. Browne indicated in his report on the sale of the Winchester bonds, there were serious questions about the city's management and accounting situation. The city had never adopted a budgetary procedure, was careless in keeping records, was never sure about the handling of funds by individuals collecting and spending money. At its May 13, 1910, meeting the city council noted that there had never been an audit made of Winchester's fiscal affairs. A majority of the councilmen voted to appropriate $541.26 to hire an expert accountant to investigate the city's records and financial status and to make recommendations for the future. The council claimed it had mandate from the people to set aright the city's financial affairs. Mayor Hughes opposed the hiring of an accountant, saying that he had been told by a local bookkeeper that there was no need to employ an accountant. Nevertheless, the council voted to employ a Mr. Escot, a Louisville accountant who was said to be "Equal to the best in the state." Once in Winchester, Escot said the

old Winchester system of record-keeping was "Primitive-incomplete-not sufficiently intelligible-the record defective." He found no checks, balances, or
comparisons of accounts of the various departments. In one case there was a
discrepancy of more than five hundred dollars. There did not exist, Escot said
in 1910, a definite knowledge of the city's fiscal condition. For instance, the
collector of taxes kept only private records, and in his personal possession.[47]
Thus it was that the mayor and city council were faced with a major restruc-
turing of the ways the city of Winchester did business in the future. By 1910
it had already taken on a significant obligation of creating and managing a
host of public services.

Changes literally stormed Winchester and its officials during the first
quarter of the twentieth century, changes which would forever set a new course
for economic, cultural, and social life in Clark County and Winchester. There
were stirring after 1910 forces which could not be resisted by a local community. The drive to create an effective sewerage disposal system and to build a
city hall were cardinal indicators of the times.[45]

Not only was it of major importance that Winchester forsake the past,
construct a city hall, and stop the flow of raw sewerage in the Town Branch,
but there was looming on the horizon a major instrumental force which would
touch deeply the lives of every human being in the county and city. The
appearance of the automobile on American streets and roads created a revolution in the national way of life. The first automobile to appear in Winchester
was said to have been fabricated in the town by a local mechanic. Though the
mayor and city councilmen were oblivious at first to the effects the automobile would have on government, they did have age-old precedental ordinances
which attempted to control a wild stamped of racing horses up and down the
streets, and daredevil buggy drivers who careened around street corners on
two wheels.[46] Then there was the accompanying menace the railroads dragged
into town of men and boys jumping on and off moving trains.[47] By the spring
of 1912 most of these nuisances were all but forgotten, but there was a new
one to be controlled. In an effort to protect life and limb in the streets of
Winchester, J. A. Ramsey and J. S. Boone sought approval by the city council
of a resolution which would clamp down on automobile drivers before they
arrived in numbers on Winchester's streets. The council approved unanimously
the resolution and ordained, "That it shall be unlawful for any person to
drive or operate an automobile or other motor vehicle on or over any of the
public streets or alleys of the city of Winchester, Kentucky, at a rate of a speed
greater than six miles an hour."[48]

The council went further in its action, providing that, "Every motor vehicle or automobile, while in use on any streets or alleys, or public place in Winchester shall be provided with good and sufficient brakes, and also suitable bells, horn or other signal, and shall be so constructed as to exhibit during the period necessary at or after sunset until not necessary, at or before sunrise, a white light visible within a reasonable distance in the direction toward which the vehicle is proceeding, and a red light in the reverse direction provided in the case of heavy fogs, if necessary such lights shall be displayed in daytime before sunset and after sunrise." There was to be levied a fifty dollar fine in cases of violation of these instructions. Fortunately, there were only a limited number of automobiles in Winchester at that date to break the speed limit, and it may be that few of them could get revved up to exceed the six-mile-an-hour speed limit.[49]

Over the years the council proved unrelenting in holding fast to its "horse and buggy" speed limit. In 1912, when automobiles were becoming more numerous in Winchester, the council again reiterated its sense of a proper speed limit. Councilman George introduced an ordinance which was adopted unanimously that the chief of police be instructed to place warning signs at all turnpike entrances to the city that motorists were to drive to the right on

Nora Lucille G. Hamilton, Secretary in the Daniel Boone Forest Office, deputy county clerk 1957-'62, appointed clerk in 1962, and was elected clerk, 1964-75.. - *Photo courtesy of the Winchester Sun*

streets and alleys, and that the speed limit was still six miles an hour.[50] This was approximately the speed at which a buggy horse traveled over the Clark County road to Ruckersville.

Possibly T. M. Walton might have owned the first automobile in Winchester. It was said that he built all of the machine except its specially milled gearing. By the time of the outbreak of World War II automobiles in Clark County and Winchester became more numerous. The Bush Brothers, descendants of the famous old pioneer family, established a garage which in time housed two full rows of cars. The garage quickly pushed the livery stable off the local scene.[51]

Once the motor age dawned in Winchester and Clark County the pace of modernization was quickened. By 1912 the city had advanced a far cry from that day in April 1882 when the town was legally designated a city or from the earlier date in 1838 when the trustees splurged and purchased a hand-drawn fire engine. Then the Rough and Ready Fire Company had pushed progress a modest notch ahead. With all its difficulties in creating an adequate water supply, including the lack of a truly effective building code and the spreading out of the Winchester limits, fire was still a capital threat as it has been in earlier years when dozens of chimneys belched forth incendiary sparks. In November 1909, the city council approved the purchase of a motorized fire truck. This vehicle was purchased from the Webb Motor Fire Apparatus Company of Vincennes, Indiana. The truck was equipped with a pump and hose lines and cost the city $4,650. Not only did the council introduce the modern age of motorized firefighting equipment to Winchester, but it closed an earlier one by selling the famous old town fire bell for twelve and a half cents a pound.[52]

With the purchase of a motorized fire truck there could be little doubt but what the automobile age had begun in earnest. Like the horse in earlier days, the car had to be serviced in garages and from gasoline pumps and tanks. On May 6, 1910, Gordon and Davis were granted a permit to bury a gasoline tank in the back of their garage.[53] In the same meeting the council once again considered the matter of driving rules for the town. In a long and detailed ordinance of thirty-one sections the councilmen came up with some conventional and some quaint driving rules. Motorists were to drive close to the right-hand curb, faster drivers could use the middle of the streets, all passes were to be made to the right, overtaking vehicles were to pass on the left, no vehicle was to be parked left-handed to the curb, all motorists were to grant pedestrians the right-of-way, no car was to stop in the middle of the street, and when turning the driver was to signal either with a whip or a hand.

Fire wagons and street cars had the right-of-way. Councilmen were reluctant to loosen the official grip on the past. In their multiple traffic rules they took a humane turn, saying, "No one was to ill treat over-load, over-drive, over-ride, or cruelly, or unnecessarily beat any horse. No driver was to crack or so use a whip as to annoy or threaten injury to citizens, or excite any horse."[54]

In pronounced legalistic fashion, the council devoted considerable space to definitions of words used in the rules, one of which was "vehicle," defined as any wheeled vehicles except streetcars and baby buggies. In adopting so incisive a set of traffic rules perhaps no councilmen realized that they were blending modern realities with nostalgic memories of two ages in the history of Clark County and Winchester. For the town never again was life to drift on at the leisurely pace of a land-based-rural-agrarian tempo. Quickly gasoline-propelled vehicles crowded horse-drawn vehicles off the roads and streets. The six-mile speed limit was honored far more in its violations than its observances. The movement of people and goods across the landscape brought a new and forceful drive to create a modern highway system out of the old debt-ridden toll turnpikes.[55]

No one on the Winchester City Council, or in Kentucky for that matter, could have predicted accurately the changes which were coming in the next two decades. In 1906 both businessmen in Lexington and councilmen in Winchester were focused mentally on the past. They were still putting faith in the construction of an interurban line connecting Lexington with Mount Sterling by way of Winchester. On June 12, 1906, officials and promoters of Kentucky Traction Company sought a permit to build a line along the Winchester streets, but a split vote in the council rejected the proposal.[56]

A month later the issue was again before the council, and this time a majority of the members approved the Kentucky Traction Company's request and a franchise was signed by Mayor W. A. Attersall and the city attorney. There apparently was no opposition to the interurban line per se; the objections pertained to the route through the city. Finally, in a rather detailed franchise document the traction company was given permission to choose a route on the condition it would take over the operation of the failing Winchester streetcar system. There seems to exist no evidence that the interurban car line was ever built. The appearance of the automobile and improved highways darkened the future of the electric cars as carriers of human passengers and local express packages.

Three railways built through Winchester in the decade of the 1880s were rugged competitors for passenger and freight traffic. The railroads no doubt stimulated the notion that Winchester would become a center for some di-

The Truman
welcoming
Committee in
October 1948. The
President on his
way back to
Washington, and
most uncertain as
to whether or not
the American voters
would choose him
or Tom Dewey in
the forthcoming
November election.
- *Photo courtesy of the
Winchester Sun*

versified industries. Acting on this prescience of what the future would bring, William M. Beckner, an active voice of the times, wrote and published a promotional handbook of the county and city in which he detailed some of the economic, social, and material assets of Winchester. He mentioned almost with an air of casualness several enterprises which might, by the wildest stretch of the imagination, be classified as industries. Among them were Thomson's tobacco warehouse, W. H. Clay and Company's planing mill, an unnamed corncob pipe factory, Attersall's carriage works, and the Winchester planing mill. All of these businesses had a direct relationship either to Clark County timber resources or to agriculture.[58]

In September 1906, McEldowney, Mattlock, and Woolcott filed a petition with the city council soliciting permission to be exempted from taxation for five years. This company promised to build a manufacturing plant with an elevator, a planing mill, and a warehouse attached. The council voted unanimously to grant this petition, setting an interesting precedent for attracting industry.[59]

In the session which granted the McEldowney company a generous exemption the council drew its purse strings tight. It received a request soliciting a $200 contribution toward defraying the expenses of a meeting of the Kentucky state development organization to be held in Winchester on October 11 and 12, 1906. J. A. McCourt proposed that that amount of the subsidy be reduced to $72, but an even split of the council vote defeated the request. The delegates to the Kentucky State Development Convention had to finance their own entertainment.[60]

Clearly the economy of Winchester and Clark County was still scaled to a frugal agrarian way of life. Seen in comparison with recent industries, it could be said that any one of the local enterprises in the decade 1900 to 1910 could be regarded as little more than service enterprises closely related to local needs. By the latter date, however, the seeds of change had been embedded firmly in the political and commercial soil of the county and town. As they moved deeper into the new century the revolutionary changes, or "progress," came on with a high degree of intensity. The appearance of the automobile in Winchester along with the building of hard-surfaced arterial highways once again placed Winchester at the hub of a system of highways which fed out into both eastern and central Kentucky. Common use of the automobile and the motor truck advanced in the years just before the occurrence of World War I. The onslaught of the war with the drives for making available all kinds of raw materials, increased food production, and tremendous expansion of the need for manpower speeded up the processes of transition for Clark County and Winchester, transferring them from being caught in the net of a calm rural-agrarian economy into more modernized communities. The introduction of the new sciences into many fields of production and life was to have a lasting impact on the future of the Clark County area. Some of the introductions came in the form of vastly improved fertilizers, in the mechanization of and in the ever-widening field of the distribution of goods. Following the cessation of the war in 1918, Winchester could not return to being a self-complacent town locked within the embrace of a tight geographical-political environment. The increased economic importance of burley tobacco in the first two decades of the century had a direct bearing on the fortunes and economic lapses of Winchester. This fact was dramatically revealed in the booming market years 1919-1920 and the crisis one of 1921.[61]

Fortunately, both Clark County and Winchester had some insulation against depression, such as that of 1921, in the diversity of the county's agriculture. This was to prove substantially true during the Great Depression of the 1930s. In many respects the county and town reaped some direct benefits from the Great Depression and its aftermath. The various federal public works programs resulted in either the refurbishing of public buildings or construction of new ones in the form of schools, improvements of roads, and expansion of some public facilities. The process of change initiated by World War I and the Great Depression was speeded up during World War II. Never again was Winchester to be the quiet county seat town of the past century.[62]

The age of the automobile brought about the phenomenal transformations in almost every phase of life in Clark County and Winchester. In town there sprang up like commercial mushrooms garages, automobile dealerships, filling stations, automobile parts stores. The rise of the self-service stores selling everything from groceries to building supplies drove the old-style stores and their forbidding counter barriers off the scene. Even drugstores in fact became variety stores where customers got the notion the stores sold everything but drugs. The hardest blow of all perhaps was dealt the old-fashioned family restaurant, which surrendered to standardized products which bore no known regional flavor. As much reflective of the tempo of life the new age as of gastronomical tastes, fast food emporiums dotted the town, as did chain self-service grocery and discount stores. Winchester fell into the trap of superficial standardization which robbed it of much of its historical personality.

The more fundamental changes in Winchester, however, occurred in its growing new industries. By 1960 the population of urban Winchester was almost equal to that of rural Clark County, and much of this population was engaged in service and manufacturing jobs.[63] After 1945 there was a steady growth in these areas. In 1947 there were 234 workers reported as being employed in manufacturing, producing $767,000 worth of goods. From that date on the area was caught up in the drive to entice industries to the town, with some substantial success.[64] In 1990 the Winchester Chamber of Commerce and the Kentucky Agricultural and Development Board listed thirty

The 1908 Winchester champion baseball team. In the 1909 championship game against Lexington Fred Toney pitched a seventeen inning game against the neighbor team allowing no hits and no runs. The game ended 1-0 for the Winchester team. - *Photo courtesy of the scrapbook of George S. Brooks the official scorer, Winchester Public Library*

Lined up and ready to go, the Police and Fire Departments. This was a long cry from the days when mud and stick chimneys were a menace in Winchester, and the town fathers passed an ordinance requiring the presence of firebuckets. This police force was a distinct advance over the "patterollers" who once roamed the streets looking for slave miscreants.

enterprises which did some form of manufacturing that ranged from bed springs, boxes, soft drinks, and men's and women's clothing to heavy-duty truck axles. In the latter decades of this century the balance between town and rural population had shifted to being mostly urban.

After 1950 labor forces flowed into Winchester from a fairly broad neighboring area; but paradoxically, a sizable stream of laborers flowed out of Clark County and Winchester to Lexington and other places of employment. Mobility of employees was a central fact in the shaping of the local economy.

The earlier discussion of the coming of the automobile to Winchester and of the city council's laboring to devise rules for driving on streets and roads was hardly a portent of what was to come in the building and administration of local and national highways. In 1912 the Kentucky General Assembly only vaguely envisioned the revolution which was imminent in the field of public roads.[65] That body created only the most modest beginnings of a unified Kentucky highway system by providing for a state road engineer. This official was admonished to begin planning a state system of roads, but to do so without giving in to political pressures. Legislative action or no action, the real driving force for improvements of the public roads was the automobile and the motor truck. One of the concluding progressive acts of the Wilson presidential administration was enactment of the first federal Highway Act of July 11, 1916.[66] The nation's entry into World War I, however, delayed real highway progress until after 1918, when once again road bridling materials and labor became available. For Clark County both the state and federal road laws ended for good the toll road era.

By 1925 the transportation revolution in the United States was well under way. In February of that year there gathered in Washington a delegation of federal highway officials and representatives from twenty-four states. They had come together to devise a uniform system of interstate highways and to create a system of numerical and directional markings for the roads. On August 3, 1925, the delegates had reached an agreement on the markings, and quickly the standardized federal highway shield became one of the most universally recognized symbols in American history. East and west road were to bear even numbers and north-south ones uneven numbers. This action had a direct bearing upon Winchester. Federal Highway 60 pierced the very heart of the town over the ancient route of the road from the Big Sandy by way of Owingsville, Mount Sterling, Lexington, Frankfort, and Louisville, and on westward to the Purchase area. In time a heavy flow of traffic from Highways 60, 89, 227, and 15 intersected in the town.[67]

On June 29, 1954, the Congress of the United States enacted the law creating a "System of Interstate and Defense Highways." This was to have tremendous bearing on the economic future of Winchester. It provided for the construction of Interstate 75, and construction was begun on this road in 1957. It was a capital artery of travel, connecting the Great Lakes with the Keys of Florida. For Winchester there were three access points, at the juncture of I-64 and I-75, at the Athens-Boonesborough point, and across the Kentucky River at the Richmond-Winchester access. Later a fourth, and directly important to Winchester, access was opened at the Man-o-War junction. By 1965 the I-75 was completed. Interstate 64, the east-west connector, linking Norfolk, Virginia with Los Angeles, California, was opened during the same period, with two access outlets to Winchester. This road was to funnel both new industries and tourist travel into the town, and it stimulated the modernization and widening of Highway 627 between Winchester and Madison County. Earlier the bridge at Boonesborough had displayed a ferry, and in 1994 a multilane modern bridge with improved access points was opened.

On February 17, 1960, Governor Bert Combs informed the Kentucky

General Assembly that plans were well under way for the construction of an eastern Kentucky parkway (the Mountain Parkway) a road which penetrated an area of eighteen counties. This road joined I-64 just east of Winchester and penetrated eastern Kentucky, actually, all the way to the Breaks of Sandy. It funneled a high volume of traffic through the Winchester periphery, once again emphasizing the town's connection with Appalachia. The Mountain Parkway was dedicated at Campton on November 1, 1963.[68]

Socially and culturally one of the fundamental changes which occurred in Clark County and Winchester history was the liberation of women. Anyone reading the minutes of the Winchester trustees, and later of the Board of City Council, from 1793 to 1930 would be almost completely oblivious to the fact that there were women in the area so far as official documentation is concerned. Occasionally, after April 1882, the name of a woman appeared in the record as the owner of a lot in front of which a sidewalk was being laid. But clearly the ordinances adopted prior to 1919 had a pronounced masculine overtone, as to both intent and application. One has to turn to church records or to the reports of the United States Census Bureau to find much information about women in Winchester. There is, of course, information about them in wills and estate settlements. Undocumented though the fact may be, it is self-evident that the women of Clark County and Winchester were major but silent participants in the areas of the family, public welfare, and social gatherings. Scores of photographs lodged in family papers reveal

The dirt road led straight through town. The sidewalks were raised above the mud line. No one along the street had ever heard the term "traffic jam". There were ample hitching posts to accommodate shoppers who came to town in buggies. Strung over head are numerous telephone and telegraph lines indicating something of the communication arts circa 1890. - *Photo courtesy of the Winchester Sun*

the participation of women in picnics and other types of folk gatherings.[69]

William Beckner's 1880s *Handbook* contains numerous photographs of persons and family homes. It has, however, only one mention of a woman, and that because she was a cattle breeder. There are numerous illustrations of the more affluent homes of the town and county. Underneath each is the caption "The Home of John W. Bean, Esq.," or "The Home of F. H. Dudley," or of J. H. Besuden, V. W. Bush, and others. In many of the illustrations there are pictured cows grazing in nearby meadows, and in a few there are almost phantom-like images of women. Beckner's publication no doubt was true to the social mores of the times.[70] Some of this readers must at times have speculated on whether behind those strait-laced Victorian walls there actually dwelled women who were kept in an Arabian-like harem?

The male fortresses of Winchester and Clark County were breached in 1897 by Nora Wilkinson, who defeated W. H. Bush in a race for county superintendent of public schools. In time she was to write some enlightened reports on the progress, or lack of progress, of education in the area. She wrote, "I believe every effort should be made to bring about greater prosperity in our country schools, for in them is the hope of our country. The town is not the best place to raise boys and girls. They have a more steady growth, physically, mentally, and morally in the country than they have in town."[71] Nora Wilkinson might not have won many Winchester town votes, but she voiced the opinion of rural America in stating her beliefs.

Once the public school movement had gained momentum in Winchester and Clark County, and the General Assembly had enacted the famous Sullivan Law in 1908, which outlined in large measure a modern public school system, and there had been conducted the two crusading "Whirl Wind" campaigns, women became far more visible in public life in all areas. During the World War I years Nancy S. Stevenson was elected county superintendent of schools; she served during the years when school consolidation and compulsory attendance were beginning to be applied.[72]

Following the joint effects of World War I, the vigorous engagement of women in war work, and the great woman suffrage campaigns, the country adopted the Nineteenth Amendment to the Constitution of the United States in 1919, dramatically elevating the status of women in public affairs. In Clark County and Winchester, as in all the nation, women became an important new element in politics, if not as officeholders then as voters. The day of the bewhiskered "town father" was over. The first woman in Clark County to be elected to a noneducational office was Lucille G. Harrison, who served first as a deputy circuit court clerk; she was appointed to the office by Judge H. O.

By 1910 the main street was covered over with asphalt, street car lines claimed center street, the hitching posts were gone, and in their place were electrical light stanchions with their grape-like clusters of globes. Most important of all the automobile had rudely shoved the horse and buggy aside, and town councilmen concerned themselves with speed limits, and driving rules. - *Photo courtesy of the Winchester Sun*

Porter, and then in 1964 she was elected to the office and served until November 1975.

Graphically, the *Winchester Sun*, September 9, 1978, published several socially revealing photographs of groups of people of the town and country. In 1904 an excursion party of ten women and twenty-three men posed for a picture before departing for the St. Louis World's Fair in 1904. Then there was the photograph of the all-male members of the Lower Howard's Creek Fish Fry Club which literally shouted maleness. Perhaps the cardinal date when women were highly visible in a public political affair was October 1, 1948, when the Harry Truman campaign train stopped in Winchester for eleven minutes for a rear platform speech. The welcoming committee for that brief ceremonial occasion was made up of a predominant number of women. In the population mix of both Winchester and Clark County, historically, the numbers of males and females remained steadily near equal.

During two plus centuries Winchester has passed through a dozen or so stages of evolutionary change, each change leaving a distinct mark on the town. One element of social relationships changed only by numerical objectivity, not in basic characteristics. In 1990 the United States Census Report indicated there were 15,799 people in Winchester, lacking just a fraction of being half the population of Clark County. Eighty-four percent of the population was native to the town. Up until 1980 only a limited number of foreign-born individuals had entered the town despite the fact the county court had the authority to formally grant the status of citizenship. Racially, there were 26,494 whites and 1,742 African-Americans in the county. The latter group showed a sharp drop in ratio, over 1850, when there were 7,709 whites and 3,974 black slaves in the county. The ancestral descent of the Winchester population remained constant over two centuries. Whites were descendants principally of four old-world national groups, English, Irish, Scotch, and German.

If the ancestral stream of humanity has remained constant, so have some of the Winchester landmarks. Modern commercial expansion has occurred largely beyond the historical perimeter of the town. In 1995 there still remains remarkable well preserved the historical architectural heart of an earlier day. Several blocks of buildings on Main Street and about the courthouse square gaze out from facades that are prime Mauve Decade Victorian. They document elegantly those decades of the closing nineteenth century when Winchester was being transposed from a country town to a city establishing numerous public services. Except for the ever-changing names of businesses and professional tenants the buildings of stand as bulwarks against the invasion of plastic America.

Mayor J. O. Simpson, J. E. Garner, or J. H. Hughes might well walk down Main Street and feel reasonably well at home, except for the automobile traffic which religiously ignores the six-mile-an-hour speed limit. Few towns in closing twentieth century Kentucky have preserved in such pristine originality so many earlier structures. Surely those must be Winchester's most precious historical monuments, which portray so vividly how it was in earlier times when "wise" town fathers-politicians sat in council granting franchises to the institutions which would be such potent forces in making Winchester a city.

Clark County Courthouse Doughboy.

CHAPTER 15

The Hands of Mars

Clark County has a fascinating military history despite the fact its area was never seriously invaded by an enemy. By the date of the formation of the county, the incoming stream of Revolutionary War veterans had almost dried up. There, however, had come a small multitude of land-hungry veterans bearing land warrants in the Virginia militia forces. Their warrants were signed by Thomas Jefferson, Patrick Henry, and other governors. Some of the veterans came west to lay claims to prodigious landholds. The early deed books of Fayette and Bourbon counties bear eloquent testimony of this fact on the face of their entries.[1]

No fact was more reminiscent of the struggles of the continental armed forces than the naming of the new county for Kentucky's most important resident military hero, George Rogers Clark.[2] Clark fully merited this honor. He had been instrumental in protecting the western frontier from major British-Indian invasions. His leadership of the successful armed expedition against the enemy strongholds of Kaskaskia and Vincennes was to have fundamental bearing on the course of the Revolutionary War in the West. Subsequently, Clark organized and led an expedition against the Miami Villages north of the Ohio River. His militiamen wrought devastating havoc against the Indian concentrations in this area. There is no documentation containing precise individual information as to what militiamen taking part in the latter expedition might have come from the future Clark County area of Fayette and Bourbon counties.[3]

Historically, the settlement pattern in future Clark County was well established before the county was officially created. After 1781 there flowed into the western country a flush stream of land-hungry emigrants. Among this throng came Revolutionary War veterans and some of the French and Indian War veterans, clutching precious land warrants as bonuses for their military services. This accounts for the fact that so many of the early Clark County leaders had served in the Virginia lines. Many of these veterans had an eye for good land with a rich future potential. Kentucky land records are filled with the veterans' entries.[4]

Representative of scores of military claims to lands in Clark County were such well-known pioneers as John Martin, John Holder, William Bush, John Strode, James and William McMillan, Thomas Lewis, William Hickman, John Vivian, and the Tracy Family Group. John Martin made a claim to more than 4,000 acres in the Stoner-Licking area; William Bush pre-empted a colonial scope of land on Lower Howard's Creek and along the Kentucky River. John Strode claimed 2,400 acres; and James McMillan, 1,041 acres.[6] In addition to these claims, John Martin and John Holder jointly established claim, with the insatiable land-grabber Matthew Walton, to 10,000 additional acres.

There were scores of Virginia veterans, like John Bean, who established warranty claims to land, founded families, and carved out modest niches in the history of Kentucky. None of the incoming war veterans, however, was so intriguing as that historically almost shadowy figure, Nathaniel Gist. Colonel Gist was the second son of the famous old adventurer and land "spy" Christopher Gist.[7] At midcentury Christopher Gist had insured himself a place in the history of the frontier. In 1751 he had come down the Ohio River and had wandered across future Kentucky as an agent for the British Ohio Land Company.[8] Tracing the personal history of Nathaniel Gist the son, however, involves the historian in a tedious search for dependable facts and in the weighing of evidence. In this instance legend and fact have become so intertwined that the truth becomes obscured. Nathaniel Gist was present with his father at Turtle Creek and Braddock's Defeat on July 9, 1755. And at the age of twenty years he went among the Cherokees as a trader and perhaps as a colonial government agent.[9] For the decade 1754-1764 Nathaniel Gist lived and operated in the area around the Long Island in the Holston River in eastern Tennessee, an era when he sought to establish a claim to the Long Island.[10] While among the Cherokees in this period he may have fathered a famous son. In the treaty of 1777, made between the Cherokees and the states of Virginia and North Carolina, there was made a reservation in favor of Nathaniel Gist.[11] Albert V. Goodpasture, writing on the paternity of Sequoyah, said, "Now Colonel Gist was living with the Cherokees on terms of intimate friendship, of which they have given the highest proofs, at the time Sequoyah was born, about 1760. The family tradition that Sequoyah was his son becomes a certainty when we consider that it was a general, almost a universal practice for white men living, even temporarily, in the nation to take Indian wives; not, generally, `until death us do part'."[12] Judge Samuel Cole Williams, the astute east Tennessee historian, wrote in some support of Goodpasture, saying that Captain Gist "was the father of the greatest of red Tennesseans.[13] The probabilities point to the period of the early 1770s as being the time of Sequoyah's birth.[14] The paternity of Sequoyah became entangled in the legend that an unlicensed Indian trader named George "Guest" was the father.[15] Again, Judge Williams wrote, "That Nathaniel Gist was the father of Sequoyah is consonant with all of many probabilities; that a wandering German peddlar from Georgia was such, in 1770, as claimed and stated by Foster in his Sequoyah, is unbelievable.[16] It may be that, to shield Gist, that story was advanced, even by his mother and her family. Guest, the peddlar, has not been traced in the archives of Georgia and South Carolina. It would be a remarkable coincidence had there been two men by the name of Gist or Guest among the Overhill Cherokees in the same half decade when few white men were to be found there."[17] In the biographical sketch of Sequoyah in the *Dictionary of American Biography*, W. J. Ghent wrote, "His father was possibly Nathaniel Gist, a trader who abandoned the mother, a woman of mixed Indian blood, before the birth of the child."[18] None of these historians said categorically that Nathaniel Gist was the known father, but they all hedged with "probabilities."

The paternity of Sequoyah had nothing really to do with the history of Clark County except as a legend about one of its major land claimants.[19] Nathaniel Gist came under historical suspicion on other counts, especially with the Virginians who had questions about his relations with British officials and the Cherokee Indians. On December 17, 1778, Gist, in George Washington's mind, was cleared of any doubts as to his loyalty; and on January 11, 1777 he was given the rank of colonel and placed in charge of one of the new regimental units created by the Continental Congress.[20] He saw action in New Jersey and in the South. On May 12, 1780, he was taken prisoner by Lord Cornwallis's forces at Charleston, South Carolina, ending his military career.[21] At the end of the war he sought land grants for his services in both the French and Indian War and the Revolutionary War.

Gist located lands in Bourbon and Clark counties, and in 1792 he began preparations to move his family and a rather large number of slaves west to Kentucky. Lyman C. Draper in an interview with James Taylor quoted him as saying, "While I was moving to Kentucky in the spring of '93 I left my com-

pany some distance before we reached Redstone (now Brownsville). I understood Col. Gist had arrived with a large number of slaves and was encamped
about a half mile above the creek from which the old fort had taken its name.
I called on Colonel Gist at his encampment. I found him sitting under his
markee which, no doubt, had protected him and his brother officers from the
storms of many a cold and dreary night. He was a venerable looking man, I
should think near 60 years of age; stout-framed and about six feet high and of
a dark complexion. It was the first time I had seen him, but, on making
myself known to him, he informed me he was well acquainted with my father
and had served, I think, in the Virginia legislature or in the state convention
together, and perhaps in both."[22] Taylor also told Draper that a handsome
seventeen-year-old boy had appeared in the camp, telling Colonel Gist he
was his son, an incident which does not seem to have involved Sequoyah.[23]
Two points relating to Gist and Sequoyah remain murky, the date of Sequoyah's
birth and precisely the date and length of his visit to the Gist family members
in Kentucky.[24]

The most essential facts about Nathaniel Gist and his family in relation
to Clark County history which can be documented, however, are that he and

Fifty Year Veterans of World War I. - *Photo courtesy of Clark Rural Electric*

his family arrived in the county in 1793, that he laid claim to six or seven thousand acres of land, that he built his famous house Canewood near the Clark-Bourbon county boundary, and that back in Virginia he had sired a family of two sons and five daughters of white lineage.[25] Gist was married to Judith Carey Bell, a granddaughter of Archibald [Carey] of the Virginia Bill of Rights fame.[26] In Kentucky his sons, Harry Carey, and Thomas N. seem to have achieved little if anything of historical significance; four of the five daughters, however, made impressive marriages. Maria Cecil married Benjamin Gratz; Anna Carey married Dr. Joseph Boswell, a Lexington physician; Eliza married Francis Preston Blair; and Sarah married Judge Jesse Bledsoe of Bourbon County. Davidilla remained single.[27]

Nathaniel Gist, as a resident of Clark County, did nothing of historical importance, except to accumulate a phenomenal amount of military bounty land. The author of the statement in the *Clark County Chronicles* no doubt was rhetorically generous when he or she wrote that the large land bounty was the reward for, "His gallant services to his country in the War of the Revolution."[28] Even General George Washington might have raised a quizzical eyebrow at this assertion. One searches in vain the pages of the histories of Kentucky for some notation on Colonel Nathaniel Gist.[29] He, like his famous house Canewood, has settled back into the dust of Indian legend and military warranted land grants, and the father-in-law of four notable Americans.

The influx of Revolutionary War veterans and other settlers to the opening Kentucky District aggravated intensely the Indian threats to the safety of the region.[30] The Kentucky counties and settlements were subjected to intermittent Indian raids. Most of those made upon the internal settlements involved relatively small parties which harassed isolated settlers and engaged in stealing horses.[31] The Indians from north of the Ohio River seem to have had an insatiable desire to own horses. The real disruptive raids, however, took place on the Ohio River above the Falls and up and down the Wilderness Trail. Kentucky, and Ohio Valley generally, were exposed to raids and disturbing depredations. The *Kentucky Gazette*, in frequent issues, contained notices of attacks on emigrant parties and the stealing of horses. So frequent were these that John Bradford set aside a column in the paper reporting the latest attacks.[32]

One of the most exciting attacks made along the Ohio River was that on the Hubble party in March 1791.[33] This attack caught the attention of President George Washington and Secretary of War Henry Knox. Between 1788 and 1791 frantic petitions had been sent to Richmond and Philadelphia begging protective relief. The petition of November 10, 1788, was truly eloquent in its appeal. The petitioner wrote, "Though forced to pierce the thicket, it was not in safety we trod. The wily savage thirsted for our blood, lurked in our paths and seized the unsuspecting hunter. Whilst we lamented the loss of a friend, a brother, a father, a wife, a child became a victim to the barbarian tomahawk, instead of consolation, a new and greater misfortune deadened the sense of former afflictions. From the nation, we receive no support; but we impeach not their justice. Ineffectual treaties, often renowned, and as often broken by the savage nations, served only to supply them with the means of our destruction. But no human cause could controul [sic] that Providence, which had destined this western country to be the seat of a civilized and happy people. The period of the accomplishment was distant, but it advanced with rapid and incredible strides. We derived strength from our falls and numbers from our losses; the unparalleled fertility of our soil made grateful returns, far disproportionate to the slight [labour] which our safety would permit us to bestow. Our fields and herds afforded us not only sufficient support for ourselves, but also for the emigrants who annually double our numbers."[34] This was a clear statement of the frontier concept of "manifest destiny." It could well have emanated from Clark County itself.

The matter of safeguarding the Kentucky frontier became so desperate by the spring of 1791 that President George Washington and Secretary of War Henry Knox asked John Brown, representative in Congress from the Kentucky District, for advice on dealing with the Indian menace in such a way that it would give assurance to the people of Kentucky of national concern. A committee composed of Isaac Shelby, John Brown, Benjamin Logan, General Charles Scott, and Harry Innis was appointed to call into service a militia corps to make a strike against the Indian villages in the Wabash, Miami, and Scioto valleys.[35] The special committee recommend that, "Brigadier Gen. Charles Scott be empowered and required to call into service any number of militia of the several counties within the Kentucky District not exceeding 326 privates, as he may think necessary for a term not exceeding sixty days, and to station them on the frontiers in such a manner as he may think conducive to public safety."[36] This action was significant to Clark County, as the militia corp offered some degree of safety to incoming settlers who took the easier route down the Ohio River to Limestone and then the short way overland to the future county area. Too, no doubt militiamen from the outlying sections of Bourbon and Fayette counties were from future Clark County.[37]

Militia action on the Kentucky frontier was made necessary because of the great inrush of emigrants to Kentucky, a flood, as described earlier, which was stimulated by the land bonus payments. They came faster than either Virginia or the central government had capabilities for defending them.[38] The Ohio River in these years was literally dotted with the flatboats of emigrating parties. Almost every month there occurred some kind of an Indian attack either along the river or along the Wilderness Trail. It must be said that some of the traveling parties were careless in using proper precautions and were trapped in ambushes.[39]

From the Indian perspective, both north and south, their great Kentucky hunting grounds were being snatched away from them by the white invasion. The two cultures were incompatible. The attacks along the river and trail and on the internal settlements were highly agitating to settlers. In July 1790, Harry Innis wrote that by 1783, 1,500 emigrants and settlers had been killed and 20,000 horses had been stolen.[40] Added to these losses was the theft or destruction of houses, goods, and even money. Although most of the really threatening Indian attacks had occurred before Clark County was created politically, they nevertheless involved the area and had a major bearing on the peace of mind of the settlers.[41]

Considerable discussion of the Indian menace took place in Danville, in Richmond, Virginia, and in Philadelphia. In response to petitions for aid in combatting the threats on the Ohio River a drive against the Miami villages got under way in midsummer 1790.[42] The force raised was a badly organized and inadequately equipped corps of ragtag volunteers who were poorly armed; some were physically unable to stand a grueling march, and most were undisciplined.[43] There was a small attachment of regulars under the command of General Josiah Harmar. It would be difficult to imagine a more inadequate force marching against a clever and watchful enemy. It was said of the volunteers that, "some of their muskets were without locks. There also was a state of insubordination among the men; and a disregard of military rule, which augured anything rather than success."[44] For this and other reasons the Harmar expedition was a miserable failure. Worse still, it stepped up Indian attacks.[45]

The stark realization that the defense of the western border was weak and disorganized at the time the Commonwealth of Kentucky and Clark County came into existence was unsettling. Earlier there was an ominous charge in General Charles Scott's appeal for volunteers. On November 11, 1791, he wrote the county lieutenants: "Srs; We have now received certain intelligence that the army have been defeated. The loss is very great. The garrison at Fort Jefferson intercepted and many, many brave wounded gallant men are now left on the road, unable to travel, and without provisions, but the flesh of the pack horses. This case requires immediate exertion. I have appointed a rendezvous of *volunteers* at Craig's Mill, [Georgetown] the 15th instant, completely equipped with arms and ammunition, and twenty day's provisions. I trust that no exertions on your part will be wanting when the safety of our country and the lives of brave men are in danger. The circumstances require the greatest dispatch, and no friend of this country can be idle."[46]

General Scott and Colonel James Wilkinson, on this occasion, led the Kentucky volunteers on an almost flying raid against the Indians in the Wabash River Valley. They killed warriors, burned villages, and twice laid waste to corn crops in the milk stage of development. This was a highly damaging raid but not a completely devastating one. The Ouiatenon villages were left intact. General Scott's hard-riding volunteers were back at the Falls of the Ohio before their twenty-day supply of provisions was exhausted.[47]

The Scott-Wilkinson strike was more or less a side blow at the Indian villages. Once more an expedition was drawn together to march against the Miami confederation of Indians.[48] Arthur St. Clair, governor of the Northwest Territory, was commissioned a general to lead the army regulars and the citizen volunteers. General St. Clair suffered from gout and was physically incapable of making even a backyard raid, let alone one against a powerful Indian concentration in rugged river country. It would be hard to imagine a more evil-starred military expedition than that led by General St. Clair.[49] It took so long to get troops assembled and under way that the vegetation along the way had become frostbitten and inedible for both horses and beef cattle being driven along with the army. St. Clair's army retraced the line of march of the disastrous Harmar expedition of the year before. His mission ostensibly was to establish a line of forts and stations from the Ohio River north to the Maumee.[50] The command set out from Cincinnati with inadequate supplies of every kind. Ammunition was in short supply and water damaged. Judge Jacob Burnet, some years later, wrote, "In regard to the negligence charged on the War Department, it is a well authenticated fact, that boxes and packages were so carelessly put up and marked, that during the action a box was opened marked `flints', which was found to contain gun locks. Several mistakes of the same character were discovered, as, for example, a keg of powder marked `for the infantry,' was found to be damaged cannon powder, that could scarcely be ignited."[51]

Again, because of mismanagement at all levels a drive against the strong Miami Confederation of tribes failed miserably, and the Ohio River frontier was left exposed to possible devastation of emigrant parties.[52] The Kentucky settlements were also left open to invasion by warring parties from the Miami country. The *Kentucky Gazette* gave extensive coverage to both the Harmar

William M. Beckner, Editor, legislator, constitutional convention delegate, author of a booster publication ushering in the new age for Clark County.

and St. Clair failures.

In 1792 President George Washington named Anthony Wayne a major general and placed him in command in the Northwest. Primarily, General Wayne's responsibilities were to rehabilitate and strengthen the United States regular army contingent and to establish a line of forts northward from the Ohio River. The plan of this expedition, arrived at after considerable discussion in Philadelphia between President Washington and Secretary Knox, was to make a major penetration of the region about the Miami and Wabash rivers. Kentucky had a high stake in the success of such a venture.

General Anthony Wayne, unlike generals Harmar and St. Clair, was an effective organizer and disciplinarian.[53] By time consuming stages he gathered an army of regulars and volunteer militiamen for a determined drive against the resistant Indian villages. Advancing northward from Fort Washington, he established a series of fortified posts. On August 20, 1794, Wayne's troops engaged the Indians in the battle at the difficult Fallen Timbers ground. In the furious but brief battle the Indians were routed, and on the following August 5, 1795, General Wayne negotiated with the confederated tribes the Treaty of Greenville.[54] By this action, and the success of Benjamin Logan and William Whitley in combatting the Cherokees along the Wilderness Trail,

Kentucky was at last freed of the Indian menace. A hero of this struggle was General Charles Scott. He, like most of his older Kentucky neighbors, was born in Virginia.[55] As a brigadier general he had fought in the American Revolution, spending part of the winter 1777-1778 at Valley Forge.[56] He moved to Kentucky in 1785, to Fayette County. On July 25, 1807, he married Judith Carey Bell Gist, widow of Colonel Nathaniel Gist. He went to live at Canewood in Clark County and during the years 1808-1812 he served as governor of Kentucky.[57] General Scott died at Canewood, and his body was buried on the grounds. In 1854 the Kentucky General Assembly appropriated $300 to have the body exhumed and reinterred in the cemetery in Frankfort.[58]

All of the military action relating to the Kentucky frontier until after the War of 1812 involved, almost altogether, citizen militiamen. The first Kentucky constitution, 1792, provided for the creation of county militia companies.[59] Chief commanding officers were to be appointed by the governor, but the militia companies were to choose their own local officers. Three of the Kentucky constitutions provided that free, able-bodied male Kentuckians (Negroes, mulattos, and Indians excepted) between the ages of eighteen and forty-five were subjected to military service. Those with religious scruples against war could hire substitutes.[60] The constitutions presumed that on regular muster days the citizen militiamen would be disciplined and drilled in preparation for conflict in battle. Muster day in Clark County, as in all of Kentucky's counties, became as much a local festive occasion as a serious military exercise. Although descriptions of what occurred on Clark County muster days are meager, it is safe to assume the military training was deficient. The lack of preparation and discipline in the Harmar and St. Clair debacles was self-evident.[61]

During the years 1800-1815 considerable militia activity took place in Clark County; sometimes it was tense and exciting, and at other times it was little more than "cornstalk muster day frolics.[62] There occurred an incident in 1803 which had the potential of major militia involvement. When there seemed to be the possibility that Spain would not honor the sale of the Louisiana Territory to the United States there arose an angry reaction in Kentucky. Clark County had a vital stake in the diplomatic transactions. To again close the Mississippi River to free commercial use would have resulted in economic disaster for the county's farmers.[63]

Almost unanimously Kentuckians approved the purchase of Louisiana and Senator John Breckinridge, an ardent supporter of President Thomas Jefferson and a proponent of the constitutionality of the Louisiana Purchase, encouraged the mustering of a sizable Kentucky militia force to wrest Louisiana by use of arms from Spain in case that country refused to accede to the sale.[64] By early fall 1803, a move was under way in Kentucky to muster into service 4,000 volunteer citizen-militiamen. These were to march on New Orleans in December that year. This militia expedition was to be under the command of General Samuel Hopkins.[65] It may have been fortunate that Spain agreed to the sale of Louisiana on November 30, 1803,[66] because later General Samuel Hopkins proved to be less than an effective commander of militia.

There was never a time when Kentucky was more involved in and concerned about foreign affairs than in the era 1787-1814. The end of the American Revolution and the negotiation of subsequent treaties by no means erased the problems of the western country. No Kentucky county was more vitally concerned with resolutions of the issues prevailing in 1800-1814 with France, Spain, and Great Britain, to say nothing of the ever-present Indian question than Clark. All three of the European countries had an influence in some way on the economic welfare and general safety of the county.[67]

When the area cut off from Fayette and Bourbon counties was formed into Clark County, there was created the responsibility of maintaining a citizen militia; this automatically was assumed in the creation.[68] The new county was formed under the authority of the constitution of 1792, which mandated the maintenance of a local militia company. This was partly influenced by the attempt of the federal government to depend upon a citizen military force rather than upon a professional army.[69] There lingered on in the region some concern about possible Indian raids, despite the fact Anthony Wayne's expedition against the northwestern tribes had been successful. Wayne's campaign, however, did not destroy the will of the various northwestern tribes to resist the spread of white population and the loss of territory. There arose a highly capable Indian leader in the person of Chief Tecumseh of the Shawnees. He had a good understanding of the threat of the white man's insatiable desire for land.

During the decade 1800-1810 Kentuckians were sensitized by the somewhat fumbling efforts of the United States to force recognition from Britain and France of free trade rights on the high seas.[70] The attempt to force Britain to recognize these rights by use of the embargo against British imports proved a failure. In the meantime the market for the products of Clark County was being badly disrupted. Nothing, however, stirred Kentucky fury more than the Chesapeake-Leopard Affair, 1807, in which a British ship captain attempted to impress American sailors.[71] There occurred in both the Kentucky

General Roger Weightman
Hanson, scion of a pioneer Clark
County family, veteran of the
Mexican War, legislator, friend of
the slave church congregation,
captured at Fort Donaldson in
February 1862, but was back in
service that August. Was mortally
wounded in the battle of Stone
River. Basil Duke called Hanson
the complete soldier. - *Photo courtesy
of the Winchester Sun*

General Assembly and in the newspaper press condemnations of the British high-handed actions. In the General Assembly, Henry Clay and Humphrey Marshall became so embroiled in the debate that they crossed the Ohio River at Louisville to fight a senseless duel on neutral soil.[72] Clay went away to the United States Senate in 1810 to fill out the unexpired term of Buckner Thruston, and subsequently was elected a congressman.[73] On his first term in the House of Representatives he was made Speaker of the House, and in this position he became a shrill prowar voice, advocating war with Britain and the annexation of Canada.[74] It is all but impossible to gauge with any precision the public responses to the national and international issues by the people of Clark County. The public records are mixed on the subject, even the ones related to maintaining a citizen militia.[75]

On November 17, Governor [General] Charles Scott issued a call to the people of Kentucky to aid the nation in the moment of threatening war on several fronts. In the call was the raising of at least 5,000 volunteers.[76] Behind this call was actually the plan to break the British-Indian collusion in the Northwest. Kentucky was too insular to be directly involved in the conflict over freedom of the seas, but Kentuckians did react angrily to the audacity of

British impressment of American seamen. Since the era of the American Revolution there was among them lingering hatred of the British, especially as their influence over the northwestern tribes of Indians was revealed from time to time.[77] This dislike of Britain was so virulent that the Kentucky General Assembly undertook to bar the citation of British court decisions rendered after 1776.

The crisis of 1807-1813 involved a mixture of political issues and conflicts on several local fronts. One nagging irritation was the Indian resistance along the Wabash River in the so-called New Purchase area where a large block of land was acquired from the associated tribes in the treaty of 1809.[78] This purchase angered the Indian leaders Tecumseh and his twin brother the Prophet.[79] In resistance to the action the Shawnees established a rather large village on the Wabash River near the mouth of Tippecanoe Creek. In this case there was a distinct difference of personality between the twin Shawnee brothers. Tecumseh was a man of unusually high intellectual and leadership qualities. He dreamed of creating a confederation of Indians as a barrier to white expansion onto Indian lands.[80] He contended that the Harrison treaty of 1809 was fraudulently made. In the fall of 1811 Tecumseh went south to communicate with the Creek and Choctaw Indians about the plan for forming a confederation. His idea was to get the tribes to adopt more of the ways of their white neighbors to avoid eventual deterioration of their conditions of life.[81]

On November 7, 1811, there occurred the battle of Tippecanoe Creek which resulted more or less in a draw between William Henry Harrison's forces and the Shawnee warriors.[82] The Indians had been stampeded into battle by the wild and mystical incantations of the Prophet. Harrison's forces were able to capture the Indian village, where they found a supply of new English guns, some of them still in the shipping wrappings.[83] The whites, however, could not call Tippecanoe a clear-cut victory. This incident, though far removed physically from Clark County, was to have a definite impact on its history. Kentuckians involved at Tippecanoe were largely from the Jefferson County area. The incident stirred further the Kentucky anger against Britain and the Northwest Indians. The war fever in Kentucky ran high in 1811.

The United States formally declared war against Britain in June 18, 1812. As a result of pressures applied by hawkish congressmen and others on President James Madison, he recommended that Congress be prepared for wide-scale hostilities.[84] By a narrow vote Congress, however, approved going to war with Great Britain and the northwestern Indians.[85]

In the latter half of the year 1811 and into 1812 war fever ran high in

Kentucky and in Clark County. Editor John Bradford of the *Kentucky Gazette*, May 26, 1812, wrote, "There soon would be 10,000 Kentuckians on the march."[86] Secretary of War William Eustice apportioned to Kentucky a requisition for 5,500 militiamen. Already Governor Charles Scott, then a resident of Clark County, in one of his last acts of his administration, ordered out 1,500 volunteers to support Brigadier General William Hull.[87] General Hull, a governor of the Northwest Territory, proved to be a hapless military officer incapable of making any aggressive move. On August 16, 1812 he committed the highly alarming act of surrendering Detroit to Isaac Brock's British force.[88] News of Hull's surrender resounded over Kentucky like a violent thunderclap. Interestingly, when news of General Hull's surrender reached Kentucky, William Henry Harrison was in Frankfort conferring with incoming Governor Isaac Shelby and others about the situation in the Wabash-Great Lakes areas.[89] By this time the War of 1812 had become one with several fronts. One front was in the Detroit-Fort Meigs-Fort Malden area.[90]

The pages of the *Kentucky Gazette* and the *Lexington Reporter* carried columns of war news. Isaac Shelby, Henry Clay, Christopher Greenup, Charles Scott, and Thomas Todd formed a self-appointed board of war and decided that Kentucky's volunteer militiamen would serve in the command of William Henry Harrison rather than that of the Tennessee War Department's appointee, General James WInchester.[91] This no doubt was a wise strategic decision. Harrison was popular in Kentucky, and Winchester had met only with moderate success in stemming the drive of Indians and the British against Fort Defiance in the southwest Michigan Territory.

On the deathly freezing night of January 23, 1813, there occurred a second and horrendous attack by the British and Indians against the American volunteers and regulars at French town and along the frozen River Raisin. Prisoners were brutally tortured and murdered by the Indians without interference from the British officers. Horror stories of this disaster reached Kentucky, and the battle cry of "Remember the Raisin!" became a recruiting tocsin.[92] Nowhere in the western country was this shrill scream heeded more fully than in Clark County. The war in the Fort Wayne-Fort Meigs-Detroit, Lake Erie corridor now became a focal point for the volunteer Clark County militia forces. Most of the volunteers seem to have been of the ninety-day variety.[93] The numerous lists of companies of volunteers in 1813 are extensive, but it is difficult to spot all those which contained Clark County volunteers, partly because some of them contained enrollees from other counties.[94] The identifiable lists contain such well-known family surnames as Bush, Sympson, Strode, Cunningham, Quisenberry, Combs, Owen, Davidson,

Hinde, Scobee, Crockett, Taylor, Bean, and others. The lists of officers and private volunteers are full, and it would require extensive research to identify all the Clark County enrollees.[95]

Among the volunteers was Leslie Combs. This twenty-year-old volunteer was a cadet in the First Regiment of Kentucky Volunteers. He was the son of Revolutionary War veteran Captain Benjamin Combs, who had established a substantial military land claim at a very early date on the Kentucky River near Boonesborough. Young Combs was attached to the command of General Green Clay and served as a messenger between generals Clay and Harrison. He was listed as a "spy." He traveled several hundred miles under perilous conditions.[96] There was also the warm human story of Leonard Beall, who volunteered as a militiaman from Indian Old Fields. He was taken prisoner. Chief Black Hoof, or Catahecassa, discovered that Leonard was from his birthplace and saved him from the murderous ordeal of running the gauntlet. There was the afterstory that Black Hoof visited Leonard in Winchester.[97]

In May 1813, Governor Shelby called up 3,000 volunteers who were placed under the command of General Green Clay of neighboring Madison County. This command contained numerous Clark County officers and volunteers. It arrived before Fort Meigs after literally cutting its way to the fort. Later in that year Governor Shelby was granted permission by the General Assembly to leave the state to command the Kentucky volunteers.[98] He left behind lieutenant governor Richard Hickman of Clark County to administer the government. In September 1813, Isaac Shelby was in his sixty-third year and was considered an aged man. True to General Harrison's wishes, Shelby, at the head of 4,000 troops, arrived at Fort Meigs in time to back up the command already in place. In this relatively large corps were Clark County militiamen under the direct command of various local company officers.[99]

On September 9, 1813, Oliver Hazard Perry, with a small fleet of gunboats engaged the British fleet under the command of Robert Barkley in battle in Put-in-Bay in Lake Erie.[100] On September 10 Perry won a strategic battle.[101] Commodore Perry was able to set the mounted company of volunteers under the command of Richard M. Johnson across the bay to attack the forces of Brigadier General Henry Proctor and Chief Tecumseh.[102] On October 5, 1813, occurred the decisive Battle of the Thames in which Proctor's troops were put to flight, and Johnson charged the Indians under the control of Tecumseh.[103]

Most historical accounts of the War of 1812 describe the recruiting of troops, their going away to fight, the battles, and the creation of military heroes. There was another side to the War of 1812 in Kentucky. There was no supplier in the state at that time capable of meeting all the needs of so large a number of volunteer troops. The volunteers who went from Kentucky to fight on the northern Ohio and southwestern Michigan frontiers were subject to rapidly changing weather conditions. At home Kentucky women industriously worked at creating clothing materials. They were credited with supplying 2,250 pairs of pantaloons, 3,144 pairs of socks, 1,176 roundabouts, 5,556 blankets, and 2,088 pairs of shoes. In addition to this inventory there was also a generous supply of food materials. Again, it is not possible to isolate the materials supplied from the counties in the Bluegrass.[104]

For the majority of the Clark County men of military age the threat of war was ended that October day on the banks of the Canadian Thames River when the forces of General Proctor and Chief Tecumseh were defeated. Though the conquest of Canada had failed, the important area around Detroit and on the southern shore of Lake Erie was definitely secured.[105] The Indian hold on the northwest region was broken. Tecumseh and the Prophet were defeated, with Tecumseh losing his dream and his life.[106] Perhaps no one can ever say with irrefutable documentary evidence who really killed Tecumseh. Richard M. Johnson later made considerable political capital by asserting that he was the hero who killed the famous Indian.[107]

Scrap for the Japs on the Chesapeake and Ohio Railroad cars in Winchester circa 1938. - *Photo courtesy of Evans*

The Clark County militiamen who had advanced onto the Northern Ohio and Michigan frontiers with William Henry Harrison and Isaac Shelby, Richard M. Johnson, James Wilkinson, General Green Clay, and the company captains faced the long, wearying march home. They passed over the route of many Indian confrontations and the scene of many physical hardships. Some of them had seen the skeletal remains of the victims of Frenchtown and the Raisin.[108] Perhaps no other war to date in which Americans had fought produced so many real and near heroes. Possibly no other military campaign in American history had been so overburdened with generals, colonels, and other officers down to fifth corporals and ensigns.[109]

Some Clark County soldiers served in other areas and in other branches of military services. Fort Meigs, Detroit, Frenchtown, the River Raisin, and the Thames, however, were the scenes of major Clark County troop participation. The War of 1812 was the high point of the Clark County citizen militia's history.

It is doubtful that many of the militiamen, officers, or citizens could have anticipated the changes which would occur in the immediate future in the history of the county and in Kentucky. For the most part the day of the importance of the militia was over, except for muster days as more or less festive occasions. As discussed elsewhere, the war brought about an era of runaway inflation, and then the economic crisis of 1819. Clark County, however, was in a more stable rural-agrarian situation to deal with the inroads of economic depression than were a majority of Kentucky's counties.[110]

The Kentucky citizen militia of frontier fame was to have one more fling at glory before it folded its colors for good. The War with Mexico was tailor-made for the volunteer militia. It would tax one's imagination to think of a military activity which would have so little meaning for Clark County as this struggle. Its citizens had gone to the polls in 1844 to cast 78.6 percent of its voting strength; 1,122 votes for the Whig Henry Clay and 314 for James Knox Polk, the Democrat.[111] Local interest in the Texas-Mexico border dispute was minimal, except for the fact of the expansion of slavery.[112]

The wave of war excitement swept over Kentucky in 1846 like an equinotial storm. The United States secretary of war called upon the commonwealth to raise volunteer troops to aid General Zachary Taylor in repelling the Mexican invasion.[113] Governor William Owsley responded that Kentuckians would heed the call gallantly. On May 8, 1846, in a somewhat comic opera battle, Taylor's forces defeated the Mexicans at Palto Alto and at Resaca de le Palma.[114] A week later the Congress formally declared war on Mexico.[115] By this date war excitement in Kentucky was at a high pitch. Colonel

Stephen Ormsby in Louisville succeeded in raising nine companies of the Louisville Legion, and they set off down river by steamboat bound for Texas.[116]

Governor Owsley issued a call, May 25, 1846, for 2,400 Kentucky volunteers, and 13,700 war-eager volunteers responded. Three regimental companies were organized in addition to the Louisville Legion; the 1st, 2nd, and 4th.[117] As it turned out the latter was the most important to Clark County. It was led by Captain John Stuart Williams.[118] Captain Williams was of geographical parts. He was born in Montgomery County near Mount Sterling on July 10, 1818. He was college educated and be became a practicing attorney in Paris. His biographical sketches are vague; Colonel Williams seems to have had no Clark County connection until after the Civil War, when he became a farmer.[119] The 4th Kentucky Regiment was associated with the 2nd Regiment of Tennessee Volunteers.[120] The attack against the Mexican forces at Atalya and Cerro Gordo involved several young officers who, later in the Civil War, would write their names indelibly in the pages of American miliary history. There were Captain Robert E. Lee, Captain George Gordon Meade, Lieutenant P. G. T. Beauregard, General Gideon Pillow, and others.[121] Captain Lee won distinction as the careful scouting engineer who platted the paths of approaches to the summit of the two ridges overlooking the vital pass of Plan Del Rio.[122]

The strategic heights of Atalya and Cerro Gordo were assaulted by the Americans on the early morning of April 17-18, 1847. The heights were defended by a large body of regular Mexican troops, plus a considerable number of the rakings and scrapings from the streets of Mexico City.[123] In command was the ubiquitous General Antonio de Lopez del Santa Anna. American troops reached the crest of Cerro Gordo on the morning of April 18. The Mexicans were routed so quickly that General Santa Anna himself fled the scene, leaving behind his carriage, his papers, and a luxuriously prepared meal.[124] Captain Robert E. Lee emerged from the battle of Cerro Gordo as the main hero. It was said that in that conflict there were present enough generals and colonels to have staffed an armed force ten times the size of General Winfield Scott's command.[125] Nevertheless, the 2nd Kentucky performed heroically, with now Colonel John Stuart Williams emerging as a hero. Because of his actions Williams was to be singled out the rest of his life by the sobriquet "Cerro Gordo."[126] In the battle William F. Durham, and Alfred H. Horton were killed; Minor T. Smith, Henry Bruce, Ira F. Storm, J. C. Langson, N. W. Kelly, and Henry D. Williams were wounded somewhat seriously. William Bruce, William Chism, James Minor, and William E. Martin were only slightly wounded.[127] The *Lexington Observer and Reporter* said the

Clark County volunteers of the 2nd Kentucky performed nobly in the last grand battle of the Mexican War.[128] Francis Lisle of that regiment, and a Clark County resident, chose to remain in the service as an informal aid to General David Twiggs in his march on Mexico City.[129]

At some point past Cerro Gordo the terms of service of the 2nd Kentucky volunteers expired and they returned to Clark County. From Jalapa on the road to Mexico City the march was virtually clear of Mexican resistance. Now the war was to be finished in the political and diplomatic areas. As indicated earlier, the Mexican War was the last great hurrah for the old-style volunteer frontier soldier. The next conflict was an internecine affair in which more regular army officers and troops were involved.

At home in Clark County and Winchester the Mexican War, except for the initial volunteering flurry, caused hardly a ripple. Life went on in its quiet routine manner. There was more concern with field crops and livestock than with the more immediate issues of internal improvements. In the midst of the war a Clark County delegation attended a public discussion of the possibility of enhancing navigation on the Kentucky River by creating slack water pools to accommodate steamboat traffic.[130]

For Clark County the thunder of Cerro Gordo did not cease with the defeat of Santa Anna's army. On the return of the veterans there followed a somewhat bizarre political afterclap. Though they had scaled the heights of Cerro Gordo as comrades at arms, there did not exist between John Stuart Williams and Roger W. Hanson the usual extraordinary but highly unpredictable character. Basil Duke wrote that had Hanson given more serious devotion to his education, he might have been less erratic in his personal behavior.[131]

Roger Hanson was never clear of personal difficulty or above committing ludicrous shenanigans. He engaged John Stuart Williams in a hot electoral contest for a seat in the Kentucky house of representatives in 1851. He ridiculed Williams' Cerro Gordo sobriquet, even charging him with fakery about the two six-pound brags Mexican cannons he had brought home from the war. Hanson told his campaign audiences that Williams had hired an Irishman to fish the cannons out of a bayou where fleeing Mexican troops had thrown them. He said Williams was the last man to scale Cerro Gordo and the first to rush down to the safety of the plain. Hanson ridiculed and embarrassed his old commanding officer from every political stump in Clark County. Williams' advisors told him he must silence Hanson or lose the race. Realizing that he might provoke his temperamental opponent to violence, the colonel armed himself with two pistols and a bowie knife, concealed beneath his coat. When the two met in the next country schoolhouse forum Williams thoroughly chastised his adversary. Hanson and his supporters withdrew from the schoolhouse to a nearby spring, ostensibly to take a drink, but in fact for Hanson to disarm himself. When he returned to the schoolroom he strutted back and forth, removing his coat, unbuttoning his shirt, and turning his pant's pockets wrong side out. He challenged Williams to do the same, which he could not afford to do because it would have revealed the pistols and knife. Despite Hanson's antics, Williams won the election by six votes.[132]

Clark County was fortunate that it did not become too deeply embroiled in the forthcoming Civil War. There is ample historical evidence to support the belief that, left to their own political, economic, and social inclinations, the people would have tolerated slavery, but would have opposed going to civil war over that or any other issue which could have been settled peaceably. Whatever sectional feelings may have prevailed in the county in 1860, voters in the majority favored the Union without disruption. In the presidential election that year 68 percent of the voters supported John Bell and the Constitutional Union party. In the election that year 44.6 percent of the registered voters were slaveholders, but John C. Breckinridge's proslavery segment of the Democratic party received only 4.9 percent of the vote.[133]

Without making a public and collective expression on the subject, a majority of the people in Clark County favored a position of neutrality for Kentucky at the moment when southern states were seceding. An interesting personal expression on the subject was that of the thirty-five-year-old Roger Hanson. He supported neutrality up to the point when it was first violated by the Confederates and then immediately by the Union forces.[134]

The history of the Civil War in Clark County is both nebulous and anecdotal. Fortunately the county, geographically, never found itself in the direct line of battling military forces. It had no industries creating the materials of war and no rich deposits of salt and iron so desperately needed by the Confederacy.[135] There was no railway line to be destroyed, and the Kentucky River along the county's border was of no strategic importance.[136] The gravest point of vulnerability was the turnpike running from Lexington to the Big Sandy River.[137] Clark County's farms produced the foodstuffs so vitally needed in the South, but no Confederate forces were able to penetrate and control the region.[138]

At least five attempts were made by Confederate armies to penetrate and exploit the rich Kentucky Bluegrass breadbasket. In September and October 1861, General Felix Zollicoffer undertook to invade the Bluegrass, but was turned back in the Battle of the Wildcat Mountain in Laurel County. Zollicoffer made a second try, this time by way of Mill Spring and Somerset; he, however, lost both the fight and his life in the skirmished of Mill Spring and Nancy.[139] John Hunt Morgan raided in the central Kentucky counties but largely to recruit men and horses.[140]

The closest the shooting war came to Clark County was General Edmond Kirby-Smith's dash up the Wilderness Road in August 1862. He engaged Union forces in a running skirmish from Kingston through Richmond to Clay's Ferry.[141] General Kirby-Smith's command reached Lexington but was forced to leave Kentucky in General Braxton Bragg's withdrawal after the Battle of Perryville on October 8, 1862.[142] There was skirmishing at Cynthiana and Mount Sterling, and soldiers in many instances seemed to have wandered almost aimlessly over the countryside.[143]

Only a couple of notations of any slight substance were made in the *Official Record of the War of the Rebellion* relating to Clark County and Winchester.[144] The Civil War history of Clark County has to be written largely in biographies of some individuals. John Stuart Williams, though at that time living in Bourbon County, enlisted in the Confederate Army in 1861 as colonel of the Fifth Kentucky Regiment. This unit was made up largely of one-year volunteers.[145] In April 1862, Williams was promoted to brigadier general,

Red Cross Parade on Winchester's Main Street during World War I.

and later to the rank of major general in command of calvary. Throughout the war General Williams fought as a commanding officer.[146]

Roger W. Hanson enlisted in the Confederate Army as a colonel in command in the 2nd Regiment of Kentucky Infantry.[147] Following the brigadier general in command of the Orphan Brigade.[148] He was mortally wounded January 2, 1863.[149] Later Basil Duke said of General Hanson that he was, "One of the most remarkable men who served in the Confederate Army. No officer was more liked and respected by the Kentucky soldiers. He possessed more thoroughly the confidence of his superiors in command.[150]

Roy Cluke of Clark County was a member of General John Hunt Morgan's brigade as a commander of infantry. After the Morgan raid on Georgetown, Roy Cluke and D. W. Chenault were authorized to raise volunteers for the Eighth and Ninth Kentucky regiments.[151] In July 1863 Cluke crossed the Ohio in Morgan's famous invasion of Indiana and Ohio. He was with General Morgan on July 26, 1863, when they were captured by Union troops at an attempted retreat across the swollen Ohio. He was imprisoned in the Ohio State Penitentiary at Columbus and was later transferred to Johnson Island, where he died of diphtheria.[152]

Throughout Kentucky in 1861-1865, brother fought against brother, neighbor against neighbor, and blood kin against blood kin. In most of their minds, however, they may have had no profound political or deep constitutional convictions concerning that the basic issues put forward as the causes of the struggle.[153] The roll calls of the two armies closely paralleled those of the pioneer Revolutionary War veterans who came seeking landholds in the area. Engaged in the southern cause were Bean, Bush, Cluke, Combs, Ecton, Gay, Boone, Hampton, Hickman, Lisle, Scobee, Williams, and Hieronymus. Out of 169 Confederate soldiers listed for the *Winchester Sun-Sentinel* by Jennie Catherine Bean most were representatives of older family groups.[154]

In treating the history of Clark County's involvement in the Civil War there has been an apparent bias in the documentation favoring the Confederacy. Nevertheless, many were enrolled in the Union muster ranks from Clark County. The United States War Department credited the state with furnishing 75,276 men to the Union Army, but estimates of those serving the Confederate cause range from 25,000 to 40,000 men.[155] The comparative numbers for Clark County may have indicated the same ratio. Among those who fought in the Union Army were the family representative names of Samuel Boone, twin brother of the Confederate Thomas Boone, Walter Combs, James H. Holloway, George N. Jackson, Colonel Charles S. Hanson, Randolph Martin, John B. Huston, B. F. Buckner, James Sympson, and G. T. Kelly.[156] In

1923 there were said to be twenty-six Union soldiers buried in the Winchester Cemetery alone.[157] One of them, Benjamin Forsythe Buckner, was born in Jacksonville, Illinois; but his father, Aylette Buckner, was a native of Bourbon County. He moved to Clark County, where he practiced law and served as circuit court clerk. Young Buckner graduated from the Kentucky Military Institute near Frankfort. He read law in his father's office and served as deputy court clerk. He joined the Union Army in 1861 with the rank of major in the Twentieth Kentucky Infantry. He was engaged in the thick of battle at Shiloh, and the following years in engagements in Tennessee and Kentucky.[158]

Clark County and Winchester fortunately escaped the fate of being scenes of pitched battles, or of being seriously invaded by the two armies. There was the minor creek bank fight between General Scott's Confederates and Union troops commanded by a Major Foley of the Tenth Kentucky Cavalry. They skirmished along Upper Howard's and Four-Mile creeks, killing one Confederate and seven or eight horses. This bit of heroics, as described by Captain Creed, occurred in July 1863. The captain, however, was not specific about the date or the end of the fight. This kind of encounter occurred many times over throughout Kentucky.[159]

A chapter of local Civil War history had a partial bearing on Clark County. When John Hunt Morgan and Thomas Hinds escaped from the Ohio State Penitentiary on November 29, 1863, Morgan made his way to Richmond, Virginia, and to an agonizing period of frustration. He was ambitious to reunite his old command and once again raid in Tennessee and Kentucky. Both President Jefferson Davis and Secretary of War Braxton Bragg refused him permission to do so; instead he recruited a new and indifferent command of volunteers. Cecil Holland, a Morgan biographer, describes them as being, "The riffraff and the criminals out of the backwash of the South who had found their way into Confederate uniforms were showing their stripe."[160]

In the spring of 1864 John Hunt Morgan at the head of his "riffraff" began his long, exhausting march through the Appalachian Highlands from Virginia by the way of Pound Gap into Kentucky. By June 8, 1864, Morgan had reached Mount Sterling, where he captured 300 Union Army prisoners and a large quantity of supplies.[161] His unruly troops pillaged stores and robbed the Mount Sterling Bank of $75,000. In doing so they threatened to burn every house in the town if the money was not handed over.[162] No one was safe from the pillaging. According to the report of one reliable Morgan officer, soldiers drew pistols on women and robbed them of their jewelry. A Mrs. Hamilton, riding into Mount Sterling with delicacies for the wounded, was robbed of her money and her horse.[163]

General Morgan and D. Howard Smith, accompanied by the 2nd Brigade, departed Mount Sterling soon after its capture and started toward Lexington by way of Winchester.[164] Behind them they had left Colonels Henry L. Giltner and Robert M. Martin in command. They had just reached Winchester when they were informed that General Stephen Burbridge's 9th U. S. Infantry had raided the Confederate encampment at Mount Sterling, which was under the command of Colonel Martin. Giltner had withdrawn his regiment and begun the march to Lexington. The people in Winchester may have been the only ones in Kentucky to owe a vote of appreciation to General Burbridge. He may have saved Winchester from experiencing the same traumatic fate as Mount Sterling.

The Civil War everywhere generated incidents of paramilitary meaning. There were at least two anecdotal accounts of wartime escapades in and around Winchester. One such was that of Alpheus Lewis, Jr., who acted as message-bearer between General Kirby-Smith's command and General Braxton Bragg right after the Battle of Richmond. He stopped by his home in Winchester for a visit when outriders of General Don Carlos Buell's forces came looking for him. He was hid securely in his mother's basement until the federal troops departed and went on his way with the message he was carrying.[165]

There was the somewhat comic anecdote of Stephen Sharpe of Kiddville. He and three companions were on leave from Kirby-Smith's regiment after the Battle of Kingston-Richmond-Clay's Ferry. A woman tollgate keeper warned them that 200 federal troops were in Winchester. The four captured a picket and "paroled" him with the false information that John Hunt Morgan's command had already crossed the Kentucky River and was headed for Winchester. They then sent a white flag into town demanding its surrender. The federals fled to Paris. Sharpe and his companions "captured" the town, climbed into the cupola of the courthouse, pulled down the national flag, and hoisted the confederate one. They issued orders for the people of Winchester to prepare a breakfast the following day for 1800 hungry Morgan troops, and then they silently skipped town.[166]

As noted above, the Civil War began and ended with the divisions of neighbors and family members, but actually Clark County and Winchester miraculously escaped being battered in the woes of "turncoat" Lexington and battle-scarred Richmond, just across the Kentucky River. Local war damages were to be assessed more in political, constitutional, and social terms. The years 1861-1865 were distinctly watershed ones for Clark County. Never again could it indulge in the complacency of the formative years of the first half of the nineteenth century.[167]

By April 1865 at least three historic phases of Clark County military activities had run a long and, sometimes, a tedious course. Long ago the Indians had been vanquished, the British had been driven back across the Canadian borders, and no Confederate and Yankee soldiers lurked about the countryside to disturb the peace. Slavery was at an end, and Clark County's people were at peace. Even in Kentucky as a whole there prevailed a spirit of relaxation. On special occasions both Union and Confederate veterans gathered in reunions, reminisced about wartime experiences, and listened to long-winded orators glorify "the cause."

The nation sought to heal its sectional wounds by holding the great Centennial Exposition in Philadelphia in 1876. Not only did the celebration take a backward look at the rise of the nation, but it also cast a longer projectory into the future. Inventive and industrial America put on display the instruments and machines which would effect enormous changes in the ways of American life.[168] During the closing decades, 1865-1900, of the nineteenth century the westward thrust of pioneering in American history had reached a stage of simmering down. The Bureau of the United States Census, in 1890, declared the frontier technically closed.[169] In the post-Civil War years Clark County reached a new stage of becoming a modern social and political entity. In fact, this was a moment in local history when people could savor in peace the simple pleasures of a rural provincial society.[170] This was a time of frequent family gatherings, public picnics, excursions to interesting places, and political barbecues when candidates bellowed out their virtues in courthouse squares. Generally in the decade 1890-1900 the people of Clark County had little knowledge or zeal for the gunboat diplomacy of the McKinley-Roosevelt years.[171] There was little in the jingoist thunder of the "yellow journalism" press which affected either the tenor or life or the fortunes of the local people. The sinking of the gunboat *Maine*,[172] Teddy Roosevelt's macho charge up San Juan Hill in Cuba, and Admiral Dewey's overnight victory in Manila Bay made exciting news in the Winchester and Lexington newspapers. There were volunteers for military service, but the war was of too short a duration to create much of a local ripple.[173]

The opening decade of the twentieth century no doubt was a mauve period, if not in fact one of innocence. Politically, Kentucky was concentrating on healing its own gaping domestic and political wounds opened by the William Goebel assassination tragedy, the eastern county blood feuds, the western counties tobacco war, and the whirlwind drives for educational reforms. All of these issues in some way bore upon the history of Clark County.[174]

After 1914, however, the traditional ways of life for most people around

Clark County draftees assembled at the rear of the courthouse prior to their departure for Camp Taylor in Louisville in September 1917. -
Photo courtesy of the Winchester Sun

the globe were exposed to change whether it be along Lower Howard's Creek, the Danube, the Thames, the Nile, or the Seine. When Central Europe that year burst into the flames of what became a world war, that it would have a fundamental meaning in Clark County was unthinkable. This was even more pronounced when voters went to the polls in 1916 to elect a president of the nation. A majority supported incumbent Woodrow Wilson; ringing in their ears was the campaign slogan, "He kept us out of war."[175] Within the months immediately following the election, the Germans renewed submarine attacks upon Atlantic shipping. This, along with the highly publicized atrocities against the people of Belgium, stirred a bitter anti-German sentiment in the county.[176]

On April 6, 1917, the United States Congress declared war on the Central Powers.[177] Just prior to this date the *Winchester Sun* carried news of the sinking of American ships by German submarines.[178] There occurred a burst of patriotism surpassing anything in the past. For instance, the Bradley Grocery Company ran a three-column advertisement in the Sun urging its patrons to, "Show your patriotic spirit by displaying OLD GLORY. If you haven't one to unfurl we have then in all sizes."[179]

A Red Cross society was formed to aid the war effort by collecting materials and rendering aid to the rapidly expanding armed forces. Eloquent Governor A. O. Stanley came to speak in the Opera House, where he urged the formation of a Navy League.[180] Twenty-five zealous prospective draftees formed a training corps to be drilled by Captain Henry Stratton.[181] In May 1917 a draft quota was set for Clark County, asking initially for sixty draftees. The *Winchester Sun* boasted that a thousand men were available.[182] Three days later 500 people gathered to watch the 2nd Kentucky Infantry march out of its encampment.[183]

By January 1918 Clark County was fully mobilized to support the war effort. At that date the local draft board was instructed to call up more men; in an early call the army requested the enlistment of forty white and fifty colored men.[184] At the same time war savings drives more than topped their quotas. Countywide donors to the Red Cross drive contributed mules, pigs, sheep, geese, and chickens along with other things to be sold at auction.[185] In addition, the local Red Cross Chapter was called upon to contribute 2,500 pairs of socks and 500 hand-knitted sweaters by the first of September.[186] This request was reminiscent of the days when the women of Clark County busied themselves spinning, knitting, and weaving clothing for the volunteers in the War of 1812.

Mobilization for war on such a vast scale created shortages of all sorts of materials. This was especially true for such foodstuffs as sugar, wheaten bread,

Reunion of Roy Cluke's Regiment in the ranks of the Morgan's Brigade. Most if not all of these men were captured in the Indiana-Ohio raid in 1863.

and meats, and also for lumber and labor.[187] The *Winchester Sun*, March 11, 1917, informed its readers that coal was in woefully short supply, a shortage created by wartime consumption and partly by the enlistment of miners in the military services.

Finally there came that glorious moment of November 11, 1918, when an armistices was signed. The *Sun* announced the news in seventy-two-point type spread across its front page.[188] The paper said that a parade of a thousand vehicles was on its way to Lexington and back home by way of Paris. It said, "At the cities visited, hundreds of cars joined the crowd from Winchester and went the circuit, there being a constant tooting of horns and shouts of the patriotic crowd. Cars were decorated with bunting and long streamers flowed in the breeze. Before the caravan left Winchester it had paraded around town through the streets.[189]

The celebration continued into the next day, November 12, 1918, when roaring bonfires were set, and the custom of shooting anvils was resurrected. This part of the celebration was presided over by Maurice "Geeny" Strode. Businesses, including the *Winchester Sun*, closed their doors in celebration.[190]

Clark County people had been highly supportive of the war effort. The newspaper boasted that they had consistently oversubscribed the community's allotment during the various bond drives. In one of the earlier ones citizens invested $802,250 in Liberty Bonds.[191] When the sixty-two-piece United States Marine Band gave a concert in Winchester on November 6, 1918, subscribers pledged an additional $900,600 in Liberty Bonds.[192]

November 11, 1918, was a cardinal date in Clark County history. The impact of World War I was to bring about changes in the county's way of life; some of them were indeed radical changes. No doubt the most fundamental one was the breaching for all time to come of the provincial barriers which had historically encompassed the county.[193] The ways of the world and its problems flowed over the land. The war had initiated new modes of personal relationships, plus an acute awareness of the bigger world. Returning veterans brought home with them changed attitudes concerning human affairs. In the more material areas modern mechanization and the new excursions into the world of chemistry brought agriculture and industry out of the nineteenth century.[194] Veterans quickly realized that as an organized body they could exert much political power. Where their Revolutionary War era forbears had come west bearing land warrants in lieu of cash bonuses for their service, World War I veterans were eligible for cash bonuses, special hospitalization and prefatory treatment in the appointment to public jobs.[195] No doubt a majority of veterans and citizens alike believed the world had been made safe for democracy.

The compromises and diplomatic and political agreements so necessary to stabilize democracy, however, eroded rapidly in the decades 1920-1940. For instance, the controversy over adopting the Fourteen Points for peace advanced by Woodrow Wilson, the League of Nations failure, and the willfulness of new national leaders paved the way for a second world holocaust of war.[196] Immediately after the surrender of Germany in 1918 historians went searching for the causes of the war. They never really reached a consensus on the subject.[197] Many of the complex issues were beyond the ken of most of the people of Clark County. Their focus was on pressing matters nearer home. Hardly had the shouting died down and the last anvil firing resounded before the county's farmers were beset by the "tobacco depression" of 1920-1921,[198] adaptation of the new sciences and machines which came out of the war, and the impact of the war and the returning veterans on the traditional agrarian way of like in the county. There occurred in both the county courtroom and the city council chamber never-ending discussions of building new roads and streets, improving public services of all kinds, improving education and public health, and entering a new era of industrialization.[199]

The people in Clark County, as for all Americans, went in search of the will-o-the-wisp, a condition which the Republican campaigners called nor-malcy.[200] Even voting patterns revealed a changed attitude when support of Republican presidential candidates went from 4 percent to 50.3 percent prior to 1920, and upward to 1920 and 1928.[201]

There prevailed in Clark County, as throughout the nation the short-sighted notion that prosperity would linger for all foreseeable time in the future. There, however, came that moment when a mist of uncertainty spread through the land. There were tell-tale signs, subtle at first, that the country was drifting into a state of economic depression. There also were other signs of changing world political conditions. Locally attention in the 1930s was too intently focused on domestic problems to permit a closer awareness of what was happening in Europe. After their rise to power the madmen Adolf Hitler of Germany and Benito Mussolini in Italy busied themselves in sweep-ing aside the international conventions, treaties, and formulas for maintain-ing world peace.[202] In this era the *Winchester Sun* largely reflected the isolated complacency in presenting the currency of news. Thus it was that a second and even bloodier world war was brewing during the late 1930s with too little attention being given the fact in the county and state.

On September 1, 1939, German armed forces invaded Poland. This in-vasion came on the heels of Germany's having negotiated a treaty of accord with Russia. The Polish incident literally set the world ablaze with a second global conflict.[203] At home in Clark County there would recur a virtual car-bon duplicate of the experiences of World War I. By January 1940 most thoughtful Americans believed that the United States would inevitably be drawn into even another war on foreign soil.[204] There was acted out in the latter 1930s a phenomenon which the people of Clark County and all other Americans bitterly regretted. The Japanese metalmongers combed the Ameri-can countryside buying scrap iron. Mile-long trains speeded to West Coast shipping ports loaded with outmoded mowing machines, discarded automo-biles, broken-down washing machines, and everything else made of iron. Just as in 1916, the United States undertook to maintain the figment, at least, of neutrality. Nevertheless, raids against American shipping by German subma-rines provoked the nation into arming its merchant vessels.[205] At the same time there was brewing in the Far East inevitable conflict. Ruthlessly, Japan was expanding its sphere of influence in Korea and the Mandate Islands and even threatened China.[206] At the moment diplomats in Washington were negotiating with those of Japan there came that treacherous event of early morning, Sunday, December 7, 1941. Japanese air forces launched a surprise devastating attack on the United States naval fleet anchored in Pearl Harbor.

This sneak attack caused the loss of 2,200 lives and the wounding of 1,109 naval personnel. Eight battleships were sunk, and other craft were severely damaged.[207]

On Monday morning, December 8, the *Winchester Sun* published, in the boldest type contained in its cases, news and condemnation of the bombing.[208] At the same time radio stations bombarded their listeners with minute-by-minute details of the attack. The United States immediately declared war against Japan. A few days later Germany and Italy retaliated by declaring war on the United States.[209] In this hysterical moment all the nation's energies and attention were focused upon fighting and winning the two-front war.

The bombing of Pearl Harbor brought the outbreak of war intimately to Clark County. The *Winchester Sun* published the names of persons from the county who were believed to be in Pearl Harbor or nearby in the Pacific area. Among them were Richard J. Toohey, Elmo Mays, Andrew Napier, Calvin Coolidge Tipton, John Codell, and Bailey Bush, Jr.[210] Robert G. White was reported to have been killed in the bombing.[211] Later the news was confirmed that George W. Scott, a former *Sun* newsboy and a storekeeper aboard the battleship *West Virginia* was the first local fatality of the war.[212]

Following Pearl Harbor 20,000-man draft quotas were set periodically for Kentucky. In the end 7,710 Clark County men and women were either drafted or volunteered to serve in the armed and special services, war related and other capabilities. The *Winchester Sun*, December 16, 1941, declared that both the county and the nation were ready to fight the war. Under the editorial heading, "Ready for the Job," the paper proclaimed, "First, we're far more prepared for war now than we have ever been, at the start, in our national history. Second, this is primarily an industrial war, and we have the best industrial equipment and resources in the world, in full operation, with steady growing output. Third, we have virtually an unlimited supply of men better adapted to the mechanized warfare than any of our antagonists are. Fourth, we have a united nation, making one vast human machine in our common purpose. Fifth, we have a habit of victory; we have never lost a war. And to cap the climax: `So conquer we must, for out cause it is just: and this be our motto; In God is Our Trust.'"[213] These were bold words uttered in a dark moment of despair. During most of the next four years the newspapers, radios, and Pathe Movie News literally crackled with accounts of battles on both fronts. At home there was great diligence in supporting war efforts.

A mass meeting of citizens was held December 8, 1941, in the county courtroom to organize a defense league. This organization was created to deal with all sorts of war needs.[214] For instance, a scrap metal drive produced ten truckloads of the vital metal aluminum.[215] The remaining iron scrap not acquired by the Japanese was collected in a substantial tonnage. Because Germany stepped up its submarine warfare against American shipping in the Atlantic and because of the naval war in the Pacific, the *Winchester Sun* appointed a special naval editor to keep track of the sea activities.[216]

Franklin W. Stevenson was made head of the commission which pledged that it would raise $5,000 initially in support of the American Red Cross.[217] Stevenson was also made chairman of the local protection league, with Allen Buckner as vice-chairman, and Mrs. Betsie Crawford, secretary.[218] Mrs. Willis Van Meter headed the Bundles for Britain committee, but after Pearl Harbor her organization became "Bundles for Blue Jackets." The income from the book *Recipes from the Bluegrass* was consigned to this organization.[219]

For every human being in Clark County World War II, in some way, struck close to home, in military service, support of the home front, and the hardships of rationing of vital materials. Most pinching of the rationing was that of sugar, meats, tires, gasoline and motor oil, building supplies, and domestic and farm equipment.[220] Locally the creation of the Signal Crops center at Avon on the border of Clark-Fayette counties and the Blue Grass Ordinance center near Richmond placed an enormous strain on Winchester, Richmond, and Lexington to provide housing for the 2,000 new families which it was said would move into the area to staff the two ordinance facilities.[221]

On May 8, 1945, the *Winchester Sun*, as it had done at the end of World War I, announced in a capital block headline victory in Europe, or V. E. Day. In a four-column illustration the paper showed GIs in Germany throwing their helmets in the air and waving their rifles. Mayor John A. Snowden proclaimed the calling of a highly subdued celebration, one entirely different from that which celebrated Germany's surrender in 1918. The people were reminded that the war was only half won. The *Sun* estimated that there were in the neighborhood of 2,000 Clark County men and women in the services, a number slightly under two-thirds more than served in the earlier war.[222] The mayor requested that where possible all businesses close their doors and that the people gather at 2:00 P.M. in their respective churches to participate in brief religious ceremonies.[223]

Reflecting the subdued spirit of the moment, the *Winchester Sun's* editor wrote, "The Nation today thanks God and its fighting force for this victory over cruel, unjust, rapacious Germany. Tomorrow it turns about face for harder work than ever, striving for the victory over cruel, unjust, rapacious Japan."[224] He soon had his wish fulfilled, as the war against Japan came to a dramatic and unprecedented close on August 6, 1945, when the first atomic bomb was dropped on Hiroshima killing approximately 130,000 persons, and three days later when a second bomb was dropped on Nagasaki, killing approximately 75,000 persons. These events were announced by the *Winchester Sun* in bold black headlines. On August 14, Japan announced its surrender, which it did more formally on September 2, 1945, aborad the battleship *Missouri* in Tokyo Bay.[225]

Almost instantaneously literally hundreds of GIs were discharged and came home to Clark County to reenter civilian life, but this time veterans came home to a world which had undergone swift and, sometimes, radical changes. Clark County men and women were called upon to serve in three more wars, in Korea, Vietnam, and the dusty thirty-day Arabian Desert Storm. There was a wide space of time between that pioneering era when riflemen armed with long-barreled flintlock rifles stood off Indian raids at Strode's and Morgan's stations and that short war against Iraq when soldiers fired highly sophisticated scud missiles and airmen flew planes with enough explosives aboard to blast out of existence every Indian in the Miami Valley. Seventy-one Clark County boys never came home from World War II; among their names were those of the ancient pioneer families who had settled the homeland.[226]

William C. Dale Power Station, Ford, Kentucky. - *Photo courtesy of East Kentucky Power Cooperative*

CHAPTER 16

The New Industrial Frontier

In a sense the industrial age in Clark County dawned in 1890 when Burt and Brabb Lumber Company transferred its operation from Michigan to Ford on the Kentucky River. During the years 1890 to 1906 this company flourished, but like all of the outside lumbermen who pillaged the timber resources of the South in this era, Burt and Brabb "cut-out-and-got-out." At Ford the company operated two sawmills, a planing mill, and a box component mill. These mills turned untold millions of board feet of prime hardwood logs into lumber and other wood products. This timber was harvested from Madison, Perry, Leslie, Letcher, Knott, Bell, Clay, and Breathitt counties.

Logs were delivered to the mills by floatation in the "tide" or freshet seasons down the Kentucky River and by railway. In the years of its operation at Ford much of the lumber was shipped to imperial Germany, and later to Great Britain as ship timbers. At the height of the mill operations the village of Ford had a population of approximately 2,500 people and all but rivaled Winchester. The boom, however, played out when the Burt and Brabb Company exhausted its timber stands. By 1912 the affairs of Ford suffered loss of population and almost of identity, until the opening of the era of rural electrification.

After the end of World War I and rapid advances made in many areas of human and economic affairs in the nation, Clark County was caught up in the web of revolutionary change. During the decades 1920 to 1960 forces were at work in Kentucky and the South brought about by changing approaches to the future. These were indeed seminal decades in the history of

Winchester and Clark County. The ramparts of the old agrarian economy and folkways were invaded, and the younger generation of natives faced an almost radical departure from the past. No longer was agriculture the dominating economic fact in local history. The county, like all its neighbors, beckoned to the new industries to locate in Winchester or in the county outskirts to the town.

Actually Clark County was not ready to attract modern energy-consuming industries in 1930. It lacked the essential central need of modern industry, a stable and abundant supply of electrical energy. The introduction of electricity to Winchester was an intriguing historical event, but not one which promised major economic changes.[1] Earlier concerns were with the lighting of streets, public buildings, and homes. In granting a franchise to the first electric company no mention was made of the application of electricity to the powering the machines or as a source of energy for an industry.

The first generator used by the Winchester Electric Company was too small and inefficient to supply more than the limited domestic needs of a small number of private and public subscribers. In thinking back on the rise of the Kentucky Utilities Company, Robert Watt, one of the founders, wrote graphically of the electric supply to central Kentucky towns. His description was accurate for Winchester. He said, "In the first decade of the present century, the electric industry was still in its infancy. There were virtually no central station services as we know it today, with large, efficient power plants, interconnected systems, and round the clock dependable service. Tiny generators served towns, and parts of towns, with competing companies frequently serving sections of the same city. These systems were wasteful, inefficient, and uneconomical. Use was limited. Service was limited. Generators, in many instances, operated only from dusk to midnight, and on Tuesday so the housewife could use her new fangled electric iron. Dozens of towns incorporated into the !KU! system had such service at the time of their acquisition by our company."[2]

Doubtless this described with unerring accuracy the situation in Winchester in 1910. The Kentucky Utilities Company came into corporate existence on August 17, 1912. At that time it began supplying electric current to seven central Kentucky towns, including Winchester.[3]

The extension of the Kentucky Utilities Company line into Winchester supplied businesses and residents of the town with electricity, but did nothing for rural Clark County residents. Thus rural dwellers were left to live through darkening evenings of the early twentieth century with wholly defective lighting. At the onset of the Great Depression in the 1930s there were few if any outlying farm homes in Clark County which had access to electrical service. This fact was documented in considerable measure by the stock carried in stores catering to rural-farm customers. They still stocked their shelves with kerosene lamps and lanterns, hand-turned corn shellers, hand-propelled washing machines, rub boards, chamber pots, flatirons, and stone milk churns and dashers. They sold wooden-metal-lined ice boxes capable of containing fifty- and-one-hundred-pound blocks of ice, and a wide assortment of hand-manipulated small tools. Even the ever-popular phonographs were spring-driven and had to be wound frequently.[4]

Outside the home farm chores were still performed by hand. The operation of such tools as saws, drills, planes, and grinders remained a laborious hand-driven process. All of these chores were lightened by the availability of electrical current, but none was so important as the adequate lighting of homes, barns, and outbuildings. Before the advent of rural electrification rural Clark County dwellers sank into a state of semidarkness. The glare of sputtering kerosene lamps and lanterns was scarcely visible a hundred yards away, and never really bright enough for comfortable night reading. If a fact-finder in 1929 had made a canvass of farm homes about Becknerville, Indian Old Fields, Trapp, and Ruckersville he or she would have uncovered doubt that electricity would ever be made available to countrymen. They might have viewed the question as a practical joke. Even Robert Watt of the Kentucky Utilities Company would have been skeptical that rural Kentuckians would ever be served by electric lines.

Two historical events far removed from the Clark County scene were in time to have fundamental bearings on the course of local domestic and industrial life in the area. On May 18, 1933, in the midst of the Great Depression, the Congress of the United States concluded the long-drawn out debate over public generation of electrical power when it enacted the Tennessee Valley Authority law.[5] Soon after that date the new agency took possession of the famous chemical producing facility at the Wilson Dam at Muscle Shoals on the Tennessee River. This plant had stood idle for approximately fifteen years and now could be converted from producing wartime chemicals to producing high nitrogenous and phosphatic commercial fertilizers.[6] The vastly enhanced quality of these fertilizers had profound meaning for Clark County farmers and, eventually, for the industrial history of Winchester. There was located in the town the fertilizer division of the Southern States Co-operative's manufacturing unit for the production of high nutritive content fertilizers, but also a distributive system for central and eastern Kentucky.[7]

It might well be open to question, but no doubt the introduction of electricity to rural Clark County was one of the most innovative moments in the region's history. The Rural Electrification Administration was brought into being on March 11, 1935.[8] The creation of this agency was solely for the purpose of supplying widely distributed rural homes and farms on an equal basis with the town dwellers, and at a reasonable monthly price range.

In 1935 only one farm in ten in America had electricity available to it.[9] In Clark County that ratio was even lower. In fact, the United States Census report seemed to indicate there were no farms with current available to them. Phenomenally, a monstrous change had occurred by 1956, when 95.9 percent were connected to a Rural Electrification Administration line.[10]

A second congressional act, adopted in 1936, gave the Rural Electric Co-operative authority to proceed with the organization of independent local cooperatives.[11] Unavailable to the cooperatives in much of the central and eastern areas of Kentucky was access to the Tennessee Valley transmission lines. The private utility companies were not interested in bearing the costs of building lines into the thinly settled country side of Clark County. In fact, it was said that Robert Watt had made the remark that he was not interested in cultivating rural patrons.

It became necessary for the rural cooperatives to make provisions for generating their own power. Eighteen cooperatives joined in financing the building of a generating plant which could furnish current. The earlier rural electrical program had faced a difficulty in supplying a level flow of current, and as a result patrons suffered either injury or total damage to their equipment and lighting systems. There was organized the East Kentucky Electric Co-operative Commission in 1941.[12] By this date the problem had become not so much a supply of current as the high cost of purchasing current from the private generating sources. Following World War II there was an ever-increasing amount of electrical current available. The main cost, however, was building of lines to sparsely settled areas and to isolated rural villages. Plans had been made by the East Kentucky Electric Co-operative prior to the occurrence of World War II to build a generating plant at Ford on the north bank of the Kentucky River.[13] These plans, however, could not be utilized until 1948, and in 1950 the co-operative made application to the Kentucky Public Service Commission for permission to construct a generating plant producing 40,000 kilowatt hours. This application was approved by the Kentucky Public Service Commission on December 14, 1950.[14]

Before the plant at Ford could be constructed and placed in production there was considerable delay while the matter was dragged through the courts at the instigation of the Kentucky Utilities Company.[15] By 1954 the legal

A workman on the line in the Bundy Tube Turning Corporation's plant. - *Photo courtesy of the Winchester Sun*

barriers had been cleared away and the generators began producing power. Quickly the demand for electrical current increased, and it became necessary to expand generating capacity at Ford. By 1960 the generating plant at Ford and the distribution and control center on Highway 60 just west of Winchester became landmarks in the rising importance of the electrical age in Clark County and much of the central and eastern Kentucky countryside.

It would be challenging for a historian or a rural sociologist or an economist to write comprehensively of the impact which the introduction of cheap electrical current had on the way of life in Clark County. Generally many of the labor-intensive tasks once performed by hand were performed after 1940 by electrical appliances. The availability of running water, indoor plumbing, and domestic refrigeration went far toward the protection of health, to say nothing of the comforts they brought to people.

Psychologically, said proponents of rural electrification, the introduction of electricity into rural homes and the lighting of interiors revealed how shabby and uninteresting the home environment was in the era of inefficient kerosene lamps. In many a home the introduction of electricity stimulated the refurbishing of house interiors. Aside from the environmental impact of electricity, the world of instantaneous opened up to even the most remote family abode along Little Howard or Four Mile creeks. Even the matter of home security was improved by the installation of night lights about rural homes. No sounder historical evidence could be presented of the efficacy of the introduction of cheap electric current to the Clark countryside than the fact that disconnections because of failure to pay light bills have been remarkably few.[16]

During the slow gestation era of the new industrial age after 1920 both Winchester and Clark County were made host to fortune by geography and geology. After the dawn of the good roads in the post-World War I years, the World War II interval, and the period of capital highway construction (1950-1980) Winchester became a strategic center of road building, just as it had been earlier when railroads were being built through the central and eastern Kentucky.[17] The old approaches to the opening and maintaining of toll roads by use of a semi-impressed labor force were but piddling gestures compared with the gigantic rock-crushing and earth-moving capabilities of the more recent years. One example will suffice. The ancient road from Winchester to Boonesborough was straightened and widened, and its river end was literally carved out of the rock. Where once a ferry transported travelers across the Kentucky River a bridge carrying two lanes of traffic was constructed. By 1990 the bridge at Boonesborough had become obsolete and a new multilane one was opened in 1994. It would be difficult to imagine a more striking physical contrast than that between this road and the Wilderness Trail which was terminated at Fort Boonesborough in 1775.

Basically the Civilian Conservation Corps set a powerful precedent in the act of opening road into eastern Kentucky which outlined the routes of a modern highway system.[18] In the post-World War II years Winchester contractors with modern mechanical boring machines, earthmovers, and paving machines completed the task begun in the Great Depression. Too, the enactment of the federal highway act of 1954 providing for the construction of the federal highway network of limited access roads gave a tremendous impetus to the Winchester contracting companies.[19] Within the decades 1950-1970 two arterial interstate roads were built across the borders of the Clark County trading area, and one other was opened nearby. The Mountain Parkway toll road in fact became a modernization of a traditional connector between Winchester and a considerable area of eastern highlands.[20] All of these modern four-lane roads created an almost insatiable demand for crushed rock, asphalt, mixed concrete, and an army of laborers.

A genuine American immigrant success story was the growth of the J. C. Codell Company. This close-knit American-Italian family had back of it a mixed history of immigration from the old world and of an American pioneering family. J. C. Codell, patriarch of the family, was born in Italy in 1885. By 1906 he had already made a beginning in the construction contracting business. He was engaged in the building of railroads. When he arrived in Winchester he not only established himself as an energetic building contractor, but he also attached his social fortunes to the Clark County past by marrying Effie Calloway, daughter of a famous pioneer family of the Fort Boonesborough era.[21]

In Clark County the Codell Company expanded rapidly as a major earthmoving enterprise. Located in Winchester, it received contracts in 1914 for construction work on both the Chesapeake and Ohio Railroad and the Louisville and Nashville road.[22] By the year the United States entered World War I the Codell Company was well established. The Kentucky General Assembly laid the initial legal mudsill of road building in Clark County and the commonwealth when it enacted the first modern highway law in 1912.[23] Though this law was a little more than a sketchy outline of the organization of a modern highway system in Kentucky which would accommodate the rising automobile traffic, it was a foundation beginning. in 1916 the Congress of the United States enacted the first of an ever-lengthening series of highway laws. The enactment of the state and federal laws had a direct bearing on the fortunes of the J. C. Codell Company. They opened contractual opportunities far beyond the boundaries of Clark County and Winchester. The company was able to capitalize on its contracting experiences prior to 1912.

The Codell family, true to its Italian antecedents, and its American pioneer background, now grew into a capital enterprise organization with eighty years of experience at digging at the face of the land. Its members maintained a close generational adhesiveness. In later years in the twentieth century the Codell Company became a major builder of highways in many areas of the rugged Appalachian Highlands in Kentucky. Their work went far toward breaking the social and economic barriers which in the past had held captive a people largely shut off from the rest of American civilization.[24]

At the same time the Codell family was expanding the scope of its activities the Allen Construction Company came into existence. Closely paralleling, if not in fact, being intertwined with the Codell Company, the Allen Company also engaged in highway construction, heavy earth moving, and large site preparation for buildings. The patriarch of this business, E. M. Allen, began his business career in the period after 1912 when the Kentucky General Assembly enacted the first highway law. E. M. Allen was associated with the J. C. Codell Company until 1949, when he withdrew and organized his own enterprise.[25]

Capitalizing on the nearby and almost inexhaustible stone resources suitable for conversion into rock construction material, the Allen Company opened or bought rock quarries in Clark, Powell, Jackson, Hart, Madison, and Menifee counties. In Clark County the company owned a quarry on the Athens-Boonesborough Road, and in 1944 it bought the one on the Kentucky River hard by the site of the historic Boonesborough.[26] In addition to producing crushed stone in literally hundreds of thousands of tons, the Allen Company processed asphalt materials at Boonesborough and at Mount Vernon in Rockcastle County. The Allen concrete mixing plants in Irvine, Berea, Danville, Richmond, and Winchester grew in importance during World War II, and in the postwar highway expansion era after 1954. The Allen Company was benefitted by the extension of two parkways. Thus the Codell and Allen companies, though operating well beyond the bounds of their home sites, contributed heavily to making Winchester and Clark County a center of the new industries which came to Kentucky after 1945.[27]

The surge of the industrial age after 1945 thrust Clark County into an entirely new movement of its history. The old term "corporation" as recorded in the corporate record book had an entirely different meaning from that of the new and modern phase of development. After 1945 the fortunes of the human population and the course of everyday life in the county were redirected toward newer and different goals. There were in 1990 concentrated within the county's borders 29,496 persons, 15,799 of whom lived in Winchester.[28] At this point the population scales were being tipped in favor of the town.

Though the new industries were to have marked bearing upon the economies of the county and town, they had limited perceptible statistical effects upon the traditional ancestral and racial composition of the population. In 1985, 15,769 or 99.5 percent of the residents of Winchester were native born, while .05 percent were foreign born.[29] Almost half of the inhabitants of the town were living in homes of long-time family occupancy. Winchester was indeed a "hometown" with all the traditional American family-household orientation.[30] From the perspective of labor potential three quarters of the population was over sixteen years of age. Nevertheless, there was a discernible imbalance of 151 nonworker dependents to each 100 workers.[31] The prosperity which the new industries brought to Clark County was selective and spotted at best. In 1989 the per capita income in the county was $10,832, and for households $21,543. Not all of Clark County's population shared in this level of income because 17.5 percent of its people were said to earn wages below the established national poverty level.[32]

The industrial profile of Clark County and Winchester changed with a degree of rapidity after 1970. The Kentucky Cabinet for Economic Development's division of research and planning indicated there were thirty-four industries in Clark County and Winchester which might be classed as such. Of this number sixteen had been established prior to 1970 and eighteen after that date. Some of the companies listed were more service oriented than industrial ones.[33] A majority of the manufacturing industries listed produced goods of a considerable variety. For instance, there was a wide diversity between the goods produced by GTE Corporation and the Freeman Corporation. The principal manufacturers in this era were Leggett and Platt, Lepages, Inc., Bluegrass Art Cast, Inc., GTE Products Corporation, Quality Manufacturing, Rockwell International Corporation, and Winchester Clothing. These were among the major employers of laborers in 1990.[34]

Among the lesser employers in the county in 1990 were Crawford Tool and Die Company, Kentucky Wood Preserving Company, Advanced Hydraulics, Machine Products, Inc., Silver Jet Corporation, and T & M Printing Company. Some of the latter rendered services rather than producing goods. In 1990 there were seven organized labor unions, among them Amalgamated Clothing and Textile Workers; International Brotherhood of Teamsters, Chauffers, Warehousemen and Helpers of America; International Union of Electronic, Electrical, Technical, Salaried, and Machine Workers; United Automobile, Aerospace and Agricultural Workers of America; Service Employees International; and United Furniture Workers of America. Seven of the companies operating with unionized labor in 1990 were Winchester Clothing, Leggett & Platt, Pepsi Cola Bottling Company, LePages, Inc., and Quality Manufacturing.[35]

Clark County and Winchester went to considerable expense to prepare a hospitable base of operations for incoming industries. In 1990 the industrial park had six manufacturing tenants who spent more than $15,000,000 in plant construction and equipment. In that year the industrial park was expanded by 242 acres; and roadways, water lines, and sewers were provided at a cost to the Winchester-Clark County Industrial Authority of $1.8 million.[36]

The new industries moved into the midst of a demographic situation of two centuries' standing. In 1989 the ancestral mix of the population was almost the same as in 1800. The white population was generally of Scotch, Irish, English, and German descent. The black, or Afro-American, population was obviously of African descent. This segment of the Clark County population reflected a marked decrease. In 1989 there were 1,742 blacks compared with approximately 6,000 black slaves in 1850.[37] Though the census gives no precise statistical information of regional origins of the internal population after 1950, it appears a reasonable supposition that, with the opening of the new and improved highways, the increased mobility of people by automobile, and the rise of the new industries, by 1990 Clark County and Winchester had received a population inflow from eastern Kentucky.[38]

By no means had Clark County become an intensely industrialized community by 1990; there still existed a substantial rural population dependent upon the traditional agricultural sources for a livelihood. Nevertheless, the nineteen industries located in the county and town had a tremendous effect upon the way of life for all the population. Not only were generous numbers of laborers and service personnel employed in the county and town, but literally hundreds of individuals went beyond the county limits to find employ-

Lumber stacks of the Ford Lumber Company in the first decade of the twentieth century. Literally millions of feet of prime eastern Kentucky timber was drifted down the Kentucky River, or brought in by railway to be sawed and distributed on both domestic and European markets. - *Photo courtesy of Myrtle Brookshire*

ment while retaining their residential, social, and cultural connections and their loyalty ties with Winchester and Clark County. Too, the statistics of industrial employment do not indicate the numbers of persons serving in nonindustrial and nonagricultural jobs.

By American standards the two centuries 1793-1993 represent an extensive scope of time. During these two centuries Clark County existed with a high degree of social and economic stability, to say nothing of complacency. Paradoxically, the county's agrarian world and way of life was provincial and isolated on one hand and dependent on outside resources on the other. The isolation and provinciality, however, were never sufficiently insulating to stave off changes exerted from well beyond the county's boundaries. Revolutionary changes abroad eventually seeped in to the county. In addition, inner social, cultural, and economic forces constantly courted change. In the ever-increasing pursuit of material fortunes old institutions were transformed, and new ones came into existence.[39] John Strode, John Baker, William Bush, William M. Beckner, Soloman Van Meter, Abram Renick, Dr. Samuel D. Martin, James E. Garner, and even Colonel Newton Holly Witherspoon might have been awed by the changes which occurred in their land. They might have drunk an Ale-8-One, grabbed a fast-food breakfast from a chain restaurant, and pitched off at sunrise to work at bending tubes, fabricating bedsprings, or stirring cauldrons of glue; or they would rush off to Lexington to a factory or to sit all day in an office in a highly plastic building. One thing is certain: these visitors from the past would find that shutting off electrical power or cutting off the cash flow from industrial wages would cause an even bigger public panic than the announcement of an outbreak of smallpox. Such a travesty as loss of power would shut the Clark County world off from the day, and the tangled affairs of romance of the soap operas would be vanished behind the veil of phantasmagoria.

The rise of the industrial era in Clark County also meant that the local banks acquired new and more demanding patrons. Both the county and the town of Winchester were in strategic geographical and fiscal positions to capitalize on the growing importance of the railroads and opening coal mines in eastern Kentucky during the closing decades of the nineteenth century. There was a hackneyed adage among Lexington bankers that they would invest in nothing "east of Winchester."[40] Perhaps this shortsightedness served well the Winchester bankers.

The banking history of Clark County is anchored in several ways to the fate of banks nationally. During the Civil War the nation faced a stringent financial crisis, in good part because of a lack of an effective national banking system. The progress of the war increased costs of goods and labor; and there was competition with the independent state banks, which issued their own currency of unstable value. On February 25, 1863, the Congress of the United States enacted legislation authorizing the issuance of a national currency backed by notes and bonds of the central government. This law, however, failed to achieve its objective, and on March 3, 1865, a second law was enacted.[41] This one imposed a 10 percent federal tax on state bank notes. There followed a great rush to Washington to secure federal bank charters. In a short space of time there were issued 1,513 charter serial numbers.[42] This law had a profound effect on banking in Winchester.

The Clark County Bank had roots reaching well back into Clark County history. This bank was organized March 11, 1845, with twenty-two signing founders who subscribed $45,000 in capital stock. Thomas H. Robinson was chosen president, and W. T. Poynter, cashier. In the closing period of the Civil War Poynter went to Washington to negotiate the procurement of a federal certificate for the Clark County Bank.[43]

Back of the enactment of wartime federal bank laws was an important chapter relating to the fiscal affairs of the nation. The law enacted on March 3, 1865, was of major importance.[44] In that frantic moment when former state banks rushed representatives to Washington to secure certification the Clark County Bank was granted certificate 995.[45] During the period 1865 to 1972 the bank amassed capital assets of $47,180,000. The Clark County Bank operated over a considerable span of time without competition. The Citizen's National Bank was organized in 1872 with capital assets of $175,000. Officials of this bank were Dr. Wash Miller, president, and A. H. Hampton, cashier.[46]

No doubt banking operations in Clark County were conducted rather quietly and with certain banking austerity. In 1885 there appeared on the local banking scene the colorful "Colonel" Newton Holly Witherspoon of Owen County.[47] He was said to have served as an officer of unspecified rank in the Confederate Army. In Winchester he began a campaign to organize a third bank, a move which met opposition on the grounds that many said the town of 3,000 inhabitants did not need another bank. The colonel was a determined man. He surely must have been cast in the same mold as some of his contemporaries like Phineas Taylor Barnum, Richard Sears, Leland Stanford, and Collis P. Huntington.[48]

In more ways than one Colonel Witherspoon embedded his imprint on Clark County and Winchester. Never a modest man, he stood out from the crowd. He built in the town a three-story fortress of a residence of no known classical architectural lines. The illustration of this architectural wonder published in William M. Beckner's *Handbook of Clark County and City of Winchester* portrayed Colonel Witherspoon in a stovepipe hat and frock coat standing as rigid as a Confederate ramrod.[49]

There seems to be some inconsistency as to the date when the Winchester National Bank opened its doors for business; was it 1885 or later? In 1890 the Winchester Bank dropped the word "National" from its title. Founding directors of the bank were J. W. Johnson, Jesse E. Gordon, J. G. Skinner, G. W. Strother, Isaac N. Cardwell, R. D. Hunter, Webb Johnson, and R. H. Ware.[50]

Colonel Witherspoon served as president of the Winchester Bank from 1885 until his death in 1921. In the latter year ownership of the bank passed to Addison Whitt, formerly of Powell County, and in 1928 to George Tomlinson, and then to E. E. Freeman, Jr., until 1961. In 1978 C. B. Pember became the Winchester Bank's president. In the latter year the Winchester Bank had assets worth $57,791,000, and four years later (1982) its assets were $74,669,000.[51] In the same year the assets of the Clark County Bank were worth $63,622,000, and those of the People's Commercial Bank, $50,192,000.[52]

Historically, the fourth and fifth Winchester banks were the People's National Bank, chartered in 1923, with J. P. Toohey, J. T. Metcalf, N. A. Powell, J. T. Stucky, J. L. McCord, Cas P. Bedford, M. T. McEldowney, and H. C. McEldowney as organizers and directors.[53] The People's Commercial Bank, which on June 30, 1982, had total capital assets worth $50,192,000.[54]

What started in the latter quarter of the nineteenth century as a gamble the railway lines would be extended into the rich coal-bearing regions of eastern Kentucky and that coal would become the prime resource within the periphery of the Winchester trading area and would benefit the local banks. Because of this there was established in the town a promising fiscal basis from which to serve the rising new industries in the latter half of the twentieth century. Historically, the fact that a substantial banking system was established in a county and town whose economy, social systems, and folkways were so deeply rooted in the land and where the agriculture and animal husbandry was so basic to the business welfare of the area was notable.

Clark County and Winchester in 1945 were in a comparable position of much of rural-agrarian America. There was some urgent need for balancing agriculture with new industries.[55] For the most part the major industries located in Clark County after 1950 were branch plants. The parent industries had their origins elsewhere and often in modest beginnings centered upon an ingenious inventive idea. Such a company is Leggett and Platt of Carthage, Missouri.[56] The origins of this company duplicated those of scores of highly successful corporate beginnings. In the golden 1880s J. P. Leggett conceived the idea of producing bedsprings with interlocking steel coils. Like many inventors, Leggett had the idea for a promising product but not the mechanical means of producing it in commercial form. Fortunately, he was able to form a partnership with a local plowmaker, C. B. Platt. Platt had the mechanical capability to manufacture the new type of bedsprings.[57]

Both Leggett and Platt had passed on to their rewards by 1930 but not before they had established manufacturing plants in Carthage, Missouri, and Louisville, Kentucky.[58] The Louisville unit expanded rapidly, and in 1946 a branch plant was located in Winchester. This unit grew, and in 1948 and 1963 the manufacturing space was enlarged. The box spring and special units division were housed in a building on New Street and Franklin Avenue. Again in 1966 and 1992 there were plant expansions. By 1995 the Leggett and Platt Company had grown far beyond C. B. Platt's village plow factory. There now were six branch plants in the eastern part of the country. In 1978 the Winchester branch was said to have produced 12 percent of the company's products.[59]

In the period when Leggett and Platt located their branch plant in Winchester the Curlee Clothing Company of St. Louis also established a branch factory in Winchester, in 1947.[60] This branch had a two-year lapse in production, 1953-1955. Nevertheless, the plant, when in production, manufactured a phenomenal number of mens sport coats and suits. A third garment industry, Loma Manufacturing, was located in Stanton in 1956, and the next year the plant was moved to Winchester. In the latter location it employed a large number of seamstresses from Clark, Estill, Powell, and Montgomery counties. This company manufactured ladies blouses for use in academic uniforms and for other kindred purposes. In 1962 the Loma Manufacturing Company employed sixty persons, but by 1992 its name had disappeared from the annual listing of Winchester manufacturers.[61]

Several branch plants of heavy metal and machine products manufacturers were located in Clark County after 1950. One of the oldest of these was the Bundy Tubing Company, which located in Winchester in 1957.[62] The Winchester branch operated in conjunction with the one in Cynthiana. The latter plant fabricated tubing, while the Winchester branch fashioned it into various forms, including fuel injection conduits, automobile wheel components, freezer tubing, medical instruments, automobile equipment, and other specialized tubing uses. This company served much of the automobile industry, especially General Motors' Oldsmobile division.[63]

The earliest heavy industry still operating in Winchester in 1995 was the (Tomlinson) Freeman Corporation. This company originated in the town in 1912, although there seems to be some discrepancy as to the correct date.[64] The Kentucky Department of Economic Development and the Clark County Chamber of Commerce list 1912, while other sources indicated 1918. Whatever the correct date, this wood-processing company was founded by George Tomlinson, a man of many parts. He served as mayor of Winchester and as president of the Winchester National Bank, and he was active in other organizations. The Tomlinson Company first produced tobacco hogsheads and wood table tops from timber harvested in nearby eastern Kentucky. By 1953 both the hogshead and table top markets had undergone basic changes. The Tomlinson Company turned to producing walnut and white oak lumber and veneer. The name Tomlinson, later Freeman, became synonymous with walnut and white oak lumber and veneer in the international timber market. In 1953 the Tomlinson Company was incorporated by Gene Freeman as the Freeman Company. Gene Freeman was the grandson of the founder George Tomlinson. This company purchased walnut and white oak stock from a broad area of Kentucky and the Ohio Valley. In turn its market for lumbar and veneer was worldwide. It was a fascinating fact that timber from the ridges of Kentucky was eventually converted into sophisticated pieces of furniture of period designs.[65]

By far the largest heavy industrial plant located in Clark County was the branch of the Rockwell International Company. In 1966 Rockwell moved into its large plant on Maple Road alongside Interstate Highway 64.[66] This plant was one of four operated by Rockwell International; the three others were located in Ohio and Pennsylvania. The one in Winchester specialized in the manufacture of rear driving axles for trucks. It also had the capacity to forge and finish drive shafts, gears, and other truck components. The plant's 2,500-pound pressure press must have been one of the largest in Kentucky. By 1978 the Rockwell plant had produced a million rear driving axles, and in 1985 the company employed 976 men and 26 women, making it the largest single employer in the county's history.[67] This dream, however, faded in 1992, when Rockwell International abandoned its elaborate operation and moved out of the county.[68] The removal of Rockwell resulted in the loss of source of high-wage employment, and in some measure also an appreciable amount of community support and leadership.

The history of Rockwell in Winchester was similar to that of manufacturing plants all across the South. In the postwar years every southern state

Young mules awaiting the day when they would be centers of interest on Clark County court day. They no doubt were born destined for the cotton fields of the Lower South. They replaced the ox as a draft animal, and in time were replaced by the tractor. - *Photo courtesy of Howard Hampton*

conducted heavy campaigns to entice industries to their communities. They made tax concessions, built plants, opened roads, and offered other advantages only to have industries come in and operate for a relatively short span of years and then move away, leaving expensive plant buildings and roads vacant and in many cases unsuitable for other uses.

The Sylvania branch of General Telephone and Electronics has had a relatively long period of operation in Winchester since early 1953. Ground actually was broken for the plant on February 11 that year.[69] This branch of the huge GTE Corporation in 1978 was producing a variety of flash bulbs, incandescent lamps, tungsten halogen lamps, and infrared lamps. The branch manager, John Kucharski, said the Winchester plant is the only one where dichroic coating is applied to reflectors. Over seventy original equipment manufacturers, including Bell and Howell, Eastman Kodak, IBM, and Xerox, use Sylvania lamps and other materials. In 1950 the Sylvania Company employed 70 male and 280 female workers, and in 1992 it had practically the same number of workers. The name of the company was changed to OSRAM Sylvania.[70]

Aside from the popularity of the local soft drink Ale 8 One, the Winchester Pepsi Cola Bottling Company franchise centralizes a five part family of flavors and distributors in Winchester. The local plant bottles at least three flavors of soft drinks, and also serves as a service and promotional center for a broader area of the company's operation. The Winchester Pepsi Cola franchise was established locally in 1965, and in 1993 it employed 76 persons.

The industrialization of Clark County and Winchester after 1945 has constituted a vital chapter in their history, economically and socially. Because of their more than a century of history in a world of radically different economics they were caught in a groundswell of change. Agriculture, lumbering, and mining in the broader trading area were losing momentum. The advent of the new forms of industrialism brought many changes in economic pursuits in the county and town. Women increasingly became important laborers, the impact of outside capitalism grew stronger, and the managers of the new plants also became leaders in the community. There appeared on the scene organized unions associating themselves with the various types of industries and manufacturing specialists. Most basic, however, was the fact that there existed in the region a fairly abundant supply of potentially willing workers.[71]

The Kentucky Department of Economic Development reported that in June 1961 the Bluegrass area with the exception of Fayette County, was, "Economically agricultural with approximately 11,925 people employed by the industry. At the same time there were 5,339 farms in the area classified as `commercial.' Of this number, 900 area farms, eighty of which were in Clark County, had an annual income of less than $2,000. Clark County had 1,727 [persons] employed in agricultural jobs in 1959."[72] This agency estimated that there were 457 men and 513 women then available in the county for industrial employment.[73] Included in the Winchester labor supply area by the Kentucky Cabinet for Economic Development were Clark, Bourbon, Estill, Fayette, Madison, Montgomery, and Powell counties, all of which were within twenty or so miles of Winchester.[74] Demographers labeled the labor force in this area a growing one. They listed 3,822 boys and girls, 80 percent of whom would within a decade be seeking industrial jobs.

As human as every aspect of Clark County history had been in the past, possibly no one had ever viewed the area's human energy in such objective terms. This was not true in the formative years when there were intensive demands for laborers. In none of the primary sources of information prior to 1940 was there much more than an almost casual statistical projection of persons available for employment in varied economic pursuits.[75]

By 1960 the new industrial age was well under way in Clark County and Winchester. There were present in the county twenty-three industries which employed 1,031 men and 895 women. These industries paid an average of three dollars an hour.[76] The industrial profile in that year was distinctly different from the one which came to exist in 1995. Among the earlier firms were Browning Turkey Farms, Inc., Curlee Clothing, Loma Manufacturing, Sylvania Electric Products, and Bundy Tubing Company. These industries in 1960 were said to have employed 1,921 laborers. Five of the companies employed at least 90 percent of the workers, and eight companies employed no women.[77]

The profile of the industrial development in Clark County by 1995 reflected marked changes which within two decades had come over the region. The base of human employment was shifting radically from its historic grounding, a fact which had already reflected itself in the way of life for a large number of families. The revered family farms, where so many of the county traditions were formed, were shrinking both in numbers and in the nature of their place in the economic system. There was by 1995 an almost complete erasure of the ancient dream of new landed Eden. Not only was there a balancing of agriculture with industry, but industry threatened to tip the scales in its favor.[78]

The new interest exerted revolutionary changes upon Clark County and Winchester. The automobile and motor truck gave a mobility to the population which made it all but transitory. In 1995 automobiles rushed through Winchester streets, over country roads, and up and down the multilane limited access roads at speeds sometimes ten or twelve times that of the twenty to thirty mile speed limit of 1910. There was an incessant roar of semitrailer trucks charging over the roads bearing burdens equal to twenty-five flatboat loads of produce in 1810. The new industrial age had settled down upon Clark County and Winchester, and its dawning raised the curtain on a new social scene and a radically changed concept of folk traditions.

Epilogue

❦

The historian learns at the outset that in writing about the American experience at the grass roots level involves perpetual mastery of the process of selectivity. Involved is the treatment of personalities, institutions and even human follies. Weekly newspaper editors learned early that it was judicious if not mandatory that they place in print as many personal names as possible, whether the individual had done no more than whittle the day away at a country store. Clark County for two centuries has fitted into the standard mold of the American county concept. In writing this history I have been challenged by the fact I had to be selective of the names and contributions of persons, of local anecdotes, and even of those commonplace incidents which have given space to the past in rural-agrarian America.

A historian might well spend a lifetime digging nuggets of information out of official records, private personal papers, commercial records, and official documents. Even so it would still be necessary to exclude much material of some relevancy. Clark County, Kentucky, like many old American and Kentucky counties was conceived and birthed in an era which literally seethed with the excitement of challenges of penetrating a raw virgin land and planting the original foundations of an Anglo-American civilization in the area. The defense against hostile resistance of competing Indian groups, the austerities of a raw environment, and the heavy demands made on human energy were the challenges to human courage and persistence. These conditions actually gave rise to a new form of local aristocracy, this, plus a generous distribution of pensioner land warrants. The earliest pioneers who made their way onto the Clark County frontier were assured a special claim on a niche in area history.

Centuries before the Euro-American settlers built the first cabins north of the Kentucky River there had already drifted across the land another people, if not of civilization, then of culture.

The land of Clark County for more than two centuries has enfolded its occupants in bonding embraces of environmental adaptations, emotional attachments, and of fortune. Geography in large measure raised the all but invisible, but realistic barriers of provincialism which tied human attachments and sentiments tightly to the land and its folk mores. Perhaps never in the mind of Clark County's people was there a thought that their homeland would never be anything but a rural-pastoral one, with Winchester being the nuclear center for county government, the professions, and local commerce. Amazingly the old frontier concept of a western eden endured in Clark County for a century and three quarters span of time. Not only did the emigrants moving onto the virgin landed frontier of Clark County bring with them many deeply grooved folk ways and provincial attitudes, but they tempered much of their nature with a rugged religious response, as demonstrated at Providence Church, in the Methodist love feasts, and in the ruggedly crusading post-Cane Ridge Revival "new lightism."

From that moment when the Clark County elders projected the plan for a new County in 1792 their area became a political enclave which reflected the larger concepts of the Commonwealth, but always with those local reservations which gave spirit and substance to the local governing process. In many respects no better example of the "Little Kingdom" power of local government can be found than in Clark County. Strong personalities have, at many intervals in the past, personified Clark County's political history. This has been true, though paradoxically, Clark County's history has in every decade reflected the impact of that of the Commonwealth of Kentucky, and of the Nation. The provincial barriers have ever had sieve-like qualities. The county, and town governments have ever functioned within the statutorily defined parameters of the state constitution and legislative processes. One reads of the acts of the Kentucky General Assembly and discovers the guidelines which steered much of the course of local county history.

Local history is a yeasty and important ingredient in the writing and interpreting of many areas of the larger national experience. Writing about a locality, however, the historian must always be responsive to the basic forces which are generated in an area, and to the elements of personality, the human lubrication of anecdotes, and even with blood relationships unto unnumbered generations when the blood strain grows thin and tattered. In no area of history does the anecdote, factual or devised, assume greater importance than at the grass roots of local human society. Often the anecdote becomes so firmly embedded in local history that it becomes difficult if not downright damaging to separate fact from folk lore. The recitation of Clark County's past has frequently been hinged on cherished anecdotes of personalities and incidents.

Though politically Clark County came into existence on the eve of the last big conflict between western settlers and the Indians, there were among its population those hoary pioneer souls who claimed personal glory from the old border confrontations. For most Clark County the great moment of mar- tial triumph was the fleeting spurt of valor and glory in the War of 1812. The march to Michigan and back in 1813-'14 was at once a grueling hardship and one of glory. From the dying rifle fire in the "Forlorn Hope" charge along the Thames River in Canada to the whirlwind conflict of "Desert Storm," Clark County people have been actively engaged, as military personnel and as patriotic citizens. A cardinal chapter in the county's history, however, was the fact it escaped the potential ravages of the Civil War, even though it was a fairly important bluegrass slave holding county. Both armies fortunately and largely by-passed the county, focusing rather upon the older and more strate- gic centers of Kentucky.

The existence of slavery in Clark County left a mixed history. There twines through the record dual threads of sharply contrasting hues. There was the humane one of owners who came into the County Court and sought emancipation papers for their slaves, and in contrast there was the one of slaves being sold to dealers who took them away to uncertain futures in the Lower South. There are sharp reflections of the institution in the Clark County Wills nd Estate Settlements.

One examines the statutory records of the Commonwealth of Kentucky with the realization that the laws and regulations relating to slavery emanated from Frankfort rather than from the courthouse and town trustee sessions in Winchester. The personal aspect of the institution were generated in more intimate relations between master and slave. There were very local rules gen- erated by the magistrates and trustees. Ultimately the freeing of the slaves made little actual impact on the overall relations of the two races. Freedman, of course, came to occupy a new position in the county in economy, politics, religion, and in the need for schooling.

After 1870 Clark County truly began the long drawn out entry into the modern agrarian-industrial age of the United States. Gradually the improved farm implements began to show up in estate inventories and on farms. The railway age, though slow in coming to the county, quickly made Winchester a center for at least three Kentucky systems. The appearance of burley tobacco wrought major changes on the land at a moment when hemp growing was fading, and Clark County was being confronted with serious competition in livestock production. The popularity of the famous old imported shorthorn cattle was being dimmed by the appearance of new dairy and beef breeds, and from the great cattle frontier in the Far West. Perhaps the peak of the shorthorn romance can be dated by the great banquet and cattle show in Winchester in 1880.

Looking back from the pinnacle of the closing years of the twentieth century it is clear that there has not been a decade during the past two centuries when Clark County did not undergo changes. The first order books of the County Court are filled with entries pertaining to the opening of roads and the readjustments of land boundaries, and those of the present era contain entries on the same subject. The evolution of intra- and extra-county roads reflect clearly economic, social, and political changes. Turnpikes, railways, and subsequently modern surfaced and numbered federal-state highways, the caul of encapsulation which so long enshrouded the region. There exists a dramatic record of Winchester's advance into modernity during the latter decades of the nineteenth century. The modern world closed in about the town.

John Baker's spring became no more than a memory blip on local history, firebuckets became museum pieces, even the proud little fire engine pushed and tugged about town by the Rough and Ready Fire Company was abandoned to the dust of antiquity. The old speed limits for horse and buggies, for the new menace, the automobile, and the motor truck became quaint historical notes. Both Winchester and Clark County responded to the forces of change wrought by a great world war followed by a biting devitalizing Great Depression. After 1918 an era of rural agrarianism began to ebb away, and in its place new industries appeared in Winchester, industries which expanded in numbers and capabilities along with the development of modern interstate highways and improved local conditions of education and social advancement. The real revolution in the way of life, and in the contents of local history, has occurred at breakneck speed in the closing decade of the twentieth century. No longer do grocerymen line up their clerks and sedate customers between counters and barrels, or bankers have their cashiers and clerks to gather around their presidents to have photos made to impress the public, instead they publicize their volumes of capital.

One historical fact is eloquently documented and that is the radical changes in domestic life from the days when families arranged the worldly possessions of deceased members for appraisers to examine and report to the court in details as those of the first families. This moment of the automobile, the television, computer, chain stores, fast food stands, and urban sprawl have all but obliterated the ancient landmarks of another era and another way of life. Hubbard Taylor, John Strode, John Baker, "Billy" Bush, "Cerro Gordo" Williams, and Dr. Samuel D. Martin would view the scene in disbelief. Even Abram Renick would stroke his square-cropped beard and perhaps frown at the daily headless rush along Highway 60 back. One can only speculate on what bit of witticism that caustic "tongue in cheek" after dinner orator James E. Garner could conjure up to put the superficial miracles of change in perspective. One thing he could say might be that Clark County and Winchester have been swept along irretrievable by the great broom of historical and impudent change.

No age, no generation of human beings, no way of life for Clark County was set imperishably in stone, and no era was historically irrelevant. The pages of history have ever remained open to the county, and to its county seat town. Pioneers still remain on the land, pioneers who will have to make adjustments and compromises with the fortunes which the swirling troubled world of modern humanity and materialism may bring their way.

List of Illustrations

Footnotes

Chapter I
The Land, Its Resources, Its People

1. W. D. Funkhouser and W. S. Webb, *Ancient Life in Kentucky*, pp. 477-52. Constantine Rafinesque, "Ancient Annals of Kentucky," Humphrey Marshall, History of Kentucky I, 22-9.

2. David Pollack, Charles D. Hockensmith, and Thomas N. Sanders, *Late Prehistoric Research in Kentucky*, "The Goolman Site: A Late Fort Ancient Winter Encampment in Clark County, Kentucky, 38-48. Funkhouser and Webb, *Archaeological Survey of Kentucky, Reports in Archaeology and Anthropology*, "Clark County," II, 84-5.

3. Pollack, *et. al.* "The Goolman Site" p. 44.

4. Funkhouser and Webb, Archeological Survey of Kentucky, Viols. I and II, Reports in Archaeology and Anthropology, passim.

5. Pollack, et. al., *Op. Cit.*, Figures 2, 7, 8.

6. Funkhouser and Webb, *Ancient Life in Kentucky*, pp. 63-4.

7. Funkhouser and Webb, *Op. Cit.*, p. 53.

8. *Ibid.*, pp. 55-57.

9. Rafinesque, *Op. Cit.*, I Appendix, p. 4.

10. Richard H. Collins, *History of Kentucky*, II, 390.

11. *Ibid.*, II, 392.

12. Funkhouser and Webb, "Clark County," *Archaeological Survey of Kentucky*, 84-5, Beckner, *Op. Cit.*

13. Funkhouser and Webb, XV.

14. *Ibid.*, p. 62.

15. Pollack, *et. al.*, pp. 44-8, Funkhouser and Webb, "Clark County," 84-5.

16. Christopher A. Turnbow and Cynthia E. Jobe, *The Goolman Site: A Fort Ancient Winter Encampment* . . . p. 1.

17. Beckner, *Eskippakithiki*, p. 281

18. Neal Hammon, "Early Roads into Kentucky," *The Register of the Kentucky Historical Society*, vol. 68 (April, 1970), pp. 9;-131. There are numerous notations of this path in Robert Kincaid, *The Wilderness Road*. It also appears P. P. Karan and Cottom, ather, Atlas of Kentucky, Map 3, p. 15.

19. *Atlas*, Map 3, p. 15.

20. U. S. Geol. Survey map, Harrodsburg, Kentucky, Topographic Series.

21. Beckner, *"Eskippakithiki*, pp. 361-64.

22. Robert M. Rennick, *Kentucky Place Names*, pp. 148-9. Rennick "Eskippakithiki," *The Kentucky Encyclopedia*, p. 297.

23. Charles A. Hanna, *The Wilderness Trail*, or *The Ventures and Adventures of the Pennsylvania Traders on the Alleghaney Path*. John M. Farragher, *Daniel Boone*, pp. 68-70.

24. Farraker, *Op. Cit.*, 69-70. John Bakeless, *Daniel Boone, Master of the Wilderness*, pp. 21-73. Lucien Beckner, "John Findley, the First Pathfinder of Kentucky, Filson Club History Quarterly, vol. I (April 1927). 11-22.

25. Reverend John D. Shane's Interview with Pioneer William Clinkenbeard "*Filson Club History Quarterly*, vol 2 (April 1828), 113. Robert W. Kingsolver, "Bluegrass," *The Kentucky Encyclopedia*, 89-90. Beckner, "Eskippkithiki," p. 372.

26. The plant poa pretenses may have had several origins. Its grow in Europe would seem to imply this.

27. *The Photographic Sheet, U. S. Geological Survey* reveals fairly *flat plain.* So does the

28. No one, perhaps, can be positively certain as to the derivative Indian word which finally evolved into "Kentucky," or the precise definition. The best definition seems to be "Land of Tomorrow," E. M. Coulter and W. E. Connelley, *History of Kentucky*, I, 1-2.

29. Thomas D. Clark, "The Frontier at War," *Frontier America*, pp. 54-79.

30. A. M. Miller, *The Geology of Kentucky*, pp. 78, 186.

31. The quality of soils, topography, and surface geography has ever been a basic fact in this area. Miller, *Op. Cit.*, 64, 187, Darrell Haug Davis, The Geography of the Blue Grass Region of Kentucky passim.

32. Miller *Op. Cit.*, Davis, Op. Cit., The Clark County reporter for the Twelth Annual Report of the Kentucky Bureau of Agriculture, Labor, and Statistics, 1897, said the soil of the county was fertile except in the southeastern and of the county which hilly, broken, and rock underlain. p. 31. Darwin G. Preston, Raymond P. Sims, A. J. Richardson, R. L. Blevins, and J. L. Taylor, *Soil Survey of Clark County* (Oct. 1964), series 1961, No. 11, pp. 4-9.

33. Under the 400 acre warranty grant, plus the 1,000 acre preemption right many of the land claimants back in Virginia never the land they acquired until they came searching for and trying to establish boundaries. Competition for the better lands was strong, and the mode of surveying was careless.

34. Incoming settlers sought a cabin site near a spring which was flush enough to run all year, near a stream with sufficient flow to turn a mill wheel, and near a river to float flatboats.

35. Darwin G. Preston, et. al. Soil Survey Clark County.

36. Ibid.

37. In 1800 the county had a rural population of 7,528 and Winchester had 122 residents. Schedule (U. S. Second Census), of persons in the District of Kentucky,. In 1830 there were 13,051 living in the county, in 1840 approximately 10,200. In 1950 there was a total population of 18,898 of whom 9,240 lived in Winchester, Statistic 1 Abstract Supplement, County and City Data Book (;956).

38. *Statistical View of the U. S.* (1850), p. 238.

39.

40. *Statistical View*, p. 238.

41. Inventory of Matthew Patton's Estate, Sept. 5, 1903, Will Book 3, pp. 35-315-330.

42. In the Patton inventory there was listed 3,271 board feet of planks, p. 327. Julia Tevis, *Sixty Years in a School Room: An Autobiography*, describes a phenomenal number of hard maple trees on Bush lands, pp. 52-3. In 1850, out of 170,102 acres, 153,096 were improved, Statistical View of the U. S. p. 238. In 1875, The U. S. Commissioner of Agriculture reported that Clark County had only 14.6 percent of its land in woods of any kind. *Report of the Commissioner, 1876*, p. 299. This was among the lowest percentage in Kentucky.

43. William Clinkenbeard described the area about Strode's Station and elsewhere int he area of future Clark County. He implies the existence of the forest without giving a specific description of it. Reverend John D. Shane's interview with William Clinkenbeard. A copy of the thirteen original pages of the interviews republished in April 1928 in *The Filson Club History Quarterly* as transcribed by Lucien Beckner, Vol. 2, pp. 95-128.

The early descriptions of land holds contained in deeds constitute a veritable catalogue of standing timber. For instance, one of the earliest deeds recorded by the Clark County clerk was to John and Benjamin Ray. The metes and bounds were, "Beginning on the Kentucky River Four Mile Creek -- on the forks of Indian Creek at two elms and two hackberries, the beginning corner of said Massey's survey of one thousand acres, thence west forty-eight poles to the Kentucky River with its meanders north seventy-two degrees, west sixty poles ... to a forked sycamore and mulberry, and elm ... north to a bush and sugar tree ... thence to two small dogwoods. (undated, p. 14), a second deed the same year listed a walnut, hackberry, sugar tree, two dogwoods, a hickory, a red oak, and a black gum. Deed Book 1, p. 21.

44. The construction of the early public buildings required an inordinate amount of timber. Plan

for a stray pen, May 27, 1794, p. 94-100. Stocks, May 27, 1794, 101-2, Prison, August 1794, pp. 128-30.

45. Compendium of Sixth *U. S. Census*, 1840, p. 264. By 1850 the production had dropped to 5, 960 pounds. *Statistical View of the U. S.*, p. 240.

46. The map published as an accompaniment of John Filson's, *The Discovery, Settlement, and Oresent State of Kentucky*, 1784, labels the spot "An abundance of cane."

47. See notes 43 and 44 above.

48. To be supplied.

49. *Statistical View* of the U. S.., p. 238.

50. *Relief Map of Kentucky*, 1924, U. S. Geological Survey map, 1990 "Lexington, Ky. quadrangle, Harrodsburg Quadrangle, 1991. *Kentucky General Highway Map of Clark County*, 1993.

51. The Kentucky General Highway Map, 1992, ed., contains a great abundance of surface data.

52. 12th *Annual Report*, Bureau of Agriculture, Labor, and Statistics, (1897), map opposite p. 31.

53. U. S. G. S. maps "Lexington" and "Harrodsburg," Ky. General Highway Map, 1992.

54. Samuel M. Wilson, *The First Kentucky Land Court*, 1779-1780, passim. Throughout the Clark County Order Books contain entries of making adjustments in land surveys. A clearer picture is in the voluminous records of the Clark County Circuit Court's case files. Aside from boundary issues the varying quality of the soils of the county had a profound bearing on their occupants. Darwin G. Preston, R. R. Sims, A. F. Richardson, R. L. Blevin, and J. J. Taylor, "Soil Survey of Clark County, Kentucky."

55. Richard H. Collins, *History of Kentucky, II*, 259, lists as present in Kentucky in 1790, 73, 677, and in 1820, 220, 955 persons.

56. The metes and bounds method of designation landmarks dates back to medieval France, and possibly to ancient Greece. It was perpetrated on Kentucky by Virginia as early as 1774.

57. A specific example, the indenture of Nicholas and Paul Merriwether to John Stumbo, May 16, 1790, for 300 acres. Deed Book I, p. 125.

58. See notes 43 and 44 above.

59. The future area of Clark County was involved in the adudication of prior claimants and confused claims by the First Kentucky Land Court, Wilson, Op. Cit. pp. 48-50.

60. W. W. Henning, Virginia Statutes, X, May 1779, pp. 50-71.

61. Thomas D. Clark, "Surveying," *The Kentucky Encyclopedia*, pp. 862-3.

62. Henning, *Op. Cit.*, X, 35-50, Wilson, Op. Cit., pp. 43-50.

63. This deed was for 200 acres more or less, Clark County Deed Book 7, June 15, 1803, p. 1.

64. No plats were filed with earlier Kentucky deeds, but there appear in the Clark County Order Books and in the filed documents in circuit court cases plats of land boundaries which were in dispute. Specific examples appeared in the Order Book for 1815 containing plats of tracts in contest along the Kentucky River.

65. See the *Clark County Precinct Map of 1877* for the earlier pattern of roads. A later one, *The Modern General Highway Map of Clark County*, 1992 ed. is even more detailed.

66. *Ibid.*

67. *Precinct Map*, 1877, Map of Clark County, Twelth Annual Report of the Bureau of Agriculture, Labor and Statistics, Op. p. 30, also list of post offices in the county in 1877, p. 33.

68. *Ibid.*

Chapter II
Travails in the New Eden

1. Charles Talbert, *Benjamin Logan, Kentucky Frontiersman*, pp. 12-30. William Stewart Lester, *The Transylvania Colony*, pp. 58-82. Thomas Perkins Abernethy, *Western Lands in the American Revolution*, pp. 102-115.

2. Robert S. Cotterill, *History of Pioneer Kentucky*, pp. 42-70. Humphrey Marshall, *History of Kentucky*, I, 16-63.

3. Nancy O'Malley, *Stockading Up*, pp. 138-169.

4. Lucien Beckner, "Eskippakithiki: The last Indian Town in Kentucky." The Filson Club History Quarterly, Oct. 1923, vol. 6, p. 367.

5. There appeared reports of the Separation Conventions after 1787 in the *Kentucky Gazette*, along with reports of the formation of the federal states as well. Neal Hammon, "Early Roads into Kentucky," *The Register of the Kentucky Historical Society*. Vol. 68, April 1970, pp. 91-131.

6. P. P. Karan and Cottom Mather, eds., *Atlas of Kentucky*, pp. 14-15.

7. The various topographical sheets relating to Clark County, United States Geological Survey. 1992 edition *General Highway Map of Clark County, Kentucky*.

8. Archibald Henderson, *Conquest of the Old Southwest* Lester *Op. Cit.*, 29-39.

9. O'Malley, pp. 138-162. That is, there was no major fort comparable to Boonesborough, Bryans Station, or Fort Harrod.

10. Reuben T. Durrett, *Bryant's Station*, pp. 41-6. Samuel M. Wilson, *Battle of the Blue Licks*, Appendices A, B, C, pp. 115-143. John Bradford's "Notes," *Kentucky Gazette*, September 15, 1826 in Thomas D. Clark, ed., *Voice of the Frontier*, pp. 11-15.

11. The settlements of William Bush and John Holder, and William Scholls were characteristic. O'Malley, *Op. Cit.* pp. 138-162.

12. Abernethy, *Op. Cit.*, p. 228.

13. This includes, Humphrey Marshall, *History of Kentucky*, Mann Butler, *History of Kentucky*, and Z. F. Smith, *History of Kentucky*.

14. John Mack Farragher, *Daniel Boone*, pp. 131-39, John Bakeless, Daniel Boone, *Master of the Wilderness*, pp. 124-139.

15. This scene was dramatized by Karl Bodmer, the Swiss artist who traveled with Prince Maxmillian of Wied Neu Wiede in 1832. He made 427 water drawings of Indians. The Boonesborough capture was the only one made east of the Mississippi River.

16. Farragher, *Op. Cit.*, pp. 114, 133, Neal Hamon, *Op. Cit.*, pp. 91-131 Karan and Mather, ed. *Op. Cit.*, p. 15, map 3.

17. *Kentucky Gazette*, "Bradford Note", Oct. 20, 1826, Clark, *Voice of the Frontier*, pp. 34-8.

18. *Richard H. Collins*, edited by W. R. Jillson, p. 372, Clark *Op. Cit.* Note p. 340, Kentucky Gazette, Nov. 17, 1826.

19. *Kentucky Gazette*, March 23, 1827.

20. Talbert, *Op. Cit.*, pp. 186-202, Lowell H. Harrison, *Kentucky's Road to Statehood*, pp. 20-34.

21. Harrison, *Op. Cit.*, pp. 60-1.

22. Delegates were named in the Proceedings of the conventions, 1787-1792. The original Proceedings are in the Kentucky Historical Collection.

23. James D. Richardson, comp. *A Compilation of the Messages and Papers of the Presidents of the United States, 1789-1908*, I, "George Washington's fourth annual address," Nov. 6, 1792, p. 128.

24. *Kentucky Gazette*, June 9, 1792.

25. Bradford Note, 44, *Kentucky Gazette* Nov. 9, 1827.

26. *American State Papers*, Vol. 4 (Indian Affairs), 340-61.

27. Charles J. Kappler, *Indian Affairs, Laws, and Treaties*, Vol. 2, pp. 18, 39, 45.

28. Bradford Note 63, *Kentucky Gazette*, Jan. 16, 1829, Clark, *Voice of the Frontier*, p. 319.

29. Humphrey Marshall, *The History of Kentucky*, 1812, 1824, Mann Butler, *History of the Commonwealth of Kentucky*, 1834, Lewis Collins, *History of Kentucky*, 1847. There were numerous topographical books which presented similar approaches.

30. R. J. Ferguson, "French and Indian War," *Dictionary of American History*, II, 342-3.

31. Deed Book, Clark County, No. 1, Nicholas and Betty Merriwether, pp. 196. Indenture between Hannaniah Lincoln of Hardin County and Nathanial Ewing for land in Clark County along the north fork of the Kentucky River, involving a survey of 1,000 acres. Deed Book 2, Oct. 25, 1796, pp. 93-5. This kind of transaction was repeated many times over.

32. C. W. Alvord, *Mississippi Valley in British Politics*, Solon J. Buck, "Proclamation of 1763,"

Dictionary of American History, IV, 353-2.

33. In the period 1775-1792, it was estimated that approximately 73,000 persons had settled in Kentucky.

34. Lester, *Op. Cit.,* pp. 22-8, Archibald Henderson.

35. John Bakeless, *Op. Cit.,* pp. 89-100, Lester, *Op. Cit.,* pp. 59-65.

36. Felix Walker, "Narrative of His Trip with Boone from Long Island to Boonesborough in 1775," J. B. *DeBow's Review,* 16 (1854), pp. 150-55.

37. Lester, *Op. Cit.,* pp. 60-65.

38. *Ibid.,* p. 65.

39. Richard H. Collins, *History of Kentucky,* I, 18, James A. James, "George Rogers Clark," *Dictionary of American Biography,* IV. 127-30.

40. W. W. Henning, *The Statutes at Large; being a Collection of the Laws of Virginia, 1619-792.* Vol. 9, pp. 257-261.

41. Marshall, *Op. Cit.,* I, 47.

42. In time, Nancy O'Malley has documented the existence of at least nineteen stations in the Clark County area. Among them Strode's, Bush's, Boyles, Baker's and McGee's. O'Malley, *Forting Up,* pp. 138-69.

43. Early the Clark County region felt the impact of the land speculators and warrant holders. The Clark County Deed Books elegantly reveal this fact.

44. Marshall, *Op. Cit.,* I, 46.

45. Abernethy, *Op. Cit.,* pp. 225-7.

46. Coulter and Connelley, *Op. Cit.,* I, 171-2.

47. Abernethy, *Op. Cit.,* p. 166.

48. The concluding section of the constitution of 1776. Quoted here is *The Constitutions of the United States of America,* (1820), p. 274.

49. Henning, *Statutes,* 10, pp. 35-50.

50. Abernethy, *Op. Cit.,* pp. 86-7, Marshall, *Op. Cit.,* I, 31-6.

51. Henning, *Statutes,* 10, pp. 35-50.

52. Newton D. Mereness, ed. *Travels in the American Colonies* (Fleming journal entries, pp. 642-6.)

53. Henning, *Statutes,* IX, Oct. 1777, pp. 355-6.

54. Samuel M. Wilson, *The First Land Court of Kentucky,* 1779-2780, p. 32.

55. Henning, *Statutes,* Vol. 10, May 1779, Chap. XIII, 5-65.

56. Mereness (Fleming Journal,). Henning, *Statutes,*

57. Mereness, *Op. Cit.,* pp. 626-34.

58. Chester R. Young, *Westward into Kentucky, The Narrative of Daniel Trabue,* p. 75.

59. Mereness (Fleming Journal, pp. 623-4),

60. Henning, *Statutes,* X, May 1779, pp. 50-71.

61. *Ibid.,* X, May 1779, pp. 50-71, Oct. 1779, pp. 10, 177, 179.

62. Second United States *Census* (1820), p.

63. There are numerous answers to this question, some of which are adventure, economic, speculative, religious, and political, Arthur K. Moore, *Frontier Mind,* pp. 25-30, Gilbert Imlay, *A Topographical Description of the Western Territory of North America,* pp. 24-36, F. A. Michaux, *Travels to the Westward of the Alleghany Mountains,* p. 53.

64. "A Memorandum of M. Austin's Journey from the Lead Mines in the County of Wythe in the State of Virginia to the Lead Mines in the Provinces of Louisiana West of the Mississippi, 1796-1797, *"American Historical Review,* V. 1899-1900, pp. 523-26.

Chapter III
Forming the "Little Kingdom"

1. There are varying estimates of the population of Kentucky in 1792. Obviously there was no

count for Clark County. Richard H. Collins, *History of Kentucky*, I, 22, says there were 61,133 whites and 12,430 slaves. The first United States *Census* stated 73,677.

2. Thomas D. Clark, ed., *The Voice of the Frontier*, (John Bradford's Note 14, Kentucky Gazette, May 11, 1827) Also, Note 37, pp. 136-7, and Note 35, pp. 139-44.

3. James Rood Robertson, *Petitions of the Early Inhabitants of Kentucky to the General Assembly of Virginia, 1769-1782*. Petition 48, 108-10, Petition 49, pp. 119-11.

4. *Ibid.*, 110-11.

5. Charles Talbert, *Benjamin Logan, Kentucky Frontiersman*, pp. 3-21, William Littell, *Political Transactions*, pp. 203-21.

6. Robertson, *Op. Cit.*, Petition 78, pp. 84-5.

7. *Ibid.*, Petitions 48, pp. 108-9, Petition 49, pp. 110-11.

8. *Acts*, Kentucky General Assembly, December 6, 1792, pp. 19-20.

9. *Ibid.*

10. *Ibid.*

11. *Ibid.*, p. 20.

12. Characteristic of literally hundreds of deeds recorded in Clark County Clerk's office is that of Nicholas and Betsy Merriwether to John Trumbo, May 15, 1796. Deed Book I, 196. The calls are largely from one marked tree to another with a stake in the line, and an indefinite point on the mouth of Slate Creek.

13. The "e" appears only seldom if ever in the George Rogers Clark Papers, James A. James, ed. George Rogers Clark Papers, 9 vol. James, The Life of George Rogers Clark.

14. Clark County Court Order Book, I, March Term 1793, p. 1.

15. *Ibid.*

16. *Ibid.*

17. *Ibid.*

18. *Ibid.*, pp. 2-3.

19. *Ibid.*, October 22, 1793, p. 60.

20. The earliest roads were from Holder's Boatyard to Strodes Fort, to Lexington, Lexington to Mount Sterling, and from Boonesboro to future Winchester.

21. Order Book I, August 27, 1793, p. 46.

22. *Ibid.*

23. *Ibid.*, August 27, 1793, p. 46. On this date, John Baker, Josiah Hart and James MaGill reported on the road between the Clark County Courthouse and Boonesboro.

24. There was no contemporary map made of the surface or roadways of Clark County before the 1830's. One has to search through the county order books to determine the existence and location of roads.

25. *Ibid.*

26. *Ibid.*, January 29, 1794, p. 82. Also January 25, 1793, p. 36.

27. *Ibid.*, July 25, 1793, p. 34.

28. *Ibid.*, October 22, 1793, p. 6.

29. *Ibid.*, March Term, 1793, p. 3.

30. *Ibid.*, July 25, 1793, the first survey was ordered to be made by James Dunlap and John Baker. Also August 27, 1793, p. 40.

31. *Ibid.*, August 27, 1793, p. 40.

32. *Ibid.*, October 23, 1793, p. 60.

33. *Ibid.*, November 27, 1793, pp. 66-7.

34. *Ibid.*, November 27, 1793, p. 68.

35. *Ibid.*

36. *Acts*, Kentucky General Assembly, December 17, 1793, p. 11.

37. Winchester, Virginia is located inside the first two tiers of the eastern face of the Appalachian Mountains, and on the main road from Charlottesville to Philadelphia, James Truslow Adams, ed.,

Atlas of American History, pp. 66. It was on the main Virginia road to Parkersburg on the Ohio.

38. *Acts*, December 19, 1793, p. 11. Also, the act was amended December 14, 1796, Littell, Laws of Kentucky, I, 367-8.

39. Clark County Court Order Book, January 27, 1794, p. 82, May 27, 1794, p. 101.

40. *Ibid.*, May 27, 1793, pp. 98-100.

41. In the pre fence era straying animals were a problem for owners, their neighbors, and the law. The Kentucky General Assembly, February 10, 1798, enacted a rather extensive law pertaining to stray boats and animals. William Littell, *The Statute Law of Kentucky*, 2, p. 76. Clark County was open range country during the closing decade of the eighteenth century. Also, Acts, June 28, 1792, pp. 34-6. The law was County Court Order Book, May 27, 1794, pp. 98-100. Amended December 18, 1794, pp. 14-6.

42. County Court Order Book, May 27, pp. 94, 101.

43. *Ibid.*, pp. 98-100.

44. *Ibid.*, pp. 101-102.

45. *Ibid.*, p. 102.

46. *Ibid.*, November 27, 1794, p. 68.

47. *Ibid.*, November Term, 1794, p. 147.

48. Basic plans for the courthouse, stocks, and stray pen, May 27, 1794, pp. 94, 100, 102.

49. *Ibid.*, November Term, 1794, pp. 147-49.

50. *Ibid.*, p. 67.

51. *Ibid.*, February Court, 1794, p. 4.

52. *Ibid.*, July 25, 1793, p. October Term 23, 1793, p. 60, February 13, 1794 9. 2.

53. Charles R. Staples, *History of Pioneer Lexington*, pp. 7-18. Also, County Court Order Book, February Term 1794, pp. 1-2.

54. *Ibid.*, p. 2.

55. *Ibid.*, October 22, 1793, p. 60.

56. February 13, 1794, 1-2.

57. *Ibid.*, p. 3.

58. *Ibid.*, p. 6.

59. *Ibid.*, p. 7.

60. Ordinance Book, Winchester Trustees, County Order Book, May meeting, 1801, p. 22.

61. *Ibid.*, February 13, 1794, pp. 2-3.

62. To be supplied - leave space.

63. Ordinance Book, Winchester Town Trustees, 1801, n. d. p. 26.

64. *Ibid.*

65. *Ibid.*

66. The Winchester Town Spring surely was fed by a strong vein of water. Nowhere in the trustee bok or the Clark County Order Books is there mention of this fact. The attempt to protect the spring reflected the sloveness of many of the users.

67. County Court Order Book, June Court, 1805, p. 26.

68. Edward Calloway et. al. admitted they owned the Commonwealth $50.00. This possibly was the earliest use of the dollar sign.

69. *Ibid.*, December Court, 1796, pp. 136-7. November term 1797, 204.

70. *Ibid.*

71. *Ibid.*

72. *Ibid.*

73. Ordinances and By Laws for the Town of Winchester, 1814, Sections 6 and 7, Ordinance Book, p. 102-3.

74. The Clark County court day resembled an ancient English market day. It was part tending to business, part socializing and listening to politicians speak, horses and knife trading, and being bamboozled by the hawkers and peddlers. It was also an important market day periodically for sale of

livestock.

75. Ordinances and By-Laws, Winchester 1814, Sections 12, 13.

76. The basic law governing mill dams was enacted by the Kentucky General Assembly, February 22, 1797. Littell, *Statute Laws*, I, 606.

77. Order Book Clark County Court.

Chapter IV
The Way of Life on the Evolving Frontier

1. Froe, shoe-making tools, saw, shovel plow, grind stone, and whiskey-making vessels. Clark County Order Book, January 21, 1787. On this date appraisers reported that James Cheatham died possessed of 3 axes, 4 hoes, and 5 "sickles."

2. Pack horses led west bore numbers of small tools in panniers. These were principally augus, axes, hoes, scythes, froes, and the necessary parts for making spinning wheels and looms. Plows, looms, spinning wheels, and all kinds of tool handles were made on the ground. There appeared numerous listings of tools and other supplies in the Kentucky Gazette, nearly all of which had been brought down stream by flatboats from Pittsburgh.

3. In building log cabins and houses workmen needed axes, pole and broad, foot axes, froes, and an augur.

4. Kentucky Gazette, May 15, 1792, and January 5, 1793.

5. Tench Coxe, *A Statement for the Arts and Manufactures of the United States of America for the Year 1810.* pp. 121-7.

6. In 1820, 6,473 persons were engaged in agriculture as compared with 41 in commerce, and 215 in manufacturing, Fourth United States *Census*, 1820.

Estate Appraisal Book, Clark County Court, estate of Joseph Smith, February 20, 1797, p. 91. Of Thomas M. Hart, September 23, 1797, p. 102.

7. Court Order Book, and the Ordinance Book of the Winchester Town Trustees. The Kentucky General Assembly in 1814, enacted a law requiring peddlers to be licensed. In 1831 the law included specifically clock peddlers, Acts, January 31, 1814, Littell, V. p. 114. Thomas D. Clark, *The Rampaging Frontier*, pp. 301-20.

8. Tench Coxe, *Op. Cit.*, pp. 121-27.

9. After the turn into the nineteenth century there appeared in the wills and estate appraisals listing furniture. Inventory of Matthew Patton's estate, Order Book, September 5, 1803, pp. 322-9. There were carpenters and craftsmen in Winchester from the early years on. The trustees of the town adopted an ordinance against these craftsmen dumping shavings and trash in the streets.

10. Prior to 1840 the court appointed appraisers recorded in detail all the properties which they were shown. For instance, the inventory of the estate of Ester Patton, November 28, 1820, Clark County Estate Settlement Book, p. 22. Ester Patton was one of the very few, if not the only, female whose estate was publicly appraised.

11. A characteristic appraisal was that of William McDaniel, December 7, 1802 in which numerous tools and utensils were listed, Clark County Estate Book, p. 69.

12. Many of the inventories listed looking glasses. See specifically the appraisal of Sam Lusk's estate, Order Book, November court, 1801, p. 237.

13. Most inventories contained listings of covers of some sort. Some listed feathers. Not often were bedsteads listed. A distinct exception was the appraisal of Peter Noe's estate. 3 bedsteads, and some "checks" (covers). Estate Settlement Book, November 23, 1802, pp. 272-1.

14. Baptist Sweet appraisal, January 6, 1803, pp. 300-07. William McDaniel appraisal, "feather bed and covering," December 7, 1802, *Ibid.*, 270. John Gordon estate, October 1823. pp. 358-60 listed counterpanes and sheets. John Baker, May 13, 1803, pp. 309-13, listed covers.

15. Drafts, having the appearance of crudely made musical scores were necessary pattern setters for the looming of woven patterns.

16. Mary Washington Clarke, *Kentucky Quilt and Their Makers*, passim.

17. Especially the appraisal of John Garden, Estate Settlement Book, October 1823, pp. 358-60. Many appraisals made similar listings.

18. Hardly an estate appraisal failed to list at least one of the three or four spinning wheels, (flax, wool, cotton).

19. *Ibid.*

20. The appraisal of William McDaniel's estate, March 7, 1803, listed a weavers loom, 4 slays, a quilt wheel, a flax wheel, pp. 290-1.

21. *Ibid.*

22. Almost universally the earlier estate appraisals listed kettles, dutch ovens, occasionally a frying pan, and pot hooks, and trammels.

23. There appeared in many of the appraisals pewter molds for spoons especially.

24.

25. Clark County Court Order Book, Special called session, May 1804, p. 317.

26. There were available several roots and berries suitable for making tea among them sassafras, maybe spice bush, sage, catnip, mint.

27. Appraisal of John Oliver's estate, June 28, 1796, Clark County Order Book, p. 71.

28. *Acts*, Kentucky General Assembly, December 19, 1804, Littell, *Laws of Kentucky*, I, 231.

29. Strangely, in no estate appraisals were any kind of barnyard fowls listed, yet bundles of feathers appeared in the listings.

30. The frequent inventories presented in the county court are collectively a social and cultural catalog of domestic life in Clark County.

31. It is quite apparent that members of the family of the deceased persons, always the head of the family, displayed such properties as were necessary to satisfy the law. There are no indications as to what was withheld.

32. County Order Book, January 24, 1799, pp. 86-9.

33. *Ibid.*

34. The Kentucky Gazette in this era published extensive lists of books and merchandise available in Lexington.

35. Clark County Estate Settlement Book, December 6, 1821, pp. 224-26.

36. *Ibid.*, Nov. 31, 1821, p. 182.

37. *Twelfth Annual Report*, Kentucky Department of Agriculture Labor, and Statistics (1897), opposite p. 31.

38. Almost universally estate inventories prior to 1849 listed "barshare" plows.

39. United States Seventh Census (1850), 153, 96 improved acres, 17, 656 unimproved with land and implements worth $4,543,412, p. 238.

40. Clark County Estates Settlement Book, (Order Book), October term of court, 1823, p. 316.

41. The ordinary everyday clothing down to 1840 and even later was for men baggy, coarse textured, and without style. The linsey-woolsey dress materials did nothing for the female form but hide it. By the latter date the women's style books like Godeys and Peters drifted into Kentucky.

42. No doubt there were musical instruments which were brought west by the Clark County pioneers. Undoubtedly, the fiddle was the favorite, and some version of the hoe down dance was popular, as were play-party games, but the records are mute on the subject.

43. Almost never did a woman's name appear as the possessor of domestic and real properties. One exception was Ester Patton listed above.

44. *Acts*, Kentucky General Assembly, December 19, 1793, Littell, *Statute Laws*, I, 194.

45. Every census from 1790 until 1860 gave special listings of slaves. Running through the entries in the county court order books, the estates settlement books, and the ordinance book of Winchester are ladened with slave notations.

46. *Acts*, February 8, 1798, Littell, Statutes 2, section 38, p. 113.

47. *Ibid.*, As real estate November 26, 1800, Littell 2, p. 374.

48. Population Tables, Second, fourth, seventh Census reports (1800, 1820, 1830, 1850).

49. See the contents of Chapter II this text.

50. *Ibid.*

51. Morehead and Brown, Statute Law of Kentucky, I, 253, 260.

52. Clark County Court Order Book, May Court, 1802, p. 60.

53. *Ibid.*, October Court, 1808, p. 281. July Court 1811, p. 467.

54. Clark County Will Book, 12, October 3, 1849, pp. 94-5.

55. It is uncertain where Patton's will was executed precisely as written. The slaves appear in the inventory of his estate November 7, 1803. Clark County Order Book, pp. 322-

56. *Ibid.*

57. *Ibid.*, December Court, 1799, pp. 171-2.

58. Clark County Estate Settlement Book, July 2, 1803, pp. 302-3.

59. *Ibid.*, January Court, 1822, pp. 128-32.

59. Clark County Estate Settlement Book, (Order Book) January Court, 1822, 32.

60. Clark County Order Book, October Court 1810. Emanuel Calloway was appointed guardian of Brenda Hazel.

61. Clark County and the Town of Winchester made some provision for indigent persons by paying individuals for care. There was for a time a poor house.

62. Order Book, 1819, p. 75-6. August Court, p. 28.

63. *Ibid.*, July Court, 1795, p. 552, October Court 1808, p. 283. February Court, 1821, p. 41, April Court 1822, p. 324.

64. Bastardy cases were Hirma Pheamster v. Eliza Dawson, Order Book February Court, 1821, p. 243, Commonwealth v. Couchman and Commonwealth v. David Donahue, p. 41.

Chapter V
Breaking the Ancient Bonds of Primeval Isolation

1. Robert L. Kincaid, *The Wilderness Road*, pp. 186-193. Neal Hammon, "Early Roads into Kentucky," *Register of the Kentucky Historical Society*, April, 1970, Vol. 68, pp. 91-131.

2. Hubbard Taylor, John M'Guire, Richard Hickman, and Neal McCann was appointed a committee of viewers to locate a road from Holder's Boat Yard to the Bourbon County line, Order Book 1, August 27, 1793, p. 48. Road from Holder's Boat Yard to the place appointed as the site of the courthouse, July 25, 1793, *Ibid*, p. 36. Locate a road from Colonel Hood's to Mount Sterling, August 27, 1793, *Ibid.*, p. 44. Mount Sterling to Iron Works on Slate Creek, *Ibid.* These surveys were but the beginning of a long and complex road locations.

3. *Ibid.*

4. *The Kentucky Gazette*, 1792-1800, regularly carried extensive lists of merchandise. At the same time merchants advertised for boatmen to float produce down river.

5. William Littell, *A Digest of the Statute Laws of Kentucky*, December 17, 1792, I, pp. 125-6.

6. Order Book, I, August 27, 1793, p. 48. July 25, 194, the surveyors reported on a road to connect with Lexington, *Ibid.*, p. 46.

7. *Acts*, Kentucky General Assembly, February 27, 1797, Littell, *The Statute Law of Kentucky*, I, 633.

8. *Ibid.*, February 25, 1797, Sec. I, p. 633.

9. Kincaid, *Op. Cit.*, pp. 188-191.

10. This road became involved in national politics, and between Henry Clay and Andrew Jackson, James D. Richardson, *Comp. Messages and Papers of the Presidents*, II, pp. 483-93.

11. There was no organized road supervisor or authority. It was necessary to depend solely upon what was called tithable labor *Acts*, Kentucky General Assembly, February 25, 1797, Littell, I, p. 633.

12. So far as the opening of Clark County to homesteading, the law of 1797 was explicit in the matter of extending roads. Later the Road Book Index to the County Order Books reflected eloquently

this facet.

13. The first road entry made in the Clark County Order Book was the appointment of the committee "to view and mark out the nearest and best road from Holder's Boat Yard on the Kentucky River to the Bourbon County line, Order Book I, p. 48.

14. *Ibid.*

15. Road surveyors were named in the official appointment law of June 1, 1800, Littell, 2, p. 294. Richard Stanton, *The Revised Statutes of Kentucky*, I, Sec. XIV, p. 525.

16. Not only did surveyors have to follow the instructions of the viewing committee, clear away trees, in some cases grade rough places, but there were always the pestiferous stumps which were axle breakers, and the soft spots in the right of way which quickly became barriers.

17. It must be kept in mind that all labor for the opening, grading, and bridging roads was essentially involuntary under the "tithing" system of warning laborers out to do stints of road work, and if they failed to shop up, they were liable to a fine.

18. C. S. Morehead and Mason Brown, *A Digest of the Statute Laws of Kentucky*, I, p. 638, p. 611. *The Kentucky Gazette* after 1792 ran frequent notices of astray animals. The fact that one of the first Clark County Order Book, I, May 27, 1794, p. 94. *Acts*, Kentucky General Assembly, February 10, 1798, Littell, Statutes, 2, p. 77.

19. *Acts*, Kentucky General Assembly, January 22, 1833, p. 85.

20. *Ibid.*, February 10, 1795, Littell 2, p. 77, November 30, 1831, p. 293.

21. Morehead and Brown, *Op. Cit.*, I, p. 507.

22. In all the actions of the county court and the road viewers the laws of the Commonwealth set the perimeters. The basic law was the one enacted February 25, 1797, and was modified from time to time.

23. *Ibid.*, Littell, I, p. 633, Sec. I. Clark County Road Book, 1792-1875 outlines an almost staggering amount of county road data.

24. Clark County Road Book, pp. 6-15, *Acts*, Littell, February 25, 1797, I, p. 633.

25. *Acts*, Kentucky General Assembly, January 22, 1833, p. 85.

26. *Ibid.*, January 29, 1830, pp. 184-5.

27. *Ibid.*, November 28, 1831, Sec. I, p. 183.

28. Edward H. Stanton, *Op. Cit.*, "Fees," Article XIV, p. 525.

29. *Acts*, February 26, 1797, Littell, I, Sec. 4, 6, pp. 1396-7.

30. *Ibid.*, Sec. 6.

31. *Acts*, January 4, 1831, p. 30.

32. *Acts*, Sec. 6, January 14, 1831, p. 30.

33. *Acts*, January 14, 1831, p. 90. This law applied to private equipment also.

34. *Acts*, February 27, 1797, Sec. 9.

35. Charles Talbert, *Benjamin Logan Kentucky Frontiersman*, pp. 284-5.

36. *Acts*, October 18, 1804, p. 203.

37. Clark County Road Book, 1793-1820, pp. 6-18.

38. *Ibid*, p. 8 and passim.

39. William Bush laid claim to at least 8,920 acres, Index for Old Kentucky Surveys and Grants in the Clark-Madison county area, pp. 25-6. In Virginia grants he owned 13,080 in the enlarged Fayette County area. Master Index Virginia Grants and Surveys, 1774-1791, p. 27. Joan Brooke-Smith and Carol Cline, Old Kentucky Surveys and Grants Index and Joan E. Brookes-Smith, compiler, Master Index Virginia Surveys and grants 1774-1791. In time these large blocks of land were subdivided into smaller holdings.

40. Mary Verhoeff, *The Kentucky River Navigation*, pp. 35-96.

41. Order Book I, July 25, 1793, p. 36.

42. Littell, *Op. Cit.*, I, pp. 125-6.

43. *Ibid.*

44. Humphrey Marshall, *History of Kentucky*, I, 126-33, Robert S. Cotterill, *Pioneer Kentucky*, pp.

179-84. Thomas D. Clark, ed. *Voice of the Frontier.* Richard H. Collins, History of Kentucky, II, pp. 634-37.

45. *Ibid.*

46. Thomas D. Clark, ed., *The Voice of the Frontier,* (John Bradford's Note 44, *Kentucky Gazette,* November 9, 1827), pp. 193-5.

47. *Ibid.,* Note 64, (*Kentucky Gazette,* 23, 1829)

48. Though legislation enacted during the 1830's and '40's was extensive the Report of J. A. Eastin, Resident Engineer, Kentucky State *Documents,* May 1, 1839.

49. There is no clear record of just when the old "tythe" or mandated labor system ceased to function. There is no hint of this in the Clark County Road Book. It is clear that the organization of toll-bearing turnpike companies and the employment of Irish labor especially brought about a change. After 1812, automobiles could be licenses and gasoline taxed.

50. *Ibid.* Neither the laws nor the delegates to the Constitutional Convention of 1849 dealt directly with public road revenue. Richard Stanton, The Revised Statutes of Kentucky. *The Report of the Debates and Proceedings of the Convention for the Revision of the Constitution.*

51. *Acts,* February 28, 1835, pp. 285-94 and 259-60. Kentucky State *Documents* (Report of A. J. Eastin, resident engineer, March 1, 1839, pp. 105-308.)

52. Mary Verhoeff, *Op Cit.,* pp. 100-10.

53. Clark County Road Book, pp. 20-25.

54. Coleman, *Op. Cit.,* pp. 233-8. The process of using crushed stone bound by some form of binding material. Named for John L. Macadam, 1756-1836.

55. The first law was enacted February 2, 1835, but was repealed on the 28th, *Acts,* February 28, 1835, pp. 35-57.

56. *Ibid.,* February 24, 1834, pp. 640-43.

57. *Ibid.,* Sec. I, p. 640.

58. *Ibid.*

59. *Ibid.,* pp. 640-3, Coleman, *Op. Cit.,* pp. 238-9. *Report of the Debates and Proceeding for the Revision of the Constitution* (1849), pp. 777-83.

60. *Acts,* Kentucky General Assembly, February 22, 1834, pp. 640-2.

61. The General Assembly enacted a uniform toll rate law March 1, 1847, pp.63-4. Coleman, *Op. Cit.,* pp.239-9.

62. *Kentucky Statesman,* December 11, 1857, Coleman, *Op. Cit.,* p. 236.

63. Coleman, *Op. Cit.,* p. 222, *An Accompaniment to Mitchell's Reference and Distance Map of the United States,* p. 297.

64. *Acts,* February 25, 1840, p. 256.

65. Clark County Court Order Books and the Clark County Road Book, *passim.*

66. The General Assembly enacted a law to absorb this road into the state's system of internal improvements, *Acts,* December 15, 1838, p. 202.

67. Coleman, *Op. Cit.,* p. 240.

68. *Ibid.,* pp. 243-_.

69. Coleman, *Op. Cit.,* pp. 233-5.

70. *Acts,* March 18, 1912, pp. 105-53.

71. *Acts,* Kentucky General Assembly, 1890, *passim,* March 11, 1912, pp. 99-100. Thomas D. Clark, *Kentucky, Land of Contrast,* pp. 85-92.

72. Report of J. A. Eastin, Resident Engineer, Kentucky State *Documents,* May 1, 1839, pp. 105-8.

73. The system of three viewers inspecting particular county roads prevailed into the first decade of the twentieth century. Too, the "tything" system prevailed. At the October session, 1886, of the county court rates were set for use of oxen and horses, plows, iron scrapers, and loads of rock. Order Book 21, p. 13. The law of 1912 actually marked the beginning of the turnpike age in Clark County.

74. Clark County's railway age did not dawn until the late 1870's and 1880's despite the fact railroads proposing to cross the county had been chartered earlier.

75. *Acts*, July 6, 1893, pp. 1404-15.

76. *Ibid.*

77. *Ibid.*

78. *Ibid.*, April 10, 1890, p.

79. *Ibid.*, March 11, 1912, pp. 96-100.

80. *Ibid.*

81. The earliest law pertaining to motor vehicles was that of March 26, 1904, *Acts*, pp. 303-6. This law was amplified in March 1914 when the General Assembly enacted an extensive and detailed law regulating motor car usage plus a licensing of vehicles. *Acts*, March 20, 1914, pp. 179-196.

82. An early, if not the first, legislation relating to automobiles was enacted March 26, 1904. *Acts*, pp. 303-4.

83. *Acts*, March 11, 1912, pp. 96-100.

84. *Ibid.*

85. *Ibid.*

86. *Ibid.*

87. *Ibid.*, March 20, 1914, Sec. 6, p. 184. The gasoline tax was imposed.

88. United States Statutes-at-Large, XXXIX, pt. I, p. 355-59.

89. Highway 60 was the only designated road in 1916 law in relation to Clark County. Kentucky had highways 25, 31, 60, and 27.

90. *Annual Report of Bureau of Public Roads*, (Federal), 1925, pp. 25-6.

91. *Ibid.*

92. The Winchester *Sun*

93. The Kentucky Road Book, 1793-1875, reflects eloquently this fact as do the Clark County Order Books, 1793-1910.

94. Technically, the *Highway Act* of 1912 marked the beginning of the end of the century and a quarter archaic system of road management.

95. Congress enacted the Rural Free Delivery Act in 1896 after an extended campaign by Populist supporters to create this service for rural Americans. The first complete county service was in Carroll County, Maryland. By 1902, there were 8,292 routes, and in 1925, 45,189 routes. It was in this era that the fourth class post offices in Clark County began to disappear and rural free delivery routes instituted. I. Howell Kane, "Rural Free Delivery," *Dictionary of American History*, IV, p. 508. Pao Haun Chu, the Post Office of the United States, *passim.*

96. The post office at Danville was established in 1792. The Kentucky Gazette, March 21, 1792. Calvin Fackler, *Early Days in Danville*, pp. 56-9. *United States Statutes-at-Large.*

97. The Kentucky *Gazette* frequently noted delay of the mails.

98. *Ibid.*, Charles R. Staples, *The History of Pioneer Lexington*, pp. 41-2, 174, 325-9.

99. Coleman, *Op. Cit.*, pp. 111, 216.

100. Morehead and Brown, *Op. Cit.*, I, p. 509.

101. Walter Gresham, Post Road Maps, Kentucky and Tennessee, 1878. Twelth Annual Report of the Bureau of Agriculture and Statistics, map, opposite p. 31 and list of Clark County post offices, p. 33.

102. Twelth Annual Report Bureau of Agriculture, p. 33.

103. I. Howell Kane, "Rural Free Delivery," *Dictionary of American History*, IV, p. 508. By 1902 there were 8,298, and in 1925, 45,189 routes.

104. *Ibid.*

105. *Ibid.*

106. The discontinuance of railway mail trains, the improvement of federal-state highways, the introduction of the motor truck changed the manner in which the mail is delivered in and out Clark County, Winchester in 1995 was the sole post office in the county.

107. There was no account by a traveler, 1792-1850, which describes a visitation to Clark County with the exception of Thomas Aflect who visited the county in April, 1841 to visit the cattle and hog

breeders.

108. General Highway Map, Clark County, 1973.

109. For example the case of

Chapter VI
The Agrarian Way

1. Tench Cox, *A Statement of the Arts and Manufactures of the United States of America for the Year 1810*, pp. 121-5.

2. This fact was fully documented in the deed books of Fayette and Bourbon counties, and later in those of Clark County. Also, Joan Brooke-Smith and Carol Cline, *Index for Old Kentucky Surveys & Grants*, passim. For historical background Thomas Perkins Abernethy, *Western Lands in the American Revolution*, and Samuel M. Wilson, *The First Land Court of Kentucky*.

3. Documentation of this condition lies in the rapidity of settlers clearing away the forest cover, erecting domiciles, streaking the landscape with winding dirt roads, harnessing the streams with mill dams, the use of the Kentucky River as a transportation artery, and the establishment of a consistent and enduring pattern of agriculture and livestock production.

4. Most of the Clark County lands were adaptable to some form of agriculture or grazing. By 1850, the county was the top group of Kentucky counties in land values, livestock production, and in value of field crops. J. B. DeBow, *Statistical View of the United States*, pp. 238, 263-4.

5. Recorded Clark County deeds reflect the progressing patterns of variations in the sizes of land holdings. See the indenture of Richard Calloway, June 15, 1803, Deed Book 7, pp. 1-2, Frequently there appeared before the county court petitioners seeking revisions of land indentures.

6. The provision of the cornpatch and cabin rights in the Virginia land law of January 1, 1778, was to cause almost infinite confusion in Kentucky. W. W. Henning, *The Statutes at Large: being a Collection of the Laws of Virginia*, 1619-1792. Also, Vol. 10, pp. 35-50.

7. The Sixth Census of the United States reported Indian corn production of 1,004, 455 bushels, tobacco 82, 410 pounds, 94, 770 bushels of wheat, and 2,229 tons of hay. p. 262.

8. The Clark County population was dependent down until the end of the first half of the nineteenth century on the Kentucky River for transporting produce outward, and upon the indifferent roads for the importation of goods. The estate inventories recorded in the county Will and Order Books document the rising standards of life.

9. Good examples of the slave labor force are to be found in the inventory of John N. Bush's estate, August 3, 1822, Clark County Estates Settlements, 1822, pp. 226-9. The estate of Jacob Pinchback, October 23, 1821, pp. 96-9.

10. *Ibid.* Estate settlement of Stephen L. Winn, April Court 1821, p. 342. James Herman's estate settlement, September 24, 1862, p. 393.

11. Littell, *Statute Laws of Kentucky*, I, 606, February 27, 1798, I, 606. *Ibid.*, December 15, 1802, Vol. 3, p. 9. *Ibid.*, January 27, 1810, Vol. 4, p. 148. Frequently petitioners appeared before the Clark County seeking permissions to construct mill dams.

12. Estates occasionally contained whiskey making equipment. An example is the inventory of Jacob Wilson's property appraised December 9, 1839. He owned a large stand of corn near his still house, still tubs, still, flake stand and worm, and a second still and equipment. Clark County Will Book 11, 1834-48, p. 517. John Oliver's Distillation Book, 1876.

13. Samuel Flag Bemis, *Pinckney's Treaty*, passim, Thomas D. Clark, ed., *Voice of the Frontier*, pp. 331-339, John Bradford's Note 65, Kentucky Gazette, February 7, 1829.

14. *Acts*, Kentucky General Assembly, December 22, 1803, *Littell*, Vol, 4, p. 134, January 25, 1803, Vol. 4, p. 167, January 9, Vol. 3, p. 526, December 13, 1820, Vol. 3, 117, 128.

15. *Ibid.*, December 17, 1796, I, 380.

16. Kentucky legislators appear to have been highly conscious of the fact that the Kentucky farmer's market was an eastern and European one, and there was specific emphasis in the laws that the quality

should be maintained.

17. *Acts*, Kentucky General Assembly, December 17, 1796, Littell, I, 380.

18. *Ibid.*, February 10, 1798, Littell 2, p. 137.

19. *Acts*, Kentucky General Assembly, January 24, 1827, p. 125.

20. Tobacco was classed as "sweet" and "Orinoco," *Ibid.*, December 19, 1795, *Littell*, I, 331.

21. *Ibid.*, December 19, 1804, Littell, 3, p. 237.

22. *Ibid.*, February 10, 1798, Littell 2, p. 137.

23. *Ibid.*, February 10, 1798, Littell 2, p. 137.

24. *Ibid.*

25. *Ibid.*

26. *Ibid.*

27. *Ibid.*

28. Clark County Order Book 4, November Court, 1907, pp. 216, 224.

29. *Acts*, Kentucky General Assembly, December 22, 1803, Littell 3, p. 124.

30. *Ibid.*, January 25, 1809, Littell 1, p. 45.

31. Clark County Order Book, 1818, pp. 35, 116, 1822, p. 45.

32. There was a rash of complaints and orders for changes among the Clark County public warehouses in 1818. *Ibid.*, October Court, 1818, p. 35, October Court, 1819, p. 116, July Court, 1822, p. 45.

33. May Court, 1822, p. 45.

34. Order Book, 1818, pp. 35, 116, 1822, p. 24

35. *Ibid.*, October term, p. 476.

36. *Ibid.*, October term, 1811, p. 476.

37. Thomas D. Clark, Kentucky Trade in Livestock, Slaves, and Hemp, unpublished masters thesis, University of Kentucky, 1929. *Kentucky Gazette*, November 14, 1822, Elizabeth L. Parr, "Kentucky's Overland Trade with the Ante-bellum South," *The Filson Club History Quarterly*, II, October 1927, II, 71-81. F. A. Michaux, Travels to the Westward of the Alleghaney Mountains, pp. 189-194, Lewis Gray, History of Agriculture in Southern United States, II, 840.

38. Mary Verhoeff, The Kentucky River Navigation, pp. 42-81. Unfortunately, there does not appear to be in existence a diary or journal of a Kentucky flatboatman from the Bluegrass county. There is a considerable volume of statutory law relating to the subject, Charles Morehead and Mason Brown, *A Digest of the Statute Laws of Kentucky*, II, 258-261. John Williams, "A Memoir," American Pioneer, I, January 1842, pp. 123-145.

39. Though no itemized inventory was published of the contents of the various Clark County warehouses, most of these commodities were covered by the Kentucky Statutues, Morehead and Brown, *Op. Cit.*, pp. 817-45, 1278, 1529.

40. Clark County Court Order Book 1, August 27, 1793, p. 48.

41. There was earlier readily available material along Lower Howard's Creek, the Red and Kentucky rivers suitable materials for the construction of flatboats. Later logs were drifted down the Kentucky. Mary Verhoeff, *Op. Cit.*, pp. 72-8.

42. *The Kentucky Gazette* carried weekly advertisements, 1792-1800 of merchants' listings of goods just received in Lexington, F. A. Michaux, *Op. Cit.*, 127-8.

43. Michaux, *Op. Cit.*, 127-8.

44. At the outset, the Indian-buffalo trail connecting the Blue Licks with the Ohio River, and with other spots in central Kentucky became a main artery of early travel. Thomas D. Clark, *Historic Maps of Kentucky*, p. 51.

45. The list of tools needed by the early settlers in Clark County was limited. This included an axe, augur, broadaxe, saw, chains, chisels, drawing knife, scythe, a metal bar for a plow, and metal parts for spinning wheels, looms, and wheat fans. These were the tools which appeared most often in family estate appraisals.

46. *Ibid.*

47. Benjamin Cassedy, *History of Louisville*, pp. 62-8.

48. Thomas D. Clark, *Voice of the Frontier*, (Bradford Note 48), pp. 208-213. William Littell, *Littell's Political Transactions*, 104-6.

49. Henry Bradshaw Fearon, Sketches of America, a Narrative of a Journey of Five Thousand Miles Made Through the Eastern and Western States of America, p. 238.

50. Frequently there appeared in the estate inventories mention of corn, wheat, rye, hemp, and flax. There does not, however, appear a specific indication that they were for seeding purposes. In a prize winning essay, "Some of the Crops of Kentucky," Richard J. Spurr, farming on the Clark County line discussed seeds. *Report of the Agricultural Society*, 1857, pp. 92-4.

51. It was a general traditional practice for farms to save seed from year to year. Many Kentuckians boasted of still using "old timey" seeds.

52. Thomas D. Clark, *Footloose in Jacksonian America*, pp. 118-20.

53. It was not until after 1850 that improved plow, harvest and processing tools and devices began to appear in the estate inventories. Even though the period 1820 to 1860 was one of major implement inventions.

54. Wheat and oat cradles appeared in estate inventories as did scythes.

55. Flour and meal were ground in the numerous mills which lined Lower Howard's Creek and the other streams. There existed in Clark County in a place or two stone of grain mill grade. Too, the streams supplied sufficient volumes of water to turn stones fast enough to mill wheat and rye flour. Chris Amos and Nancy O'Malley, Milling and Related Industry in the Boone Creek Drainage, Fayette and Clark Counties, pp. 9-15.

56. Tench Cox, *Op. Cit.*, p. 125. J. B. D. DeBow, *Statistical View of the United States*, pp. 240-1 lists corn, production income as compared with non-farm income.

57. Order Book Clark County Court, February 23, 1807, pp. 228-231.

58. The fact that the Kentucky General Assembly concerned itself at various intervals with the construction, maintenance, and inspection of products being shipped south documents this fact. The collected laws are contained in Morehead and Brown, *Op. Cit.*, II, pp. 817-51, and 1529, and Verhoeff, *Op. Cit.*, pp. 73-78.

59. J. B. D. DeBow, *Statistical View* (1850), pp. 238-9.

60. *Ibid.*, p. 240.

61. *Ibid.*, Table CCI, 182, Tench Cox, *Op. Cit.*, 1529. Verhoeff, *Op. Cit.*, p. 125, Chris Amos and Nancy O'Malley, *Op. Cit.*, pp. 27-9.

62. DeBow, *Op. Cit.*, C. C. I, 92.

63. This was especially true when contrasted with the southern states, and outside the range of the operation of the new plows and harvesting machines in the Northwest.

64. *The Western Farmer and Gardner*, January 1840, II, 73-4, p. 94-5.

65. Samuel D. Martin, *"Report to the Commissioner of Patents,"* (Agriculture), Document 59, 1855, p. 126.

66. Richard H. Collins, *History of Kentucky*, December 21, 1857, I, 79.

67. Martin, *Op. Cit.*, p. 186.

68. *Ibid.*, p. 190.

69. William Stewart Lester, *Transylvania Colony*, p. 59, Robert L. Kincaid, *The Wilderness Road*, pp. 99-103, John Bakeless. Daniel Boone did not bring his family and others to Boonesborough in August 1775, John Bakeless, *Daniel Boone Master of the Wilderness*, pp. 110-116, John Mack Farragher, pp. 89-92.

70. Lucien Beckner, "Eskippakithiki: The Last Indian Town in Kentucky," *The Filson Club History Quarterly*, October, 1932, Vol. 6, p. 377. Robert W. Kinsolving, "Blue Grass," *The Kentucky Encyclopedia*, pp. 89-90.

71. Thomas Aflect, "Notes from Kentucky," *Western Farmer and Gardener*, April 1841, Vol. II, 162.

72. Winston J. Davie, *Kentucky, It's Resources and Present Condition*, Legislative Document No. 1, p. 312.

73. William Axton, Tobacco and Kentucky, pp. 62-74 United States 10th.

74. Census, "Culture in Kentucky Agriculture," III, 74-5. *Biennial Report*, Department of Agriculture, Labor, Livestock, Industry Board, and Forestry, 1935, reported that Clark county produced 3,716,561 pounds of burley tobacco on 4,566 acres, p. 76. In 1870 the county had produced 5,384,137 pounds of burley. (Agriculture) Table XCV, 730. Clell Coleman, *The Truth About Kentucky*, reported that in 1993 the county produced 2,310,000 pounds on 3,040 acres, p. 113.

75. pp. 79-84.

76. 1900-1960.

77. Russell A. Anderson, "Jethrow Wood," *Dictionary of American Biography*, XX, 463-4, Herbert A. Keller, "Cyrus Hall McCormack," XI, 607-8, Carl W. Mitman, "John Deere," V, 193-4. Nearer home were Benjamin Franklin Avery and E. C. Brinley of Louisville and Middletown, Biographical *Encyclopedia of Kentucky*, p. 496.

78. *Franklin Farmer*, 1837-1855, *Kentucky Farmer*, 1859-1861.

79. The Kentucky farm periodicals were founded to publicize advances in farming, and to promote the establishment of an agricultural and mechanical college. Robert W. Scott, *Report of the State Agricultural Society*, pp. 5-10.

80. *Ibid.*

81. *Ibid.*, p. 5.

82. *Ibid.*, p. 11.

83. *Ibid.*

84. *Ibid.*, p. 19.

85. *Ibid.*, p. 11.

86. *Ibid.*, p. 305.

87. *Ibid.*, p. 128.

88. The various raids of skirmishes which occurred in Clark County were really minor. There appears to have been no serious disruption of farming or livestock production. Fortunately John Hunt Morgan's unruly raiders did not harm in Clark as they did in Montgomery County. Cecil Holland, Morgan and his raiders, pp. 321-8.

89. For comparative date see the agricultural tables of Kentucky as compared with those of the northwestern farm states in the ninth, eleventh, and fourteenth United States Census reports on agriculture, 1870, 1890, and 1920.

90. Though new and improved farm implements flooded the market after 1870, Clark County farmers appeared rather conservative in their use.

91. J. B. D. DeBow, *Statistical View*, p. 326.

92. *Ibid.*, pp. 237-8.

93. The death of most landholders resulted in subdivisions of landed property. A specific case was that of Charles Goldman at the mouth of Red River and Bull Run Creek which was divided into a lower tract, and one for heirs. Clark County Estate Settlement Book, November Court 1840, pp. 430.

94. United States *Fourteenth Census* (Kentucky), p. 74. The majority of the farms averaged 140 acres or less. Of the 169,600 acres in the county, 154,568 were farm lands.

95. *Ninth Census,*

96. In 1890 hemp poundage produced in Clark County was 1,620,000 pounds. *12th Annual Report, Agriculture, Labor and Statistics*, p. 492.

97. *Ibid.*

98. In 1880 corn production had dropped to 791,202 bushels as 1,056,206 in 1860. Compendium of the Tenth Census, Table XLVII, 774, and the Eighth Census (1860), VII, 59-65.

99. *Eighth Annual Report of the Commissioner of Agriculture* (Kentucky), part III, 78.

100. Hemp was not listed as a crop in Clark County in the Fourteenth U. S. *Census*, (Agriculture-Kentucky), Table IV, 98.

101. *Ibid.* Kentucky fescu '31 was to appear later.

102. *Ibid.*, there was listed in 1920 612 horses and 360 mules, Table II, 86. In 1950, however, only 48.7 percent of Clark County farms had tractors, *Statistical Abstract Supplement (County and City Data*

Book 1956), Table 2, p. 129.

103. In 1950, 95.9 percent of Clark County residents had available electricity, County and City Data Book, Table 2, p. 120.

104. In 1950, there were 1,407 automobiles, 722 motor trucks, and 830 tractors, *Ibid.*, p. 121.

105. *Ibid.*, p. 114.

106. *Ibid.*

107. Axton, *Op. Cit.*, pp. 97-115.

108. With the appearance of white burley and the railroads, tobacco warehousing shifted from the Kentucky River to Winchester. An example, Thompson's Warehouse, W. A. Beckner, Hand-Book of Clark County and the City of Winchester, p. 5.

109. Agricultural Adjustment Act, 1933, *Statues at Large of the United States*, pt. I, XIVIII, 31-2, Agricultural Adjustment Act, *Ibid.*, XIIX, 282-3. Rural Electric Administration, *Ibid.*, Title IV, 818-9.

110. W. J. Davie, *Kentucky, It's Resources and Present Condition*, 1st annual report, 1878, p. 315.

Chapter VII
Lords of the Pasture

1. Jedediah Morse, *The American Geography*, pp. 402-8. Thomas D. Clark, *Agrarian Kentucky*, pp. 24-40. Gilbert Imlay, *A Topographical Description of the Western Territory of North America*, pp. 148-51. Robert Peter, *History of Fayette County*, pp. 179-94.

2. Arthur M. Miller, *The Geology of Kentucky*, pp. 179-83. W. E. Jackson, *Kentucky Forest Trees*, pp. 15-21, Mary E. Wharton and Roger Barbour, *Trees and Shrubs of Kentucky*, passim.

3. Many of the estate appraisals contained listings of leather, shoe-making tools and lasts, candle molds, and beef hides. Most harness and shoes were home made.

4. Lewis C. Gray, *History of Agriculture in the Southern United States*, II, p. 840.

5. *Report* of the Commissioner of Patents for the Year 1854, p. 14.

6. Will Book I, Clark County, March 27, 1801.

7. *Western Farmer and Gardner.*

8. Though no one kept a record, by inference it can be asserted that thousands of Clark County hogs went afoot to market.

9. 15,000 Kentucky hogs were driven through Franklin, Tennessee in November, 1837 bound for the southern market. *The Franklin Farmer*, I, p. III, December 2, 1837.

10. Except for whiskey cured Kentucky port was one of the most popular commodities sold South.

11. Robert Wilmot Scott, "Sheep Husbandry in Kentucky," *Second Report* of the Commissioner of Agricultural Society, 1860, pp. 206-17. "Improved Sheep," *Report* of the Commissioner of Agriculture (U. S.) for the Year 1860.

12. The magistrates at the November, 1805 meeting of the Clark County Court awarded bouties for wolf scalps to Moses Sharp, Samuel West, Bartlett Woodward, James Chambers, Thomas Baldwin, Richard Oldham and others. Clark County Order Book 3, November, 1805, p. 65.

13. A Kentuckian writing under the pen name "Umbra" submitted a revealing essay on early Kentucky sheep and woolen fleece to the *Western Farmer and Gardner*, April, 1841, II, pp. 156-160.

14. No one made a note of when the horse first appeared in Clark County. No doubt John Findley was mounted when he visited Eskippakithi in 1754. Later in 1769, the Boone-Finley party came mounted. When they left the Yadkin Valley on May 1, 1769, their train contained ten to fifteen horses. Surely some of these crossed the river to Clark County. John Mack Faragher, *Daniel Boone, the Life and Legend of an American Pioneer*, p. 76. Certainly, the Boone Findley party had horses with them on Lulbegrud Creek.

15. These were the horses listed in the estate inventories. Universally, horses were listed and described by color and markings. For instance, Joseph Smith's estate inventory listed a bay horse, a yellow mare, a dark bay mare, a sorrel horse, an old mare, a bay filly, and a black filly, Clark County Order Book 2, February 29, 1797, pp. 89-90.

16. This fact was clearly indicated in the numbers listed in estate inventories, the listing of saddles, plows, and later horse-drawn vehicles, but more especially in the matter of opening rural roads.

17. Under the "Crime and Punishment" section of the *Revised Statutes of Kentucky,* Richard H. Stanton, ed., p. 401, persons were forbidden to ride a bull, or stallion near a place of public worship, or to have them cover a mare or cow. By act of the General Assembly, February 7, 1798, counties and towns were protected by section 2, which forbade the standing of stud horses within the in-lots of towns. C.S. Morehead and Mason Brown, *A Digest of Kentcuky,* II, p. 1508.

18. The Commonwealth required that the county courts set rates for lodging, liquor, and horse care. William Littell Statute Laws of Kentucky I, 194.

19. As indicated, the horse was a beast of burden, a matter of substantial value, and, in the early years, attractive to Indian raiders.

20. There were few, if any, horse breeders in Clark County comparable to Robert Aitcheson Alexander, Abe Buford, Benjamin W. Dudley, or Elisha Warfield. Robert Peter, *History of Fayette County, Kentucky,* pp. 131-76.

21. In 1850, Clark County had 8,287 "Horses, asses, and mules." *Statistical View of the United States,* p. 238.

22. Henry Clay to Henry Clay, Jr., December 1, 1833, Hopkins and Hargreaves, The Papers of Henry Clay, vol. 8, pp. 669-670. Henry Clay to Thomas Clay, November 25, 1833, p. 668.

23. Samuel D. Martin to the Commissioner of Patents, August, 1852, *Report* of the Commissioner of Patents for Agriculture, pp. 312-13.

24. In time, Clark County cattle breeders like the Patton brothers, Matthew Patto, Isaac Cunningham, Abram Renick, Isaac Van Meter, Samuel D. Martin, and William Duncan were to cattle what the Fayette County breeders cited above were to the horse industry.

25. This reference was to Joshua 21:40 relating to the divisions of the cities, and 32:1.

26. *The Franklin Farmer,* June 9, 1838, I, p. 317.

27. Lewis F. Allen, *History of the Shorthorn Cattle,* pp. 158-9.

28. *Ibid.*

29. Lewis Allen, *History of the Shorthorn Cattle,* p. 158-9.

30. *American Herd Book*

31. *The Franklin Farmer,* December 2, 1837, I, III. Paul C. Henlien, *Cattle Kingdom in the Ohio Valley,* 1783-1860, p. 28.

32. Lewis C. Gray, *Op. Cit.,* I, p. 849.

33. *Ibid.*

34. *Ibid.*

35. Inventory of Matthew Patton's Estate, Clark County Order Book 3, September 3, 1803, pp. 323-29.

36. *Ibid.,* p. 328

37. Clark County Order Book 2, 1804, pp. 315-16, The inventory, pp. 323-33. He meant to care for Ester generously, though he proved for the sale of their domestic properties.

38. Trade between the United States and Britain was interrupted by Embargo Act, 1807 and the Non Intercourse Act of 1809. United States States-at-Large.

39. "Henry Clay to Lewis Sanders," September 13, 1817, James F. Hopkins and W. M. Hargreaves, ed. *The Papers of Henry Clay,* Vol. 2, pp. 380-81. "McDonald and Ridgely to Henry Clay, May 1, 1817, *Ibid.,* p. 345.

40. *The Franklin Farmer,* June 9, 1838, I, pp. 317-19.

41. "The Importation of 1817," *Western Farmer and Gardener,* June, 1840, II, p. 83. Anna Virginia Parker, *The Sanders Family of Grass Hills,* pp. 22-4.

42. *The Franklin Farmer,* December 2, 1837, p. 111, October 4, 1837, p. 56.

43. Allen, *Op. Cit.,* p. 168.

44. Lewis Allen, *Op. Cit.,* pp. 168-70.

45. Dr. Martin was appointed in September, 1837 to be the agent to receive and record pedigree

records, *The Franklin Farmer*, October, 1837, I, p. 55, June 1839, II, p. 323.

46. *The Western Farmer and Gardener*, June, 1845, v. 241.

47. *Ibid.*

48. This was especially true of the Renicks. Breeders in Ohio and Kentucky shared in the importations.

49. Allen, *Op. Cit.*, pp. 68-70, p. 166.

50. Caywood, *Op. Cit.*, p. 18, 19.

51. Henlein, *Op. Cit.*, p. 78.

52. Lucien Beckner, "Kentucky's Glamorous Shorthorn Age," *Filson Club Quarterly*, January 1952, Vol. 26, pp. 216-7, Franklin Farmer, November 2, 1839.

53. *Western Farmer and Gardner*, August 1841, II, p. 277.

54. Ben F. Van Meter, *Diary*, "A Voyage to Europe," p. 1. *The Diary of Charles F. Garrard, The Register*, Kentucky Historical Society, June, 1932, Vol. 30, p. 51.

55. *Ibid.*

56. Kentucky *Statesman*, August 13, 1853.

57. *Ibid.* Also, "Importation of Cattle," *The Register*, Kentucky.

58. Historical Society, October, 1936, Vol. 27, p. 421.

59. *Ibid.*

60. Eighth United States *Census*.

61. To answer an ancient question. Shorthorn bulls were bought by some western cattlemen to be bred to the longhorn cows to improve the range stock. The *Report* of the U.S. Commissioner of Agriculture, 1876, pp. 418-19, Lucien Beckner, "The Kentucky Shorthorn Age," *The Filson Club History Quarterly*, January, 1932, Vol. 26, p. 42.

62. *Ibid.* Becknee, pp. 42-43.

63. *Ibid.*, p. 44.

64. *Ibid.*

65. *Ibid.*

66. The menu and program for the dinner are included in Martha F. Van Meter; Diary of "A Voyage to Europe" as tip in sheets. Ben, the diarist went along as a young boy with the importation party in 1853.

67. Beckner, *Op. Cit.*, pp. 45-7. John Sharp Williams was the golden tongued United States Senator from Mississippi. He attended the Kentucky Military Institute. In 1880, he was a highly successful practicing attorney and public speaker, Charles S. Snyder, "John Sharp Williams," *Dictionary of American Biography*, XX, pp. 277-8.

68. Bill of fare contained in Van Meter, *Diary*, "A Voyage to Europe." Beckner, *Op. Cit.*, pp. 45-6.

69. The great banquet of July 27, 1880, not only celebrated the high standing of Clark County shorthorn breeders, it, in fact, marked the beginning of the decline of the local shorthorn history. Beckner, *Op. Cit.,* pp. 50-1.

70. U. S. Eleventh *Census*, Beckner, *Op. Cit.*

71. There are no more Pattons or other short horn survivors in Clark County.

72. J. B. D. DeBow, *Statistical View of the United States* (Compendium of the Seventh *Census*), pp. 236, 238.

73. Compendium of the *Sixth United States Census*, p. 263.

74. Tenth U. S. Census, *Report of Statistics in Agriculture*, p. 154. Eleventh Census, *Ibid.*, General Tables p. 329.

75. Twelth *Census*, General Tables, p. 443.

76. Thomas, Aflect, *Western Farmer and Gardner*, April, 1941, pp. 155-6.

77. John Bradford, "Notes on Kentucky," *Kentucky Gazette*, March 23, 1827, May 18, 1827, November 16, 1827. Thomas D. Clark, ed., *The Voice of the Frontier*, pp. 109-10, 139-44, 190-5.

78. *Western Farmer and Gardner*, October 1841, III, 5-11, March 1941, II, 122.

79. *Ibid.*, October 1940, III, 9-10, February 1940, 116-20.

80. *Ibid.*, June, 1941, II, 16.

81. *Ibid.*, February, 1940, II, 119-20.

82. *Ibid.*, February, 1840, II, 120. May 1841, II, 200-1.

83. Anna Virginia Parker, *The Sanders Family of Grass Hills,* pp. 19-21.

84. *Western Farmer and Gardner,* II, June 1841, p. 212.

85. Richard H. Collins, *History of Kentucky,* I, 82.

86. Anna Virginia Parker, *The Sanders Family of Grass Hills,* pp. 19-21.

87. *Report* of the Kentucky State Agricultural Society to the Legislature, p. 128.

88. *Ibid.*, p. 305.

89. *Ibid.*, 18567, pp. 136-41.

90. *Ibid.*, pp. 361-3.

91. *Ibid.*

92. In none of the published lists of prizes in the Report of the Kentucky Agricultural Society, The Franklin Farmer of Kentucky.

93. J. Allan Smith, College of Agriculture, University of Kentucky.

94. Winchester *Sun,* "Centennial Edition" (Agriculture) September 9, 1978, p. 2.

95. In none of the published prize lists in the Report of the Kentucky State Agricultural Society, *The Franklin Farmer,* the *Kentucky Farmer* are hams mentioned.

96. *Statistical View of the United States,* 1854, p. 238.

97. Kentucky Agricultural Statistics, p. 10.

98. The earlier statistics are from the *Report of the Bureau of Agriculture, Labor and Statistics,* 1893, p. 234. In 1880 the number of mules there were 1,881 mules, and in 1881, 662, Ibid. 1882, p. 195.

Chapter VIII
Winchester County Town

1. The Clark County Order Books, 1-3, 1793-1812, passim. Road Book, pp. 6-14.

2. Charles R. Staples, *The History of Lexington,* 1779-1800, pp. 92-211. Richard H. Collins, History of Kentucky, II, 66-79.

3. County Order Books, I, August 27, 1793, p. 44, 46, 68,206. Road Book, pp. 6-20.

4. *Acts* Kentucky General Assembly.

5. William Littell, The Statute Laws of Kentucky, December 6, 1792, I, p. 119.

6. Winchester Trustee Minute book, August 29, 1814, articles 5, 6, 7, pp. 102-3.

7. The Winchester population, according to decennial census reports, 1800, 96, including 18 slaves, 1830, 600? 1840, 1,047. In 1850, the census taker did not report the number. In 1860, 1,142 and 1870, 786. error, the population was 1,400.

8. The population in 1830 was possibly 1,216. The population statistics at best for the earlier years are so questionable. Winchester in the decade 1830-1840 was making the transitions from log cabin and wood stick chimneys to more substantial buildings. The sanitary regulations were in effect, and the street system was being expanded and improved.

9. Trustee Minute Book, August 29, 1814, articles 8, 10, 28 p. 104 pertained to safety.

10. *Ibid.*, meeting of Trustees adopted extensive ordinances requiring fire buckets. In 1826-27, the trustees ordered that both large and small fire ladders be purchased, Trustee Minutes p. 235. In 1829, the ladders were painted, p. 211. An ordinance was adopted July 13, 1831 ordering citizens to comply strictly with the former fire bucket law. August 10, 1831. The trustees ordained A. L. Ferguson and James Duncan to repair the town cistern for fire protection.

11. Repeatedly the early trustees discussed the protection of the town spring against trashing and pollution.

12. Trustee Book, 1805, p. 26.

13. *Ibid.*, pp. 26-7, March 23, 1805, pp. 32-3, 43.

14. *Ibid.*, October 29, 1809, pp. 161-2.

15. *Ibid.*, p. 40.

16. January term trustees, 1812, pp. 61-3, 1816, p. 37, 1818, pp. 171-4.

17. *Ibid.*

18. *Ibid.*, July 20, 1818, p. 175.

19. See note 10.

20. *Ibid.* September 9, 1829, p. 259. This law was repealed almost instantly.

21. *Ibid.*

22. *Ibid.*

23. *Ibid.*

24. *Ibid.*, January 20, 1835, p. 372.

25. *Acts*, Kentucky General Assembly, December 12, 1831, pp. 95-7.

26. *Ibid.*, p. 96.

27. *Ibid.*

28. Trustees Minute Book, August 10, 1831, n. p.

29. *Ibid.*, November 1831, n. p.

30. *Ibid.*, June 21, 1830, p. 271.

31. *Ibid.*, September 28, 1822, p. 202, August 13, 1817, p. 146.

32. *Ibid.*, January, 1830, pp. 270. September 1822, p. 203.

33. *Ibid.*, p. 202.

34. "Ordinances and By-Laws for the Town of Winchester, August 29, 1814, Trustee Minute Book, p. 99.

35. *Ibid.*, December 20, 1835, n. p.

36. *Ibid.*, December 3, 1831, n. p. This was an amendment to the Ordinances and By-Laws.

37. *Ibid.*, December 20, 1839, n. p.

38. *Ibid.*, December 14, 1835, n. p.

39. This ordinance was in conformity with the somewhat complex Kentucky slave code as represented in periodic acts of the Kentucky General Assembly.

40. Trustees Minute Book, December 3, 1831, n. p.

41. *Acts*, Kentucky General Assembly, 1843.

42. Trustees Minute Book, February 17, 1840, pp. 217-19. Ordinances and By-Laws, August 29, 1814, p. 106.

43. *Ibid.*, Section 13, p. 44, 219.

44. *Ibid.*, February 17, 1841, pp. 234-5. *Acts*, Kentucky General Assembly.

45. *Acts*, February 15, 1838, p. 204.

46. *Ibid.*, March 1, 1848, pp. 423-4.

47. *Ibid.*, February 25, 1848, pp. 293-4.

48. There is a question as to the validity of the 1850 count. There is a footnote in the Kentucky section of the Seventh Census Report saying no report had been made on Winchester. Richard H. Collins, *History of Kentucky*, II, 130.

49. *Acts*, March 2, 1857, p. 268.

50. *Ibid.*, March 3, 1857, p. 272.

51. *Ibid.*, March 21, 1857, pp. 464-5.

52. Trustee Minute Book, June 3, 1851. Also June 16, 1861, n. p.

53. *Ibid.*, June 2, 1856, n. p.

54. *Ibid.*, April meeting, 1856, n. p.

55. *Ibid.*, June 2, 1856, n. p.

56. *Ibid.*, August 15, 1855, April 12, 1858, n. p.

57. *Ibid.*, December 7, 1864, n. p.

58. *Ibid.*, December 30, 1864, n. p.

59. (Lexington) *Observer and Reporter*, December 4, 1869.

60. *Acts*, Kentucky General Assembly.

61. *Ibid.*, March 18, 1870 pp. 501-8.

62. *Ibid.*, p. 507.

63. *Ibid.*, p. 508.

64. *Ibid.*, p. 507.

65. *Ibid.*, p. 508.

66. To be supplied - leave space.

67. To be supplied - leave space.

68. Trustees Minute Book, October 22, 1881, 90.

69. *Ibid.*, p. 294.

70. This arrangement did not work, and on November 4, 1898, the Council $1,100 to Winchester Street Railway Company, Minute Book Winchester City Council, November 4, 1890, p. 803, August 11, 1890, p. 370.

71. *Ibid.*, February 3, 1891, pp. 391-93.

72. *Acts*, Kentucky General Assembly.

73. Minute Book, February 3, 1880, pp. 107-9.

74. *Ibid.*, p. 504.

75. *Ibid.*, March 8, 1894, pp. 491, 496, 498.

76. A part of court day in Clark County was the variety which the hawkers and peddlers gave the occasion. The peddling of patent medicines, cheap john jewelry, table ware, and clothing was as much a part of Kentucky pageantry on court day as jockey row.

77. Minute Book City Council, March 1894, p. 496.

78. *Ibid.*, p. 498.

79. *Ibid.*, July 2, 1881.

80. *Ibid.*, July 26, 1881, p. 69.

81. *Ibid.*, October 18, 1881, p. 80.

82. *Ibid.*, October 14, 1881, p. 85.

83. *Ibid.*, October 19, 1881, p. 85.

Chapter IX
The Seeds of Religious Faith

1. Pioneering in a virgin country obviously challenged human character. Warring with Indians, the wild scrambled to possess land, the stress of creating a new state, and opening the drover and down river flatboat trade. All shaped the western character. Even the crudity of the human domicile played a role.

2. John B. Boles, *The Great Revival, 1789-1805*, p. 11.

3. John Taylor, *A History of Ten Baptist Churches*, of which the Author has been an Alternately Member. There were three groups of traveling churches. The first was that led by Captain Billy Bush in 1784. S. J. Conkwright, History of the Churches of Boone's Creek Baptist Association of Kentucky, pp. 17-25, Thomas D. Clark, *Kentucky Land of Contrasts*, pp. 40-54, George W. Ranck, *The Traveling Church*, passim.

4. John B. Boles, The Great Revival, 1787-1805, pp. 1-24.

5. Taylor, *Op. Cit.*, pp. 12-18, J. H. Spencer, *A History of Kentucky Baptists*, I, pp. 28-47, Conkwright, *Op. Cit.*, pp. 16-9.

6. There was no central st of rules or constitution for the Regular Baptist Congregations. See George F. Doyle, a Transcript of the First Record Book of Providence Church, pp. 163-169. The congregations were constantly revising their so-called constitutions. The general doctrinal rules were outlined in "History and Doctrine, and Organization Union Mountain Baptist Association, North Carolina," *Census of Religious Bodies*, p. 262.

7. The two major requirements were that the prospective minister have an "experience," and that he pass muster with a board of deacons.

8. Clark, *Op. Cit.*, pp. 40-44.

9. Julia Tevis, *Sixty Years in a School Room: An Autobiography*, presents an interesting portrait of her grandfather, pp. 40-48, A. Goff Bedford, *The Proud Land*, contains extensive mentions of the entire Bush family.

10. *Ibid.*

11. Chester R. Young, ed., *Westward into Kentucky, the Narrative of Daniel Trabue*, pp. 69-78. Newton W. Merennes, *Colonel William Fleming's Journal of Travels in Kentucky*, 1779-80, pp.

12. Doyle, Transcription of Providence Minutes, p. 1.

13. Doyle, Transcription, p. 2, Conkwright, *Op. Cit.*, p. 23.

14. Conkwright, p. 27.

15. Doyle Transcription, pp. 167-70.

16. Frequently the congregations revised their basic rules and "constitution," but never their basic beliefs. Throughout the minutes of the church meetings at Providence there were rule revisions.

17. In Providence Church, as in all other Regular Baptist congregations, the governance of the group rested with the male members.

18. Quisenberry, *Op. Cit.*, p. 23.

19. The Separatist Baptists tolerated the drinking of a certain amount of whiskey, but not too much. On August 13, 1796, they John Lile and Beal Kelly "from us for drinking two much spirituous lickers frequently and other conduct not justified, Doyle, *Op. Cit.*, p. 25.

20. Doyle, *Op. Cit.*, passim.

21. *Ibid.*, pp. 12-13.

22. *Ibid.*, June 13, 1792, p. 17.

23. *Ibid.*, July 11, 1793, p. 20.

24. *Ibid.*, December 13, 1792, p. 18.

25. *Ibid.*, June 12, 1793, p. 20.

26. Nov. 13, 1795, p. 23.

27. Richard H. Collins, *History of Kentucky*, I, p. 22.

28. Doyle, *Op. Cit.*, October 5, 1796, pp. 25-7, July 11, 1801, p. 39.

29. *Ibid.*, February 13, 1802, p. 44.

30. *Ibid.*, June 13, 1792, p. 17, March 12, 1795, p. 23, June 10, 1797, p. 28, February 14, 1800, p. 36.

31. *Ibid.*, June 13, 1818, p. 101.

32. There is no indication of the Great Revival in the Providence Minute Book. Spencer, *Op. Cit.* makes only slight mention of it in connection with Alexander Campbell, II, pp. 118-21.

33. Spencer, *Op. Cit.*, II, 118, Taylor, *Op. Cit.*

34. Taylor, II, p. 119.

35. James R. Rogers, *The Cane Ridge Meeting House*, p. 62, John B. Boles, *Op. Cit.*, pp. 65-9.

36. Doyle, *Op. Cit.*, pp. 163-70.

37. *Ibid.*, passim.

38. Spencer, *Op. Cit.*, II, p. 120.

39. *Ibid.*, p. 121.

40. This was especially true when the Methodists and Disciples of Christ arrived on the scene.

41. By 1830, a new generation had come to maturity in Clark County. At the same time the emotional religious stirrings along with the rise of conflicting religious theological philosophics and the strenghening of other denominations inevitably produced changes.

42. Boles, *Op. Cit.*, pp. 125-64.

43. Some of the early sermons which have appeared in print reflect a somewhat emotional but repetitious quality. The Methodist circuit riders could be quite emotional in the delivery of their sermons, often times stirring congregations to the point of shouting.

44. The membership of the early Baptist churches included many of the most prominent family names. See Doyle, Transcription of First Record Book, Conkwright, *History of the Churches of Boone's Creek Baptist Association*, and Spencer, *A History of Kentucky Baptists*, II.

45. *Ibid.*

46. A. H. Redford, *History of Methodism in Kentucky*, I, p. 347.

47. Redford, I, p. 209, W. E. Arnold, *History of Methodism in Kentucky*, I, p. 167.

48. Redford, I, p. 209, Arnold, I, p. 114.

49. Arnold, I, pp. 96-7.

50. *Ibid.*, I, pp. 96-184.

51. *Ibid.*, quoting the Southwest Quarterly, I, pp. 135-6.

52. *Ibid.*, I, pp. 136-137.

53. *Ibid.*, I, p. 135.

54. Redford, *Op. Cit.*, I, pp. 391-3, Arnold, pp. 177-8, 185-6, 1889.

55. Arnold, I, p. 94, p. 256.

56. Julia Tevis, *Op. Cit.*, p. 42, Redford, I, p. 391, Arnold, I, p. 185.

57. Arnold, I, pp. 185-92, Redford, I,

58. Redford, I, pp. 392-3, Arnold, I, p. 185.

59. The Methodist Church in America was formerly created in the Baltimore Conference on December 24, 1784. The United Methodist Church of Winchester was the earliest formal Methodist Church established in Clark County, Winchester Sun.

60. *Ninth United States Census*, Table XVIII, p. 540.

61. *Twelfth United States Census*, "Special Reports on Religious Bodies, Kentucky, Table 4, p. 317.

62. *Sixth United States Census*, "Statistical View of the United States," p. 637.

63. *Seventh United States Census*, "Churches and Church Property," Table XIV, p. 637. United States Census, "Presbyterian Churches in the United States," Table 7, p. 68.

64. Alonzo W. Fortune, *The Disciples in Kentucky*, pp. 106-08, Boles, *Op. Cit.*, pp. 63-9, Rogers, *Op. Cit.*, pp. 54-69.

65. Fortune, p. 37.

66. *Ibid.*, pp. 114-132.

67. *Ibid.*, p. 383.

68. *Acts*, Kentucky General Assembly, Chapter 325, p. 207.

69. *Ibid.*, Chapter 387, February 12, 1858, p. 433.

70. *Religious Bodies in the United States*, I, p. 736.

71. *The Winchester Sun* (Centennial Edition), September 9, 1978, p. 16.

72. Fortune, *Op. Cit.*, p. 398.

73. *The Winchester Sun*, September 9, 1978, "Schools/Churches," p. 1.

74. *Ibid.*

75. "African Union Methodist Protestant Churches," Religious Bodies in the United States, p. 455. August 10, 1802, the deacons of Providence Church consented that "Mr. George G. Taylor do consent his Negro man George be at liberty to exercise his gift of exhortations..." Doyle Transcription, p. 46.

76. *The Winchester Sun*, September 9,1978 "Schools and Churches," p. 1.

77. A Transcript of the First Record Book, Providence Church, 1784-1833, pp. 16, 44-5, 57.

78. This was especially true of the Winchester churches. See chapter on the Town of Winchester.

79. "African Union Methodist Protestant Church," *Religious Bodies*, p. 455.

80. *Ibid.*, p. 483.

81. *Winchester Sun* (Cent. ed.) September 9, 1978, p. 11.

82. *Ibid.*

83. *Ibid.*, p. 9.

84. *Religious Bodies in the U. S.*, pt. II, Table 4, p. 319.

85. Statistically, the division between church and non-church members remained almost equally divided. There, of course, was a large portion of the population under the age of affiliating with a church.

86. Basic social issues were liquor, petty crimes, fornication, controversies over interpretations of church policy, and of the Scriptures in this order.

87. Thomas D. Clark, *Footloose in Jacksonian America.* The temperance movement of the 1830's grew in force. See pp. 21, 28, 188, 191. Daniel Dorchester, *The Liquor Problem of All Ages,* (1884) and John A. Krout, *The Origins of Prohibition* (1925)

88. At times it was difficult to separate the spiritual from the temporal in everyday life. The leaders of the county and of Winchester were also leaders in their churches.

89. In 1910, Clark County had a population of 16,694 and a church membership of 7,774, "General Tables," *Special Report of Religious Bodies,* Table 4, pt. I, p. 317.

90. In 1906, Clark County had a population of 16,694 and a collective church membership of 7,774; 3,021 were of the Baptist faith. *Religious Bodies,* pt. II, p. 317.

91. *U. S. Seventh Census,* 1850, Eleven churches had seating for 4,400 persons and the collective church properties were valued at $15,000.00. Table XIV, p. 634.

92. *Ibid.*

93. In 1870, there were thirty-four congregations housed in twenty-seven church houses with 9,700 seating capacity with a property worth of $71,300.00. Ten of the churches were Baptist with 2,600 seatings. *Ninth United States Census,* "Selected Statistics of Churches," Table XVIII, p. 540.

94. In 1980, there were fifty-one churches and synagogues in Clark County with a combined membership of 15,821. *Kentucky Facts,* pp. 114-5.

Chapter X
Education

1. W. C. Caywood, Jr., *Kentucky Mayor, the Story of John E. Garner,* p. 18.

2. *Second United States Census,* 1800, "Kentucky, Schedule of the Whole Number of Persons in the District of Kentucky, p. 2.

3. Good examples of expression and handwriting is to be found in the Clark County Order Book 1 and in the Winchester Trustee Book 1. 1793

4. Luther M. Ambrose, The County Academy System in Kentucky, an unpublished doctoral dissertation, University of Kentucky, Tables 40, 43 pp. 671-2. C. W. Hackensmith, Out of Time and Tide, pp. 24-23.

5. *Second United States Census,* p. 2.

6. *Ibid.*

7. *Ibid.*

8. As an example of a Clark County Estate Inventory, see Matthew Patten, Will Book. Also the estate appraisal of Joseph Smith, Order Book, No. 2, January 24, 1797, pp. 86-9.

9. Joseph J. Bullock, "Report on the condition of education in Kentucky," in Barksdale Hamlett, *History of Education in Kentucky,* pp. 16-19. By the fourth grade it was presupposed that students could write a legible hand, cipher to the "rule of three," and describe land boundaries.

10. Henning's *Statutes at Large of Virginia,* X, 1779-8, pp. 287-8. *Acts,* Kentucky General Assembly, February 2, 1818, p. 526.

11. Henning, *Op. Cit.,* X, 287-8.

12. Christian County, Ky. Deed Book C, . 28. Caldwell County Deed Book D, p. 360. For the most part available academy lands were located well away from settlements. See Ambrose, *Op. Cit.,* Table 43, p. 972.

13. *Acts,* Kentucky General Assembly, Dec. 12, 1794, pp. 48-50.

14. William Littell, *The Statute Laws of Kentucky,* III, pp. 217-9, 474.

15. William Littell, *The Statute Law of Kentucky,* II, 217.

16. This was especially true for the period from June, 1791 to May, 1792. There appeared frequently in the Kentucky Gazette rather long essay discussions as to the desirable form of government.

17. Richard Stanton, *The Revised Statutes of Kentucky,* I, 85a-117.

18. *Ibid.,* I, 107.

19. Christian County, Kentucky, Deed Book C, p. 28, Caldwell County Deed Book D, p. 360.

20. Littell, *Statute Laws of Kentucky*, II, 244, Thomas D. Clark, *Historic Maps of Kentucky*, (John Melish Map of Kentucky, 1816), p. 71-2.

21. Part of Christian County was added to Caldwell County, *Acts*, Kentucky General Assembly, February 1, 1819, 1st session, p. 712.

22. Christian County Deed Book C, December 20, 1821, pp. 28-9.

23. This was the land described in Christian County Deed Book C, November 18, 1809, p. 28.

24.

25. p. 345.

26. *Ibid.*

27. *Ibid.*

28. No notice of a session of the academy ever having been taught prior to this date has appeared. Fred A. Engle, History of education in Clark County, Kentucky, an unpublished M. A. thesis, University of Kentucky, p. 7.

29. Lexington, Kentucky, Reporter, April 6, 1813.

30. Martin explained that "the young ladies would be instructed in the necessary and useful parts of a complete education," a euphemistically reference to becoming housewives.

31. Lexington Reporter, April 6, 1813.

32. Luther Ambrose, *Op. Cit.*, p. 178, Engle, *Op. Cit.*, p. 8, Lexington Reporter, May 13, 1815.

33. *Acts*, Kentucky General Assembly.

34. Christian County Deed Book C., p. 28.

35. Ambrose, *Op. Cit.*, p. 176, *Acts*, Kentucky General Assembly, 1873-74, p. 254.

36. The Winchester Trustee Ordinance Book.

37. The legislative act of January 30, 1830, Chapter CCCLXXXVII, pp. 272-80 was only a tentative outline of a public school system. The major act was that of February 10, 1838, pp. 274-83.

38. Niles Weekly Register (supplement, "Law Cases," XXII, 152-7. A. M. Stickles, *The Critical Court Struggle*, pp. 5-42.

39. Kentucky unluckily did not share in the plan for the support of public educationas outlined in the Northwest Ordinance of 1787.

40. *Acts*, Kentucky General Assembly, 1920-21, December 18, 1821, 351-55. Thomas D. Clark, *A History of Kentucky*, p. 205, McVey, *Op. Cit.* 161-2, *Acts*, 1824-25, p. 157.

41. Journal of the Senate of the Commonwealth of Kentucky, November 30, 1822, pp. 162-222, Journal of the House of Representatives, Commonwealth of Kentucky, December 11,, p. 232.

42. *Acts*, Kentucky General Assembly, January 29, 1830, pp. 272-80.

43. Hackensmith, *Op. Cit.*, p. 65.

44. This law was enacted largely because a group of citizens made a drive to establish a system of public schools. See Thomas D. Clark, *Footloose in Jacksonian America*, p. 136.

45. Clark County Order Books, passim, 1830-1846.

46. Clark County Order Books, October Court, 1843, p. 226.

47. *Ibid.*

48. October Court, 1846, p. 457.

49. *Acts*, Kentucky General Assembly, February 13, 1838, pp. 274-83.

50. *Ibid.*

51. Journal, House of Representatives of the Commonwealth of Kentucky, 1838-39, p. 23.

52. Niles Weekly Register, XXIII, pp. 153-55, Stickles, *Op. Cit.*, pp. 29-31.

53. Journal of the Senate, Commonwealth of Kentucky, December 5, 1836, pp. 17-18.

54. Journal House of Representatives, December 4, 1838, p. 23.

55. Sixth Census, United States, "Aggregate Amount of Each Description of Persons within the District of Kentucky," June 1, 1840, p. 278. *Statistical View of the United States*, 1854 (Compendium of the Seventh Census), pp. 236-37. Table 41, Preliminary Report Eight Census, 1860, p. 260.

56. Kentucky Auditor's Report.

57. *Statistical View of the United States*, p. 237.

58. *Acts*, Kentucky General Assembly, February 16, 1838, p. 274.

59. *Ibid.*

60. Report of the Debates and Proceedings for the revision of the Constitution for the State of Kentucky, 1849, p. 901.

61. Fred A. Engle, *Op. Cit.*, Table I, p. 25.

62. *Acts*, Kentucky General Assembly, February 10, 1845, pp. 46-8. This law defined for the first time the duties and terms of the public superintendent of education. For a biographical sketch of Ryland T. Dillard see Barksdale Hamlett, *Op. Cit.*, p. 33.

63. Hamlett, p. 54.

64. Engle, *Op. Cit.*, Table I, p. 25.

65. *Ibid.*

66. Report and Proceedings, Constitutional Convention, 1849, pp. 377, 380.

67. Dr. Andrew Hood is an almost fugitive historical figure. His father was at Strode's Station and at Hood's Station. Nacy O'Malley, *Stockading Up*, pp. 150, 162. His son, however, exerted no influence in the constitutional convention - education or otherwise.

68. *Report of the Debates and Proceedings of the Convention for the Revision of the Constitution*, p. 880.

69. *Ibid.*, p. 1117.

70. *Report of Debates*, December 1, 1849, pp. 730-1. Dr. Hood voted against providing for the office of lieutenant governor and to keep the state capital in Frankfort, p. 1,105.

71. Engle, *Op. Cit.*, Table I, p. 25.

72. *Ibid.*

73. *Ibid.*

74. Hamlett, *Op. Cit.*, p. 43.

75. *Ibid.*, pp. 48-9.

76. Ryland T. Dillard wrote a clear statement of the Kentucky public school house in the years 1845-1860. He confirms Mayor John E. Garner's statement on the subject. Hamlett, *Op. Cit.*, p. 47.

77. *Ibid.*, p. 43, 75-8.

78. Journals of the Last Five Separation Conventions, Kentucky Historical Society. Thomas P. Abernethy, "Journal of the First Kentucky Constitutional Convention, Journal of Southern History, February, 1935, I, 67-78.

79. In 1860, Clark County was overstocked with school districts. There were 39 of them to serve potentially 2,041 children, but only 828 maintained even a gesture of sustained attendance. Engle, *Op. Cit.*, Table I, p. 25.

80. Hamlett, *Op. Cit.*, p. 80.

Chapter XI
Life in Thraldom

1. There were in Fayette 10, 538 whites, and 7, 921 slaves, in Bourbon 9, 751 whites and 5, 204 slaves. In Clark 8,147 whites 4,577 slaves. Fourth U. S. *Census*, "aggregate amount of each Description of Persons within the District," p. 88.

2. Felix, Walker, "Narrative of His Trip with Boone from Long Island to Boonesborough in 1775," *DeBow's Review*, 1854. vol. 16, pp. 150-55. John Mack Farragher, *Daniel Boone*, p. 116, Thomas D. Clark, *Voice of the Frontier*, John Bradford's Note 4, *Kentucky Gazette*, Sept. 15, 1826.

3. There were 1,535 slaves in Clark County in 1800. Second *United States Census*, p. 2.

4. J. Winston Coleman *Slavery Times in Kentucky*, 4-14, Farragher, *Op. Cit.*, p. 152.

5. Richard H. Collins, *History of Kentucky*, I, 254-95, II, 64-37, Humphrey Marshall, *History of Kentucky*, I, 12634.

6. *The Kentucky Encyclopedia*, pp. 298-9, Robert S. Cotterill, *History of Pioneer Kentucky*, 179-82.

7. U. S. Eight *Census*.

8. At the remaining residence of Hubbard Taylor, Samuel D. Martin, and others.

9. Never did the Kentucky field crops or livestock grazing afford the same seasonal rhythms for use of slave later as did the cotton, sugar cane, and rice crops of the lower South.

10. Dr. Martin's Colbyville farm, though a fairly large and diversified one, it was never comparable to a true slave plantation in the South.

11. Richard H. Stanton, Revised Statutes of Kentucky, I, 203-4.

12. U. S. Eight *Census*, "Farms Containing three acres or more (Agriculture), p. 201.

13. U. S. Fifth *Census*, in 1840 there were 6,178 whites and 3,998 slaves, p. 275. In 1850 there were 7,709 whites and 4,480 slaves. Statistical View of the U. S., p. 242.

14. Second U. S. *Census*, p. 2. The Kentucky State Auditor reported in 1830 8,565 whites and 4,496 slaves. Kentucky State Documents 263, p. 25.

15. Estill County was created in 1808, Acts, Kentucky General Assembly, _____Powell County was created in 1852, *Ibid.*

16. Collins, *Op. Cit.*, II (Clark County) 258

17. Statistical View of the United States, 1850, p. 236.

18. Eight U. S. Census.

19. Although the record is either vague or does not exist as to the precise labors which slaves performed in Clark County it must be assumed the greater number were owned by farmers, and that they helped clear the land, cultivate crops, and perform other agrarian tasks.

20. Slaves were not included in the list of "tithes" obligated by law. They were considered as real estate, and could be used in meeting the "tithe" obligation in the same way ox and horses were supplied in road work. Charles S. Morehead and Mason Brown, *Digest of the Statute Laws of Kentucky*, I, p. 566.

21. C. S. Morehead and Mason Brown, A Digest of the Statute Laws of Kentucky, II, 1476. Bellmore v. Caldwell, Bibb 2, p. 76.

22.

23. By no means were all the estates in Clark County appraised by court appointed commissioners. Although there is no discernible rule as to what estates were appraised at from the contents, however, that only the more affluent ones were appraised, and in the reports in the Order books, 1793-1860, there were slave listings in almost every estate's viewing.

24. George Doyle, Transcription Minutes of Providence Church, p. 20.

25. George Ranck, The Traveling Church, Thomas D. Clark, Kentucky Land of Contracts, pp. 40-54.

26. *Ibid.*, p. 33.

27. *Ibid.*, p. 42.

28. *Ibid.*, p. 36.

29. *Ibid.*, p. 44-5.

30. *Ibid.*, p. 46.

31. *Ibid.*, p. 60.

32. *Ibid.*, p. 119.

33. Trustees Ordinance Book, n. p.

34. Provisions for religious instruction of slaves appeared in wills recorded in the various will books. Often an owner expressed affection for a slave.

35. Trustees Ordinance, Nov. 1831, n. p.

36. *Acts*, Kentucky General Assembly Nov. 29, 1799, Littell, vol. 2, p. 264, Morehead and Brown, A Digest of the *Statute Laws of Kentucky*, II, 1257-8.

37. Clark County *Democrat*, June 26, 1896.

38. Trustees Ordinance, Nov. 1831, n. p.

39. *Act* of the Kentucky General Assembly, December 22, 1802. Littell, vol. 3, p. 63.

40. J. Winston Coleman, *Slavery Times in Kentucky*, pp. 115-45.

41. Ivan E. McDougle, *Slavery in Kentucky*, 1792-1865, passim. This fact was reflected in the rise of the slave trade after that date, and the passage in 1833 of the anti-importation law. *Acts*, Kentucky General Assembly, Feb. 2, 1833, p. 258.

42. There are notations through the County Court Order Books, and estate inventories of slave rentals.

43. In Clark County the source of the slave employment was predominantly agricultural. In 1840, 3,117 persons were engaged in this field, Sixth U. S. *Census*, p. 277. In 1850 Clark County had invested in manufacturing $39,000 with 86 individuals so employed, yielding a return of $50,116 of which $28,440 was of home manufacture, *Statistical View*, p. 241.

44. *Acts*, Kentucky General Assembly, sec. 31, Littell Laws, vol. 3, p. 113.

45. James H. Dickey, *Western Luminary*, October 4, 1826, Estwick Evans, *A Pedestrious Tour*, p. 216, Coleman, *Op. Cit.*, pp. 144-50.

46. J. Winston coleman, *Slavery Times in Kentucky*, p. 144.

47. Thomas N. Allen, *Chronicles of Old Fields*, pp. 88-9.

48. *Ibid.*, pp. 901.

49. *Acts*, Kentucky General Assembly, December 19, 1798, pp. 125-28.

50. Generally, Clark County fell under the mandates of the above slave code.

51. Richard H. Stanton, *The Revised Statutes of Kentucky*, I, p. 147.

52. The law of 1833 forbade the bringing of slaves into Kentucky for resale outside the state. Article X of the 1849 applied to conditions of emancipation of slaves and their removal from the state. Oates was caught in the high state of emotions prevailing in 1860. Richard H. Stanton, *The Revised Statutes of Kentucky*, I, p. 147.

53. Clark County Court Order Book, Feb. Term, 1860, pp. 73-4.

54. *Ibid.*, May term, 1865, p. 596.

55. This personal description of physical features appeared many times in both the County Court Order Books, and in the Ordinance Books of the Winchester Trustees.

56. The Kentucky General Assembly provided by law the process of the emancipating a slave, Morehead and Brown, *Op. Cit.*, I, 254-60.

57. A rather surprising number of owners from time to time came before the Clark County Court seeking manumission of slaves under the terms of the Article X of the 1849 Kentucky Constitution, and earlier Stanton, *Op. Cit.*, p. 147, Morehead and Brown, *Op. Cit.*, I, pp. 259-60.

58. To be supplied.

59. As meticulous as Dr. Martin was in keeping records, his journal book is not numbered, nor did he include day dates.

60. Clark County Order Book, 12, May Term, 1850, p. 342.

61. Clark County Court Order Book, May Term, 1853, p. 615.

62. To be supplied.

63. Order Book, 17, Jan. Term, 1862, pp. 215-217.

64. *Ibid.* Feb. Term, 1862, p. 9.

65. Ninth United States Census.

66. Sr. Martin's general account book, July, 1864, n. p.

67. Dr. Martin's general account book, 1861-1864, passim.

68. *Ibid.* Nov. 1862, Dec. 1862.

69. *Ibid.* passim.

70. Richard D. Sears, *A Practical Recognition of the Brotherhood of Man*, II-IV. E. Merton Coulter, The Civil War and Readjustment in Kentucky, pp. 265-7.

71. Sears, *Op. Cit.*, p. 4-34.

72. *Journal* of the Senate of the Commonwealth of Kentucky, 18.

73. Coulter, *Op. Cit.*, pp. 257-86.

74. The freedom of slaves by the end of the Civil War placed an entirely new responsibility in chancery concerning the children of ex-slaves which the county court attempted to solve by creating a system of enforced peonage on the abodned children. Perhaps this was the only course the court could have persued under the context of the times.

75. Order Book, Clark County Court.

76. *Ibid.*

Chapter XII
The Golden Harvest

1. In 1840, out of a population of 10,803, 711 individuals were listed as having been born out of the state and 78 were foreign born. *Statistical View of the United States*, pp. 236-7.

2. In almost ever case native sons and daughters went elsewhere in their creative years, beginning with Joel Tanner Hart.

3. In context of the late twentieth century definition of the "basics" the Clark County schools were concerned solely with the "three R's."

4. Richard H. Collins, *History of Kentucky*, II, pp. 129-40.

5. Robert Peter, History of Fayette County, Kentucky, 1882, and Benjamin Cassaday, *The History of Louisville from Earliest Settlement to 1852.*

6. Collins, *Op. Cit.*, II, 129-40.

7. Not a single traveler-visitor of American or European origins left a note of his or her visitation to Clark County. Thomas D. Clark, *Travels in the Old South*, 1527-1860.

8. This was a serious loss in the documentation of Clark County's river trade. There, however, are journals describing the flatboat experience of the Ohio River. George Sample, "Sketch of Western Settlement, The American Pioneer, II, pp. 157-8. T. Wilkeson," Early Recollections of the West," *Ibid.*, pp. 158-64.

9. Goff Bedford, Land of Our Fathers and The Proud Land, Vols. I and II is a veritable catalogue of Clark County people, their forebears and family relationships. So are historical essays published in the *Winchester Sun*, p. 19.

10. This was true of Hart, Tevis, Conkwright, Tate and Quisenberry.

11. Joel Tanner Hart is easily Clark County's most distinguished artist. He was the son of Jesiah and Judith Tanner Hart. He was born in Clark County, February 10, 1810 and died in Florence, Italy, March 2, 1877. His father, Josiah, was an active land surveyor, county official, and flatboat trader. His name appeared frequently in the early records of Clark County and the town of Winchester.

12. James F. Hopkins and Wilma Mary Hargreaves, eds., *The Papers of Henry Clay*, I, Clay to James Monroe, July 29, 1812, pp. 697-9. Same September 21, 1812, pp. 728-30. To William W. Wesley, July 2, 1812, pp. 685-32, "Answer to," *Boston Repository*, pp. 692-5.

13. Samuel Woodson Price, *The Old Masters of the Bluegrass*, p. 150, J. Winston Coleman, *Three Kentucky Artists*, pp. 4-5.

14. J. Winston Coleman, *Three Kentucky Artists*, pp. 4-6.

15. *Ibid.*, pp. 4-5, Price, p. 150.

16. *Ibid.*

17. *Ibid.*

18. *Ibid.*

19. Henry Clay proved to be Hart's most popular and profitable human subject.

20. Coleman, *Op. Cit.*, p. 6, Price p. 152.

21. *Ibid.*

22. Edwin G. Nash, "Shobal Vail Clevenger," *Dictionary of American Biography*, IV, pp. 212-13.

23. Robert F. Seegar, ed. *The Papers of Henry Clay*, "Henry Clay to Henry Clay, Jr., Vol. 8, pp. 600-4.

24. See the illustration of the Cassius M. Clay bust included in this chapter.

25. Cassius M. Clay, *The Life of Cassius M. Clay, Memoirs, Writings, and Speeches*, I, p. 222. Coleman, *Op. Cit.*, p. 7.

26. *Ibid.*

27. *Ibid.*

28. Joel T. Hart to Thomas Nelson, November 7, 1845, quoted by J. Winston Coleman, p. 22.

29. C. M. Clay, *Op. Cit.*, I, 112-3, Hart to Clay, January 25, 1865.

30. Coleman, *Op. Cit.*, p. 10.

31. *Ibid.*, p. 13. Price *Op. Cit.*, p. 158.

32. Price, p. 159.

33. Hiram Powers (1905-1873) was a native of Woodstock, Vermont. His family moved to Cincinnati where he too fell under the influence of Shobal Vail Clevenger. His masterpiece was the "Greek Slave." Adeline Adams, "Hiram Powers," *Dictionary of American Biography*, XV, pp. 158-60.

34. C. M. Clay, *Op. Cit.*, I, p. 225.

35. Price, *Op. Cit.*, pp. 154-6.

36. *Lexington Observer and Reporter*, November 14, 1860. Kentucky Statesman, February 7, 1860. C. M. Clay, *Op. Cit.*, I, pp. 227-8.

37. *Acts*, Kentucky General Assembly, February 20, 1874, p. 8.

38. Coleman, *Op. Cit.*, p. 17. Lexington Press, December 21, 1873.

39. *Lexington Herald*, May 15, 1897.

40. *Acts*, Kentucky General Assembly, 1883-4.

41. *Lexington Press*, June 19, 1887. Authorization for the reinterment was given by the Kentucky General Assembly, *Acts*, Vol. I, May 15, 1886, pp. 273-4. Hart's remains were placed in an honorable space. Governor Proctor Knott introduced Colonel William Beckner who spoke for an hour and a half. In conclusion, P. Wat Hardin read a poem by Rosa Vertner Jefferies.

42. Julia Tevis, *Sixty Years in a School Room, An Autobiography*, pp. 42, 53.

43. *Ibid.*, p. 40.

44. *Ibid.*, pp. 41-57.

45. A. H. Redford, *The History of Methodism in Kentucky*, L, p. 291.

46. *Ibid.*, pp. 40-51.

47. *Ibid.*, p. 42. Redford, History of Methodism, II, 391.

48. Tevis, *Op. Cit.*, pp. 46-49.

49. The "Bush Colony" covered much of the territory surrounding Lower Howard's Creek. Joan E. Brookes-Smith, compiler, *Master Index Virginia Surveys and Grants*, p. 27. Actually most of the Bush lands were absorbed in numerous family subdivisions.

50. Tevis, *Op. Cit.*, pp. 49-50.

51. "Billy" Bush's obsession with the dream of finding Swift's silver mine associates this myth with Clark County, almost every county in eastern Kentucky shares the legend of Swift's silver. Thomas D. Clark, *The Kentucky*, pp. 20-31.

52. Julia A. Tevis was not only kin to many of the earliest Clark County pioneer families, she heard their stories of beginning settlement of the land.

53. *Ibid.*, pp. 54-7.

54. *Ibid.*, pp. 40-3.

55. *Ibid.*, pp. 52-3.

56. *Ibid.*, pp. 257-64, George L. Willis, *History of Shelby County*, Kentucky, pp. 107-8.

57. *Ibid.*, pp. 313-47, Jo Della Alband, "History of Education of Women in Kentucky," an unpublished masters thesis, University of Kentucky, 1934, pp. 46-7.

58. Alband, pp. 46-7.

59. Nellie Adams and Bertha Fox Walton, *Cousins by the Dozens*, pp. 80-1.

60. *Ibid.*

61. *Ibid.*, p. 120, John Wilson Townsend, *Kentucky in American Letters*, II, 172-81. Though Pleasant Jefferson Conkwright was born in Bristow, Oklahoma, he possibly was conceived in Clark County. Datus Smith, Jr. and Herbert S. Bailey, Jr., "Some Personal Recollections of P. J.," Princeton University *Library Chronicle*, LVI, No. 2, Winter 1995, p. 185.

62. Mark Argetsinger, "Harmony Discovered," p. J. Conkwright in the Tradition of Classical

Typography," *Ibid.*, pp. 183-252.

63. Datus Smith, Jr., *Op. Cit.*, p. 189.

64. *Ibid.*

65. Argetsinger, *Op. Cit.*, pp. 197-200.

66. *Ibid.* Illustration of Conkwright designed book titles placed between, pp. 272-93.

67. Princeton University *Library Chronicle*, pp. 300-14.

68. *Report of the Special* Centennial Committee, University of Kentucky, 1965.

69. P. J. Conkwright designed the symbolic statue which was placed in front of the University Medical School, and an imprint which appeared on the University's centennial literature.

70. On the occasions of his visitations in Lexington annually the author had frequent conversations with P. J. Conkwright. He designed three books which I edited, and all three received distinguished graphic arts attention.

71. Argetsinger, *Op. Cit.*, Between pp. 228 and 229, 292-3.

72. John Bakeless, *Daniel Boone Master of the Wilderness*, p. 55, John Mack Faragher,m *Daniel Boone*, p. 83.

73. *Ibid.*

74. This often quoted journal is owned by the Calk Family of Mount Sterling, and Lexington.

75. This informative book was written as a doctoral dissertation. Professor Lester received one of the earliest, if not the earliest doctorate in history from the University of Kentucky.

76. *Transylvania Colony* has a high degree of pertinency to the history of Clark County. Many of the county's early settlers came to the region by way of Boonesborough. Dr. Lester made one of the earliest and most extensive use of the Draper and Durrett collections, p. 282.

77. Goff Bedford in his two volumes, Land of Our Fathers and The Proud Land, dealt in detail with a multiplicity of historical facts, local personalities, and the significance of the communities within a community. The catalog of personal names alone constitute a significant roll call of the human beings once present in Clark County. Using the annalistic approach, these volumes are mines of voluminous information.

78. An all but undiscovered fact by historians is the one that local public records yield an unending stream of information of American public life at the grass roots.

79. *Ibid.*, (*The Proud Land*), p. 614.

80. R. Gerald Alvey, *Kentucky Bluegrass Country* brings into focus the everyday life and times of the region, with specific references to Clark County, passim.

81. *Ibid.*

82. Like the earlier travelers who visited the Bluegrass Region of Kentucky and went away to publish pontifical descriptions of what they saw, Alvey writes with the assurance of a careful researcher and observer.

83. *Ibid.*, pp. 9-15.

84. R. Gerald Alvey, *Homer Ledford man and Craftsman*, p. 168.

85. *Ibid.*, p. 243.

86. *Ibid.*

87. *Ibid.*, p. 30.

88. Paul K. Conklin, *The Southern Agrarians*, p. 14.

89. Joy Bale Boone, "Allen Tate," *The Kentucky Encyclopedia*, p. 867, Conklin, *Op. Cit.*, pp. 14-22.

90. Conklin, pp. 14-22.

91. John Wilson Townsend, Kentucky in American Letters, II, pp. 27-8.

92. Conklin, pp. 57-88.

93. *Ibid.*, pp. 160-4.

94. Townsend, *Op. Cit.*, II, p. 275. Who Was Who in America, 1897-1942, I, 1006.

95. As a newspaper editor, Quisenbury had a better perspective on life about him than did his contemporaries.

96. Though there is no specific reference to Clark County, the background history of the region

which became the Daniel Boone Forest is pertinent to the county. Robert Collins, *A History of the Daniel Boone National Forest*, pp. 1-183.

97. *Ibid.*, p. 281.

98. *Acts*, Kentucky General Assembly, December 27, 1810, pp. 12-15.

99. Anderson Chenault Quisenberry, "A Brief Historical Sketch of the Newspapers of Winchester," p. 1.

100. Lynee Boxly, "History of the Public Library," a brief hand written sketch of the beginnings of the present Winchester Library. The notation is undated.

101. Dr. Martin must have spent almost as much time at his desk writing articles and keeping records of cattle pedigrees and his medical practice accounts he did on his farm than in the practice of medicine. See *Report* of the Commissioner of Patents, (Agriculture, Vol. II, 1853, and 1854, pp. I, 3134, (1854), pp. 14, 115, 126, 186, 190-1.

102. The library's chronology is given in Boxley, *Op. Cit.*, and Jean Ann Kerr, a chronoly, January 24, 1995.

103. Kerr, *Op. Cit.*

104. *Ibid.*

105. Boxley, Kerr.

106. Kerr.

107. Thomas Parvin no doubt had some experience as a printer. His importance, however has caused considerable controversy. W. R. Jillson.

108. George M. Ranck, *History of Lexington*, Kentucky, pp. 233-5.

109. *Ibid.*, p. 234-5.

110. Quisenberry, *Op. Cit.*, 1-14. The History of newspaper publishing in Clark County is a badly disrupted one; a fact reflected in the *Kentucky Union List of Newspapers*.

111. Quisenberry, p. 15.

112. *Ibid.*, p. 16.

113. *Ibid.*, p. 19.

114. *Ibid.*, p. 20.

Chapter XIII
In the Shadow of the Courthouse

1. Repeatedly the Kentucky General Assembly revised and extended the laws pertaining to the counties and their administration. This was also true in relation to the town of Winchester. For almost all of two centuries *Acts* contained generous numbers of local laws. *Acts*, Kentucky General Assembly, 1792-1992.

2. This fact was adequately reflected in the contents of the Clark County Order Books, the recorded proceedings of the town trustees, and subsequently, the Winchester City Council.

3. County officials were from the public ranks, they were readily available to constituents, and had intimate knowledge of the mores, turns of the public mind, and of local needs.

4. Frequently, it is difficult to differentiate purely local legislation from the more general laws, and certainly from the great body of Kentucky statutes.

5. *Ibid.*

6. James R. Robertson, *Petitions of the Early Inhabitants of Kentucky to General Assembly of Virginia*, 1769-1792, Petitions 28, pp. 85-6, 48, pp. 100-110, 49, pp. 110-11.

7. Charles S. Morehead and Mason Brown, *A Digest of the Statute Laws of Kentucky*, I and II, I, 274-509, II, 812-1542.

8. Hubbard Taylor, 1792-1820, was no doubt the most significant personal figure in Clark County. He was a land surveyor and claimant, a legislator, constitutional convention member, a leading figure in politically creating and organizing Clark County. Prior to the creation of Clark County, he served in the Kentucky House of Representatives from Fayette. James McMillan was a founding father and local

political figure. A. Goff Bedford, The Proud Land, Vol. 2, said that by 1800 the McMillan influence had ended, pp. 248-50.

9. Both the Kentucky legislative record and that of Clark County are silent on the kind of preliminary maneuverings prior to the creation of the county. However, the fact that a group of citizens was named in the act gives some considerable insight. *Acts*, Kentucky General Assembly, December, 1792, vol. XIV. (The Taylor Letters, pp. July 9, 1792, pp. 339-40, May 27, 1792, p. 304-7.

10. *Kentucky Gazette*, June 9, 23, 1792.

11. Hubbard Taylor, "Condensed Statement of some of the Occurrences of My Past Life."

12. William T. Hutchinson and William M. E. Rachel, eds., *The Papers of James Madison.*

13. *Ibid.*

14. *Ibid.*

15. By 1840, the laws pertaining to the Kentucky counties had become voluminous, Morehead and Brown, Two Vol., I, 274-425, II, 706-72. The first two Kentucky constitutions were almost silent on the subject of the county. The act of the General Assembly creating Clark County outlined briefly the political structure of the county. Robert Ireland, *The County in Kentucky History*, pp. 1-17.

16. Hubbard Taylor to James Madison.

17. Richard H. Collins, *History of Kentucky*, I, 774.

18. This seemed inferred in Hubbard Taylor's "Condensed Statement."

19. Although the area of Clark County consisted of a sizable slice of eastern Kentucky, the population was concentrated about the projected location of the county seat. The original area was rapidly reduced by the creation of Montgomery County in 1796. Estill in 1808, Powell in 1852. The matter of creating county seats within horseback rides of citizens was often put forth. There were other more pressing matters such as local offices, control of taxes, and the opening of roads and policing.

20. Morehead and Brow, *Op. Cit.*, I, sheriffs, 1453-70, clerks, II, 1158-60, 1373-82, surveyors, II, 102, 53, 1594-99, 1501-4.

21. The presence of at least three streams in the condensed area of Clark County was a significant economic, social, and political fact.

22. There is no documented reference to the size of the Clark County's area of population in 1792.

23. There were various political and personal cross-currents which explained why Strode's Station was not chosen the county seat. No doubt the greater reason was the lack of an adequate water supply.

24. *Acts*, Kentucky General Assembly.

25. Clark County Order Book 1.

26. *Ibid.*, Smith was a land speculator. He owned land on the creek at Little Mount. He and Isaac Davis built a cabin on the future site of Mount Sterling. Richard Ried, Historical Sketches of Mount Sterling, p. 8.

27. Clark County Order Book, 1, December 20, 1792.

28. *Ibid.*

29. *Ibid.*

30. *Ibid.*

30. Nancy O'Malley, Stockading Up: A Study of Pioneer Stations in the Inner Bluegrass, pp. __, Collins, I, 131.

31. Clark County Court Order Book, 1793.

32. *Ibid.*

33. Clark County Will Book 2, The will of James Bodkin, August 8, 1804, pp. 1-4, is a good example of Clark County wills.

34. Morehead and Brown, Vols. I and II, I, pp. 133-83, II, pp. 818-1542. This *Digest* covers the full range of duties of the county court.

35. Hubbard Taylor to James Madison, May 8, 1792, April 16, 1792, The Papers of James Madison, Vol. 14, pp. 218-19, 284. Journal of The First Constitutional Convention of Kentucky, Held in Danville April 2-18, 1792. Lowell H. Harrison, *Kentucky's Road to Statehood*, pp. 94, 111.

36. Taylor to Madison, May 8, 1792.

37. Thomas D. Clark, ed., *Voice of the Frontier*, p. 241, Richard H. Collins, *History of Kentucky*, I, 369, II, 774.

38. Robert S. Cotterill, "James Clark," *Dictionary of American Biography*, IV, 133-4, "Chilton Allen," V, *Biographical Encyclopedia of Kentucky*, p. 149, "Richard Hawes," *Ibid.*, p. 142.

39. Cotterill, *Op. Cit.*, IV, 133-4.

40. *Ibid.*

41. Richard H. Collins, *History of Kentucky*, I, 133, 350, 364.

42. Cotterill, *Op. Cit.*, IV, 133-4.

42. Arnot M. Stickles, *The Critical Court Struggle in Kentucky 1819-1829*, pp. 8-15.

43. *Ibid.*

44. *Acts*, Kentucky General Assembly, December 25, 1820, pp. 185-95, December 5, 1822, pp. 114-26, Samuel M. Wilson, *History of Kentucky*, II, 123-7.

45. L. Ethan Ellis, "Dartmouth College v. Webster, "*Dictionary of American History*," II, 111, Carl Brent Swisher, "McCullough v. Maryland," *Ibid.*, III, 364.

46. Stickles, *Op. Cit.*, pp. 30-9.

47. Cotterill, *Op. Cit.*, IV, 133-4.

48. Richard H. Collin, *Op. Cit.*, II, 774. Victor R. Howard, "James Clark," Lowell H. Harrison, *Kentucky's Governors*, 1792-1985, pp. 4-3.

49. Collins, *Op. Cit.*, I, 41.

50. *Acts*, Kentucky General Assembly, February 16, 1838, pp. 274-83.

51. *Journal*, Kentucky Senate.

52. Cotterill, *Op. Cit.*, IV, 133-4.

53. *Biographical Encyclopedia of Kentucky*, p. 142.

54. *Ibid.*

55. *Ibid.*

56. Harrison, ed., *Kentucky's Governors, 1792-1985*, pp. 71-2. Collins, *Op. Cit.*, I, 774.

57. *Biographical Encyclopedia of Kentucky*, p. 142, Harrison, 71-2.

58. Collins, I, 113, Harrison, Harrison, *Kentucky's Governors*, pp. 71-2.

59. *Biographical Encyclopedia of Kentucky*, p. 142.

60. By 1836, a new generation, this time of native sons, had come on to take active roles in Clark County politics. Over the years political contests and maneuverings became active if not furious affairs.

61. James F. Hopkins and Mary Wilma Hargreaves, eds., *The Papers of Henry Clay*, I, 2-3.

62. *Ibid.*, I, 3.

63. *Kentucky Gazette*, February 28, 1799, Hopkins and Hargreaves, I, 10-14.

64. *Ibid.*, I, 95-6.

65. Robert McNutt McElroy, *Kentucky in the Nation's History*, pp. 224-5. George Dennison Prentice, *Biography of Henry Clay*, pp. 22-25. Collins, *Op. Cit.*, II, 205-6.

66. Kentucky Gazette, August 2, 1798, Hopkins and Hargreaves, eds., *Op. Cit.*, I, 8.

67. A. Goff Bedford, *The Proud Land, A History of Clark County, Kentucky*, p. 164.

68. Melba Porter Hay, ed., *The Papers of Henry Clay*, "candidate," "compromiser," "elder statesman," January 1, 1844, June 29, 1852, Vol. 10, pp. 788-90.

69. *Ibid.*

70. The issue of slavery in Clark County hinges on somewhat limited ownership, on restrictive activities, of slaves, volunteer manumission, and the slave trade. In 1860, there were 6,578 whites and 4,706 slaves. Table No. 48, p. 260, Preliminary Report of the Eighth United States *Census*, 1860.

71. Repeatedly there appeal Martin, Bush, Van Meter, Hart, Duncan, Taylor, Quisenberry, Sudduth, Garner, Simpson, Hanson, et. al.

72. Cotterill, *Op. Cit.*, IV, 133-4.

73. There is a generous listing of these names, and descriptions of many personal activities of this group in A. Goff Bedford, *Op. Cit.*, *passim.*

74. The subject of the actual voting processes in Kentucky history have never been clearly defined

by historians. Under the first constitution Kentucky voters were required to cast paper ballots, under the second voting was viva voce. The australian or secret ballot was first used in 1885 in a Louisville municipal election, Richard H. Stanton, *The Revised Statutes of Kentucky*, I, 430-56. W. E. Connelley and E. Merton Coulter, *History of Kentucky*, I, 476-80.

75. George Caleb Bingham's paintings became popular pieces of western art. George H. Genzmer, "George Caleb Bingham," *Dictionary of American Biography*, II, 274-5.

76. Report of the *Debates and Proceedings of the Convention for the Revision of the Constitution*, pp. 313-14.

77. Adoption of the secret ballot in Louisville led to its adoption for the state of Kentucky as a whole by the Constitution Convention of 1890. *Acts*, Kentucky General Assembly, 1891, 1892, 1893, specifically, June 30, 1892, pp. 114-21.

78. Jasper B. Shannon and Ruth McQuown, *Presidential Politics in Kentucky*, 1824-1948, p. 2.

79. Hopkins and Hargreaves, eds, *Op. Cit.*, from Clark County delegation June 3, 1825, I, 412-13, To Michael Taul et.al, June 7, I, 418-19.

80. Cotterill, "James Clark," *Dictionary of American Biography*, IV, 133-4.

81. Shannon and McQuown, *Op. Cit.*, p. 5.

82. *Ibid.*, p. 8.

83. *Ibid.*, p. 7.

84. *Ibid.*, the Whigs received 83.4 percent of the 1,200 votes cast, p. 14.

85. Democrats 391 votes, Union Party 611, Republican and Lincoln party one vote. *Ibid.*, p. 35.

86. *Ibid.*, pp. 32, 35.

87. *Ibid.*, p. 35.

88. Only 820 Clark County voters cast a ballot out of a potential voter enrollment of 1,714. *Ibid.*, p. 39.

89. *Ibid.*, pp. 37, 39.

90. *Ibid.*, p. 50.

91. The *Lexington Herald*, November 15, 1899.

92. Shannon and McQuown, p. 93.

93. *Ibid.*, p. 96.

94. *Ibid.*, p. 128.

95. William M. Beckner, in contrast to Dr. Andrew Hood in 1849, was exceedingly active in the Constitutional Convention of 1890. See Index, Volume 4, pp. 6086-97, of the published proceedings.

96. *Ibid.*

97. Boswell H. Hodgkin, *Education Bulletin*, XVII, January 1590, *Ibid.*, June, 1949.

98. *Journal*, Kentucky Senate, 1838-9, December 4, 1838, pp. 3-19.

99. The Kentucky General Assembly in 1974 voted to offer an amendment to negate and rewrite the judiciary article of the Kentucky Constitution. The voters approved the amendment in 1975 and it became a part of the Constitution in 1976. Kentucky Revised Statutes annotation, Section 109.

Chapter XIV
Winchester an Emerging City

1. *Acts*, Kentucky General Assembly, February 2, 1882, pp. 60-100.

2. Ordinance Book, Winchester City Council, February 8, 1882, p. 108.

3. *Ibid.*

4. *Ibid.*, February 10, 1882, p. 110.

5. *Ibid.*, May 5, 1882, p. 121.

6. *Ibid.*, February to June, 1882, pp. 86-124.

7. *Ibid.*, p. 152.

8. *Ibid.*, March 12, 1886.

9. *Ibid.*, June 4, 1886, p. 201.

10. *Ibid.*

11. *Ibid.*, December 2, 1886, p. 217.

12. *Ibid.*, December 3, 8, 7, 1886, 1887, pp. 217, 220, 228.

13. *Lexington Transcript*, August 7, 1883, Thomas D. Clark, *A Century of Banking History in the Bluegrass*, p. 6.

14. Ordinance Book, December 3, 1886, p. 217.

15. *Ibid.*, December 3, 1886, p. 218.

16. *Ibid.*, December 7, 1888, p. 297.

17. Winchester's problems with was first discussed, *Ibid.*, September 2, 1887, p. 24.

18. As early as March, 1887, p. 242, J. H. Frazier and N. A. Attergast were appointed a committee of two review proposals for establishing a public water works.

19. *Ibid.*

20. *Ibid.*, June 16, 1888, pp. 275-8.

21. There was considerable discussion in the Lexington Transcript, March 2, 1881, January 19, 1883, and the extension of a line to Winchester, October 14, 1881, and June 14, 1883. Clark, History of Banking, pp. 6-7.

22. William Channing Langdon, "Alexander Graham Bell," Dictionary of American Biography, II, 148-52. Kenneth E. Dawson, The Presidency of Rutherford B. Hayes, pp. 60-1.

23. Lexington Transcript, January 19, 1883.

24. Clark, History of Banking, pp. 6-7.

25. Ordinance Book, May 4, 1894, pp. 537-9.

26. *Ibid.*, p. 537.

27. *Ibid.*, pp. 538-9.

28. *Ibid.*, November 11, 1898, p. 804.

29. *Ibid.*, June 2, 1905, p. 452.

30. The issue of raising sufficient revenue to operate the various public city services was one which constantly haunted the City Council. In the matter of only casual purchases the Council was extremely cautious.

31. Ordinance Book, February 3, 1882, p. 107. Reports, Kentucky Court of Appeals.

32. Ordinance Book, December 2, 1897, p. 719. The final agreement on the bank tax issue resolved a dispute between the Winchester banks and the City Council. Apparently, the agreement was the first typewritten document to be placed on record in the ordinance book.

33. *Ibid.*

34. For many Kentucky mountaineers, Winchester was the first stopping place either for those escaping arrest or as parties. This was especially true in the case of the Hargis-Cockrill feuding in Breathitt County. Thomas D. Clark, *Kentucky Land of Contrast*, pp. 207-33.

35. Ordinance Book, 4, 1901, pp. 113-4.

36. The dates pertaining to the electrical, street car, water and ice-making facilities are numerous. Perhaps the key one was the agreement reached on October 4, 1901 when E. S. Jouett and J. M. Benton appeared before a called meeting of the council to intercede for their clients from Wilkes-Barre, Pennsylvania. Ordinance Book, pp. 113-4.

37. Holbrook and Pickrell were awarded the contract on October 12, 1901 to erect the light poles and to furnish electric current to both private and public customers. *Ibid.* October 12, 1901, pp. 119-124. In this instance, the action of the council appears confusing.

38. *Ibid.*, July 13, 1902, p. 151.

39. *Ibid.*, July 23, 1906, pp. 582-94.

40. *Ibid.*, April 4, 1902, pp. 175-6.

41. *Ibid.*, March 22, 1905, p. 420.

42. *Ibid.*, October 22, 1904, p. 381.

43. *Ibid.*, pp. 381-3.

44. *Ibid.*, p. 387.

45. *Ibid.*, October 15, 1909, p. 136. May 24, 1910, pp. 252-3.

46. *Ibid.*, May 29, 1910, pp. 252-3, pp. 252-3.

47. *Ibid.*, p. 253.

48. This ordinance pertaining to the use of carriages and the automobile on Winchester streets was detailed and by modern city traffic standards quaint. *Ibid.*, May 24, 1910, pp. 241-44. May 20, 1910, pp. 256-8.

49. *Ibid.*, January 1, 1913, p. 651.

50. *Ibid.*, June 2, 1905, p. 463.

51. *Ibid.*, December 16, 1912, 651.

52. *Winchester Sun*, "History II," September 9, 1978, p. 5.

53. Ordinance Book, November ?, 1909, pp. 85-6.

54. *Ibid.*, May 6, 1910, p. 241.

55. *Ibid.*, 245-6.

56. *Acts*, Kentucky General Assembly, March 11, 1912, pp. 96-100.

57. *United State Statutes-at-Large*, XXXIX, part I, pp. 155-9.

58. Ordinance Book, July 23, 1906, p. 583.

59. William M. Beckner, *Hand-Book of Clark County and the City of Winchester*, pp. 18-9, 27.

60. By the time the legalistic maneuverings were ended the automobile ushered in a new means of interurban travel.

61. Ordinance Book, September 7, 1906, p. 611.

62. *Ibid.*

63. William Axton, *Tobacco and Kentucky*, pp. 102-9, William E. Connalley and E. Merton Coulter, *History of Kentucky*, II, 1182-5.64. Good roads, the automobile and motor truck, the arrival of chain stores, the rise of industrial employment, the shrinking of numbers of family farms - all these things wrought significant changes on both Winchester and Clark County. The limits of the city were extended far beyond anything the City Council could have conceived in 1900. Even Strode's Station became an urban enclosure.

64. Good roads, the automobile and motor truck, the arrival of chain stores, the rise of industrial employment, the shrinking of numbers of family farms - all these things wrought significant changes on both Winchester and Clark County. The limits of the city were extended far beyond anything the City Council could have considered in 1900. Even Strode's Station became an urban enclosure.

65. By 1990, the population scales had tipped heavily in favor of Winchester. Clark County had a population 29,496 and Winchester had 15,799. General population characteristics of Kentucky, U. S. *21st census*, June 1992, Table I, pp. 1.

66. This fact is eloquently reflected in the periodic publication of economic data by the Chamber of Commerce and the Agricultural and Industrial Board of Kentucky.

67. The act of 1912 was little more than a provision for the appointment of an engineer to gather technical information and design some arterial roads. *Acts*, Kentucky General Assembly, March 11, 1912, pp. 96-100.

68. *United States Statutes-at-Large*, XXXIX, part I, D L4.

69. This configuration is reflected on the face of the General Highway Map of Clark County, prepared by the Transportation Office of Transportation Planning in cooperation with the United States Department of Transportation Federal Highway Administration.

70. George W. Robinson, Jr., *The Public Papers of Governor Bert T. Combs*, "Address in Winchester," March 23, 1860, pp. 483-4.

71. Carolyn Sledd possessed a sizable collection of Taylor-Prewitt family photographs, *Winchester Sun*, September 9, 1978, "History II, "Arts," p. 7, "History" II, 3, "Schools/Churches," p. 10.

72. William M. Beckner, *Handbook*, pp. 1-19.

73. *Winchester Sun*, September 9, 1907, "Three Women Served herein Full Time Offices, "History" II, p. 6.

74. *Ibid.*

Chapter XV
The Hand of Mars

1. Samuel M. Wilson, *Catalogue of Revolutionary War Soldiers and Sailors, Commonwealth of Virginia Surveys and Warrants 1774-1791*, pp. 27, 93, 204, 219.

2. James A. James, *The Life of George Rogers Clark*, James, ed. *George Rogers Clark Papers* (8 Vol.)

3. James, *Life of George Rogers Clark*, pp. 109-46; *Kentucky Gazette*, October 27, 1826.

4. Joan E. Brookes-Smith, comp., *Master Index Virginia Surveys and Grants, 1774-1791*, passim. Wilson, *Catalogue*, pp. 190-272.

5. Brookes-Smith, pp. 204, 27, 219, 93.

6. Richard Bean, John Bean, 1766-1849, of Clark County Kentucky. His Story and His Descendants (unpublished mss.), pp. 20-1.

7. J. Stoddart Johnston, ed. *First Explorations of Kentucky, Journals of Dr. Thomas Walker, 1750, and Christopher Gist, 1751*. W. J. Ghent, Christopher Gist," *Dictionary of American Biography*, VII, pp. 223-4. Samuel Coles Williams, "The Father of Sequoia.

8. Nathaniel Gist, "*The Chronicles of Oklahoma*, XV, March 1937, pp. 1-2.

9. J. Stoddard Johnston, ed., *First Explorations of Kentucky. Journals of Dr. Thomas Walker and Christopher Gist. passim.

10. Stanley Pargellis, "Braddock's Defeat," *American Historical Review*, Vol. 31, October-July, 1935-6, pp. 253-69. Williams, Father of Sequoia," p. 5.

11. Williams, p. 9. Albert V. Goodpasture, "The Paternity of Sequoya, the Inventor of the Cherokee Alphabet," *Chronicles of Oklahoma*, pp. 124-5.

12. Goodpasture, p. 126.

13. *Ibid.*, p. 129.

14. Williams, "The Father," p. 9.

15. *Ibid.*

16. *Ibid.*, p. 10.

17. *Ibid.*

18. *Ibid.*

19. Goodpasture, "The Paternity of Sequoia," p. 586.

20. Wilson, *Catalogue of Revolutionary War Soldiers and Sailors*, p. 218.

21. Benjamin Sharpe, "Nathaniel Gist," *The American Pioneer*, I, pp. 237-8. John D. Gillespie, Christopher Gist of Maryland and some of his descendants, typescript, Owen Scrap Book, p. 35.

22. *Ibid.*, p. 37.

23. Lyman Draper interview with James Taylor.

24. W. J. Ghent, "Christopher Gist," 1706-1759, *Dictionary of American Biography*, VII, pp. 323-22.

25. Sequoia stopped in Lexington briefly, perhaps only a day, when he was on his way to Washington as an envoy from the Cherokees, Ghent, "Sequoia," *Dictionary of American Biography*, XVI, 586, Len Cobb, in an unidentified Winchester Sun, Owen Scrap Book.

26. "Clark County Chronicles," *Winchester Sun*, January 4, 1922. Gist Family Genealogical Table, Owen Scrap Book.

27. John D. Gillespie, "Christopher Gist of Maryland," Typescript. Owen Scrapbook.

28. "Clark County Chronicles," December 28, 1922, W. E. Smith, "F. P. Blair," *Dictionary of American Biography*, II, pp. 330-332.

29. Wilson, *Land Bounty Grants*, p. 218, says Gist received 6,666-2/3 acres in bounty grants, "Chronicles of Clark County," December 28, 1922.

30. Nathaniel Gist claimed land bounties for service in both the French and Indian War and the American Revolution.

31. 1784, estimated 30,000, 1788, 62,000, 1792, 74, 677. Lowell H. Harrison, *Kentucky's Road to Statehood*, pp. 8, 24, 91. Richard H. Collins, *History of Kentucky*, I, p. 22.

32. Thomas D. Clark, ed., *Voice of the Frontier*, pp. 109-10. James Robertson, *Petitions of the Early Inhabitants of Kentucky to the General Assembly of Virginia*, Petit. 5, p. 42.

33. *The Kentucky Gazette*, October 8, 12, 1791, March 17, 1792.

34. *The Kentucky Gazette*, January 25, 1791. "Report of Brig. Gen. Scott, June 28, 1791, "*Am. State Papers*, (Indian Affairs) Vol. 4, pp. 131-32.

35. William Littell, *Political Transactions*, p. 104.

36. Clark, *Voice of the Frontier*, p. 149, Littell, "Appendix" XXVII, pp. 60-1.

37. Littell, "Appendix" XXVII, p. 117.

38. *Ibid.*

39. This was true for a large segment of the Clark County pioneers, and especially for those who came from around Winchester, Virginia, and from Maryland and Pennsylvania.

40. Population increase, 1784, 30, 000; 1792, 73, 677.

41. Littell, *Political Transactions*, p. 35, *Kentucky Gazette* December 3, 1789. Humphrey Marshall, *History of Kentucky*, I, 357, 363-76.

42. "Harry Innes to Mj. Gen. Knox," July 7, 1790. Littell, *Political Transactions*, XXIII, 118, Charles G. Talbert, *Benjamin Logan*, pp. 246-252. Jacob Burnet, *Notes on the Early Settlement of the Northwestern Territory*, 88-93.

43. Clark, *Voice of the Frontier*, pp. 132-5, Littell, *Political Transactions*, Appendix XXII, XXIII, XXIV, pp. 114-16.

44. Burnet, *Notes*, p. 102.

45. *Ibid.*

46. *Kentucky Gazette*, March 14, 1790, *American State Papers* (Indian Affairs), Vol. 4, pp. 197-88. Burnet, *Notes*, pp. 105-7.

47. Marshall, *History*, I, p. 358.

48. *Lexington Reporter*, June 25, 1791, *Kentucky Gazette*, July 16, 1791. Burnet, *Notes*, pp. 115-16.

49. *Kentucky Gazette*, July 10, December 10, October 6, 1791. Marshall, *History*, I, pp. 358-9.

50. Burnet, *Notes*, p. 128.

51. Metcalfe, *Indian Wars*, pp. 144-45, Clark, *Voice*, pp. 156-63. Burnet, *Notes*, pp. 132-3.

52. *Kentucky Gazette*, October 5, 1793, *Am. State Papers* (Indian Affairs), Vol. 4, p. 359. Clark, *Voice*, pp. 202-3, Burnet, *Notes*, pp. 132-3, pp. 155-82.

53. Clark, *Voice*, pp. 318-31, *Kentucky Gazette*, July 11, 1875.

54. Wilson, "Charles Scott," *Dictionary of the American Biography*, XVI, p. 487. Clark, *Voice*, pp. 149-50.

55. Samuel M. Wilson, Yearbook of the Society of the Society sons of the Revolution, pp. 124-30.

56. Wilson, *Dictionary of American Biography*, XVI, p. 487. An unidentified periodical page, Owen Scrap Book, entitled, "Mrs. Benjamin Gratz."

57. *Acts*, Kentucky General Assembly, Resolution 14, March 10, 1854, p. 192.

58. Article VI.

59. Second Kentucky Constitution, Art. 3, Sec. 28-30. Richard G. Stone, *A Brittle Sword*, pp. 24-39, Burnet, *Notes*, pp. 102-4.

60. Joseph Thacker, M. A. Thesis, "The Kentucky Militia, 1792-1812, University of Kentucky, 1947. Glenn Clift, Cornstalk Militia.

61. *Kentucky Gazette*, January 4, 1828. Clark, *Voice*, pp. 220-26, January 2, 9, 1829.

62. Lowell H. Harrison, *John Breckinridge, Jeffersonian Republican*, p. 166.

63. *Ibid.*

64. Thomas D. Clark and John D. W. Guice, *Frontier in Conflict*, pp. 2, 42.

65. Britain in the Northwest, France and Spain in the Old Southwest and the Mississippi River.

66. First Kentucky Constitution, Article VII, C. S. Morehead and Mason Brown, *A Digest of the Statute Laws of Kentucky*, II, pp. 1147-97.

67. E. M. Coulter and W. E. Connelley, *History of Kentucky*, I, pp. 547-51, Robert M. McElroy, *Kentucky in the Nation's History*, pp. 315-20.

68. *Lexington Reporter*, June 21, 1808, *Kentucky Gazette*, June 21, 1808.

69. James F. Hopkins and Mary Wilma Hargraves, "Henry Clay to Thomas Hart Clay, January 4, 1809, "*The Papers of Henry Clay*, I, pp. 398-9.

70. Robert Remini, *Henry Clay, Statesman of the Union*, p. 58.

71. *Annals of Congress*, 11th Congress, 3rd session, pp. 55-64. *Niles Weekly Register*, I, pp. 357-8.

72. Bennett Young, *Battle of the Thames, Roster of Volunteers*, pp. 211-269. Coulter and Connelley, *History of Kentucky*, II, pp. 547-8.

73. McElroy, *Kentucky in the Nation's History*, pp. 332-36, Mann Butler, *History of Kentucky*, p. 343.

74. Marshall, *History of Kentucky*, II, Acid comment on Governor Harrison, pp. 518-21, *Niles Weekly Register*, 2, p. 108.

75. Dorothy Burne Goebel, *William Henry Harrison, A Political Biography*, pp. 106-8, "William Henry Harrison," *Dictionary of American Biography*, VIII, pp. 347-8.

76. Dorothy Burne Goebel, *William Henry Harrison, A Political Biography*, pp. 106-108, Katherine E. Crane, "Tecumseh," *Dictionary of American Biography*, XVIII, pp. 358-60, Alfred Pirtle, *The Battle of Tippecanoe*, pp. 11-15.

77. Crane, *Op. Cit.*, p. 359.

78. Clark and Guice, *Frontiers in Conflict*, pp. 124-26. Pirtle, *Op. Cit.*, p. 15, Marshall, *History of Kentucky*, II, pp. 437-8.

79. Pirtle, *Op. Cit.*, pp. 51-62. Goebel, *Op. Cit.*, p. 124.

80. Marshall, *Op. Cit.*, II, pp. 494-522.

81. *United States Statutes at Large*, June 18, 1812, J. Richardson, *A Compilation of the Messages and Papers of the Presidents*, I, pp. 512, 545.

82. *Ibid.*, I. pp. 491, 544, 586.

83. Collins, *History of Kentucky*, I, 27; *Niles Weekly Register, Kentucky Gazette*, September 1, 1812.

84. Coulter and Connelley, *History of Kentucky*, I, pp. 552-3.

85. Mahon, *Op. Cit.*, pp. 31-42.

86. *The Kentucky Gazette*, May 26, 1812, *The Reporter*, May 23, 1812.

87. John K. Mahon, *The War of 1812*, pp. 158-65, Coulter and Connelly, *History of Kentucky*, I, p. 559.

88. Coulter and Connelley, *Op. Cit.*, I, p. 556.

89. *Kentucky Gazette*, August 23, September 7, 1812, *The Reporter*, August 15, 22, 29, 1812.

90. *Report of the Adjutant General of the State of Kentucky*, "Soldiers in the War of 1812," pp. 126, 220, 306, 360, Isaac Cunningham's Mounted Volunteers," 12021, Typed company roster, Kathryn Owen Scrap Book, p. 56.

91. Stephen, son of John Strode, was in the battle of the Raisin. Owen, Scrap Book, p. 56. Adjutant General *Report*, various company rosters.

92. *Ibid.*

93. Adjutant General *Report*, "War of 1812," p. 220.

94. "Clark County Chronicles," October 25, 1923.

95. *Acts*, Kentucky General Assembly, 1913, Resolution, p. 109.

96. Collins, *History*, I, 27, Mahon, *War of 1812*, pp. 177-79, McElroy, *Kentucky in the National History*, p. 346.

97. *Kentucky Gazette*, October 12, 1813. *Lexington Reporter*, October 23, 1813.

98. *Gazette*, October 12, 1813, *Lexington Reporter*, October 23, 1815, Mahon, *Op. Cit.*, pp. 172-75.

99. Bennett H. Young, *Battle of the Thames*, pp. 75-83, "Forlorn Hope," p. 84, "Death of Tecumseh, pp. 87-93, *Kentucky Gazette*, October 13, November 1, 8, 1813.

100. Young, *Battle of Thames*, "Forlorn Hope," 84, death of Tecumseh, pp. 89-93.

101. *Lexington Reporter*, February 6, 1813, *Kentucky Gazette*, February 2, 1813.

102. Claims made on parts of Canada, *Kentucky Gazette*, October 21, 1813. November 8, 1813.

103. Leland W. Meyer, *Richard M. Johnson*, p. 129, Thomas Perkins Abernethy, "Richard Mentor

Johnson," *Dictionary of American Biography*, X, pp. 114-16.

104. Katherine Elizabeth Crane, "Tecumseh," *Dictionary of American Biography*, XVIII, pp. 358-60.

105. McMahon, *Op. Cit.*, pp. 381-86.

106. Collins, *History of Kentucky*, I, 27.

107. *Report* of Adjutant General of the State of Kentucky, pp. 126, 220, 366, *Military History of Kentucky*, Clark County sent 11 companies to the War of 1812, p. 80.

108. United States 3rd *Census*, 1820.

109. Shannon and McQuown, *Presidential Politics*, p. 18.

110. Though many Clark County volunteers fought in the Mexican War, the home scene remained quiet.

111. J. G. Massey, acting secretary of war, to Governor William Owsley, October 27, 1847. Owsley Papers, Kentucky State Archives, Frankfort.

112. Otis A. Singletary, *The Mexican War*, pp. 31-2, 51, Robert S. Henry, *The Story of the Mexican War*, pp. 60-5.

113. J. D. Richardson, *Messages and Papers of the Presidents*, IV, pp. 437-43, Henry, *Op. Cit.*, pp. 51-2.

114. J. Stoddard Johnson, *Memorial History of Louisville*, I, 220088. This volume contains Ernest McPherson, "History of the Louisville Legion.

115. *Ibid.*, p. 150.

116. *Report* of the Adjutant State of Kentucky, "Mexican War Veterans, pp. 150-7.

117. *Biographical History of Congress*, p. _, *Biographical Encyclopedia of Kentucky*, p. 177.

118. *Lexington Observer and Reporter*, May 17, 1847. Henry, *Op. Cit.*, 294-5.

119. Charles L. Dufours, *The Mexican War, A Compact History*, 1846-48, pp. 217-224, Singletary, *Op. Cit.*, pp. 80, 96, 133.

120. J. Frost, *The Mexican War and Its Warriors*, pp. 163-7, Henry, *Op. Cit.*, 283-4.

121. Henry, p. 287, Singletary, pp. 76-82.

122. *Ibid.*

123. *Lexington Observer and Reporter*, May 12, 1847, Henry, *Op. Cit.*, pp. 307-9, Singletary, *Op. Cit.*, pp. 102-17.

124. *Lexington Observer and Report*, May 12, 1847, *Biographical Encyclopedia of Kentucky*, p. 177. Owen Scrap Book, p. 58.

125. *Report* of the Adjutant General of the State of Kentucky, "Mexican War Veterans," p. 150.

126. May 17, 1847.

127. Lyles was a private, Adjutant Report, p. 152.

128. *Kentucky State Documents*, Collins, *History*, I, p. 54.

129. Basil W. Duke, *Reminiscences of General Basil W. Duke*, C. S. A.

130. *Ibid.*, pp. 141-42.

131. Shannon and McQuown, *Presidential Elections*, p. 35.

132. *Biographical Encyclopedia of Kentucky*, pp. 557-8.

133. Historically there was an iron works in Clark County,m but it was hardly of military significance.

134. J. Winston Coleman, *Steamboats on the Kentucky River*, pp. 24-31, Mary Verhoeff, *The Kentucky River Navigation*, pp. 102-9.

135. Thomas D. Clark, *Historic Maps of Kentucky*, Map 6. H. S. Tanner, A New Map of Kentucky, Map 7, John Bertholomew, *Kentucky and Tennessee. An Accompaniment to Mitchell's References and Distances Map of the United States*, p. 297.

136. Attempts were made by General Felix Zollicoffer, Kirby-Smith, John Hunt Morgan, and Braxton Bragg.

137. Thomas D. Clark, *A History of Laurel County*, pp. 211-219.

138. Cecil F. Holland, *Morgan and His Raiders*, pp. 132-58.

139. Joseph Park, *General Edmund Kirby-Smith*, p. 612.

140. Lowell H. Harrison, *The Civil War in Kentucky*, pp. 43-57.

141. Captain John C. Creed, Scott's Raid, First of a series on the Civil War and Events in Clark County, an unidentified newspaper clipping (Winchester Sub.), Owen Scrap Book, p. 68.

142. *Official Record, War of the Rebellion*, XVI, pp. 990-1.

143. Ed Porter Thompson, *History of the Orphan Brigade*, pp. 329, 563, 691, Duke, *Reminiscences*, p. 286.

144. *Battles and Leaders of the Civil War*, IV, pp. 476-7, Thompson, *Op. Cit., p. 563.*

145. Thompson, *Op. Cit.*, pp. 375-80, *Battles and Leaders*, III, pp. 630-31.

146. Thompson, *Op. Cit.*, p. 279.

147. *Ibid.*

148. Duke, *Reminiscences*, p. 138.

149. Thompson, pp. 155-158.

150. Holland, *Morgan and His Raiders*, pp. 247-58, Owen, Scrap Book, p. 65.

151. Owen, *Op. Cit.*, p. 69.

152. Owen, *Op. Cit.*, p. 63.

153. Harrison, *Op. Cit.*, pp. 94-5. H. M. Coulter, *Civil War and Readjustment in Kentucky*, p. 295.

154. *Ibid.*, "Clark County Civil War Soldiers," p. 60.

155. *Ibid.*, p. 62.

156. *Biographical Encyclopedia of Kentucky*, p. 413.

157. Owen, *Op. Cit.*, "Civil War Days," Captain John Creed, "Scott's Raid in Clark County," Published in *Winchester Sun*, February 8, 1906.

158. Holland, *Op. Cit.*, p. 322.

159. *Ibid.*, p. 321. Howard Swiggett, *The Rebel Raider*, pp. 252-55.

160. Holland, *Op. Cit.*, pp. 321-22. Swiggett, *Op. Cit.*, pp. 253-4.

161. *Official Record*, Sec. I, Vol. XXIX, 1, 77. Holland, *Op. Cit.*, p. 322.

162. Holland, *Op. Cit.*, p. 323.

163. "Civil War Days in Clark County, Wade's Mill Area, *Winchester Sun*, August 21, 1923.

164. *Ibid.*

165. The war brought the end of slavery. The opening of the western live stock ranges, and the industrialization of the country all had a bearing on Clark County's future.

166. Frank Monoghan, "Centennial Exposition, Philadelphia," *Dictionary of American History*, I, p. 333.

167. *Eleventh Census* of the United States, Part I, (Population), XXVII-VIII.

168. Monoghan, *Op. Cit.*

169. Frederick L. Paxson, "William McKinley," *Dictionary of American Biography*, XII, pp. 105-9. Walter B. Norris, "Destruction of the *Maine, Dictionary of American History*, III, p. 327. H. S. and M. G. Merill, *The Republican Command, 1897-1913*, pp. 485-4.

170. *The Oxford Companion to History*, p. 884. Theodore Gronert, "Yellow Journalism, "*Dictionary of American History*, V, p. 505.

171. Company C, 2nd Regiment of Infantry was made up largely of Clark County volunteers (82), *Report* of the Adjutant General of the State of Kentucky (War with Spain), pp. 54-6.

172. Hughes, Shaeffer, and Williams, *That Kentucky Campaign*, Passim, James Klotter, *William Goebel, The Politics of Wrath*, John Ed Pearce, *Days of Darkness*, pp. 98-9, Thomas D. Clark, *Kentucky, Land of Contrast*, pp. 213-33.

173. In 1916, Clark County had a heavy turn out at the polls. 83.5 of the enrolled voters voted, giving Woodrow Wilson a 59.7 majority.

174. James Morgan Reed, *Atrocity Propaganda, 1914-1919*, pp. 32-50, H. C. Peterson, Propaganda for War, pp. 58-68.

175. *Public Laws, The Statutes at Large of the United States of America*, Vol. 40, Pt. I, p. 425, *Winchester Sun*, August 7, 1917.

176. *Winchester Sun*, April 2, 1917.

177. *Ibid.*, April 3, 1917.

178. *Ibid.*, April 2, 1917.

179. *Ibid.*, April 23, 1917.

180. *Ibid.*, May 9, 1917.

181. *Ibid.*, May 12, 1917.

182. *Ibid.*, July 2, 1918.

183. *Ibid.*, July 1, 1918.

184. *Ibid.*

185. *Winchester Sun*, 1917-18. passim.

186. *Winchester Sun*, November 11, 1918.

187. *Ibid.*

188. *Ibid.*, November 12, 1918.

189. *Ibid.*, November 5, 1918.

190. *Ibid.*, November 7, 1918.

191. Veterans returning home to Clark County at war's end brought with them new world, political and social perspectives. While they were away at war there occurred prohibition, the rise of political power of women, the introduction of a chemical era, and of new machines of all sorts.

192. Farm production underwent changes in the use of high grade fertilizers and the increased use of tobacco, especially in cigarettes.

193. J. Allan Smith, *College of Agriculture University of Kentucky Early and Middle Years, 1865-1951*, pp. 148-57.

194. "Veterans' Benefits," *United States Statues-at-Large*, XLII, Pt. I, Title I, pp. 147-58.

195. Address to Congress, January 8, 1918, J. B. Scott, ed., *Official Statement of War Aims.*

196. Sidney B. Fay, *The Origins of the World War*, pp. 32-49, Bernadotte Schmidt, *The Coming of the War*, IV, pp. 257-308.

197. Coulter and Connelley, *History of Kentucky*, II, pp. 177-87, W. E. Axton, *Tobacco in Kentucky*, pp. 101-6.

198. Order Books, Clark County Court, 1920- Minuyes Winchester City Council, Ordinance books, 1920-

199. In the presidential campaign of 1920, Warren C. Harding said, "America's present need is not heroics, but healing; not nostrums, but normalcy... ."

200. Shannon and McQuown, *Presidential Elections*, pp. 98. 107.

201.

202. *The New York Times*, September 1, 1939, Johnson, ed., Oxford Companion to American History, p. 575.

203. Samuel Eliot Morrison, *The Two Ocean War, A Short History of the United States Navy in the Second World War*, pp. 26-45.

204. Morrison, *Op. Cit.*, pp. 46-76, *Winchester Sun*, December 8, 1941.

205.

206. Morrison, *The Two Ocean War*, pp. 35-8.

207. *Winchester Sun*, December 8, 1941.

208. *Winchester Sun*, December 8, 1941.

209.

210. *United States Statutes at Large*, Chapter 564, Vol. 55, 1041-42, December 11, 1941, Part I, pp. 796-7.

211.

212. *Winchester Sun*, December 8, 1941.

213. *Ibid.*

214. *Ibid.*, December 16, 1941.

215. *Ibid.*

216. *Ibid.*, July 26, 1941.

217. *Ibid.*

218. *Ibid.*, December 16, 1941.

219. *Winchester Sun,* December 13, 1944.

220. December 13, 1941.

221. *Ibid.*, January 1, 1942.

222. *Ibid.*

223. *Ibid.*, May 8, 1945.

224. *Ibid.*

225. *Ibid.*

226. Morrison, *The Two-Ocean War,* pp. 570-75.

227. *Kentucky in World War I.* 1917-1918, Vol. I, 50. World War II data compiled by Fred B. Caldwell. *Fatalities in World War II for Clark County,* 71. Kentucky Department of Military Affairs, Military Records, and Research, Frankfort.

Chapter XVI
The New Industrial Frontier

1. From the beginning of settlement, the people of Clark County were dependent on their timber resource. In later years, the great mill of Burke and Brabbitt produced a phenomenal amount of lumber. Ford became the destination of the mountain log runs. Burke and Brabbitt Papers, Special Collection, University of Kentucky. There are no specific statistics on Clark County lumber. Kentucky in 1880 produced 305,680,000 board feet. In 1900, 420,820,000; in 1920, 765,968,000. *Statistical Abstract, U. S. Census,* 1920, Table 168, p. 252.

2. Robert Watt, *Kentucky Utilities Company,* p. 9.

3. *Ibid.*

4. The Belknap Hardware Catalogs, Louisville, 1900-1940, passim. Electricity and Service, pp. 10-11, *Winchester Sun,* September 9, 1978, "Progress," p. 6.

5. *United States Statutes-at-Large,* March, 1933-June, 1934, XLVIII, p. 58-68.

6. *Ibid.* _____Thomas D. Clark, *The Emerging South,* p. 66.

7. The Southern States, Fertilizer Division, was established in Winchester in 1948. *Resources for Economic Development,* 1990, p. 11.

8. *United States Statutes at Large*

9. *Abstract United States Census,* 1935.

10. In 1956, 95.9 of the homes in Clark County had available electricity. *Statistical Abstract Supplement, County and City Data Book,* Table 2, p. 127.

11. *United States Statutes.*

12. Electricity and Service, p. 22, *Winchester Sun,* "Progress," September 9, 1978, p. 6.

13. After a bitter court struggle with the Kentucky Utilities Company, The Kentucky Public Service Commission granted a certificate of convenience to the East Kentucky Power, *Electric Service,* p. 29.

14. *Ibid.*

15. *Ibid.*, Chapter 5, pp. 27-30.

16. *Ibid.*, Chapter 6, pp. 31-44, Thomas D. Clark, *The Emerging South,* pp. 96-101.

17. *Acts,* Kentucky General Assembly, March 18, 1912, pp. 114-6. *United States Statutes-at-Large,* XXXIX, pt. I, pp. 355-9. Vol. 68, May 6, 1954, pp. 72-3, June 29, 1956, Vol. 70, pp. 734-31.

18. Thomas D. Clark, *The Greening of the South,* pp.

19. *U. S. Statute-at-Large,* May 6, 1954, Vol. 68, pp. 72-3, Vol. 70, June 29, 1956, pp. 734-87.

20. George W. Robinson, ed., *The Public Papers of Bert T. Combs,* March 5, 1963, November 1, 1963, pp. 369-74, pp. 483-4.

21. *Winchester Sun,* "Progress," September 19, 1978, p. 2.

22. *Ibid.*

23. *Acts,* Kentucky General Assembly, March 11, 1912, pp. 90-100.

24. *Winchester Sun*, "Progress," September 9, 1978, p. 2.

25. *Ibid.*, p. 7.

26. *Ibid.*

27. *Ibid.*, pp. 2, 7.

28. *United States 21st Census*, (population), Table 1, Kentucky, p. 4.

29. *Ibid.*, "Selected Social Characteristics, Table I, Kentucky, p. 4.

30. *Ibid.*

31. *Ibid.*

32. *Ibid.*, Table 57, Summary of Economic Characteristics, p. 57.

33. *Resources for Economic Development*, Winchester, Kentucky, 1990, pp. 10-11.

34. *Ibid.*

35. *Ibid.*, p. 12.

36. *Ibid.*, pp. 36-7.

37. *United States 20th Census*, 1880, "Race by Sex," Kentucky, pp. 928.

38. *Ibid.*, "Selective Social Characteristics, Table I, Kentucky, p. 4.

39. In this era the family farms were shrinking in number, the stripping of Bluegrass seed waned, tobacco faced an uncertain future largely because of the reduced acreage for small farmers.

40. Thomas D. Clark, *A Century of Banking History in the Blue Grass*, pp. 69-84. Banks in Louisville and Lexington were conservative in their loan policies. State law also restricted banking to county limits.

41. *United States Statutes-at-Large*, March 3, 1865, XIII, p. 486.

42. Donald L. Kemmerer, "Banking," *Dictionary of American History*, I, 156-8.

43. *Winchester Sun*, September 9, 1978, "Progress," p. 5.

44. *United States Statute-at-Large*, March 3, 1865, XII, p. 486.

45. *Ibid.*

46. W. E. Beckner,

47. *Winchester Sun*, September 9, 1978, "Progress," p. 5.

48. *Ibid.*, p. 15.

49. Beckner, *Op. Cit.*,

50. *Winchester Sun*, September 9, 1978, back page advertisement, "Heritage,", p. 13.

51. *Seventh Annual Report*, Kentucky Banking Commissioner, June 30, 1982, p. 22.

52. *Ibid.*

53. *Ibid.*

54. *First Annual Report*, Kentucky Banking Commissioner, 1913, p. 156.

55. *Ibid.*, *Winchester Sun*, "Progress," September 9, 1978, p. 5.

56. In the era after World War I there was a strong drive in Kentucky to attract industries to the region. This was characteristic of the entire South. James C. Cobb, *Industrialization & Southern Society*, 1877-1984, pp. 27-50, Thomas D. Clark, *The Emerging South*, pp. 104-23.

57. *Winchester Sun*, "Industry," September 9, 1978, pp. 4, 8.

58. *Ibid.*

59. *Ibid.*, p. 4.

60. *Ibid.*, p. 8.

61. *Ibid.*, pp. 5-7.

62. *Ibid.*, "Industry," p. 4.

63. *Ibid.*

64. *Ibid.*, p. 8.

65. *Ibid.*

66. *Ibid.*, "Industry," p. 6.

67. *Ibid.*

68. *Ibid.*, "Industry," p. 10.

69. *Resources for Economic Development*, 1983, p. 7, (1969), p. 5. Letter to the author from Betty

Berryman, January 24, 1995.

70. Berryman to Clark, January 24, 1995.

71. *Winchester Sun,* September 9, 1978, "Progress," p. 3, "Industry," p. 2, *Resources for Economic Development,* 1994, p. 10.

72. *Ibid.*

73. *Ibid.,* 1993, p. 11.

74. The issue of *Resources for Economic Development, Winchester, Kentucky,* 1993, gives a rather full profile of industrial progress in Winchester and Clark County up to 1993.

75. *Ibid.,* p. 12.

76. *Ibid.,* June 1961, pp. 3-7.

77. *Ibid.,* p. 4.

78. *Ibid.*

79. *United States 18th and 19th Census Reports.* In 1980 the Bureau of the Census presented a rather full detailed report on the human resources in Clark County, Tables 1, *Selected Social Characteristics,* 1990, Kentucky, Table 16, Table 58.

80. *Industrial Resources,* June 1961, pp. 3-7.

81. *Ibid.,* pp. 5-6.

82. Family farms were reduced in number, and industrial employment was on the rise annually. The Winchester Chamber of Commerce published a community profile in 1994 which was highly reflective of changes.

Bibliography

Federal Documents

American State Papers, Indian Affairs, 1789-1815, Vols., I & II, Washington, D.C., 1932.
Biographical Directory of the United States Congress, 1771-1989, Washington, D.C., 1989.
Harrodsburg Quadrangle Map, U.S. Geological Survey, Reston, Va., 1991
Kappler, Charles J. *Laws and Treaties,* Vols., I & II, Washington, D.C., 1904.
United States Census, 1790-1990, Washington, D.C.
Census of Agriculture, 1840-1987, Washington, D.C.
1978 Census Maps of Lexington-Fayette Metropolitan Area, Series 4280, Washington, D.C., 1980.
Reports of the Commissioners of Agriculture 1853-1870, Washington, D.C., 1854-1871.
Slave Census, 1830-1860, Washington, D.C.
Special Report on the History and Present Conditions of the Sheep Industry in the United States, Washington, D.C., 1892.
Stillman, Richard P. *The U.S. Sheep Industry,* Washington, D.C., 1990.
Report of the Commissioner of Patents for the Year 1852, Washington, D.C.
United States Statutes At Large 1930-1960, Washington, D.C.
Works Progress of Administration's Writers Program. *Fairs and Fair Makers of Kentucky,* Frankfort, Ky., 1942.

State Documents

Acts, General Assembly of Kentucky, Frankfort, 1792-1991.
Agri-Business Potential in Clark County, Kentucky, Frankfort, 1963.
Bluegrass Development District. *Winchester-Clark County* Master Plan for Parks and Recreation Development, Lexington, Ky., 1974.
Breckinridge, Robert J. *Special Report of the Superintendent of Public Transportation to the Senate,* Frankfort, 1851.
Commonwealth of Kentucky. *Reports of the Auditor of Public Accounts,* Frankfort, 1839-1992.
Directory of Kentucky Breeders of Pure Bred Livestock, Frankfort, 1924.
Biennial Reports of the Bureau of Agriculture, Labor and Statistics of the State *of Kentucky,* Frankfort, 1889, Louisville, 1987.
Kentucky Historic Farms: An Awards Program for Recognizing Kentucky's Century-old Farms, Frankfort, 1990.
Industrial Directories for Winchester and Clark County, Frankfort, 1953-1992.
Kentucky State Documents, Frankfort, 1840-1920.
Littell, William. *A Digest of the Statute of Law of Kentucky: Being a Collection of All the Laws of the General Assembly, of a Public and Private Nature, From the Commencement of the Government to May Session 1822,* 2 Vols., Frankfort, 1822.
Stanton, Richard H. *The Revised Statutes of Kentucky Approved and Adopted by the General Assembly,* 1851-1852, and In Force from July 1, 1852, 2 Vols., Cincinnati, 1860.
Report of the Adjutant General of the Commonwealth of Kentucky, *Soldiers in the War of 1812,* Frankfort, 1891.

Clark County Documents

Clark County Board of Education Meeting Minutes, 1878-1992.
Clark County Book of Incorporation, Winchester, 1875-1960.
Clark County Court Order Books, Winchester, 1792-1992.
Clark County Deed Books, Winchester, 1791-1992.
Clark County Distilling Book, Winchester.
Clark County Road Book, Winchester.
Clark County Soldiers Discharged, Winchester.
Clark County Court Will Books, Winchester, 1792-1992.

Winchester City Documents

Meeting Minutes of Winchester City Trustees, Winchester.
Meeting Minutes of the Winchester City Council, Winchester.
Periodicals and Pamphlets
Aegetsinger, Mark. "P.J. Conkwright in the Tradition of Classical Typography," *Princeton University Library Chronicle*, Vol. LVI, Winter 1959.
Beckner, Lucien, ed. "John D. Shane's Interview with Benjamin Allen in Clark County," *Filson Club History Quarterly*, Vol. 5, April, 1931.
Butler, Mann. "Details of Frontier Life," *Register of the Kentucky Historical Society*, Vol. 62, July 1964.
Carver, Gayle R., "Joel Hart Tanner: Kentucky's Poet-Sculptor," *Register of the Kentucky Historical Society*, Vol. 38, Jan. 1940.
Draper, Lyman C. *Draper's Notes of His Interview With Joseph Scholl*, State Historical Society of Wisconsin, Draper MSS 22S.
Eslinger, Ellen. "Migration and Kinship of the Trans-Appalachian Frontier: Strode's Station, Kentucky," *Filson Club History Quarterly*, Vols. 62, January 1988.
Garrard, Charles T. "Imported Cattle in Kentucky," *Register of the Kentucky Historical Society*, Vol. 60, January 1932.

Harrison, Lowell. "Kentucky Born Generals in the Civil War," *Register of the Kentucky Historical Society*, Vol. 64, April 1966.
"Introduction of Imported Cattle to Kentucky," *Register of the Kentucky Historical Society*, Vol. 29, October 1931.
Jillson, Willard R. "A Sketch of Thomas Person, First Printer in Kentucky," *Register of the Kentucky Historical Society*, Vol. 34, Oct., 1936.
Rice, Otis. "Importation of Cattle into Kentucky," *Register of the Kentucky Historical Society*, Vol. 49, Jan., 1951.
Riddle, Garlock Mable. "John Constant-A Kentucky Pioneer," *Register of the Kentucky Historical Society*, Vol. 32.
"Some Personal Recollections of `P.J.'," *Princeton Library Chronicles*, Vol. LVI, Winter 1995.
Williams, Samuel Cole. "The Father of Sequoyah: Nathaniel Gist," *The Chronicles of Oklahoma*, Vol. XV, March 1937.
Van Meter, Ben F. "Diary of a Voyage to Europe," *Kentucky Statesmen*, March 11, 1953.

Newspapers

Clark County Democrat, Winchester, Ky.
Clark County Republican, Winchester, Ky.

Clark County Weekly, Winchester, Ky.
The Daily Democrat, Winchester, Ky.
The Gateway Sentinel, Winchester, Ky.
Jeffersonian Democrat, Winchester, Ky.
The National Union, Winchester, Ky.
The Semi-Weekly Sun, Winchester, Ky.
The Smooth Coon, Winchester, Ky.
The Sun-Sentinel, Winchester, Ky.
Winchester Advertiser, Winchester, Ky.
The Winchester Chronicle, Winchester, Ky.
The Winchester Democrat, Winchester, Ky.
Winchester Democrat, Winchester, Ky.
Winchester Sentinel, Winchester, Ky.
The Winchester Sun, Winchester, Ky.
Lexington Morning Herald, Lexington, Ky.
Lexington Herald, Lexington, Ky.
Lexington Leader, Lexington, Ky.
Lexington Herald-Leader, Lexington, Ky.
Courier-Journal, Lexington, Ky.

General Works

Allen, Lewis F. *History of Short-Horn Cattle: Their Origins, Progress and Present Conditions,* Buffalo N.Y., 1872.

An Accomplishment to Mitchell's Kentucky and Distance Map of the United States, Philadelphia, 1935.

Ardery, P.L. *American Agricultural Implements, A Review of Inventions and Developments in the Agricultural Industry of the United States,* Chicago, 1973.

Asimov, Isaac. *Asimov's Chronology of Science and Discovery,* New York, 1989.

Axton, W. F. *Tobacco and Kentucky,* Lexington, Ky., 1975.

Bayless, D.L. *An Economic Study of Spring Lamb and Wool Production in the Inner Bluegrass,* Lexington, Ky., 1938.

Bean, Jennie Catherwood. *Confederate Soldiers: Correct List of Those Who Enlisted in the Confederate Army from Clark County, Kentucky,* N.P., 1938.

Bean, Richard M. *John Bean, 1766-1849, of Clark County, Kentucky,* Lexington, Ky., 1991.

Beckett, Mary R. *Flora of Clark County, Kentucky In Relation to Geological Regions,* Lexington, 1956.

Beckner, W. M. *Hand-Book of Clark County and the City of Winchester, Kentucky,* Chicago, 1889.

Bedford, Goff A. *Land Of Our Fathers, A History of Clark County,* Mt. Sterling, Ky., 1977.

Beecher, Catherine Esther and Stowe, Harriet Beecher. *The American Woman's House,* New York, 1869.

Beirne, Francis F. *The War of 1812,* New York, 1949.

Bell, Ron. *Disorganized Crime: True Stories of Unlucky Thieves & Stupid Robbers,* Atlanta, Ga., 1994.

Blandford, Percy W. *Old Farm Tools and Machinery, An Illustrated History,* Fort Lauderdale, Fla., 1976.

Boidvery, Richard. *The Bibliographer of Kentucky Archaeology: 1784-1981,* Lexington, Ky., 1982.

Breckinridge, Robert J. *The Great Deliverance and the New Carrier,* Philadelphia, 1865. *Denominational Education,* Philadelphia, 1854.

Buck, Paul H. *Road to Reunion,* New York, 1937.

Burke, James L. *A Stained White Radiance,* New York, 1992.

Burt and Brabb Lumber Company Records, 1890-1939. University of Kentucky, M. I. King Library, Special Collection.

Caywood, W.C. Jr. *Kentucky Mayor, The Humor and Philosophy of John Edwin Garner, Winchester's First Citizen,* Winchester, Ky., 1950.

Clark County Historic Society, *Clark County Chronicles*, Winchester, Ky., 1922-1924.

Clark, Mary Washington. *Kentucky Quilts and Their Makers*, Lexington, Ky., 1976.

Clark, Thomas D. *Footloose in Jacksonian America: Robert W. Scott and His Agrarian World*. (Frankfort, The Kentucky Historical Society, 1989). *Historic Maps of Kentucky*, Lexington, Ky., 1979. *The Emerging South*, New York, 1968. *Kentucky Land of Contrast*, New York, 1968.

Clark, Thomas D. and Guice, John D.W. *Frontiers in Conflict, The Old Southwest 1795-1830*, Albuquerque, N.M., 1989.

Clark, William Joseph. *Diary of William Joseph Clark*, University of Kentucky, M.I. King Library, Special Collection.

Clay, Brutus. *Ohio Farmer*, N.P., 1855.

Cobb, James. *Industrialization and Souther Society, 1877-1984*, Lexington, Ky., 1984.

Coleman, J. Winston. *Joel T. Hart, Kentucky Sculptor*, Lexington, Ky., 1962. *Steamboats on the Kentucky River*, Lexington, Ky., 1960. *A Bibliography of Kentucky History*, Lexington, Ky., 1949. *Famous Kentucky Duels*, Lexington, Ky., 1971.

Conkwright, S.J. *History of the Churches of Boone's Creek Baptist Association of Kentucky*, Winchester, Ky., 1923. *The Clark County Court Houses*, N.P., 1930.

Coward, Joan Wells. *Kentucky In The New Republic, The Process of Constitution Making*, 4Lexington, Ky., 1979.

Coulter, E.M. *The Civil War and Readjustment in Kentucky*, Chapel Hill, N.C., 1926.

Davis, Darrell H. *The Geography of the Blue Grass Region of Kentucky*, Frankfort, Ky., 1927.

Davison, Kenneth E. *The Presidency of Rutherford B. Hayes*, Westport, Conn., 1972.

Doyle, George F. *A Transcript of the First Record Book of Providence Church, Clark County, Kentucky Records 1789-1833*, Winchester, Ky., 1924.

East Kentucky Power Cooperative 1941-1991, Winchester, Ky., 1991.

Fay, Henry Bradshaw. *The Origins of the World War*, 2 vols., New York, 1930.

Falwell, Marshall. *Allen Tate: A Bibliography*, New York, 1969.

Funkhouser, William D. and Webb, W.S. *Archaeology Survey of Kentucky*, Lexington, Ky., 1932.

Graham, William B. *Railroads in Kentucky Before 1860*, Lexington, Ky., 1932.

Hamlett, Bardsdale. *History of Education in Kentucky*, Frankfort, Ky., 1914.

Harrison, Lowell. *John Breckinridge, Jeffersonian Republican*, Louisville, Ky., 1969. *Kentucky Road to Statehood*, Lexington, Ky., 1992. *The Civil War in Kentucky*, Lexington, Ky., 1975.

Harrison, Molly. *The Kitchen in History*, Berkshire, Eng., 1972.

Hazelton, John M. *History and Hand Book of Hereford Cattle*, Kansas City, Mo., 1935.

Henlein, Paul C. *Cattle Kingdoms in the Ohio Valley 1783-1860*, Lexington, Ky., 1959.

Hughes, R.E., Schaefer, F.W. and Williams, E. L. *That Kentucky Campaign: Or the Law, the Ballot and the People in the Goebel-Taylor Contest*, Cincinnati, 1900.

Ireland, Robert M. *Little Kingdoms, The Counties of Kentucky*, Lexington, Ky., 1977. *The County in Kentucky History*, Lexington, Ky., 1976.

Jillson, W.R. *Early Kentucky Literature*, Frankfort, Ky., 1931. *Bibliography of Clark County, Kentucky*, Frankfort, Ky., 1963. *The First Printing in Kentucky*, Louisville, Ky., 1936. *Geology of the Mina Dome in Clark County*, Frankfort, Ky., 1963. *Early Clark County, Kentucky: A History1674-1814*, Frankfort, Ky., 1963. *The Geology of Clark County, Kentucky*, Frankfort, Ky., 1963.

Jobe, Cynthia. *Phase II Testing of Pre-Historic Sites Within the J.K. Smith Power Station, Clark County, Kentucky*, Lexington, Ky., 1980.

Jouett Family Papers. University of Kentucky, M.I. King Library, Special Collection.

Johnson, Thomas H. *The Oxford Companion to History*, New York, 1960.

Johnston, J. Stoddard. *Memorial History of Louisville From Its First Settlement to the Year 1896*, Chicago, 1896.

Karam, B. and Mather, Cotton. *Education Atals of Kentucky*, Lexington, Ky., 1977.

Kentucky Union Land Company Records, 1783-1918. University of Kentucky, M.I. King Library, Special Collection.

Kleber, John E., ed. *The Kentucky Encyclopedia*, Lexington, Ky., 1992.

Klotter, James C. *William Goebel. The Politics of Wrath*, Lexington, Ky., 1977.

Lamar, Howard R. ed. *The Reader's Encyclopedia of the American West*, New York, 1977.

Long, Jamie B. *Women in Kentucky Industries*, Lexington, Ky., 1927.

Lovegrove, H.T. *Crop Production Equipment*, London, 1968.

Lynch, Daniel. *Development of State and Local Debt in Kentucky*, Lexington, Ky., 1965.

Lynch, Lawrence. *A Statistical Model of Intercounty Commuting*, Lexington, Ky., 1966.

Mahon, John K. *The War of 1812*, Gainesville, Fla., 1872.

Dr. Samuel Martin Records. University of Kentucky, M.I. King Library, Special Collections.

Merrell, Horace Samuel and Galbraith, Marion. *The Republican Command, 1897-1913*, Lexington, Ky., 1971.

Michaux, F.A. *Travels West of the Allegheny Mountains*, N.P., 1793.

Midkiff, Rush H. *An Economic Analysis of Beef Cow Herds in Kentucky*, Lexington, Ky., 1987.

Miller, Arthur M. *Geology of Kentucky*, Frankfort, Ky., 1919.

Miller, R.C. *The Sheep Industry of the Kentucky Mountains*, Lexington, Ky., 1920.

Meyer, Leland Winfried. *The Life and Times of Colonel Richard M. Johnson of Kentucky*, New York, 1932.

Moore, Arthur K. *The Frontier Mind, A Cultural Analysis of the Kentucky Frontiersman*, Lexington, Ky., 1957.

Morehead, Charles S., Brown, Mason. *A Digest of the Laws of Kentucky of Public and Permanent Nature*, 2 Vols., Frankfort, Ky., 1834.

Norwak, Mary. *Kitchen Antiques*, New York, 1975.

Nourse, James. *Journey to Kentucky in 1775*, Greenfield, Ind., 1925.

O'Malley, Nancy. *Stockading Up: A Study of Pioneer Stations in the Inner Bluegrass Region of Kentucky*, Lexington, Ky., 1987. *Searching for Boonesborough*, Lexington, Ky., 1989.

Owen, Kathryn. *Civil War Days in Clark County*, Winchester, Ky., 1963. *Old Graveyards of Clark County*, Winchester, Ky., 1975. *Old Homes and Landmarks of Clark County, Kentucky*, Winchester, Ky., 1967. *Scrapbooks, 2 Vols.*

Palmer, Eddie. *History of the Forest Grove Christian Church*, N.P. 1971.

Partridge, Michael. *Farm Tools Trough the Ages*, Reading, Eng., 1973.

Patrons of Husbandry. *Kentucky Patrons of Husbandry Records 1873-1939*, N.P., N.D.

Paul, Virginia. *This Was Sheep Ranching: Yesterday and Today*, Seattle, 1976.

Perkins, Bradford. *The Cause of the War of 1812, National Honor or National Interest?*, New York, 1962.

Perrin, William H., ed. *History of Fayette County*, Chicago, 1882.

Peterson, H.C. *Propaganda for War, The Campaign Against American Neutrality 1914-1917*, Norman, Okla., 1939.

Pickett, Thomas E. *The Testimony of the Mounds: Considered With Especial Reference to the Pre-Historic Archaeology of Kentucky and the Adjoining States*, Maysville, Ky., 1875.

Pirtle, Alfred. *The Battle of Tippecanoe*, Louisville, Ky., 1900.

Pollock, David, ed. *Late Prehistoric Research in Kentucky*, Frankfort, Ky., 1984.

Price, Samuel Woodson. *The Old Masters of the Bluegrass: Jouett, Bush, Grimes, Frazer, Morgan, Hart*, Louisville, Ky., 1902.

Purdy, Herman R. *Breeds of Cattle*, New York, 1987.

Quisenberry, Anderson C. *A Brief Historical Sketch of the Newspapers of Winchester*, Winchester, Ky., N.D. *Clark County and the Battle of the Thames*, N.P., 1938. *Kentucky in the War of 1812*, Frankfort, Ky., 1915. *Revolutionary Soldiers in Kentucky*, Baltimore, Md., 1968. *Revolutionary War Soldiers in Clark County*, N.P., 1938.

William W. Ranney Papers. University of Kentucky, M.I. King Library, Special Collections.

Read, John Morgan. *Atrocity Propaganda 1914-1919*, New York, 1941.

Reid, Richard. *Historical Sketches of Montgomery County*, Lexington, Ky., 1920.

Richardson, James D. *A Compilation of the Message and Papers of the Presidents 1789-1908,* Vol. IV, Washington, 1908.

Riley, John J. *A History of the American Soft Drink Industry: Bottled Carbonated Beverages 1807-1957,* Washington, 1958.

Robert, Joseph C. *The Story of Tobacco in America,* Chapel Hill, N.C., 1967.

Robinson, George W., ed. *The Public Papers of Bert T. Combs 1959-1963,* Lexington, Ky., 1979.

Rogers, James R. *The Cane Ridge Meeting House,* Cincinnati, 1910.

Sanders, Alvin H. *The Story of The Herefords,* Chicago, 1914. *A History of Aberdeen-Angus Cattle,* Chicago, 1928. *Short-Horn Cattle,* Chicago, 1901. *Short-Horn Cattle: A Series of Historical Sketches, Memoirs and Records of the Breed and Its Development in the United States and Canada,* Chicago, 1918.

Schwartz, Douglas W. *Conceptions of Kentucky Prehistory, A Case Study in Archeology,* Lexington, Ky., 1967.

Schmidt, Beradlentle. *The Coming of the War 1914,* 2 vols., New York, 1930.

Smith, J. Allan. *College of Agriculture, University of Kentucky, Early and Middle Years 1865-1951,* Lexington, Ky., 1981.

Stewart, J.L. *The Burden of Time: The Fugitives and Agrarians; the Nashville Group of John Crowe Ransom, Allen Tate and Robert Penn Warren,* Princeton, N.J., 1965.

Stickles, Arnt M. *The Critical Court Struggle in Kentucky 1819-1829,* Bloomington, Ind., 1929.

Stone, Richard G. *A Brittle Sword--The Kentucky Militia 1776-1912,* Lexington, Ky., 1977.

Stuart, T.G. *The Origins and Derivation of the Names of Towns and Places in Clark County, Kentucky,* N.P., 1923.

Sulzer, Elmer Griffith. *Ghost Railroads of Kentucky,* Indianapolis, Ind., 1967.

Swiggett, Howard. *Rebel Raider, A Life of John Hunt Morgan,* New York, 1934.

Talbert, Charles Gano. *Benjamin Logan, Kentucky Frontiersman,* Lexington, Ky., 1962.

Hubbard Taylor Papers. University of Kentucky, M.I. King Library, Special Collections.

Tevis, Julia A. *Sixty Years in a School Room,* Cincinnati, 1878.

Thompson Family Papers. University of Kentucky, M.I. King Library, Special Collections.

Thompson, Ed Porter. *History of the Orphan Brigade,* Louisville, Ky., 1898.

Townsend, John Wilson. *Kentucky in American Letters 1784-1912,* 3 vols., Cedar Rapids, Iowa, 1913.

Turnbow, Christopher, ed. *Cultural Radiocarbon Determination of Kentucky,* Lexington, Ky., 1981.

Turnbow, Christopher. *Archaeology Excavation of* Goolman, Devary and Stone Sites of Clark County, *Kentucky,* Lexington, Ky., 1983.

Turner, Robert G. *The Locational Characteristics of* the Role of the Kentucky Department of Commerce in *the Location of New Manufacturing Plants,* Lexington, Ky., 1969.

Verbugge, James A. *The Financial Resources of Eastern Kentucky,* University of Kentucky, Masters Theses, 1965.

Verhoeff, Mary. *The Kentucky River Navigation,* Louisville, Ky., 1917.

Walford-Lloyd, E., ed. *The Southdown Sheep,* Chichester, Eng., 1924.

Warfield, William. *American Short-Horn Importations,* Chicago, 1884.

Watt, Robert McDowell. *Kentucky Utilities Company,* Forty Years of Service to Rural Communities in the *Blue Grass State,* New York, 1939.

Wentworth, Edward N. *America's Sheep Trails: History and Personalities,* Ames, Iowa, 1948.

Wharton, Mary E. and Barbour, Roger W. *Trees and Shrubs of Kentucky,* Lexington, Ky., 1973.

Who Was Who 1897-1942, Vol. 1, Chicago, 1942.

Wilson, Samuel M. *Battle of the Blue Licks,* Lexington, Ky., 1927. *The First Land Court in Kentucky 1779-1780,* Lexington, Ky., 1923.

Winchester, Kentucky City Directory, Chillicothe, Ohio1965.

Wing, Joseph E. *Sheep Farming in America,* Chicago, 1912.

Wolfe, E. R. *An Analysis of Factors Affecting the Local Financing of Public Education in Kentucky,* Lexington, Ky., 1976.

Young, Bennett, H. *History of the Battle of the Blue Licks,* Louisville, Ky., 1897.
Young, Chester Raymond, ed. *Westward Into Kentucky,* Lexington, Ky., 1981.

Index

Patrons

Adams. Cole M and Lisle H
Adams, Julia H and Steven D
Adams, Nellie Fox
Allen Jr, Mr. and Mrs. James B
Allen, Mr. and Mrs James Bradley
Appraisal Associates of Kentucky
Arnold, Dick and Doris
Atchison, Paul and Kay
Avent, Mr. and Mrs. John J
Baber, Paul and Jo Gravett
Baldwin, Mr. and Mrs. Robert L
Ballard, John Edward and Joyce Baber
Ballard, Dr. Billy C
Barnes. Alice and Josh
Bedford, A Goff
Berryman, Robert and Betty
Blakemore, J N
Bloomfleld, Clarence V and Mary S
Brooks, Rose Mary Codell
Cantrell, David and Georgia
Caudill, Michael N
Chism, Marion R and Lillie M
Clay, Mr. and Mrs. James W
Codell, Anna Laura Sudduth
Codell, Family of J Hagan
Collins, Dr. John
Collins, Robert F
Coney, David C
Coney Jr, Mr. and Mrs Robert S
Corns, Arthur and Jerri
Curry, Family of E E
Curry, William Nelson
Curtis, Dorsey
Disney, Family of Larry
Downing, Mr. and Mrs. Frank
Ecton, Mr. and Mrs. Walter G
Edgington, E.L. and Betty
Falmlen, Ben and Barbara
Flynn, Maurice D and CIydella R
Fox, Eldon and Mary Eleanor
Gamble, Dick and Martha
Glenn, Dr. and Mrs. James
Graham, Drew and Lorra
Gravett, Clyde and Beulah Lisle
Gravett, David and JoAnn Parker
Gravett, Donald and Jo Rankin
Gray, Dr. John and Dr. Anita
Guerrant. Rev. and Mrs. Wallace
Haggard, Mr. and Mrs. Paul F
Hays Jr, Family of J Smith
Heflin, Mr. and Mrs Clyde
Hensley, Paul and Mary
Hodgkin, Douglas G
Hodgkin, John D
Hodgkin, William H and Mischelle

Holt, Howard and Susan
Houlihan, Mr. and Mrs. John Spencer
Hunt, Mr. and Mrs. David N
Hunt, Mr. and Mrs. William G
Jenkins, Glenn and Nellie
Johnson, Harry C and Lillie R
Jones, Edsel T
Juett, Arnold and Marie
Kincaid, Gene and Elaine
Kirby, Jim and Sharon
Langley, Clifford R and Shirley N
Lawson, Gary and Joyce
Logsdon, Ed and Jean
Ludwig, Charles and Bernie
Lytle, Brenda G
McCammish, Mark and Shirley
McCrary, Mr. and Mrs. Stuart K
McCready Jr, Mr. and Mrs. Richard F
McIntosh, Thomas L and Marjorie W
Meers, Richard E
Miller, Elizabeth
Miller, Mr. and Mrs. Kenneth H
Moberly, Dr. and Mrs. Harold S
Molloy, Mr. and Mrs. James M
Monohan, Richard N
Muncie, Mr. and Mrs. Thomas D
Murray, John and Sharon
Newell, Henry and Alice
Norton, Stephen and Sarah
Nunan, Mr. and Mrs. John F
Oliver, Ralph and Lois
Owens, Mr. and Mrs. Cabbell
Pace, Family of Leon P
Pennington, James F
Pound, J Taylor
Puckett, Family of Virgil and Mary Jane Kash
Pumphrey, William R and Martha S
Quisenberry, Mrs. J H
Rankin, Robert C and Holly Gibson
Richardson Sr, Family of Paul W
Rompf, John H and Elizabeth L
Rose, John A
Rose, Mr. and Mrs. Robert L
Rosenthal, Vincent and Zella
Rowady, Family of Ed
Rowady, Mr. and Mrs. Michael A
Sams, Danny and Cecilia
Sanford, Family of Charles and Martha
Sattler, Mrs. Charles G
Saunier, Ed and Shannon
Schoolmaster, Family of Thomas G
Seay, Margaret Hodgkin
Shearer, Ada
Shearer, Family of Ben
Shearer, Mr. and Mrs. Walsa P

Shearer, Mr. and Mrs. William P
Skinner, Dr. and Mrs. Rankin D
Sledd, Herbert and Carolyn McCann
Smith, Dr. Clifton R
Smith, Wayne and Betty Ratliff
Snowden, Jess F and Betty L
Sphar II, Mr. and Mrs. A R
Sphar Jr, Family of William P
Steven D. Adams Real Estate Services
Stone, Edward and Dorothy
Stone, Mr. and Mrs. William E
Talbott Sr, Family of J Scott
Tatman, Family of James S
Taylor, Stuart Dudley and Betsy Keyes
Tucker, Family of Roy J and Gladys R

Van Meter, Holly
Venable, Family of Charles S and
 Martha Fishback
Vivion, Robert and Dorothy
Wagers, Gardner and Susan
Walson, Arthur and Billie Jo
Walson, Family of Pete and Gola Palmer
Walson, Jeffrey and Allyson Clark
Westlund, Arnie and Kaaren
Wheeler, Family of Earl B
Whiteman, Family of Gayle
Wiedemann, Clara Houlihan
Williams, Danby
Wilson, Woodrow and Dianne
Witmer, Mr. and Mrs. Clay Reed

Advance Subscribers

Adams, Elizabeth Franklin
Adams, Julia Hylton
Adams, Robert D
Aldridge, Betty and L C
Allen Jr, Mr. and Mrs. James B
Allen Concrete and Supply Inc.
Baldwin, Robert L
Barnes, Shirley Hardin
Bedford Dr. A Goff
Branham, Henry
Bridgewater, Craig and Linda
Brooks, Rose Mary C
Bryant, Ray
Calvert, Rick and Paula
Cheatham, Nell Sue
Clemons, Rondal R
Codell, Anna Laura Sudduth
Coleman, James J and Barbara
Coney Jr, Mr. and Mrs. Robert S
Conner, Harriet B
Croucher, Jennilyn
DeVary, Coburn
Eldridge, Lucinda G
Fannie Bush Elementary PTA
Fantz, Lloyd E
Fox, Ernest A
Fox, James B
Fugitt, Roy and Margaret P
Golden, Dr. William Young
Haggard, Mr. and Mrs Robert B
Heffner, Gary and Cora
Hudgens, Jean Whiteside
Hufnagle, Judy M
Hunt, Elizabeth B
Indian Old Fields Homemakers
Jacobs, Fritz and Audeen
Jones, Joseph R and Margie C

King, Mattie Hunt
Kirby, James and Sharon
Kohlbecker, Mr. and Mrs. Carl
Langley, C R (CAP)
Latham, Ralph and Elizabeth
Moyer, J Donald
Mozingo, Wade K
Noplis, Bonnie P
Norris, Don and Evelyn
Oliver, Carol Ann and Doug
Pennington, Dr. and Mrs. James F
Phillips, Francis Pryor
Phillips, Jack Howard
Quality Manufacturing Inc.
Raney, Mary Combs
Rhoades, Virginia May
Richardson Sr, Mr and Mrs. Paul W
Ringo, David Leer
Sainte, Deborah and Robert
Skaggs, Susan
Sledd, Herbert and Carolyn M
Smith, Mr. and Mrs. Russell
Snowden, Elizabeth Duty
Snowden, Ruth V
Strode Station Elementary School
Sudduth, Dr. Martha Cooper
Thornberry, G H
Tyler Jr, Mrs. John O
Vivion, Robert Smith
Whisman, John and Anne
Wiedemann, Clara Houlihan
Wiler Jr, John L
Wilhite, J R and Donna
Winchester Insurance Co.
Winchester SUN
Wiseman, Larry Gravett